Knowledge Discovery, Transfer, and Management in the Information Age

Murray E. Jennex
San Diego State University, USA

A volume in the Advances in Knowledge Acquisition, Transfer, and Management (AKATM) Book Series

Information Science REFERENCE
An Imprint of IGI Global

Managing Director: Lindsay Johnston
Production Editor: Jennifer Yoder
Development Editor: Erin O'Dea
Acquisitions Editor: Kayla Wolfe
Typesetter: Christina Henning
Cover Design: Jason Mull

Published in the United States of America by
Information Science Reference (an imprint of IGI Global)
701 E. Chocolate Avenue
Hershey PA 17033
Tel: 717-533-8845
Fax: 717-533-8661
E-mail: cust@igi-global.com
Web site: http://www.igi-global.com

Library of Congress Cataloging-in-Publication Data

Knowledge discovery, transfer, and management in the information age / Murray E. Jennex, editor.
pages cm
Includes bibliographical references and index.
Summary: "This book brings together the latest empirical research in knowledge management practices and information retrieval strategies to assist organizations in effectively and efficiently utilizing the data at their disposal"-- Provided by publisher.
ISBN 978-1-4666-4711-4 (hardcover) -- ISBN 978-1-4666-4712-1 (ebook) -- ISBN 978-1-4666-4713-8 (print & perpetual access) 1. Knowledge management. 2. Information retrieval. 3. Information storage and retrieval systems. 4. Management--Data processing. I. Jennex, Murray E., 1956- editor of compilation.
HD30.2.K63623 2014
658.4'038--dc23
2013040297

This book is published in the IGI Global book series Advances in Knowledge Acquisition, Transfer, and Management (AKATM) (ISSN: 2326-7607; eISSN: 2326-7615)

British Cataloguing in Publication Data
A Cataloguing in Publication record for this book is available from the British Library.

Advances in Knowledge Acquisition, Transfer, and Management (AKATM) Book Series

Murray E. Jennex
San Diego State University, USA

ISSN: 2326-7607
EISSN: 2326-7615

Mission

Organizations and businesses continue to utilize knowledge management practices in order to streamline processes and procedures. The emergence of web technologies has provided new methods of information usage and knowledge sharing.

The **Advances in Knowledge Acquisition, Transfer, and Management (AKATM) Book Series** brings together research on emerging technologies and their effect on information systems as well as the knowledge society.**AKATM** will provide researchers, students, practitioners, and industry leaders with research highlights surrounding the knowledge management discipline, including technology support issues and knowledge representation.

Coverage

- Cognitive Theories
- Cultural Impacts
- Information and Communication Systems
- Knowledge Acquisition and Transfer Processes
- Knowledge Management Strategy
- Knowledge Sharing
- Organizational Learning
- Organizational Memory
- Small and Medium Enterprises
- Virtual Communities

The Advances in Knowledge Acquisition, Transfer, and Management (AKATM) Book Series (ISSN 2326-7607) is published by IGI Global, 701 E. Chocolate Avenue, Hershey, PA 17033-1240, USA, www.igi-global.com. This series is composed of titles available for purchase individually; each title is edited to be contextually exclusive from any other title within the series. For pricing and ordering information please visit http://www.igi-global.com/book-series/advances-knowledge-acquisition-transfer-management/37159. Postmaster: Send all address changes to above address.

Titles in this Series

For a list of additional titles in this series, please visit: www.igi-global.com

Knowledge Management Practice in Organizations The View from Inside
Ulla de Stricker (de Stricker Associates, Canada)
Information Science Reference • copyright 2014 • 318pp • H/C (ISBN: 9781466651869) • US $205.00 (our price)

Knowledge Discovery, Transfer, and Management in the Information Age
Murray E. Jennex (San Diego State University, USA)
Information Science Reference • copyright 2014 • 300pp • H/C (ISBN: 9781466647114) • US $175.00 (our price)

Harnessing Dynamic Knowledge Principles in the Technology-Driven World
Mark Nissen (Royal Oaks, USA)
Information Science Reference • copyright 2014 • 291pp • H/C (ISBN: 9781466647275) • US $175.00 (our price)

Emerging Pedagogies in the Networked Knowledge Society Practices Integrating Social Media and Globalization
Marohang Limbu (Michigan State University, USA) and Binod Gurung (New Mexico State University, USA)
Information Science Reference • copyright 2014 • 352pp • H/C (ISBN: 9781466647572) • US $175.00 (our price)

Knowledge Management and Competitive Advantage: Issues and Potential Solutions
Michael A. Chilton (Kansas State University, USA) and James M. Bloodgood (Kansas State University, USA)
Information Science Reference • copyright 2014 • 387pp • H/C (ISBN: 9781466646797) • US $175.00 (our price)

Ontology-Based Applications for Enterprise Systems and Knowledge Management
Mohammad Nazir Ahmad (Universiti Teknologi Malaysia, Malaysia) Robert M. Colomb (University of Queensland, Australia) and Mohd Syazwan Abdullah (Universiti Utara Malaysia, Malaysia)
Information Science Reference • copyright 2013 • 423pp • H/C (ISBN: 9781466619937) • US $175.00 (our price)

Knowledge Management and Drivers of Innovation in Services Industries
Patricia Ordóñez de Pablos (Universidad de Oviedo, Spain) and Miltiadis D. Lytras (The American College of Greece, Greece)
Information Science Reference • copyright 2012 • 349pp • H/C (ISBN: 9781466609488) • US $175.00 (our price)

Customer-Centric Knowledge Management Concepts and Applications
Minwir Al-Shammari (University of Bahrain, Bahrain)
Information Science Reference • copyright 2012 • 315pp • H/C (ISBN: 9781613500897) • US $175.00 (our price)

Table of Contents

Detailed Table of Contents

The crisis of our time is very much a crisis of knowledge. There is no easy way of "solving" the crisis. "Solving" the crisis demands for a real shift of mind, implying new ways of thinking and knowing about what is the real. The most important task of today, therefore, is to see and to open up a new world: a world of the possible, with its hitherto uncharted and unexplored complexity territory. For the sake of mastering complexity, understanding real complexity is urgently needed. The problem of complexity for organizations is the way organizations and companies attempt to respond to complexity. To confront and master complexity, the focus should be on the conditions of possibility, hitherto unknown. These conditions are about the possibility of triggering self-generative, self-organizing processes with potential nonlinear effects within dynamic, hyperconnected networks. These effects can be generated by the process of amplifying changes within these networks. This amplifying is about the amplifying of learning, of thinking, and of knowing. In practice, this means that new thinking in complexity is urgently needed to master the complexity involved. This approach is compared with the recent approaches advocated by big firms and companies in their embracing of complexity. This chapter shows how they are unable to discover and explore the very potential of complexity for their own Complex Organization (CO). They are very much in need to master complexity for the sake of fostering creativity, novelty, and innovation in their own organizations.

The knowledge elicitation process allows for the acquiring and transferring of knowledge. Actually, this process presents difficulties when selecting the appropriate elicitation technique. This chapter presents a classification of the elicitation techniques used in software engineering and the relationship between the elicitation techniques and some elements of knowledge management such as assets knowledge, epistemological dimension of knowledge and the knowledge creation phases. This classification provides a guideline to select a technique or a set of techniques for knowledge elicitation based on phases of Nonaka's model. Additionally, the chapter presents the use of product patterns in knowledge elicitation, and defines a product pattern as formal representation mechanism for each of the knowledge assets defined and presented in this chapter.

This chapter discusses the usage of metadata in libraries in Serbia. So far metadata have been used for describing printed documents available for patrons in library holdings and for describing digital documents available in online repositories. Paper presents some specific aspects of metadata usage primarily in regards to automation of digital data delivery for patrons. The advent of information technologies provides librarians in Serbia, as well as their colleagues in other countries, with powerful tools to describe digital objects and interconnect them making those related digital objects effectively available for users via an emergent, more semantic web.

In this chapter, the authors investigate the correlation between characteristics of the four social networks and employee task and contextual performance. The chapter focuses on the degree centrality and betweenness centrality of the four social networks (Job Advisory, Work Discussion, Friendship and Email Networks) of a Chinese state-owned enterprise as well as the individual attributes of knowledge sharing behavior and IT capability. The findings of this research are 1) employee contextual performance is uncorrelated with the network characteristics; 2) it is significantly and positively correlated with knowledge sharing behavior, but significantly and negatively correlated with individual IT capability, and 3) task performance is correlated, both positively and negatively, with various network characteristics, but not with knowledge sharing behavior and individual IT capability. In addition to discussing the cultural dimension of these results, the authors draw theoretical and managerial implications based on our research framework and findings.

There is no way to acquire, store, and disseminate knowledge other than semiotically. Yet semiotics is hardly acknowledged in science, and not at all as science. Were it not for the fame of a few writers (Barthes, Derrida, and especially Eco), associated more with the semiotics of culture, few would even know that such a knowledge domain exists. In the age of computers, genetics, and networks—all of underlying semiotic condition—semiotics would at best qualify as pertinent to an obscure past, but insignificant for current endeavors. Gnoseologically, there is little to gain from acknowledging the shortcomings of semiotics. Epistemologically, quite a bit is at stake in grounding semiotics among the fundamental sciences. For this to come about, new interrogations become necessary: Why knowledge? What is knowledge? What kind of knowledge? How is knowledge acquired? One way or another, the answer will acknowledge semiotic processes as a necessary factor. The perspective advanced in this chapter relies on an understanding of the living, and, in particular, of the human being, that ascertains anticipation as definitory. The future is made part of the present via semiotic processes. This is significant because in the age of neurons, suggestive of brain activity and of attempts to emulate it, to distinguish between knowledge supporting human activity, embodied in new technologies, and knowledge essential to the unfolding of the living becomes very difficult.

With the prevalence of affordable e-Readers in the consumer marketplace and library users increasingly having access to lendable e-Books from their local library institutions, library administrators continue to have difficulty in determining the immediate and long term effect of these technologies on their organizations. This chapter attempts to provide administrators with a brief overview of the current e-Reader and e-Book technology landscape and describe trends and issues. To help Administrators better understand their library users' experiences and expectations with e-Readers and e-Books, the researcher conducted a survey of 70 individuals. This survey is a follow-up to 2012's E-Readers and E-Books in Public Libraries: Measuring Library Patron Expectations research project. Using the same survey questions, format and potential respondent pool, One Year Forward demonstrates that patrons are increasingly demanding access to e-Books and e-Readers. Library patrons are finding these services more easy to use than in the past. Users clearly see value in these services both now and in the future. The results of this research project should be difficult for any library administrator to ignore.

This chapter is an evaluation of the efficiency of 3D Collaborative Virtual Learning Environments to facilitate the implementation of collaborative learning activities. Firstly, there is a presentation of the state of the art regarding open source as well as proprietary platforms. Afterwards, the use of a case study reveals issues concerning the suitability of open source Collaborative Virtual Learning Environments, rationalizing the choice of executing a collaborative learning scenario in Second Life. The specific scenario is then presented culminating in evaluation results related to the appropriateness of Second Life with regards to its technical and pedagogical affordances. Finally, students' suggestions and reactions towards such a novel didactical approach are discussed.

Since business processes may address complex behavioral requirements resulting from the integration of several items, i.e. tasks, business entities (also called artifacts), control flow rules and data flow rules, they need notations able to accommodate several viewpoints. This chapter proposes a notation, ARTS, aimed at integrating the traditional activity-oriented viewpoint and the artifact-oriented one. The major benefits are the unification of the control flow and the data flow and a clear representation of the choices to be carried out by the participants. The basic features are illustrated with the help of three

Preface

INTRODUCTION

2012 was the year of Big Data with 2013 continuing this focus. We are living in a time when there is an explosion in the availability of data, information, and knowledge. More data, information, and knowledge are being generated/created, collected, stored, and analyzed then at any other time in recorded history. Organizations are infatuated with the technologies that are used to generate, create, and store this data, information, and knowledge; technologies such as the Cloud, Big Data, Data Warehouses, Data Mining, the Internet of Things, Social Media, Smart Grids, and Smart Technologies. Organizations are expected to implement these technologies lest they be left behind their competitors. But are organizations better off using these technologies and gathering and storing all this data, information, and knowledge? Are there risks is storing large amounts of data, information, and knowledge, and if yes, what are they? Finally, are the risks of storing this much data, information and knowledge worth the return? These are difficult questions to answer and are the challenges that knowledge management is striving to meet.

Storing large amounts of any resource of potential value involves the risks of theft and destruction. Additionally, if the data, information, and knowledge are used to support decision making there is the risk it could be modified without the organization knowing. These are significant risks as there are many vulnerabilities and methods for attacking stored data, information, and knowledge and the consequences of their occurrence are quite high. Attack methods such as hacking and data thefts from individuals, competing companies, or other nation states are increasing and causing increased concern. Product designs, including defense systems, have been stolen. Customer databases have been downloaded and the personal identification and credit card information contained in them utilized for criminal gain. The same can be said for employee databases and to some degree patient databases. Critical infrastructure is under attack making the availability of systems a risk. All this drives up the cost of protecting these assets and organizations are finding it reasonable to be spending 10% or more of their information systems budget on just security. Ultimately individuals and organizations have to balance this risk against the value they can create from the data, information, knowledge, and systems they possess. There needs to be investment in security technologies as this is required by law and the principle of due diligence. But how much should organizations and individuals spend and how much security should they install? The answer should rely on the value that is created but usually isn't. Instead organizations and individuals spend what they must for the data, information, knowledge, and systems they without actually asking how much value they create or even if it is worth keeping all the collected data, information, knowledge, and systems.

There has always been a focus on value, investors and owners want to see a return on investment and push managers to show value. However, there does tend to be a lag on measuring actual value when doing something new or innovating. This is what is happening in many organizations, analytics and big data are new initiatives, investments made with much promise but not necessarily a known value proposition. How does data, information, and knowledge turn into value? Value comes from improving services or products and in creating new services or products. Organizations do this by improving or creating new activities in the organizational value chain. Major activities in the value chain include managing inbound logistics, operations, outbound logistics, sales, and customer service/support. Improvements can include managing warehouses better by minimizing storage times, shortening delivery and/or wait times, reducing wastage, improving quality of services, etc. These improvements can be accomplished by utilizing "big" data collected on the processes or products and learning more about their customers and/or where there are areas for improvement and or discovering market needs or identifying areas of opportunity for new products and/or services. This is the process of sense making and it can be a wicked problem with large data sets. Sense making generally starts by identifying patterns/trends of significance in the data sets. Data mining and analytics tools are used to identify these patterns/trends; but these tools cannot determine significance. Human analysts have to make sense of identified patterns/trends before they are useful as knowledge. How do analysts make sense of patterns/trends? They need to place the patterns/trends into context where context is the collection of relevant conditions and surrounding influences that make a pattern/trend unique and comprehensible to the users of the pattern/trend's knowledge. Analysts then need to create a shared context of understanding, where context of understanding incorporates context and experience, with the organization so that the newly identified knowledge can be transferred to those that can put the pattern/trend knowledge to work. To put patterns/trends into context analysts use their experience to generate mental models of how to use or apply the pattern/trend knowledge (Degler & Battle, 2000). Experience comes from the analyst's own experience with the knowledge domain, other's shared experience with the knowledge domain, and/or a collective experience with the knowledge domain (Note that in the context of this sentence knowledge domain refers to the domain or source of data from which the patterns/trends were identified). Additionally, analysts need to understand the organizational and national cultures from which the patterns/trends originate. The end result is that analysts put the identified patterns/trends into a cultural and contextual framework (i.e. this is the pattern/trend knowledge) that allows the organization to understand and use the pattern/trend knowledge to generate value.

So how does knowledge management fit into the "Big Data" process? Knowledge management is about capturing experiential knowledge and applying it to future situations (Jennex, 2005). Knowledge management focuses on getting the right knowledge to the right people at the right time and is associated with knowledge workers, where knowledge workers are defined by Davenport (2005) as those who think for a living and whose main assets are knowledge. Analysts are knowledge workers who apply the principles of knowledge management, i.e. by reusing experiential knowledge, to create new knowledge by putting patterns/trends into cultural and contextual frameworks that are then used to create value.

Knowledge management plays another significant role in the use of Big Data, Data Warehouses, Data Mining, and Analytics. How does the organization know or decide on what data, information, and knowledge is needed or at least is likely to lead to value creation? This is a particularly important question for the creation of data warehouses as they are designed to support specific decision making and are not easily or cheaply modified. In other words, you need to know before you build the data warehouse what data and information is needed. Additionally, as previously discussed there are costs and risks associated with building systems for capturing and storing data, information, and knowledge. Organizations can attempt to capture and store everything, but not only is this expensive and risky, it also probably lead to information overload, or having so much data, information, and knowledge that decision making and action taking become paralyzed while managers try to find the perfect data, information, and knowledge. Knowledge management can help resolve this dilemma by helping the organization formulate a knowledge strategy and an organizational knowledge structure.

Jennex and Bartczak (2013) put this problem of too much data, information, and knowledge and the role knowledge management plays in solving the problem into perspective with Figure 1. Figure 1 shows that the purpose of knowledge management is to extract the portion of available data, information, and knowledge that is useful to the organization from all that is available. Organizations determine what data, information, and knowledge is needed by identifying the intelligence they need to achieve their strategic goals. Intelligence is that key actionable knowledge that organizations can use to make critical decisions, decisions that affect the value generation capability of the organization.

The term intelligence is taken from the intelligence "activity" realm, which implies a function that seeks to generate actionable knowledge to be used in the formulation of strategies and tactics to accomplish a specific goal, such as beating an opponent during wartime or to determine what actions should be planned. This term is not chosen lightly as it does fit into the data, information, and knowledge hierarchy meaning that it is the interpretation of data, information, and knowledge to create courses of action or make specific decisions. Also, the solid arrows that represent KM are shown to be double-headed as the hierarchy may travel in either direction. In fact, it is expected that while the learning process will tend to generally be a bottom-up process, meaning that it starts with the interpretation of data, organizational learning and KM will generally be top-down processes where it is first determined what actions or decisions need to take place or be made and from there it is identified what intelligence, then knowledge, then information, then data is needed to support taking the specific actions or making the specific decisions. This is function of interest for this discussion.

Figure 1. The revised knowledge pyramid (Jennex & Bartczak, 2013)

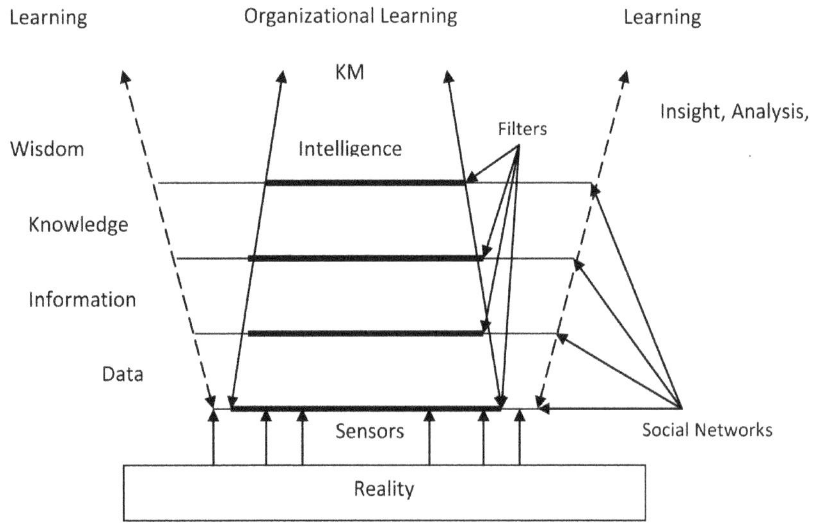

The other major point of interest in Figure 1 is the application of filters. While the general learning process seeks to push data, information, knowledge, and wisdom out to all who wish to use it, KM does not. As stated earlier, KM seeks to support specific decision making and thus needs specific data, information, knowledge, and intelligence. Additionally, KM seeks to share this with the right people at the right time. This implies that KM filters data, information, and knowledge to generate specific, actionable intelligence that is shared with specific, limited users. Moreover, these filters can also be described as analytical tools (i.e. data mining, data warehouses, analytics) used to segregate data, information, and knowledge into that which is needed from that which is not.

The combination of identifying critical data, information, and knowledge with the identification and/or creation of filters forms the basis for an organizations knowledge management or knowledge strategy. Knowledge management strategies are used to guide organizations in determining what their knowledge needs are, where and how knowledge should be obtained, how it should be stored, and how and who needs to apply it. Knowledge management strategy is incorporated into knowledge management critical success factors and modeled in the Jennex and Olfman KM Success Model (Jennex & Oflman, 2006). Knowledge management strategy has also been found to be an indication of knowledge management success and is a part of the knowledge management success definition proposed by Jennex, Smolnik, and Croasdell (2009, 2012). Knowledge management strategy has been found to be a key differentiator between those organizations who successfully captured and used knowledge and those organizations that did not (Jennex, Olfman, & Addo, 2003; Jennex, 2012, 2013). Organizations should apply knowledge management strategy to determine what data and information is needed and what technologies should be used and what decision making they support.

So what are the components of a KM strategy? Jennex and Addo (2005) used the literature, Jennex, Oflman and Addo (2003), and the longitudinal case study reported in Jennex (2008) (performed between 1996 and 2004) to generate the components of a KM strategy as being:

- Identification of users of the KMS
- Identification of sources of knowledge
- Identification of knowledge to be captured
- Identification of goals/expectations of the KM initiative by identifying ties to organizational strategy
- Identification of how captured knowledge is to be stored and represented
- Generation of top management support
- Establishment of process for adding, removing, and/or modifying knowledge to the KMS
- Establishment of metrics for knowledge use
- Establishment of feedback process on the effectiveness of knowledge use
- Identification of the amount of context to be captured with the knowledge

Additionally, it is expected that these organizations will undertake the following activities:

- Modification of processes/procedures as a result of Organizational Learning
- Creation of new processes/ procedures as a result of Organizational Learning
- Creation/Modification of KM support tools to support the KMS and knowledge use
- Increased utilization of personnel who create, share, and/or utilize organizational knowledge at higher levels of authority/responsibility

- Use of lessons learned reports or post activity assessment to review and capture what was learned during organizational activities
- Creation of a learning organization.

How do organizations create a knowledge management strategy for their large amounts of data, information and knowledge? The following are the basic steps:

Create a Mission/Vision Statement for How the Data, Information, and Knowledge is to be Used:

- Answer why the initiative is being pursued
- Describe the final desired state/condition
- State who are the stakeholders/users
- Says what initiatives (Big Data, KM, Data Warehouse, etc.) are to be used

Create a Goals Statement:

- State what the goals of having the large amounts of data, information, and knowledge
- Outline how success is to be measured

Create a Value Statement:

- Describe the value to be gained by the large amounts of data, information, and knowledge for all involved parties
- Make it as quantitative as possible and have a timeline of expected benefits
- Include costs needed to gain the benefits

Identify the Metrics to be Used to Measure Goal and Value Achievement:

- Create a roadmap for implementing the goals of having data, information, and knowledge that includes activities to be accomplished along with a timeline and identified resource allocation.

Create the Data, Information, and Knowledge Statement:

- Specify data, information, and knowledge being used
- Specify sources of the data, information, and knowledge
- Specify format of the data, information, and knowledge
- Specify how the data, information, and knowledge will be captured
- Specify how the data, information, and knowledge will be used

Create the Technology Statement Specifying Technologies Needed to Support the Initiative Including Infrastructure:

- Specify technologies for repositories for the data, information, and knowledge
- Specify technologies for transferring/sharing the data, information, and knowledge
- Specify the infrastructure needed to support the above technologies

- Create a plan for developing and implementing needed technologies
- Create a plan for developing needed infrastructure

Create an Issues Statement:

- Identify key issues with the initiative (such as security, privacy, etc.)
- Define rules/limitations needed to address the issues
- State consequences of the issues

Create an Implementation Plan:

- Identify issues that may prevent adoption and how each will be overcome
- Identify the implementation strategy
- Create the timeline and resources needed to implement the initiative
- Identify expected and potential risks and unexpected outcomes
- Create contingency plans for coping with unexpected issues
- Identify targeted users for adoption of the data, information, and knowledge
- Identify implementation suspension criteria should the project go wrong

So what does this mean for this book? While knowledge management strategy is understood to be important, knowledge management researchers are focusing on determining new processes and tools to support the design and implementation of these strategies. This book presents eleven chapters of research focused on understanding how knowledge is used, how it is adopted and transferred, and methods and tools for analyzing organizations to aid in determining what knowledge is needed. This research reflects the needs of organizations to make sense of the flood of data and information and to determine how to interpret it into critical knowledge/actionable intelligence. Understanding how to make sense of the data/information flood is what will determine which organizations will prosper and which organizations may drown in data/information flood.

The following paragraphs outline the focus and content of the eleven chapters of this book. I welcome you to peruse and to use this research to either further your own research or to support your knowledge management strategy formulation.

CHAPTER SUMMARIES

Chapter 1: The Crisis of Knowing in the Age of Complexity

The crisis of our time is very much a crisis of knowledge; that is, a lack of knowledge about the complexity of the complex world we live in. We 'simply' do not know what we do not know. This is true for the complexity of a nonlinear complex reality. Complexity is still taken for granted. Ignorance on complexity is still dominating our worldview. Those leading complex organizations are trying to confront the complexity of the world, but at the same time they show their ignorance on the very complexity involved. Harnessing complexity is a hardy perennial for these complex organizations and their managers. They do not seem able to explore the very potential of complexity for their own organizations, in terms of fostering creativity, novelty and innovation. The only remedy for this is first to recognize their ignorance on the topic of complexity. To confront complexity, they need to become (more) knowledgeable about the very dynamics of complexity. They need to view the system with new eyes by the use of a new lens: a complexity lens. Only then they might become able to organize complexity for the opening of new spaces of possibility in a 'world of the possible'. This is the very promise of complexity for organizations.

Chapter 2: Product Patterns to Support Knowledge Acquisition Management

Knowledge elicitation process allows acquiring and transferring the knowledge. Actually, this process presents difficulties to select the appropriate elicitation technique. This paper presents a classification of the elicitation techniques used in software engineering and the relationship between the elicitation techniques and some elements of knowledge management as assets knowledge, epistemological dimension of knowledge and the knowledge creation phases. This classification provides a guideline to select a technique or a set of techniques for knowledge elicitation based on phases of Nonaka's model. Additionally, is presented the use of product patterns in knowledge elicitation, and are defines a product pattern as formal representation mechanism for each of the knowledge assets defined and presented in this paper.

Chapter 3: Metadata in Serbia: Describing Library Collections, Towards a More Semantic Web

This chapter discusses the usage of metadata in libraries in Serbia. So far metadata have been used for describing printed documents available for patrons in library holdings and for describing digital documents available in online repositories. Paper presents some specific aspects of metadata usage primarily in regards to automation of digital data delivery for patrons. The advent of information technologies provides librarians in Serbia, as well as their colleagues in other countries, with powerful tools to describe digital objects and interconnect them making those related digital objects effectively available for users via an emergent, more semantic web.

Chapter 4: Social Networks and Employee Knowledge Sharing and Performance: A Chinese Case Study of a State-Owned Enterprise

In this chapter, the authors investigate the correlation between characteristics of the four social networks and employee task and contextual performance. The chapter focuses on the degree centrality and betweenness centrality of the four social networks (Job Advisory, Work Discussion, Friendship and Email Networks) of a Chinese state-owned enterprise as well as the individual attributes of knowledge sharing behavior and IT capability. The findings of this research are 1) employee contextual performance is uncorrelated with the network characteristics; 2) it is significantly and positively correlated with knowledge sharing behavior, but significantly and negatively correlated with individual IT capability, and 3) task performance is correlated, both positively and negatively, with various network characteristics, but not with knowledge sharing behavior and individual IT capability. In addition to discussing the cultural dimension of these results, the authors draw theoretical and managerial implications based on our research framework and findings.

Chapter 5: Semiotics is Fundamental Science

There is no way to acquire, store, and disseminate knowledge other than semiotically. Yet semiotics is hardly acknowledged in science, and not at all as science. Were it not for the fame of a few writers (Barthes, Derrida, and especially Eco), associated more with the semiotics of culture, few would even know that such a knowledge domain exists. In the age of computers, genetics, and networks—all of underlying semiotic condition—semiotics would at best qualify as pertinent to an obscure past, but insignificant for current endeavors. Gnoseologically, there is little to gain from acknowledging the shortcomings of semiotics. Epistemologically, quite a bit is at stake in grounding semiotics among the fundamental sciences. For this to come about, new interrogations become necessary: Why knowledge? What is knowledge? What kind of knowledge? How is knowledge acquired? One way or another, the answer will acknowledge semiotic processes as a necessary factor.

The perspective advanced in this chapter relies on an understanding of the living, and, in particular, of the human being, that ascertains anticipation as definitory. The future is made part of the present via semiotic processes. This is significant because in the age of neurons, suggestive of brain activity and of attempts to emulate it, to distinguish between knowledge supporting human activity, embodied in new technologies, and knowledge essential to the unfolding of the living becomes very difficult.

Chapter 6: One Year Forward: The 2013 Update to the E-Readers and E-Books in Public Libraries Survey

With the prevalence of affordable e-Readers in the consumer marketplace and library users increasingly having access to lendable e-Books from their local library institutions, library administrators continue to have difficulty in determining the immediate and long term effect of these technologies on their organizations. This chapter attempts to provide administrators with a brief overview of the current e-Reader and e-Book technology landscape and describe trends and issues. To help Administrators better understand their library users' experiences and expectations with e-Readers and e-Books, the researcher conducted a survey of 70 individuals. This survey is a follow-up to 2012's *E-Readers and E-Books in Public Libraries: Measuring Library Patron Expectations* research project. Using the same survey questions, format and potential respondent pool, *One Year Forward* demonstrates that patrons are increasingly demanding access to e-Books and e-Readers. Library patrons are finding these services more easy to use than in the past. Users clearly see value in these services both now and in the future. The results of this research project should be difficult for any library administrator to ignore.

Chapter 7: Open Source vs. Proprietary Collaborative Virtual Learning Environments

This chapter is an evaluation of the efficiency of 3D Collaborative Virtual Learning Environments to facilitate the implementation of collaborative learning activities. Firstly, there is a presentation of the state of the art regarding open source as well as proprietary platforms. Afterwards, the use of a case study reveals issues concerning the suitability of open source Collaborative Virtual Learning Environments, rationalizing the choice of executing a collaborative learning scenario in Second Life. The specific scenario is then presented culminating in evaluation results related to the appropriateness of Second Life with regards to its technical and pedagogical affordances. Finally, students' suggestions and reactions towards such a novel didactical approach are discussed.

Chapter 8: An Integrated Notation for Business Process Models

Since business processes may address complex behavioral requirements resulting from the integration of several items, i.e. tasks, business entities (also called artifacts), control flow rules and data flow rules, they need notations able to accommodate several viewpoints. This chapter proposes a notation, ARTS, aimed at integrating the traditional activity-oriented viewpoint and the artifact-oriented one. The major benefits are the unification of the control flow and the data flow and a clear representation of the choices to be carried out by the participants. The basic features are illustrated with the help of three versions of a simplified hiring process. This chapter also deals with the structure of work lists, which are the major interface between the participants and their tasks. The organization of the work lists leverages the artifacts to emphasize human choices; for this reason, the traditional linear structure is replaced with a network one, which shows the artifacts along with their states, correlations and valid options.

Chapter 9: The Relationship between Gardner's Multiple Intelligence and Kolb's Learning Style

In a diverse work environment, it is important to have diverse leaders, managers, and people with different talents and intelligence in order to deal with different problems. In this case, each individual can know their own strength and weakness, and know which position works best for them. The concept of learning styles is used to describe individual differences in the way people learn. Kolb has identified four statistically prevalent learning styles- diverging, assimilating, converging, and accommodating. On the other hand, Gardner's Multiple Intelligence Theory is very helpful to recognize that people have differing aptitude in different subject areas. This chapter documents a study in which the participants consisted of 153 bachelor students of Management from the Multimedia University of Malaysia. They were given two questionnaires, one for Kolb's learning style and other for Gardner's Multiple Intelligence inventory and a correlation was conducted. The results showed that there was a significant relationship between Kolb's Learning Style and Multiple Intelligence. The relationship could be seen particularly in Abstract Conceptualization(AC) and Multiple Intelligences which were Nature, kinesthetic, music, word, interpersonal, and picture. There were also a slight relationship between Concrete Experience(CE) and kinesthetic and nature; and also between Active Experimentation(AE) and Music. There was no relationship between Reflective Observation (RO) and Multiple Intelligences. The results also indicated that the majority of the participants are between AC and AE which means they are convergers and the second in lead was between AE and CE, which means they are accommodators. Having the right information for companies can be beneficial since knowing how their employees learn can lead to a diverse workplace that would have significant results on organizational structure, planning, development, and operation.

Chapter 10: Argument Extraction in Opinion Analysis: Identifying the Reasons behind Consumer Evaluations

In this chapter, the authors present foundational elements related to argument extraction in opinion texts to design a model of how consumers develop argumentation in such texts. A second goal of the chapter is to analyze and synthesize user preferences and therefore user value systems from these arguments. The authors show that (1) that the association of an evaluative expression with a discourse structure such as an elaboration, an illustration, or a reformulation must be interpreted as an argument and (2) that the link between a consumer statement and a related argument often requires domain knowledge and dedicated inference schemas. This chapter develops a conceptual semantics of these discourse structures.

Chapter 11: Current Trends and Developments, Future Requirements, and Predictions for Computer Mediated Communications and E-Collaboration

This chapter provides a revision and update to the authors' original 2012 research that discussed fifteen semi-structured interviews carried out with international industry experts and thought leaders within the computer mediated communications and e-collaboration field. The original interviews focused on 5, 10, and 15-year time frames, and sought to elicit predictions on the components and services of future platforms, as well as their likely impact on business processes and value chains. Affinity Diagramming/ KJ Analysis techniques on the original interview transcripts exposed a number of key tenets that are now revisited, discussed in a current context, revised and updated in this chapter. Following a similar structure to the 2012 paper, the authors discuss the origins of the field, main providers and platforms, related software developments technologies, W3C standards, video conferencing, telepresence, cloud computing and Enterprise 2.0. The authors provide a synopsis of the original interviews and have updated their conclusions and findings in light of most recent research and developments. With reference to future requirements, they have also updated their discussions on a next generation architecture proposal/model with additional insights from the authors' research work and that of others in the computer mediated communication and e-collaboration field.

REFERENCES

Davenport, T. H. (2005). *Thinking for a living*. Boston: Harvard Business Press.

Degler, D., & Battle, L. (2000). Knowledge management in pursuit of performance: The challenge of context. *Performance Improvement*, *39*(6). doi:10.1002/pfi.4140390609

Jennex, M. E. (2005). What is knowledge management? *International Journal of Knowledge Management*, *1*(4), i–iv.

Jennex, M. E. (2008). Impacts from using knowledge: A longitudinal study from a nuclear power plant. *International Journal of Knowledge Management*, *4*(1), 51–64. doi:10.4018/jkm.2008010105

Jennex, M. E. (2012). *Identifying the components of a knowledge management strategy*. Paper presented at 18th Americas Conference on Information Systems.

Jennex, M. E. (2013). Knowledge management success in an engineering firm. *Engineering Management Reviews*, *2*(3), 65–74.

Jennex, M. E., & Addo, T. B. A. (2005). *Issues in knowledge management strategy*. Paper presented at the Information Resource Management Resource Conference.

Jennex, M. E., & Bartczak, S. E. (2013). a revised knowledge pyramid. *International Journal of Knowledge Management*, *9*(3). doi:10.4018/ijkm.2013070102

Jennex, M.E., & Olfman, L. (2006). A Model of Knowledge Management Success International Journal of Knowledge Management, 2(3), pp. 51-68.

Jennex, M. E., Olfman, L., & Addo, T. B. A. (2003). The need for an organizational knowledge management strategy. In *Proceedings of the 36th Hawaii International Conference on System Sciences, HICSS36, IEEE Computer Society.*

Jennex, M. E., Smolnik, S., & Croasdell, D. (2012). Where to look for knowledge management success. In *Proceedings of the 45th Hawaii International Conference on System Sciences, HICSS45, IEEE Computer Society.*

Jennex, M. E., Smolnik, S., & Croasdell, D. T. (2009). Towards a consensus knowledge management success definition. *VINE: The Journal of Information and Knowledge Management Systems*, *39*(2), 174–188. doi:10.1108/03055720910988878

Chapter 1
The Crisis of Knowing in the Age of Complexity

Ton Jörg
University of Utrecht, The Netherlands

ABSTRACT

The crisis of our time is very much a crisis of knowledge. There is no easy way of "solving" the crisis. "Solving" the crisis demands for a real shift of mind, implying new ways of thinking and knowing about what is the real. The most important task of today, therefore, is to see and to open up a new world: a world of the possible, with its hitherto uncharted and unexplored complexity territory. For the sake of mastering complexity, understanding real complexity is urgently needed. The problem of complexity for organizations is the way organizations and companies attempt to respond to complexity. To confront and master complexity, the focus should be on the conditions of possibility, hitherto unknown. These conditions are about the possibility of triggering self-generative, self-organizing processes with potential nonlinear effects within dynamic, hyperconnected networks. These effects can be generated by the process of amplifying changes within these networks. This amplifying is about the amplifying of learning, of thinking, and of knowing. In practice, this means that new thinking in complexity is urgently needed to master the complexity involved. This approach is compared with the recent approaches advocated by big firms and companies in their embracing of complexity. This chapter shows how they are unable to discover and explore the very potential of complexity for their own Complex Organization (CO). They are very much in need to master complexity for the sake of fostering creativity, novelty, and innovation in their own organizations.

DOI: 10.4018/978-1-4666-4711-4.ch001

INTRODUCTION

We have to deal with what we do not understand,

and that demands new ways of thinking.

-Paul Cilliers, 1998, p. 2

In this contribution we want to go deeper into the crisis of our time and its consequences for organizations and companies, operating in our society, commonly conceived as a kind of 'information society' or 'knowledge society'. According to the French thinker Edgar Morin, we may speak about a so-called 'poly-crisis' (see Hessel, 2011, p. 43). We argue that the crisis of our time can be taken as being both a financial, economic, political and scientific crisis. The crisis is very much the crisis of Western Culture. According to Sandywell (1996), we may speak about a crisis of Western reason. We 'simply' lack an adequate understanding of the crisis we are in. To understand the very crisis we are in, and its effects on Complex Organizations (CO's) and their management, we need to become more reflective on the *nature* of this crisis. We argue here that the deep nature of the crisis is still very much hidden. After reading the papers, journals and more specialist literatures, we are of opinion that nobody seems to have a kind of bird's eye view of the crisis. Consequently, nobody seems to know what is underlying the very crisis we are still in. We seem 'simply' not able *to view the system with new eyes*.

We want to argue here that the crisis is very much the crisis of our common way of knowing: that is, about the very *limits* of our knowing. The crisis we are in is very much the crisis of a *learned* incapacity to make the link between the known known and the field of the unknown unknown (see Table 1). The crisis is very much a crisis of our *learned* ignorance: the ignorance about the unknown unknown. It is the crisis of complexity, of complex phenomena, which we still take so much for granted. We take not only complexity for granted but also the very notion of reality. We have 'simply' disregarded the very complex nature of reality: that is, the nonlinear complex reality (Mainzer, 2004). Our view of complexity of reality is 'simply' *insufficiently complex*. The map we have of reality is a reduced version of this reality. We seem *insufficiently* aware of our assumptions about reality, being so reduced. We seem *insufficiently* aware that reality can be different: nonlinear and complex. This is very much true for innovation. Innovation is a complex topic being part of our nonlinear complex reality. But we 'simply' do not know how to deal with this complexity. Dealing with the complexity of reality demands a new approach and new ways of thinking about reality. The crux of our crisis is that "we don't have the right vocabulary to precisely describe what we're studying" (Mitchell, 2011, p. 301). We are a kind of *prisoners of description*. Henceforth, we need a new approach, with a new language, a language of complexity, with a new vocabulary, with new terms, concepts and metaphors, so to be able to describe reality as a nonlinear complex reality. We have to *learn* to use the term reality in a new way, based on a new way of thinking. We urgently need a new kind of map about what is the real(m) of our sciences. That is, a map about the complex dynamics of reality. We need this map to overcome our learned ignorance and learned incapacity in dealing with reality. This map is linked to the complexity of knowing. We need a more complex map to deal with the hitherto *unknown* territories of complexity of a nonlinear complex reality. These territories are the territories of the complexity of knowing, but also of innovation, novelty and creativity (cf. Kuhn, 1999, p. 90). To be able to deal with this complexity, we need a new way of thinking: of thinking in complexity (see Jörg, 2011).

'SOLVING' THE CRISIS

From seeing through a lens to seeing the lens.

-Kuhn, 1999, p. 6

There is no easy way of 'solving' the crisis. What seems certain is that we cannot 'solve' the crisis with the knowledge which is now available. We cannot 'solve' the crisis with the knowledge from the field of the known known (See Table 1). 'Solving' the crisis demands for a real shift of mind: of new ways of thinking and knowing about [what is] the real. It is therefore no surprise that there is no such thing as an easy 'solution' for this crisis. This description of the state of art may explain why nobody seems able to find the path of 'solving' the very crisis we are in. For this reason we may speak not only about the tragedy of the crisis as unforeseen. We may as well speak about the tragedy of *misunderstanding* the crisis. The crisis is very much the crisis of the unexpected and misunderstood phenomena, being more complex than ever thought before. The unexpected in this is very much about the *unknown*. Experts, whom we trusted, were not very expert and knowledgeable about the field of the unknown. They didn't know very well what could be done or should be done about the very crisis. Their knowledge was very much bounded by the discipline they worked in. Their lack of knowledge became clear to others, operating in other fields and disciplines of knowledge. Consequently, reputations got lost very quickly and the struggle to survive became very prominent.

Table 1. Description of fields of knowledge

Fields of knowledge	Known	Unknown
Known	Certain	Uncertain/Latent
Unknown	Amnesia/Blind Spot	**Ignorance**

The demonstrated lack of knowledge about the unknown is not only about the known unknown but also, and even more so, about the *unknown* unknown. This, we argue, might be viewed as the key for a new opening in our thinking about the world as a more complex world. This opening might be viewed as opening a new window on the world. This hitherto unknown complex world may show up to be a 'world of the possible' (Kauffman, 1993, p. 375). Within this new world we may open up new vistas of possibility, with new spaces of possibility, hitherto unknown. Kuhn (1999) speaks for good reasons about "spaces of *infinite* possibility" (p. 51; emphasis added). These spaces are the spaces of what Melanie Mitchell describes as "uncharted territory" (Mitchell, 2011, p. 303). Opening of this new world of the *possible* asks for a shift of mind about (what is) the real in this complex world. We need to open up the black box of this unknown world, to see what is actually *in* it and how complexity may be 'at work' in the real. This is part of the adventure of complexity (Kuhn, 1999). We have to step outside of the system and learn to think outside of the box, to be able to view the system with new eyes, with a new lens: a *complexity* lens (cf. Kuhn, 1999, pp. 7, 11; emphasis added). It is through such a tool of a new way of seeing and thinking that organizational life may be viewed with new eyes.

We should not only be ready to *embrace* complexity. We also need to learn to live with complexity by facing the very complexity of our world. Doing so, we may better understand the power of complexity operating in this world. It is the very power of complexity as 'self-potentiating' (see Rescher, 1998, p. 21). Once we better understand how complexity can be 'at work' in this complex world, we might benefit from a deeper understanding of "how complexity can help identify organizational processes and potentialities" (Kuhn, 1999, p. 2). This, we think, is the very promise of complexity.

THE TRAGEDY OF THE CRISIS

In order to arrive at what we do not know
You must go by a way which is the way of ignorance.

-T. S. Eliot, in "East Coker"

The tragedy of the crisis of today may be viewed as the tragedy of modernism, showing its fundamental incapability to function as an adequate source for *mastering* the crisis: that is, the very complexity of the crisis. The tragedy is about the fallibility of our knowledge and our common ways of knowing, based on modernism; that is, of our inability to harness the effects of the crisis in a satisfying way. The crisis we are in, at all levels, is very much "the crisis of knowledge," as put forward by Paul Cilliers (1998, p. 121). We have never learned to embrace and face the complexity of our world in an adequate way. Actually, we have *discarded* complexity, even though Nietzsche has warned us that "[T]he 'most simple' cases are *very complex*, - one cannot be surprised enough about that!" (in his work "Morgenröte;" all emphasis in original). We actually had very much trouble to take complexity seriously: not only in science but also in practice, like the practice of managing complex organizations (see special edition HBR, September 2011; see also Kuhn, 1999). Below, we go deeper into an analysis of the reasons for this situation. Our main argument has to do with our deep ignorance about the world, which is a fundamental *complex* world (see Vitek & Jackson, 2008). This ignorance is very much the ignorance, which is based on modernism. It is very much the ignorance, based on linear thinking. According to Klaus Mainzer, "linear thinking may be *dangerous* in a non-linear complex reality" (Mainzer, 2004, p. 407; emphasis added). We seem not able to escape the danger of such thinking. We 'simply' do not know what we do not know; that is, we do not know about the very complexity of our world. There is a deep gap between the map we have and the territory of this very complex world: a gap between the view we hold of reality and the real world. This gap shows the deep ignorance about the world we live in. This ignorance is not innocent but a real danger for our sciences and society at large: that is, for complex organizations (CO's) and companies that want to deal with the problem of complexity for their own organization or company. Some scholars, and others as well, do know that the century we live in, the 21st century, might be viewed as "the century of complexity," as prophesized by Stephen Hawking (2000). But the problem of complexity is very much the problem that we cannot see complexity as real in our world:

The world we actually inhabit, as opposed to the happy idealization of modern scientific mythology, is filled with wonderful and im-

portant things we have not seen because we have not looked.

-Laughlin, 2005, p. xvi

We may conclude from this description of the state of art that, although the complexity of reality is real, we 'simply' do not know how to think about a world in terms of a *complex* world. We take complexity too much for granted (Bak, 1996). This makes that we are not only ignorant about the complexity of this complex world, but we even do not know *how* to arrive at what we do not know (see the quote by T. S. Eliot, above). We still seem not able to open the sciences to deal with the complexity of our world. We seem not able to explore the uncharted territories of our complex world. We may call this 'the problem of complexity'. The map we have of complexity is 'simply' *not* the territory. We lack a theory of complexity which may be of use for dealing with the *real* complexity of our world, being part of "a nonlinear complex reality" (Mainzer, 2004). We are not able to "deal with the theoretical dynamics of complexity" (Minati, Abram, & Pessa, 2012, p. vi), which is so much part of our world. We actually need new thinking in complexity to understand this complexity: how complexity really 'works' in the complex world. Only then we may become able to deal with complexity. We argue here that the most important task of today is to open up a new world of the possible, with its uncharted and *unexplored* territories of complexity and spaces of possibility. This is not an easy task. It demands for several steps to be taken:

1. First, we need to become aware of the need for a new approach of complexity, starting with recognition of our ignorance about the real complexity of the real world.
2. Second, we need to understand what complexity is 'really' about, to be able to harness complexity by the development of tools for new thinking in complexity.
3. Third, once we learn to understand how complexity may be 'at work' in the real, we may finally better be able *realize* its potential to open up new spaces of the possible in a world of the possible.

After making these steps, we may become aware that reality has become a different reality: that is, a nonlinear complex reality. We may explore this still very much *unknown* reality. Doing so is actually opening new spaces of possibility. This opening of new spaces of possibility can be done by learning to know what might be the very *conditions* of possibility in the new world of the *possible*. The challenge here is to turn conditions of impossibility (linked to modernism) into conditions of *possibility* for the future. We may learn, then, how to deal with complexity more effectively by turning complexity into *advantageous* complexity (see Jörg, 2011). All of this new kind of thinking in complexity is linked to the deeper understanding of the real *power* of complexity for complex organizations (CO's). Understanding this very power of complexity is the key for opening the field of learning, knowing, thinking and innovation. But, again, it demands for a shift of mind and a readiness to make this shift. It demands for viewing the system with new eyes, by stepping outside of the system and by thinking outside of the box. Several steps need to be taken, to become able to see and think the new way: that is, to see with a new lens, a complexity lens, and to think in complexity about the real complexity of a nonlinear complex reality.

NEW THINKING IN COMPLEXITY

The difficulty lies, not in the new ideas, but in escaping from the old ones.

-J. M. Keynes, 1936, p. xxiii

The urgency of dealing with the complexity is increasing as the problem of increasing complexity in our society becomes more and more urgent. New thinking in complexity might therefore be linked to the practical of our society. This may be illustrated by a recent edition of Harvard Business Review (HBR, September 2011). In this edition, the editors put the spotlight on the very problem of complexity. Their focus on "embracing of complexity" is done for good reasons. Complexity has always been very much neglected or 'simply' discarded. We mainly tend not only to take complexity for granted but also to *deny* the very problem of complexity. So, it is time indeed to change our view on complexity and take a different stance: one which is more positive about complexity. Putting the spotlight on complexity, in the HBR issue on complexity, one speaks warmly about "Embracing Complexity," in an interview with Michael Mauboussin (2011). The central topic, however, is about "Managing Complex Organizations." One of the articles in this edition is about "[L]earning to live with complexity" (Sargut & Gunther McGrath, 2011). So, it seems that complexity has become a topic of real concern for organizations and companies.

Big companies, like the international accountancy partners of KPMG, fully recognize the need to deal with complexity for their own business purposes. They organized a survey among their partners in 22 countries to learn from these partners how urgent the problem of complexity is for them. The report they published was titled "[C]onfronting complexity" (KPMG, 2011). Based on this report, they proudly used the slogan "cutting through complexity™" as their Trade Mark. So, they became convinced that their view of the world had been too simple to deal with the complexity of this world. But in their view of complexity they show more an urgency of *taming* complexity than that of *understanding* complexity.

Based on the urgency of the problem of complexity, we may wonder what might be the promise of complexity for the 21st century. But first, we have to deal with the problem of complexity: why thinking about complexity has hampered our thinking about the world for so long. We should, however, also be critical about the urgency of *confronting* complexity. The approach seems to know already what this complexity is about. We think, however, that there is a real danger of misunderstanding complexity: in how complexity may actually 'work' in the real. The description of the problem of *confronting* complexity in the KPMG report shows the lack of an adequate view of complexity and an adequate vocabulary of complexity to describe what they are actually dealing with. They seem not aware of the state of art in the field of complexity. Melanie Mitchell is clear about this state: "we don't have the right vocabulary to describe what we're studying" (Mitchell, 2011, p. 301).

The basic misunderstanding in the KPMG report is the neglect of complexity being very much a network concept. Not many scholars or managers of companies seem to have noticed the warning, made by Barabási (2003), that most attempts to deal with complexity and to construct a theory of complexity "have overlooked the deep link between it and networks" (p. 238). This is essential for new thinking in complexity (Jörg, 2011). Network thinking is the missing link for all of our disciplines, in developing a better understanding of complexity. Complex systems, like living systems, are "dynamic networks of many self-organising entities or agents" (Kuhn, 1999, p. 38). We dare to say that all of those who have disregarded this link to networks have missed the unexpected but wonderful opportunity to see the world in a new way and to develop the potential to open up a new world of the possible. Complex reality is a different reality indeed, but still very much unknown. Complex reality is simultaneously dynamic, relational, interconnected and network-like (see Jörg, 2011; Mesle, 2008; Spretnak, 2011). The power of complexity is very much present *in* and *through* the new kind of dynamics of these networks, with their specific network features (Minati, Abram, & Pessa, 2012, p. vi). It is the very same power which we may see as being 'at work' in nature as complex adaptive systems (CASs). The big question, then, is "what are the conditions of their wonderful operating in the real world?" Another question is "what can we learn from this wondrous world?" It should be clear by now that the steps of thinking, needed to answer these questions, are not simple steps. It is necessary to get ready for making these steps, to overcome our cognitive limitations to deal with the problem of complexity. But first, one has to recognize that one *wants* to be ready, and to make these steps, before actually getting ready and become able to think the new way. All of this is about "getting yourself into the right mind-set to deal with complexity" (see HBR issue, 2011, p. 92). All of these changes of seeing and thinking in a new way are very much needed to turn the dynamic network of self-organizing entities or agents in a complex organization into a more intelligent network. Turning the organization or company into a smarter organization demands not only a new way of seeing, through a complexity lens, but also a new way of *organizing* the company. The focus should be more on *organizing* complexity to create novelty and innovation in organizations.

THE CRISIS AND THE PROBLEM OF COMPLEXITY

We are hampered by cognitive limits.

-Sargut & Gunther McGrath, 2011, p. 72

We are convinced that the problem of complexity is related to the crisis. We argue here that the deeper cause of the crisis is strongly linked to our *inability* to deal with the real complexity of our world. This inability, we think, is strongly related to our cognitive limitations to harness complexity. It is not only the limitations to fully comprehend the complex organizations to manage (see the HBR edition), but also to comprehend the full complexity of all kind of complex phenomena of our world. Albert-László Barabási (2003) has made clear that "earlier attempts to construct a theory of complexity have overlooked the deep link between it and networks" (p. 238). Ignoring this deep link is not innocent. It implies the danger of a *misunderstanding* complexity: not only for a theory of complexity but also for the practice of dealing with complexity in complex organizations and companies.

If real complexity is about the complexity of networks, then a theory of networks should deal with the dynamics of networks that are constitutive for real complexity. With real complexity, we mean the dynamic complexity of deeply interconnected loop networks of many self-organizing entities or agents (see

Kuhn, 1999, and above). Only by taking this kind of complexity into account, we may become able "to make sense of the unpredictable and the indefinable in today's *hyperconnected* business world" (Sargut & Gunther McGrath, 2011, p. 69). This demands a shift of mind and a readiness to think the new way. Only then we might be able to link theory with practice: the theory of real complexity with the reality of complexity of a complex business world. We need a new language of complexity, with a new vocabulary, to deal with this hitherto unknown complexity, being part of the field of the unknown unknown (see Table 1).

We think the deeper problem of the crisis is the lack of capability to deal with the problem of complexity, which makes that we cannot comprehend and deal with the complexity of our world, 'simply' because of our cognitive limitations. The complexity we have to face seems to be too complex to be mastered! So, we get easily paralyzed in our thinking about the world as a complex world. The main reason is that we lack an adequate view and an adequate way of thinking about this complex world. If the map is not the territory, we 'simply' need to change our map. We argue here that the map is not sufficiently complex to represent the complexity of our world, and to build adequate knowledge about this complex world. We have to replace our known map of the world into a more complex map. This brings us to the question "how the new map might look like?" Can we get a more realistic map of the real complex world? This brings us to the problem what the real world itself might be like. So there are two problems which are related: the nature of the territory and the map we may have of the territory. To be able to deal with these problems, we need to think in a new way. We need to think *about* reality in a new way and we need to think about how to *comprehend* complexity of our complex world. This implies a broadening of our worldview. We need new thinking in complexity to deal with the real complexity of our world. Our way of seeing and thinking must be *sufficiently* complex to deal with complexity. *Embracing* complexity, we think, is not enough. *Confronting* complexity is also not enough, because it expresses only an attitude of facing the complexity of our world. Confronting complexity, however, does not help very much in *understanding* the very complexity of our nonlinear complex reality. Paul Cilliers is very right in his assessment that "[W]e *have to* deal with what we do *not* understand, and that demands *new ways of thinking*" (Cilliers, 1998, p. 2; emphasis added). We do need new thinking in complexity to deal with a nonlinear complex reality, which is very much a kind of *new* reality for our sciences (cf. Mainzer, 2004; Jörg, 2011). We now have to face the complexity of our world: not just by embracing or confronting complexity but by developing a deeper understanding about how complexity may be 'at work' in the real world. This world is a complex, *hyperconnected* world. We do need a kind of *hypercomplex* map of this world, which is a map about *dynamic* networks of entities or agents. This is the most important task for our time of multiple crises. This new map is opening a new world: the world of the *possible*. Opening the world of the possible is the task for our 21st century, slowly becoming the century of complexity. It is through new thinking in complexity about dynamic networks that we may develop new ways of knowing about this complex world of the possible. It is opening new spaces of possibility indeed: the complex spaces of a *hyperconnected* world. We may place this unexpected opening of new spaces of possibility within a new hyperconnected world of the *possible*. The new thinking in complexity, however, strongly demands for overcoming the inherent cognitive limits of our thinking.

NEW THINKING IN COMPLEXITY ABOUT A HYPERCONNECTED WORLD

Based on a new account of reality as a nonlinear complex reality, we may start to confront the real complexity of our hyperconnected business world. We may do so, first, by embracing the very complexity of this complex world. We may start to live with the complexity of this world by developing a new window on this world and to develop new ways of seeing and thinking about the complexity of this world. So, the learning to *live* with complexity implies the learning to *think* in complexity in new ways. We should never take the complexity of our world for granted. We will only be able to deal with this complexity by viewing the system with new eyes, by the use of a new complexity lens, and by the development of new tools of thinking about this very complexity of the world. We may start to realize that complexity is about dynamic networks, with entities or agents linked in a hyperconnected way. This may imply the notion of a so-called 'relational reality' (Spretnak, 2011), with dynamic, cyclic (reciprocal) relationships, interconnected in a hyperconnected way. We may even think about a hypercyclic, web-like world, operating, in three or more dimensions (Kauffman, 1993). With Kauffman (1995), we may ask the important but difficult question "What is the weave?" Not only the entities or agents as elements within the network, but also the effects, are always interconnected within this kind of hyperconnected, web-like networks. Our thinking about the complexity of this kind of networks demand for a network way of thinking in complexity. The complexity being at work within the dynamic network can operate as a *generative* kind of complexity, which is potentially nonlinear in its effects over time (Jörg, 2011). We may describe the states of the entities or agents in the dynamic network as dynamic states within a multi-dimensional so-called 'state hyperspace' (Globus, 1995). The generative complexity involved in these dynamic networks may become self-potentiating indeed (Rescher, 1998). These terms and concepts are part of a new vocabulary to see the world with new eyes, and describe the world accordingly. The map we may 'construct' of the complex, hyperconnected network should be close to the hyperconnected business world, to be relevant for managers and the management of complex organizations or companies. This map may be dynamic and fluid itself, corresponding to the dynamic states of the entities or agents within the state hyperspaces. These states may be described in terms of dynamic, evolving trajectories, patterns or landscapes. The knowledge one may acquire about these states is not always about a certain state but may be about a fluid kind of state: about dynamic patterns and landscapes in many dimensions, evolving over time within multi-dimensional state hyperspaces (see Jörg, 2011). This knowledge may be about the patterning of the dynamic landscape of interdependent entities evolving over time. Knowing is not anymore about certainty of states of entities or agents, but about the very quality of the trajectories, patterns and landscapes of entities or agents operating in the organization. This quality may be described and understood as the very *quality* of relationships between the entities or agents in the organization (Kuhn, 1999; Jörg,

2011), now conceived as a complex organization. This description and understanding goes largely beyond the cognitive limits of our common reasoning.

It might be clear that all of this new thinking in complexity about a hyperconnected business world demands for a new language, with a new vocabulary, which is based on the new framework of complexity (see Jörg, 2011). In this new framework, we may link the concept of complexity with a generative notion of hypercomplexity, being linked to spaces with many dimensions. With this new language, it will be possible to describe the degree of complexity, conceived as generative complexity, as being based on the degree of connectivity and the degree of interactivity within these relationships. It will also be possible to link the degree of complexity with the rather unknown concept of 'generativity', being the power of a network to *generate* potential nonlinear effects. All of these new conceptions of complexity is about the new theory of complexity (Jörg, 2011). This theory is very much about 'the complexity of complexity' (Jörg, 2011, Ch. 13). This theory enables to conceive of potential nonlinear processes and effects within complex spaces of the possible, like the so-called 'butterfly effect', the 'Matthew effect' and the 'Comenius effect'. All of these effects are a kind of *multiplier* effects, to be conceived as effects of amplification, thriving on the interaction between the entities or agents within the network. These effects are about amplifying changes within dynamic networks, with effects on the entities or agents operating within these networks. This amplifying may be the amplifying of learning, of thinking and of knowing (cf. Senge, 1990; Nonaka, 2004). This amplifying of learning corresponds with the concept of 'generative learning', described by Senge (1990, p. 14). The effects, described here, imply the fundamental possibility of *enlarging* the space of the possible within a world of the possible. The effects can be conceived as taking place within new "spaces of *infinite* possibility" (Kuhn, 1999, p. 51; emphasis added).

The challenge for now is to link the fundamental with the practical (see Jörg, 2011, p. 228). We want to do so by making a link to the actual case of the international office of KPMG, and their specific approach to deal with complexity by *confronting* complexity. "Confronting complexity" is the title of the recent report they made, which is based on data from a survey among 22 countries all over the world (KPMG, May 2011). In this report, mention is made of the ambition to help the reader, being a partner of KPMG:

to better understand the causes and impact of complexity, and ways to integrate actions into your strategies that will not only help you to manage the challenges that lie ahead, but also to take better advantage of new opportunities (p. 1).

THE CASE OF KPMG

For business, increasing complexity is not just an inconvenience. It can radically affect the way that businesses are managed, challenging profitability with new costs, adding new risks and creating opportunities.

-KPMG, 2011, p. 2

We think it might be of general interest to describe the case of KPMG and their way of confronting complexity for the future of the company and their partners, operating as agents in this company. We therefore aim to analyze the results of their effort to do a survey among their partners in 22 countries all over the world. Although they made a report about each of the countries involved, we focus only on the general results and conclusions. Our focus, then, is on giving a diagnosis of their alleged *confrontation* of complexity. We do so because it might be of general interest to see how a big company like KPMG tries to deal with the problem of increasing complexity in a world which is experienced as becoming a more complex world.

A DIAGNOSIS OF CONFRONTING COMPLEXITY

It's easy to confuse the merely complicated with the genuinely complex.

-Sargut & Gunther McGrath, 2011, p. 70

We start our diagnosis by taking into account the rationality and relevance of the decision to do such a large survey about the topic of complexity among their partners. How rational was the decision to organize a survey about the problem of complexity for KPMG and their partners all over the world? Somehow they had the notion of 'embracing complexity' as being of value for their partners in their organization. Clearly they had the idea that something didn't go so well in their company. This state of art seems to have been the source of some worries about the future of this company, operating in many countries all over the world. That made KPMG to start a survey with questions about the experience of complexity in practice by the partners of the firm. Those who were responsible for the survey seemed to wonder if the increasing complexity of society, as it manifests itself in the practice of their partners, was a common, shared experience in the 22 countries they addressed for their survey. Implicitly, they seem responsible for taking a critical stance towards the problem of facing of this increasing complexity by the partners. Probably this was the reason that they used the notion of 'confronting complexity, as they used this phrase in their final report "Confronting Complexity" (KPMG, 2011). Implicitly, however, they were also responsible for the optimistic prospects of coming to clear conclusions by doing the survey. They seemed to hold a rather optimistic view of defining and transforming their way of viewing the world as a more complex world and the possibility of renewal of their practice. The final result of their survey was even more optimistic in their prospects about the future of KPMG, as demonstrated by the use of the new slogan "cutting through complexity" in their own logo. This brings us to the specific language in use for describing the results and their conclusions in the final report (KPMG, 2011).

Below, we will give a sketch of the positive elements of the way KPMG has confronted complexity: see Table 2. We will also take account of the less positive elements of their efforts and their conclusions, i.e. about the way they have translated the conclusions to a new policy for practice. We do so because of our ambition to draw some lessons about the problem of complexity for complex organizations (CO's); lessons, which may be of value for other companies and organizations. Our diagnosis may be of particular value for the discussion about the functioning of CO's and the management of these CO's.

What goes right in dealing with the increasing complexity of a complex world is their way of approaching complexity as a challenge to deal with in a direct, constructive way, by doing a large survey. This is a remarkable

Table 2. Positive and less positive elements of confronting complexity by KPMG

Positive Elements	Less Positive Elements
• recognition of complexity as a critical issue for business and the business agenda • taking complexity into account as a challenge to deal with in a constructive way for business • doing a survey on the topic of complexity • the implicit idea of defining the practice anew • the implicit idea of possible transformation of the company • the idea of a new approach of local practice by individual partners	• no awareness of 'the crisis of knowledge' as linked to the problem of complexity of our postmodern society (Cilliers, 1998, p. 121) • no awareness of what they do not know: the field of the unknown about complexity • the use of the term 'confronting complexity' • no clear concept of complexity to start with • no clear concept of complexity to end with • the notion of simplifying complexity • the notion of 'cutting through complexity' • the use of the concept complexity as insufficiently complex • no clear idea of the power of complexity for the management of CO's • no idea of a new framework of complexity that shows the bootstrapping power of complexity for use in CO's • no understanding of the link between complexity and innovation

decision, taking into account the general problem of managing complex organizations, which is not an easy task. Those responsible for the decision were rather optimistic in their readiness of embracing complexity. They describe increasing complexity not just as an inconvenience, but *also* as creating *opportunities*, and rightly so! However, their readiness to deal with complexity shows a danger, which is a very common danger in science: the eagerness of coming to conclusions. In this case to conclusions which are of direct importance for the partners and their practice, in their facing the increasing complexity of the world. These are described in their final report.

So, we may now come to the less positive aspects of the approach taken by those involved in the report. As can be read from Table 2, they take complexity as a concept too much for granted. They do not seem aware of the very 'crisis of knowledge', as put forward by Paul Cilliers (1998, p. 121), in his book titled "Complexity and Postmodernism," in which he links this crisis to the very *conditions* for knowledge (Cilliers, 1998, p. 121). This crisis of knowledge, we argue, is linked to the fields of the unknown. From the report itself, it may be derived that they do not take into account what literature about complexity may tell about the problem of complexity and how to deal with it. The authors of the report do not treat complexity as being very much part of the field of the unknown about the world as a complex world. They 'simply' make no mention of the link between complexity and the concept of networks and the functioning of these networks in complex organizations, operating as dynamic networks within a hyperconnected business world. The mental map of complexity 'simply' does not correspond to the real complexity of the world. As a result they actually *simplify* complexity from the very start. They also end up with simplifying complexity. In their report "Confronting Complexity," about the research findings and insights, they make mention of "a world striving for simplicity" (KPMG, 2011, p. 2). Doing so, they are disregarding the *fact* that complexity can be self-potentiating (see Rescher, 1998, p. 28). It is this very *fact* that may create the opportunities they like to mention. However, they do so only in a limited way, without awareness of the real power of complexity.

In Table 3, we give a summary of critical remarks about the report "Confronting Complexity." In their descriptions of confronting complexity, they do *not* show a mental map which is about the real complexity of the world. So, the real complexity of a complex world 'simply' remained hidden: the complexity of a nonlinear complex reality (Mainzer, 2004), operating within a dynamic, network-like architecture of bootstrapping configurations (Jörg, 2011). It is the very power of bootstrapping relations within complex, dynamic networks of interconnected loops that nonlinearity of effects, like multiplier or bootstrapping effects, may show up in the real (Jörg, 2011). Such effects may show up as effects of generative processes, showing the power of complexity as self-potentiating indeed (cf. Rescher, 1998).

To recap, the case of KPMG is a clear example of what Paul Cilliers (1998) has called 'the crisis of knowledge' (p. 121). Cilliers is right that this crisis is "a direct result of the complexity of our postmodern society" (ibid., p. 121). The problem, then, is how to get knowledgeable about the very complexity of our society. This problem is clearly not solved by KPMG. They have missed the chance to become more knowledgeable about this complexity. They were clearly not aware of the danger of *misunderstanding* complexity. In drawing the conclusion of 'cutting through complexity', they could not escape the danger Cilliers (again) warns us for, namely that "[I]n 'cutting up' a system, the analytical method *destroys* what it seeks to understand" (ibid., p. 2; emphasis in original). They did not seem aware of the danger of linear thinking for the analysis and understanding of complexity, as phrased by Klaus Mainzer: "linear thinking may be dangerous in a non-linear complex reality" (Mainzer, 2004, p. 407). They did not seem able to escape the danger of such thinking. The question is "how KPMG will fare with their conclusion of cutting through complexity?"

Table 3. Critical remarks about the KPMG report "Confronting Complexity"

• it shows the danger of misunderstanding complexity by underestimating the complexity of complexity • no clear idea about the gap between the (mental) map of complexity and the complex world itself • no clear idea of the building stones of complexity linked to a complex reality • no awareness of how effects of complexity might be 'at work' in complex organizations • a lack of awareness of the link between complexity and the network-like character of complexity • no clear idea of taking advantage of new opportunities by confronting complexity • no conviction or mental map of the power of complexity for complex organizations (CO's) • a rather vague idea about the causes and impact of complexity on the management of CO's • no notion of complexity as self-potentiating in its dynamics in CO's as network organizations • no notion of 'network intelligence' and the opportunity to foster this intelligence by thriving on complexity • no notion of the architecture of complexity in network-like CO's • no notion of the bootstrapping configuration of CO's as a complex system

HOW KPMG WILL FARE IN CONFRONTING COMPLEXITY

Organized complexity is the fount of life, liberty, and novelty on the planet earth.

-Wilden, 1987, p. 309

In taking a limited view of complexity by simplifying complexity from the very start, KPMG and their partners will not become knowledgeable about the fields of the unknown. Consequently, they will remain ignorant about the real power of complexity for their organization. This ignorance, again, is not innocent! As a consequence, they keep on being ignorant about the unknown, and will not become knowledgeable about the promise of complexity for the complex organizations they are advising for in their role as consultants. They remain ignorant about how complexity thrives on (human) interaction within interactive human relationships. They will remain ignorant about "the full generative power of interaction" (Bruner, 1996, p. 119). They will remain ignorant of the possibility of "learners who bootstrap each other" (ibid., p. 21) in a community of learners as a community of interaction. By taking an approach of cutting through complexity, they will not become able to exploit the power of networks of a hyperconnected business world, thriving on the power of complex relationships within this world, empowered by the strong interaction, generating potential nonlinear effects over time. So, they will remain ignorant about the link between complexity and innovation, with organized complexity being the fount of novelty and innovation (see quote above by Wilden, 1987, p. 309).

In their report they do not show a path of how to advance their knowledge about complexity. On the contrary. We may illustrate their way of thinking by the following quote:

It is not the nature of the complexity that a company faces that will determine its success; it is the extent to which the company can analyze the problem, identify the most effective way to address it, and then implement appropriate action. In doing so, the challenges of complexity can be turned into opportunities for growth.

-KPMG, 2011, p. 3

In this quote, in which the wrong use of words is emphasized, everything comes together what is taken wrongly about how complexity might be 'at work' in a company. It is 'simply' putting their 'new' approach of complexity in an old bag. It is demonstrating a kind of misunderstanding complexity that is lacking any promise of complexity for the future of CO's. What is actually needed for harnessing complexity in CO's is almost the opposite of what has been stated in this quote! The problem of *increasing* complexity that they notice in their report does not correspond to an increase of knowledge about complexity: in how it may be 'at work' in CO's, operating in a hyperconnected business world. There is no sign of becoming more knowledgeable about the dynamics of complexity within dynamic hyperconnected networks in the hyperconnected business world, with dynamic, generative complexity operating in this world. They will therefore 'simply' lack the tools of new thinking in complexity, which are needed to turn organizations and their network-like configuration into more intelligent network-like organizations. They will not become able to develop knowledge about how to turn the intellectual capacity of their organization and the complexities of everyday social interaction into a more socialized intellect of the complex network, which a complex organization actually *is* (see Sandywell, 1996, pp. xii, xviii).

DISCUSSION

... there is no denying that the world we live in is complex and
that we have to confront this complexity
if we are to survive, and, perhaps, even prosper.

-Paul Cilliers, 1998, p. 112

Based on our theorizing about the complexity of the real world, and the description of the case of KPMG, we may now come to some general conclusions about the complexity of complex organizations (CO's) and the management of this complexity in CO's. The basic conclusion is that CO's, like KPMG, need to develop a more appropriate way of becoming knowledgeable about how to confront and manage complexity. The real problem of complexity is the way companies attempt to respond to complexity (see also Morieux, 2011). It should be clear for the managers of these companies that complexity cannot be taken for granted. This has important consequences. The real challenge for CO's and their managers is to find the key to open up a new view of complexity of a complex world and to view the word with new eyes by using a new lens: a complexity lens. The first step to be made is to recognize our ignorance about complexity *before* starting to think about the role of complexity in CO's. Doing so, it becomes possible to discover the *virtues* of ignorance (Vitek & Jackson, 2008).

It is not advisable to talk about embracing complexity or confronting complexity without knowing what complexity might be really about. Managers may start to become aware that the topic of complexity is very much about knowing what you do *not* know. Thinking about complexity is very much like thinking about the hitherto field of the unknown. We may put the question "how do we know what we can know about a complex, nonlinear world?" (see Mainzer, 2004, pp. 431, 438) Facing the complexity of an increasingly complex world can therefore be a paralyzing kind of experience: of facing real ignorance. Yet, it is this very ignorance on complexity which can as well become a dramatic point of departure for *new* ways of seeing and knowing: that is, for a real shift of mind (cf. Senge, 1990). We may start to use a new lens: a *complexity lens*. We may, then, view this complex world with *new eyes*. This is the lesson to be learned from the history of our sciences. The development of quantum physics started with a deep ignorance about the subject. It took many decades to become able to arrive at what they did not know: the field of knowledge about quantum physics. All of the problems to deal with in this topic of physics had the basic starting problem of how to deal with the assumed reality. The real problem was to *escape* the reality as a kind of 'delivered' reality, 'delivered' by the history of the field. The Danish physicist Niels Bohr, however, knew very well that physicists had to *learn* to use the term 'reality' in a new way (see Pirsig, 1999). Only then it would be possible to develop new ways of thinking and new tools of thinking about the subject of study. From hindsight, one may conclude that a 'real' *reinvention* of reality was needed to develop the new, hitherto unknown field of physics.

Dealing with the subject of complexity and its manifestation in complex organizations asks for a similar task of *reinvention* of the field: that is, the field of complexity and complex organizations (CO's). These CO's operate within a complex system, being part of a complex reality, which should be taken as a fundamental nonlinear complex reality. This reality is relational, network-like: about dynamic, interdependent entities or agents, evolving over time. The network is a dynamic network with evolving elements, operating as a hyperconnected network. The complexity being 'at work' in these networks should be taken as *generative* complexity, operating in dynamic networks as a kind of *hyper*complexity (Morin, 2008; Jörg, 2011). The linear and the nonlinear of complexity are fully integrated in this new kind of reality. The dynamics of generative complexity is responsible for the different kind of multiplier effects, described above, which are hitherto unknown (see also

Jörg, 2011). These effects are about amplification of learning, and knowing. These effects are thriving on the interaction within communities of learning and interaction. It is the interaction between individual human beings, with their full generative power of interaction, that may lead to new possibilities like "learners bootstrapping each other" (Bruner, 1996, p. 21) and to "the amplification and development of new knowledge" (Nonaka, 2004, p. 166) in the complex network of a CO.

We may conclude that you can only manage complexity in CO's by becoming knowledgeable about the *real* complexity of the CO. It is necessary to think about how hypercomplexity may be linked to knowledge about a dynamic, hyperconnected network (Jörg, 2011). Only by taking this kind of hypercomplexity into account it will possible to become knowledgeable about how complexity may be 'at work' in the CO's, operating as a hyperconnected organization within a hyperconnected business world.

CONCLUSION

Summarizing, it may be argued that confronting complexity is not that easy as commonly assumed in management literature. One 'simply' cannot take complexity for granted. Real complexity is more complex than we might always have thought, or are able to dream of. We may therefore come to the conclusion that *there is no simple path to understanding complexity*! Neglecting this message implies a real danger: the danger of misunderstanding complexity. This implies the misunderstanding of the potential generative nature of a complex organization with its feature of 'generativity', being the power to generate nonlinear effects. This feature may also be linked to generativity as a state of being of the individual, in terms of his/her potential of "being *generative*" in a community of learners or community of interaction (cf. Senge, 1990, p. 13; emphasis added).

To become aware of the real promise of complexity we have to *reframe* complexity and take account of "the complexity *of* complexity" (see Chapter 13, in Jörg, 2011). Complexity should actually be taken as dynamic *hyper*complexity, operating in dynamic networks of interconnected loops. To deal with this real complexity of a *hyper*connected business world, we first need to become aware of the need for an 'altered account of reality' (Kauffman, 2009). This means that we may envision a larger, augmented version of reality (Jörg, 2011). The most important task of today for all kind of managers of companies and CO's is to *expand* their view of reality, so to become able to view the system of their organization with new eyes.

Managers of all kinds of CO's need to think of their organization as a complex dynamic network. Not as a simple flat network but more in terms of a complex hyperconnected network, with complexity being 'at work' in many dimensions, as potential nonlinear processes and their corresponding effects of amplifying: of amplifying knowledge, learning and thinking. Once they become aware of the hypercomplex nature of their CO, as a hyperconnected network, they may become better able to *realize* the very potential of this complex network. They may become knowledgeable about the power of complexity in their organization: in how the organization may thrive on the very complex dynamics within a hypercomplex network. This kind of networks may be described as a complex architecture of dynamic configurations in many dimensions. These configurations may be described in terms of bootstrapping configurations, leading to processes of bootstrapping each other in communities of learning or communities of interaction in organizations. Of course, getting knowledgeable about such complex networks, and their dynamics over time, is not an easy job. This is also very much true for *organizing* complexity in a CO. To organize complexity you need to understand complexity, operating as generative complexity in organizations. It is not easy to foster the full generative power of interaction in a dynamic network organization.

Once, managers become more knowledgeable about the possibilities of the new framework of complexity, they may start to *learn* to know how conditions of *possibility* within the new framework of complexity may open up a new world of the *possible* in their organization: a world which has remained unknown for them for so long. To confront complexity, then, means organizing complexity for the sake of fostering the full generative power of interaction within communities of interaction; a power that is able to generate the multiplier effects, described above. These hitherto unknown effects may be linked to the amplification of knowledge, the triggering of novelty, and the enhancing of innovation. To harness complexity, then, means turning complexity into effective complexity for the organization.

REFERENCES

Bak, P. (1996). *How nature works: The science of self-organised criticality*. New York: Copernicus Press. doi:10.1007/978-1-4757-5426-1

Barabási, A.-L. (2003). *Linked. How everything is connected to everything else and what it means for business, science, and everyday life*. New York: Penguin Group.

Capra, F., Juarrero, A., Sotolongo, P., & Van Uden, J. (Eds.). (2007). *Reframing complexity*. Mansfield, MA: ISCE Publishing.

Globus, G. (1995). *The postmodern brain*. Amsterdam, The Netherlands: John Benjamins Publishing Company. doi:10.1075/aicr.1

Hawking, S. (2000, January 20). *San Jose Mercury News*. Retrieved May 5, 2012, from http://www.comdig.com/stephen-hawking.php

Hessel, S. (2011). *Doe er iets aan! (transl. from French)*. Amsterdam, The Netherlands: Van Gennep.

Jörg, T. (2010). A theory of learning for the management of knowledge in learning communities and complex organizations. *International Journal of Knowledge and Systems Science*, *1*(1), 27–42. doi:10.4018/jkss.2010010103

Jörg, T. (2011). *New thinking in complexity for the social sciences and humanities – A generative, transdisciplinary approach*. Dordrecht, The Netherlands: Springer. doi:10.1007/978-94-007-1303-1

Kauffman, S. A. (1993). *The origins of order. Self-organization and selection in evolution*. Oxford, UK: Oxford University Press.

Kauffman, S. A. (1995). *At home in the universe*. New York: Oxford University Press.

Kauffman, S. A. (2009). Foreword. The open universe. In R. Ulanowicz (Ed.), *The third window. Natural life beyond Newton and Darwin* (pp. ix–xvii). West Conshohocken, PA: Templeton Foundation Press.

Keynes, J. M. (1936). *General theory of employment, interest, and money*. London: Macmillan.

KPMG. (2011, May). *Confronting complexity. Research findings and insights*. Retrieved May 5, 2012, from http://www.kpmg.com/global/en/issuesandinsights/articlespublications/pages/confronting-complexity-report.aspx

Kuhn, L. (1999). *Adventures in complexity. For organizations near the edge of chaos*. Devon, UK: Triarchy Press.

Laughlin, R. B. (2005). *A different universe. Reinventing physics from the bottom down*. New York: Basic Books.

Luhmann, N. (2002). *Theories of distinction. Redescribing the descriptions of modernity*. Stanford, CA: Stanford University Press.

Luhmann, N. (2003). The cognitive program of constructivism and a reality that remains unknown. In L. E. Cahoone (Ed.), *From modernism to postmodernism: An anthology* (2nd ed.). London: Blackwell Publishing Ltd.

Mainzer, K. (2004). *Thinking in complexity* (4th ed.). New York: Springer Publishers. doi:10.1007/978-3-662-05364-5

Mauboussin, M. J. (2011). Embracing complexity. *Harvard Business Review*, (Sept): 89–92.

Mesle, R. (2008). *Process-relational philosophy. An introduction to Alfred North Whitehead.* West Conshohocken, PA: Templeton Press.

Minati, G., Abram, M., & Pessa, E. (2012). Preface. In G. Minati, M. Abram, & E. Pessa (Eds.), *Methods, models, simulations and approaches towards a general theory of change: Proceedings of the Fifth National Conference on Systems Scienc*e (pp. v-vii). Singapore: Worlds Scientific. Retrieved 20th of April 2013 at http://www.complexityinstitute.it/wp-content/uploads/2013/01/indice-libro-Minati.pdf

Mitchell, C. M. (2011). *Complexity. A guided tour.* New York: Oxford University Press.

Morieux, Y. (2011). Smart rules: Six ways to get people to solve problems without you. *Harvard Business Review*, (Sept): 78–84. PMID:21939130

Morin, E. (2008). *On complexity.* Cresskill, NJ: Hampton Press.

Nietzsche, F. (1881). *Morgenröte. Gedanken uber die moralischen Vorurteilen.* Chemnitz: Verlag von Ernst Schmeltsner.

Nonaka, I. (2005). A dynamic theory of organizational knowledge creation. In K. Starkey, S. Tempest, & A. McKinlay (Eds.), *How organizations learn* (2nd ed., pp. 165–201). London: Routledge.

Rescher, N. (1998). *Complexity. A philosophical overview.* New Brunswick, NJ: Transaction Publishers.

Sandywell, B. (1996). *Reflexivity and the crisis of Western reason. Logological investigations* (Vol. 1). London: Routledge. doi:10.4324/9780203420171

Sargut, G., & Gunther McGrath, R. (2011). Learning to live with complexity. *Harvard Business Review*, (Sept): 69–76. PMID:21939129

Senge, P. (1990). *The fifth discipline.* New York: Doubleday.

Spretnak, C. (2011). *Relational reality. New discoveries of interrelatedness that are transforming the modern world.* Topsham, ME: Green Horizon Books.

Vitek, B., & Jackson, W. (Eds.). (2008). *The virtues of ignorance. Complexity, sustainability, and the limits of knowledge.* Lexington, KY: The University Press of Kentucky.

Vygotsky, L. (1987). *Thought and language* (A. Kozulin (Trans. Ed.)). Cambridge, MA: The MIT Press.

Watzlawick, P. (Ed.). (1984). *The invented reality. How do we know what we believe we know? Contributions to constructivism.* New York: W.W. Norton and Company.

Wilden, A. (1987). *The rules are no game.* London: Routledge & Kegan Paul.

Chapter 2
Product Patterns to Support Knowledge Acquisition Management

Diana-Marcela Vásquez-Bravo
Carlos III University of Madrid, Spain

Fuensanta Medina-Domínguez
Carlos III University of Madrid, Spain

Maria-Isabel Sánchez-Segura
Carlos III University of Madrid, Spain

Antonio Amescua
Carlos III University of Madrid, Spain

ABSTRACT

The knowledge elicitation process allows for the acquiring and transferring of knowledge. Actually, this process presents difficulties when selecting the appropriate elicitation technique. This chapter presents a classification of the elicitation techniques used in software engineering and the relationship between the elicitation techniques and some elements of knowledge management such as assets knowledge, epistemological dimension of knowledge and the knowledge creation phases. This classification provides a guideline to select a technique or a set of techniques for knowledge elicitation based on phases of Nonaka's model. Additionally, the chapter presents the use of product patterns in knowledge elicitation, and defines a product pattern as formal representation mechanism for each of the knowledge assets defined and presented in this chapter.

1 INTRODUCTION

For several years it has stressed on the importance of knowledge for organizations seeking to survive in today's competitive market, and it has demonstrated a clear relationship between knowledge and organizational success (Baruch & Juergen, 2004; Nonaka & Takeuchi, 1995; Webster & Jensen, 2006; OECD, 2010).

Knowledge management is presented as a discipline which focuses on the development of knowledge. The phases of knowledge

DOI: 10.4018/978-1-4666-4711-4.ch002

management are identification, capture, organization, distribution, preservation, use and measurement (Rus, Lindvall & Sinha, 2001; Kuhn & Abecker 1997).

Within knowledge management process, many authors have argued that one of the major bottlenecks in the process of building a knowledge-based system is the process of acquiring knowledge that corresponds with the phases of identifying and capturing the knowledge life cycle (Greenwell, 1988; Debenham, 1989; Brulé & Bount, 1989; Meyer & Booker, 1991; Kuhn & Abecker 1997; Mason & Pauleen, 2003).

Knowledge elicitation refers to the process of extract and makes accessible the knowledge of an organization. However, this activity is currently in experimental period due to the difficulty that represents to elicit the knowledge of the people, represent it adequately this knowledge and make it accessible to all members of an organization (See Figure 1).

Knowledge elicitation involves acquiring and transferring the knowledge of human beings (as such it exists in the minds of experts in a specific domain) to an abstract and effective representation, to organize it, to model it and finally to express this knowledge in an understandable and reusable format through a formal representation.

Knowledge elicitation process presents difficulties as in the elicitation techniques used, because of they are not complete enough to capture all the relevant knowledge for a specific domain, as in the same process of elicitation because a lot of the information that people knows is less than information verbalized. "We can always know more than we can tell, and we will always tell more than we can write down". Within Software Engineering field, one of the first phases in software product development is the requirement elicitation that allows characterizing the product type to be developed as well as the needs and features of the environment for which is being developed the software product.

Figure 1. Knowledge elicitation process

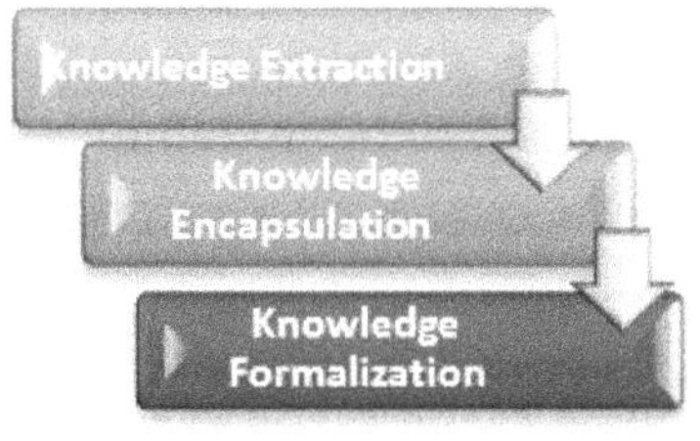

This means that software engineers have enough experience in requirement elicitation area. This is extrapolated and equivalent to knowledge elicitation.

On the other hand in knowledge management field there is not a catalog of knowledge elicitation techniques, so this work is going to approach on identifying of the requirement elicitation techniques coming from the software engineering field and that can be applied on knowledge management field as well as their classification based on the applicability and the knowledge creation model phase where these are applied. Furthermore, it is proposed for the selected knowledge elicitation techniques categories, the type of knowledge asset that is can be generate.

So, the different techniques of software engineering applied to knowledge elicitation will be analyzed. The knowledge asset types that exist and the knowledge life cycle phases to conclude with a proposal that combines the three elements previously mentioned, that may be used as discernment element by the time to choose the knowledge elicitation technique type that better adjust in each moment according to a particular situation and the knowledge asset type that is going to elicit.

The chapter is structured in 4 sections as detailed next. Section 2 is dedicated to related works about the spiral model of knowledge creation (Nonaka & Takeuchi, 1995). Knowledge assets, product patterns, and requirements elicitation techniques provided by software engineering as tools that allow the eliciting of knowledge are discussed, section 3 describes the proposal of the authors, and finally in section 4 the obtained conclusions of this work are presented.

2 BACKGROUND

In this section the spiral model of knowledge creation (Nonaka & Takeuchi, 1995), knowledge assets, requirements elicitation techniques provided by software engineering as tools that allow to elicit knowledge and the product patterns are discussed. Finally, in this section a classification of requirements elicitation techniques used in knowledge elicitation (this classification has been developed by the authors to achieve the scope of this research).

2.1 Spiral Model of Knowledge Creation (Nonaka & Takeuchi, 1995)

It has been analyzed the contributions of different authors that go into the knowledge management models in depth. Next, the works of several authors (Wiig, 1988; Grant, 1997; Tejedor & Aguirre, 1998; Alexander, 1979; Nonaka & Takeuchi, 1997) are described concisely. It is worth mentioning that the analyzed works have choose as a basis the Nonaka's spiral model of knowledge creation owing to this model presents a continuous process of knowledge creation described by phases that facilitates knowledge creation, use and transformation, is a model recognized by many scientific community authors and has been used as a reference in numerous works related on the topic.

The spiral model of knowledge creation proposes a knowledge creation process through a spiral knowledge generation model, described through knowledge conversion phases. In this work, the knowledge is classified as:

- **Tacit Knowledge:** Knowledge highly informal, personal, un-verbalized, intuitive and derived from experience. This knowledge is applied on specific contexts including cognitive elements (mental models) and technical elements (applicable to specific works).
- **Explicit Knowledge:** It is characterized for being formal and systematic knowledge that can be expressed without ambiguities through writing, mental maps, schematics, databases, etc.

Making use of this classification, the spiral model of knowledge (Nonaka & Takeuchi, 1995) is presented as an interactive process between tacit and explicit knowledge that has dynamic and continuous nature, making up a permanent spiral of knowledge transformation carried out in 4 phases.

- **Socialization:** To convert tacit knowledge into tacit knowledge through the knowledge transfer from one person to other by means of social interaction and shared experiences among the members of the organization.
- **Externalization:** To convert tacit knowledge into explicit knowledge represented in concepts, models and articulation of best practices or lessons learned.
- **Combination:** To convert explicit knowledge into explicit knowledge by means of categorizing, reclassifying and synthesis of explicit existing knowledge.

- **Internalization:** To convert tacit knowledge into explicit knowledge, allowing to persons to acquire explicit knowledge and to expand their tacit knowledge, so that new knowledge can be developed.

Although the Knowledge creation model (Nonaka & Takeuchi, 1995) describes knowledge transformation phases, this model does not identify which elicitation techniques can be used for knowledge elicitation in each of the 4 phases.

2.2 Knowledge Assets Involved in Knowledge Management

To manage the organizational knowledge in a much more efficient way, its flows, the critical management points and other factors, it is beneficial to divide and classify knowledge as it is proposed in (Freeze & Kulkarni, 2007). The method is indicated next. This knowledge assets classification has been chosen due to the existing importance that organizations develop an integrated approach of knowledge management that covers all knowledge potential components and make the most of the particular components in order to reach the strategic aims of business.

Next, it is briefly described the five knowledge assets proposed by (Freeze & Kulkarni, 2007) and that have been taken as the basis of this research work.

Data includes the facts summarized in simple values or figures; it is about very explicit knowledge that comes from processes, operations, experiments or polls. As knowledge asset, its importance lies on the ability to be associated inside a context to turn into strategic information and to create value and utility for decisions choosing.

Experience is a knowledge way, skill or ability coming from observation, from the facts and events experience and coming from events that happen in person's life. As experts as theirs experiences are source of big knowledge quantity in an organization. Knowledge coming from the experience is highly tacit, related to a specific domain, coming from the experiences, formal education and collaboration.

The *learning lessons* correspond to the knowledge set obtained through analysis and thought about an experience, project, process or situation in an organization. To acquire and to document the learning lessons contribute to transform the tacit knowledge into explicit knowledge, which facilitates it is spreading to all levels of the organization.

The *knowledge documents* represent knowledge codifying in highly explicit way. The source of codifying knowledge may be internal to the organization or may come from external sources. These assets may have specific structured formats like the case of technical reports, project reports, research reports and other publications. They also may be explicit in an unstructured way like images, diagrams, presentations, multimedia files, on-line handbooks, tutorials, etc.

The *Proceedings and politics* is the knowledge asset that represents the organizational knowledge required for the organization works in efficient and coherent way. The proceedings and politics document collects regulations and work flows of the routine operations of the organization; these are designed to provide the know-how of a process. The source of this type of asset may be the tacit aspects of the assets Learned lessons and experience. This asset can be transferred in knowledge way to the employees through the delivery of organization rules, routines, culture, structures and technologies, for helping the learning.

2.3 Techniques Software Engineering Provide

The software engineering requirements elicitation process is composed of the following activities: capture, discovery, acquisition, analysis, specification, and validation of requirements. It is worth noting that the elicitation process is not only a technical process before the construction of a system, but it is also seen as a social process that involves different individuals and groups of people with different levels of knowledge, abstraction and communication.

The majority of the models that capture requirements are based on specific techniques such as those presented in Table 1. There are also some elicitation methodologies proposed by some authors, for example, Robertson's requirements methodology that includes a process model that details the activities of requirements capture, with inputs, outputs and recommended techniques for each activity (Robertson et al. 1999).

Other authors have defined specific process models, establishing the use of scenarios for requirements elicitation (Hsia et al., 1994; Holbrook, 1990). There are also general top-down elicitation approaches (Gause et al., 1989; Pressman, 2006), but very few provide an approach to the process-view.

Based on the review and classification of the techniques analyzed, is presented a summary of the elicitation techniques of requirements and/or knowledge elicitation. These techniques correspond to an important subgroup of the universe of existing techniques. In Table 1, is presented a short description of each technique, the knowledge epistemological dimension that can be obtained through the application of this technique, if the acquired knowledge can be used to describe processes or activities, or to clarify and classify concepts, and finally determines if the knowledge was acquire from direct or indirect source (Direct is denoted with D, Indirect is denoted whit I), this according to the type of interaction with the domain expert.

2.4 The Product Patterns as Knowledge Elicitation Technique

A Pattern in Software Engineering is an artifact that represents solutions to problems that arise in application development. These solutions are based on experience and may be reused in similar conflicts that occur in different contexts (Alexander, 1979; Buschmann et al., 1996; Gamma et al., 1994). The term Product Pattern, coined by the authors (Garner & Mann, 2003; Medina-Domínguez et al., 2008) encapsulates the knowledge and experience related to the development of any software product, understanding software product as anything produced during the software lifecycle.

The product patterns facilitates the understanding of the organization assets and the knowledge representation, due to these correspond to a generalization or reusable abstraction that may be used as a starting point for future solutions (Medina-Domínguez et al., 2009; Sánchez-Segura et al., 2010).

3 DESCRIPTION OF THE PROPOSAL

The performed analysis has allowed to establish the relationship between elicitation techniques provided by software engineering and some key elements of knowledge management methods studied, as well as the identification of the concepts that have enabled the authors to classify the techniques found according to these determinants factors to choose an elicitation technique. According to this, the

Table 1. Summary of the elicitation techniques/knowledge elicitation

Techniques	Description	Tacit	Explicit	Process/ Activity	Concepts	Type
Card Sorting	It allows to know how the user mentally organizes the information, categories and priorities in his mind.	♦			♦	D
Scenarios	It consists in the description of a sequence of actions and events for a specific case in the domain.	♦		♦		I
Product Pattern	A Pattern in Software Engineering is an artefact that encapsulates and represents solutions to problems that arise in application development. These solutions are based on experience and may be reused in similar conflicts that occur in different contexts.	♦	♦	♦	♦	D
Structured Interview	It consists in interviewing the user with a set of prepared questions		♦	♦		D
Critical success factor (CSF)	It is a technique to analyze factors that ensure the success for an organization, and that represent the management area, that must receive special and continual attention to achieve high performance.		♦		♦	D / I
Unstructured Interview	It consists in interviewing the user about a specific domain with a set of questions without planning		♦	♦		D
Brainstorming	A group of users provide ideas about a specific domain, without emphasis on evaluation.		♦	♦	♦	I
Text analysis	It consists in examining existing and related documentation, contributes with obtaining knowledge, domain requirements, identification of reusable components and concepts.	♦	♦		♦	I
Repertory grid	It consists in asking the user for the applicable attributes to a set of entities and their values. It is an array of attributes.	♦		♦	♦	D
Multi-dimensional scaling	Multidimensional scaling represents a set of statistical techniques used in information visualization for exploring similarities or dissimilarities in data.	♦		♦	♦	I
Concepts mapping	This technique can help to understand the relationships between concepts. It is simple, uses hierarchies, and visual representation.	♦	♦		♦	D
Task analysis	It consists in the observation of the user while he is doing his activities. This technique provides knowledge of the processes, actions and interactions in the real environment.	♦	♦	♦		D
Participant observation	It analyzes the current practice of users in the domain.	♦		♦		D
Behavior analysis	The expert analyzes over long periods of time to users in their workplace. The aim is to describe the functional relationships between response classes and classes of stimulus. Explanation of behavior.	♦		♦		D
Protocol analysis	The user performs a task and provides detailed information quietly about how it is performed.	♦	♦	♦		D
Prototyping	The user provides information on a prototype of the desired system.		♦		♦	D

authors have established some considerations to guide the user in choosing the technique to be applied as appropriate.

The proposal in this work includes:

- Identification and establishment of the interaction between different types of knowledge assets and the way how may be possible to create and to provide feedback organizational knowledge, on the basis of the spiral model of knowledge creation (Nonaka & Takeuchi, 1997).
- Classification of elicitation techniques that has been analyzed in each phase of the spiral model of knowledge creation that will contribute to the choice of the technique or group of elicitation techniques suggested as the most appropriate for use in each one of the phases according to the type of knowledge asset.
- Proposal of Product Patterns as knowledge elicitation technique.
- Proposal of use of the Product Patterns as representation formalism of each knowledge asset identified and defined in this paper.

3.1 Interaction between Knowledge Assets and Nonaka's Model

As it was mentioned before, each knowledge asset must be considered individually and differently according to their phase in the life cycle of it (Birkinshaw & Sheehan, 2002). However, knowledge assets may be take part in the 4 phases of knowledge creation.

It is possible that from a type of knowledge asset a new one can be generated or this asset can be to provide feedback and be expanded, improved or updated through the application of the knowledge elicitation techniques identified and classified for each stage of knowledge conversion.

In Table 2, the first column indicates the types of starting knowledge asset, while the first row indicates the new asset that can be generated or to provide feedback if it is the same type asset. It achieved through the application of the techniques of a particular phase of conversion. The phases are detailed in the squares: S: Socialization, E: Externalization; C: Combination; I: Internalization.

3.2 Classification of Elicitation Techniques in the Nonaka's Model (Nonaka & Takeuchi, 1997)

Next, a classification of the studied elicitation techniques is introduced. Using this classification, it is possible to establish relationships between these categories and the knowledge conversion phases of (Nonaka & Takeuchi, 1997).

In Table 3, it is shown a summary of some of the most relevant characteristics of the studied

Table 2. Relationship between types of knowledge assets and the stages of spiral model of knowledge creation

	Expertise	Knowledge Documents	Data	Policies & Procedures	Lessons Learned
Expertise	S/ E	E	E	E	S/E
Knowledge Documents	I		C	C	I
Data	I	C		C	I
Policies & Procedures	I	C	C		I
Lessons Learned	S/ E	E	E	E	E / C

Table 3. Guideline to select knowledge elicitation technique

Classification	Techniques	Tacit	Explicit	Process/ Activities	Concepts	Type	Applicability	Knowledge creation Phase
Structured Elicitation Techniques	Card Sorting	♦			♦	D	KE	E I
	Scenarios	♦		♦		I	KE/ RE	
	Structured Interview		♦	♦		D	KE/ RE	
	Critical success factor		♦		♦	D / I	RE	
Unstructured Elicitation Techniques	Unstructured Interview		♦	♦		D	RE	S E I
	Brainstorming		♦	♦	♦	I	RE	
Formal Analysis Techniques	Text analysis	♦	♦		♦	I	KE/ RE	C
	Repertory grid	♦		♦	♦	D	KE/ RE	
Representation techniques	Multi-dimensional scaling	♦		♦	♦	I	KE	E C
	Concepts mapping	♦	♦		♦	D	RE	
Observation-based techniques	Task analysis	♦	♦	♦		D	KE/ RE	S I
	Participant observation	♦		♦		D	KE/ RE	
	Behaviour analysis	♦		♦		D	KE	
	Protocol analysis	♦	♦	♦		D	KE	
	Prototyping		♦		♦	D	KE/ RE	

In the squares "Knowledge elicitation": KE, "Requirement elicitation": RE, "Direct": D, "Indirect": I; and the knowledge creation phases are denoted: "Socialization": S, "Externalization": E, "Internalization": I, and "Combination": C.

techniques. In first column a classification of the requirements elicitation and knowledge elicitation techniques widely used in software engineering in five categories is shown.

Some of these techniques are applied in requirement elicitation, knowledge elicitation, or both areas. For this reason in the Applicability column, is referenced the discipline that used the technique. The knowledge elicitation is denoted by Knowledge E., and requirement elicitation is denoted by Requirement E.

In the same way, in Knowledge creation Phase column is presented the relationship between the categories for elicitation techniques and the knowledge creation model phases (Nonaka & Takeuchi, 1997). The aim of relationship establishment is to propose a convenient combination between knowledge conversion phases (Nonaka & Takeuchi, 1997) and the suggested techniques by the authors to create or provide feedback for the knowledge assets on each phase (See Table 3). The establish relationship in this work, between the knowledge conversion phases and elicitation techniques is justified under next assumptions:

In first instance, the socialization is applied for unstructured elicitation techniques. Inside this category, techniques as the open interview and the brainstorming make tacit to tacit knowledge conversion easier through the knowledge and experience transference from one person to another, through social interactions.

In the same way this knowledge conversion type can be carried on through the techniques based on observation, because these facilitate the social interactions between the employees of different levels of the organizational structure (e.g. behavior analysis in view of particular situations, to discover how the experts solve the problems and to perform their tasks, to provide tacit knowledge to the people that provide feedback about individual knowledge).

The externalization has the purpose to convert tacit to explicit knowledge, for this it is possible to apply the categories of unstructured elicitation techniques, structured elicitation techniques and mapping based techniques. The first two techniques satisfy the need to extract knowledge from the people for each problem domain. The structured elicitation techniques allow knowledge acquisition in tidy way and create scenarios to guide the interviewed person in the answers in presence of certain circumstances; moreover these contribute in concepts clarifying and classification. The mapping based techniques benefit the externalization of the acquired knowledge through the usage of mental maps, correlations establishment, hierarchies and visual representation of knowledge elements.

Combination consists on explicit to explicit knowledge conversion. For this, the usage of mapping based techniques and formal analysis is proposed as elements that allow identifying, analyzing and classifying explicit knowledge. In addition to this, this categories combination facilitates the fusion, categorization and summarized representation of existing knowledge.

The internalization allows to acquire explicit knowledge to the people of the organization and to expand their tacit knowledge. This may be supported in structured elicitation techniques, unstructured elicitation techniques and based on observation techniques. Through structured social interactions formally or informally, the scenario deployment or the brainstorming can be transform and provide feedback to the people knowledge. The same thing happens with the based on observation techniques that allow the person to learn through the observation of others behavior, their answer to particular situations and the task execution way. In the squares Knowledge elicitation: KE, Requirement elicitation: RE, Direct: D, Indirect: I; and the knowledge creation phases are denoted: Socialization: S, Externalization: E, Internalization: I, and Combination: C.

3.3 Proposal of the Product Patterns as Knowledge Elicitation Technique

A Product pattern is an element that allows to encapsulate and reuse knowledge. In addition, the authors propose in this work the Product Pattern as a knowledge elicitation technique that facilitates the knowledge elicitation in the 4 phases of Nonaka's Model.

The Product pattern facilitates transformation of knowledge into the 4 phases as follows:

- **Socialization:** Product pattern allows sharing tacit knowledge acquired from the experiences of different users through the lessons learned from its use.
- **Externalization:** Product pattern will allow materializing the elicitation of the experience of software engineers (tacit knowledge) to an artifact that encapsulates and represents the knowledge (explicit knowledge).
- **Internalization:** Product pattern will be the artifact (explicit knowledge) from which the software engineers will nurture of knowledge and experience of others software engineers. In this

way, engineers will be able to develop their knowledge and experience (tacit knowledge).

- **Combination:** Through the use of the product pattern (explicit knowledge) the software engineer may elicit knowledge and expertise. This will enrich this product pattern or it will elicit knowledge for a new product pattern.

The Product Pattern as a knowledge elicitation technique provides a guide that consists of a set of questions that must be answered by software engineers to elicit explicit knowledge and tacit knowledge that is necessary when making a software product. While software engineers use this guide to elicit their knowledge, such knowledge is encapsulated in the Product Pattern artifact, which have the properties defined for a reusable artifact, which is a necessary characteristic for an adequate management of knowledge.

Table 4 shows on the left column the questions that must be made to elicit the knowledge of software engineers and on the right column it is showed the field name of the product pattern that will store knowledge for subsequent reuse in software projects. Once that identification and establishment of the interaction between different types of knowledge assets with the stages of Nonaka's model has been presented, and it is in turn, has been related with categorization of elicitation techniques, introducing to the reader a proposed technical to choose in according to the categorized by type of knowledge asset in matter, it proceeds to present an integrated approach to the solution of these elements in relation to product patterns. The authors have elicited and have represented knowledge and experience of expert engineers of the technical analysis and design Craig Larman methodology: the software management project processes and activities of the XP methodology using the knowledge elicitation technique of Product Patterns. Finally, we have implemented a wiki that provides a Process Asset Library (PAL) as a central repository of expert knowledge in software engineering which can be accessed via web at URL: http://kovachi.sel.inf.uc3m.es

3.4 Proposal of use of the Product Patterns as Representation Formalism of Each Knowledge Asset

The authors recommend the use of Product Patterns to create knowledge assets that should be created during the execution of a software project. In order to use them, project managers or software developers are able to use one or more product patterns to perform the activities of a project, following on the following rule:

```
If you find yourself in this
context
(and) with this problem
(and) entailing these forces
Then
map a product pattern in your
project (and) look for product
patterns
```

Making use of the Guide of Knowledge Elicitation through the use of Product Patterns presented in Table 4, the authors present to next, a product pattern for each knowledge asset described in section 2.2 (Data - Table 5, Expertise - Table 6, Lessons Learned – Table 7, Knowledge Documents – Table 8, Policies and Procedures – Table 9).

The structure used to describe each knowledge asset, corresponds with the same structure it was presented in Table 4.

Table 4. Description of guide of knowledge elicitation through the use of product patterns

Guide for Knowledge Elicitation	Product Pattern
¿What is the name of knowledge asset that you are going to elicit? ¿How will name the artifact of knowledge (Product Pattern xx)? *Recommendation:* *Descriptive name, the name can be a word or short phrase related to the product pattern.*	Name
¿Is there any relationship between this software product and other (e.g., These belong to the same phase of software development, Precedence relationship to develop the software processes, static or dynamic relationships between this pattern and others)?	Related Patterns
¿Which preconditions must be present to apply this knowledge (product pattern)? ¿What is the state that the system has to present to apply this product pattern? *Recommendation: Provide the pre-conditions under the pattern are applicable - a description of the initial state before the pattern is applied.*	Initial Context
¿What is the state or configuration of the system after the pattern has been applied?	Result Context
¿What do you want to do? *Recommendation: Describe the problem to be solved.* ¿What is the problem that is solved when the product patterns are applied?	Problem
¿Which are the restrictions under which the product pattern is applied? ¿What feature should have the organization, respect to: Organization size, number of employees, communications infrastructure, geographically distributed maturity-business, organizational management layers, billing? ¿What feature should have the project, respect to: Experience of the development team in language and tools; experience of development team in the type of application and platform to develop, volatility of the platform; restrictions on execution time, reuse of requirements, continuity of staff; paradigm?	Forces
¿What steps must be performed to obtain the desired product? *Recommendation:* *Perform an activity diagram that shows the process that must be performed to obtain the product.* ¿What is the time that is estimated for this process?	Solution
¿What roles participate in the steps to obtain software product?	Roles
¿Is required some software product to develop the process described in the "solution" field of the product pattern?	Entries
¿What lessons learned have you got of the software product realization? ¿What positive or negative experience do you have about realization of the software product?	Lessons Learned
¿What template may be used to facilitate the realization of software process?	Templates
¿What examples can you provide?	Examples
¿Which product is obtained after perform the steps detailed in the Solution field? ¿Which product is obtained when the pattern is used?	Exit
In this field the level of maturity that is obtained is detailed once the product pattern is made. The maturity levels are based on two process models, CMMI and SPICE. This is useful when the product pattern represents a product included in some software improvement approach: Name (text), Level in which this product is allocated in a process improvement program (text)	Capability Level
¿What references can be useful to facilitate the development of the steps described in the Solution field?	Information's Resources
¿What basic knowledge must have the user to use product patterns?	Basic Knowledge

Table 5. Product pattern of knowledge assets: Data

Guide for Creation of Knowledge Assets	Product Pattern
Product Pattern of Knowledge Assets: Data	Name
• Knowledge Documents	Related Patterns
• A process, activity, or phase of project of the organization has been executed. There are quantitative or qualitative results of the result of such implementation. • It has conducted a survey to users, developers, or people involved in a project of the organization. There are quantitative or qualitative results of the result of such surveys.	Initial Context
A new document from Category: Data has been obtained. This document details quantitative and qualitative information, related to data of a procedure, activity, phase of a project, or survey about a project of the organization.	Result Context
• It requires a document containing the data obtained from the execution of a process, activity or project phase of the organization. These data must be expressed with precision and detail. • It requires a document containing the data obtained of a survey related to a particular project. These data must be expressed with precision and detail.	Problem
Type of Variables: Variables quantitative and qualitative Situations: • Apply these knowledge assets when there are survey data in its most simple state and has not been carried out any type of analysis for interpretation. • Apply these assets when procedures, activities or phases of a project are executed, and its execution provides qualitative and quantitative information, expressible as data.	Forces
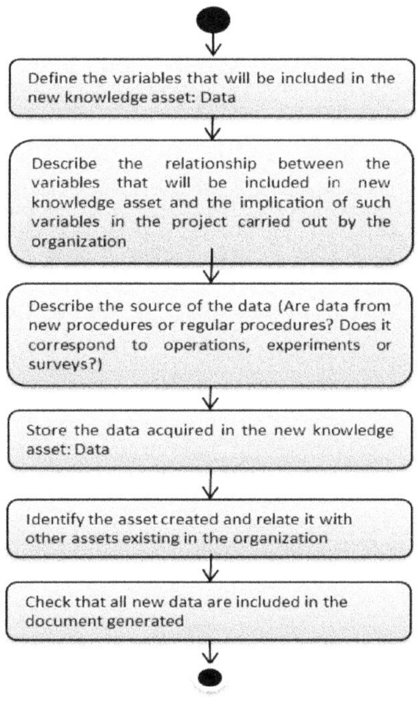	Solution
• Project Manager • Developers • Analyst	Roles
• Documentation of the implementation of procedures, activities or phases of a software project. • Quantitative and qualitative information expressible as data obtained from surveys conducted with the people involved in a project of the organization.	Entries
Register in this paragraph the lessons learned in the creation of document: Data. This information may be about the tool used, the format of product pattern used to construction of asset: Data, or the storage format of the data obtained.	Lessons Learned

continued on following page

Table 5. Continued

Guide for Creation of Knowledge Assets	Product Pattern
The storage template of the data is the format suggested by the organization to save the knowledge asset.	Templates
Data document in the format specified by the organization	Exit
• Basic Knowledge of Statistics. • Knowledge about the project, the relevant data of project and the impact of such data on the results of the project.	Basic Knowledge

Table 6. Product pattern of knowledge assets: Expertise

Guide for Creation of Knowledge Assets	Product Pattern
Product Pattern of Knowledge Assets: Expertise	Name
• Knowledge Documents • Lessons Learned	Related Patterns
• It has implemented a procedure, activity or project phase of the organization, for this reason; there are experiences and learning of the people involved in such implementation. • It has implemented a procedure, activity, or project phase of the organization and the people have acquired new skills. For this reason is required to store the new tacit knowledge in the knowledge repository of the organization.	Initial Context
Is obtained a new document from category: Experience. This document details the information related to knowledge or skills of individuals, derived from observation or experiences acquired during the execution of the procedures, activities, or phases of a project. The knowledge described in this type of asset is highly tacit, concerning a specific domain and the main sources are the formation of people and the collaboration between coworkers.	Result Context
Is required a document that describe the experiences and expertise of the employees of the organization with respect to a particular domain. This document must be precise and detailed.	Problem
Apply this type of asset when has been executed procedures, activities, or phases of a project that return information highly tacit about the experiences during such execution, and when this knowledge represents highly impact on activities.	Forces
	Solution

continued on following page

Table 6. Continued

Guide for Creation of Knowledge Assets	Product Pattern
• Project Manager • Developers • Analyst	Roles
• Documents of the execution of procedures, activities, or phases of a software project. • Tacit knowledge that describes the experience of the people involved in the execution of a procedure, activity, or project phase of the organization	Entries
Register in this paragraph the lessons learned in the construction of document: *Expertise*. This information may be the format of product pattern to construct the asset, or the storage format of the experience gained.	Lessons Learned
The template to store Experiences is the format specified by the organization for such type of knowledge asset	Templates
Experience Documents in the format specified by the organization	Exit
• Skills and knowledge acquired during the development of activities related to the role of each person in the organization • Capacity of Abstraction • Capacity of Analysis • Domain of language	Basic Knowledge

Table 7. Product pattern of knowledge assets: Lessons learned

Guide for Creation of Knowledge Assets	Product Pattern
Product Pattern of Knowledge Assets: Lessons Learned	Name
• Knowledge Documents • Expertise	Related Patterns
When a procedure is executed, activity, or phase of a project of the organization, and such knowledge has been put in consideration, through its analysis by the people involved, next step is to generate new knowledge result of the experience of actual facts. Finally, this tacit knowledge must be registered in the repository of knowledge in the organization.	Initial Context
A new document of *Lessons Learned* is obtained. This document describes the information related to the knowledge derived from the analysis and reflection about events that occurred in the execution of the procedures, activities, or phases of a project of the organization.	Result Context
Is required a document that explicitly the lessons learned by the employees of the organization with respect to a particular domain.	Problem
Apply this type of asset when there are new knowledge's based on analysis and reflection about events in the execution of procedures, activities, or phases of a project. This knowledge is highly tacit, it is consensus, it may be negative or positive about the experiences lived, and help in the identification of activities and decisions which reduce the negative impacts on the activities of the organization.	Forces

continued on following page

Table 7. Continued

Guide for Creation of Knowledge Assets	Product Pattern
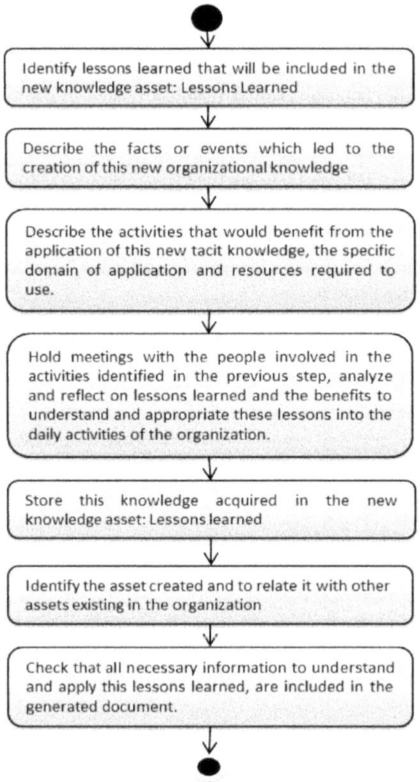	Solution
• Project Manager • Developers • Analyst	Roles
• Documentation of the implementation of procedures, activities, or phases of a software project. • Tacit knowledge product of analysis and reflection about the experiences and events that occurred in the implementation of such procedures, activities, or phases of an organizational project.	Entries
The template to store Lessons Learned is the format specified by the organization for such type of knowledge asset	Templates
Document of lessons learned in the format specified by the organization.	Exit
• Skills and knowledge acquired during the development of activities related to the role of each person in the organization. • Capacity of Analysis. • Domain of language.	Basic Knowledge

Table 8. Product pattern of knowledge assets: Knowledge documents

Guide for Creation of Knowledge Assets	Product Pattern
Product Pattern of Knowledge Assets: Knowledge Documents	Name
• Lessons Learned • Expertise	Related Patterns
Has been identified new knowledge that positively impacts the performance of procedures, activities, or phases of projects of the organization. Such knowledge may be internal or external source to the organization.	Initial Context

continued on following page

Table 8. Continued

Guide for Creation of Knowledge Assets	Product Pattern
Is obtained a new asset of category Knowledge Documents, in which is detailed information related to knowledge derived from analysis of events that occurred in the execution of the procedures, activities, or project phase of the organization. The knowledge can be stored in different representation formats, but such representation must be strictly structured. The source of this knowledge can be internal or external to the organization.	Result Context
It is desired to prepare a document that describes explicitly the organizational knowledge. The source of this knowledge can be internal or external to the organization. The documents generated can be: technical reports, documented procedures, statistical analysis, process mapping or activities, project reports, images, graphics, diagrams, presentations, multimedia files, manuals, online tutorials, and other publications.	Problem
This type of asset is applied when there are new knowledge from internal or external source to the organization. Such knowledge must be explicit and it expressed in a structured format.	Forces
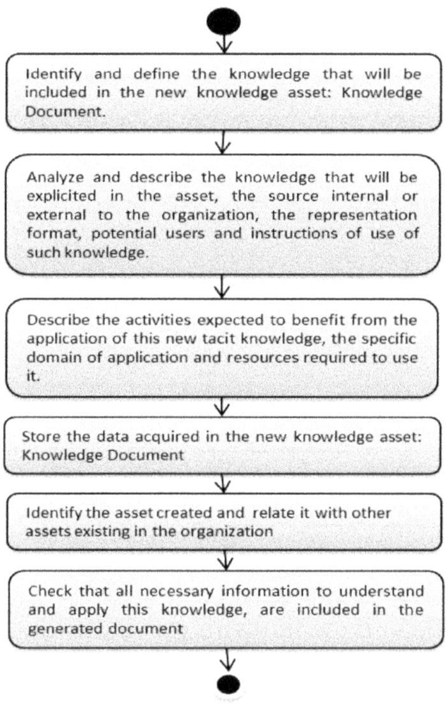	Solution
• Project Manager • Developers • Analyst	Roles
• Documentation concerning to implementation of procedures, activities, or phases of a software project. • Tacit knowledge that comes from analysis and reflection about the experiences acquired in the implementation of procedures, activities, or phases of a project. • Technical reports, project reports, statistical analysis, and data.	Entries
The template to store the active: Knowledge Documents is available to different representation formats. All these formats should be indicated by the organization for these knowledge assets.	Templates
Document of Knowledge in the format specified by the organization	Exit
• Skills and knowledge acquired during the development of activities related to the role of each person in the organization. • Capacity of Analysis. • Domain of language.	Basic Knowledge

Table 9. Product pattern of knowledge assets: Policies and procedures

<table>
<tr><th>Guide for Creation of Knowledge Assets</th><th>Product Pattern</th></tr>
<tr><td>Product Pattern of Knowledge Assets: Policies and Procedures</td><td>Name</td></tr>
<tr><td>• Knowledge Documents</td><td>Related Patterns</td></tr>
<tr><td>This knowledge asset must be used when there is a new policy or organizational procedure that impacts the performance of organizational activities, the behavior or conduct of employees, and the communication protocols, as well as the organizational structure.</td><td>Initial Context</td></tr>
<tr><td>A new document that contains policies and procedures about the activities of the organization is obtained.</td><td>Result Context</td></tr>
<tr><td>It requires a document that explicitly the policies and procedures that govern the activities of the organization. This document must be precise and detailed.</td><td>Problem</td></tr>
<tr><td>Apply this type of asset when there are updates or are introduced new policies and procedures that govern the activities of the organization.</td><td>Forces</td></tr>
<tr><td>
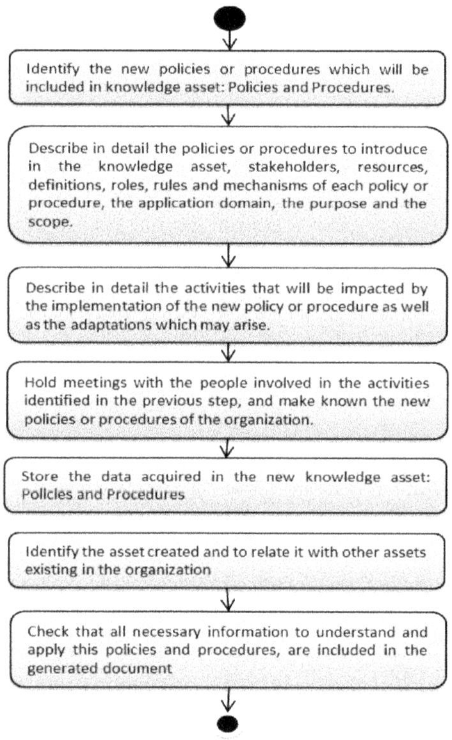

</td><td>Solution</td></tr>
<tr><td>• Manager
• Project Manager</td><td>Roles</td></tr>
<tr><td>Documents with the description of procedures, activities or protocols that are carried out in the ordinary activities of the organization.</td><td>Entries</td></tr>
<tr><td>The template to describe the policies and procedures is the format specified by the organization for this knowledge asset.</td><td>Templates</td></tr>
<tr><td>Document of Policies and Procedures in the format specified by the organization.</td><td>Exit</td></tr>
<tr><td>Knowledge about:
• Protocols existing in the organization
• Development of activities of organizational projects
• The domain language and,
• Capacity of Analysis</td><td>Basic Knowledge</td></tr>
</table>

4 CONCLUSION AND FUTURE WORKS

The knowledge elicitation is an active part of knowledge management. It involves the elicitation, acquisition and the transfer of experts´ knowledge on a specific domain, to a formal representation that allows understanding, use and reuse such knowledge in a particular domain.

Some of the problems presented in knowledge elicitation process are: the lack that has the knowledge elicitation techniques to capture the tacit and explicit knowledge that covers the 4 phases of the Nonaka's spiral model of knowledge creation, the coverage of epistemological dimensions of knowledge, and few formal mechanisms for knowledge representation.

Therefore, the authors provide a guide to select knowledge elicitation technique. For this, in this paper was presented the interaction between the different knowledge assets and how the organizational knowledge can be created and provided feedback starting from the basis of Nonaka's spiral model of knowledge creation (Nonaka & Takeuchi, 1997), the classification of the elicited techniques analyzed on each one of the Nonaka's spiral model of knowledge creation phases that will provide which elicited technique is more appropriate for use in each one of the phases, the guide of Knowledge elicitation through the use of Product Patterns as knowledge elicitation technique, and the results of the proposal, the use of the Product Patterns as representation formalism of each knowledge asset identified and defined in this paper: Data, Expertise, Lessons Learned, Knowledge Documents, and Policies and Procedures.

The authors recommend the use of Product Patterns to create knowledge assets that should be created during the execution of a software project in the organization. The project managers or software developers are able to use one or more product patterns to perform the activities of a project. The use of product patterns facilitates acquiring and representing all relevant information about each knowledge asset, such as Name, Related Patterns, Initial Context, Result Context, Problem, Forces, Solution, Roles, Entries, Lessons Learned, Templates, Examples, Exit, Capability Level, Information's Resources, and Basic Knowledge.

ACKNOWLEDGMENT

This work has been partially funded by the Spanish Ministry of Science and Technology through the project TIN2011-27244.

REFERENCES

Alexander, C. (1979). *The timeless way of building*. Oxford, UK: Oxford University Press.

Baruch, L., & Juergen, D. (2004). The dominance of intangible assets: Consequences for enterprise management and corporate reporting. *Measuring Business Excellence*, *8*(1), 6–17. doi:10.1108/13683040410524694

Birkinshaw, J., & Sheehan, T. (2002). Managing the knowledge life cycle. *MIT Sloan Management Review*, *44*(1), 75–83.

Brulé, J., & Bount, A. (1989). *Knowledge Acquisition*. New York: McGraw-Hill.

Buschmann, F., Meunier, R., Rohnert, H., Sommerlad, P., & Stal, M. (1996). *Pattern oriented software architecture. A system of patterns*. New York: John Wiley & Sons.

Debenham, J. (1989). *Knowledge system design*. Sidney, Australia: Prentice Hall.

Freeze, R., & Kulkarni, U. (2007). Knowledge management capability: Defining knowledge assets. *Journal of Knowledge Management*, *11*(6), 94–109. doi:10.1108/13673270710832190

Gamma, E., Helm, R., Johnson, R., & Vlissides, J. (1994). *Design patterns: Elements of reusable object-oriented software*. Boston: Addison Wesley.

Garner, S., & Mann, P. (2003). Interdisciplinarity: Perceptions of the value of computer-supported collaborative work in design for the built environment. *International Journal of Automation in Construction.*

Grant, R. (1997). The knowledge-based view of the firm: Implications for management practice. *Long Range Planning*, *30*(3), 450–454. doi:10.1016/S0024-6301(97)00025-3

Greenwell, M. (1988). *Knowledge engineering for expert systems*. Chichester, UK: Ellis Horwood Limited.

Kuhn, O., & Abecker, A. (1997). Corporate memories for knowledge management in industrial practice: Prospects and challenges. *Journal of Universal Computer Science*, *3*(8), 929–954.

Mason, D., & Pauleen, D. (2003). Perceptions of knowledge management: A qualitative analysis. *Journal of Knowledge Management*, *74*, 38–48. doi:10.1108/13673270310492930

Medina-Domínguez, F., Sanchez-Segura, M., Mora-Soto, A., & Amescua, A. (2008). *Patterns in the field of software engineering. Encyclopedia of Information Science and Technology* (2nd ed.). Hershey, PA: Idea Group Publishers.

Medina-Domínguez, F., Sanchez-Segura, M., Mora-Soto, A., & Amescua, A. (2009). Reverse engineering and software products reuse to teach collaborative web portals: A case study with final-year computer science students. *IEEE Transactions on Education*, *53*(4), 595–607. doi:10.1109/TE.2009.2037313

Meyer, M., & Booker, J. (1991). *Eliciting and analyzing expert judgment. A practical guide*. London: Academic Press.

Nonaka, I., & Takeuchi, H. (1995). *The knowledge creating company: How Japanese companies create the dynamics of innovation*. New York: Oxford University Press.

Nonaka, I., & Takeuchi, H. (1997). *The knowledge-creating company*. New York: Oxford University Press.

Organization for Economic Cooperation and Development. (2010). *Measuring innovation: A new perspective*. OECD Publishing.

Rus, I., Lindvall, M., & Sinha, S. (2001). Knowledge management in software engineering, the Data & Analysis Center for Software (DACS) state-of-the-art-report.

Sánchez-Segura, M., Medina-Domínguez, F., Amescua, A., & Mora-Soto, A. (2010). Improving the efficiency of use of software engineering practices using product patterns. *Information Sciences*, *180*(14), 2721–2742. doi:10.1016/j.ins.2010.03.028

Tejedor, B., & Aguirre, A. (1998). Proyecto Logos: Investigación relativa a la Capacidad de Aprender de las Empresas Españolas. *Boletín de Estudios Económicos*, *53*(164), 231–249.

Webster, E., & Jensen, P. (2006). Investment in intangible capital: An enterprise perspective. *The Economic Record*, *82*, 82–96. doi:10.1111/j.1475-4932.2006.00296.x

Wiig, K. (1988). *Management of knowledge: Perspectives of a new opportunity*. Arlington, VA: The Wiig Group.

Chapter 3
Metadata in Serbia:
Describing Library Collections, Towards a More Semantic Web

Adam Sofronijevic
University of Belgrade, Serbia

Natasa Dakic
University of Belgrade, Serbia

Jelena Andonovski
University of Belgrade, Serbia

ABSTRACT

This chapter discusses the usage of metadata in libraries in Serbia. So far metadata have been used for describing printed documents available for patrons in library holdings and for describing digital documents available in online repositories. Paper presents some specific aspects of metadata usage primarily in regards to automation of digital data delivery for patrons. The advent of information technologies provides librarians in Serbia, as well as their colleagues in other countries, with powerful tools to describe digital objects and interconnect them making those related digital objects effectively available for users via an emergent, more semantic web.

INTRODUCTION

Metadata is structured information that describes, explains, locates, or otherwise makes it easier to retrieve, use, or manage an information resource (National Information Standards Organization, 2004). Metadata or data about data are as old as librarianship and are being considered and are still considered to be a prime product of librarianship practice (Coyle, 2005). In order to keep, preserve and organize data librarians need to describe them. Therefore when we talk about metadata we often talk about librarianship (Good, 2002; JISC Digital Media, 2010). Usually metadata are employed through one of the meta-

DOI: 10.4018/978-1-4666-4711-4.ch003

data schemas and the knowledge of these is considered to be one of the more important items in a librarian education (Greenberg, 2005). Recently, overwhelming progress of the digital have made metadata essential for anyone dealing with vast number of digital objects and therefore many experts with different and complementary skills are involved with metadata, even in the framework of a single project, making the issue of metadata a complex and even the social one (Hall & Khoo, 2013). Metadata are often perceived as a tool for making digital objects more visible and accessible and the Web more efficient (Shukair et al., 2013). In such a complex world metadata usage in libraries is dynamically changing especially in regards to Open Access initiatives, options for free availability of catalogue records and relations with commercial publishers (Flynn, 2013).

Metadata usage in libraries in Serbia so far was mostly related to the general librarianship practice. In the past metadata was mostly considered a tool for achieving the means of describing printed collections. The fine art of classification was considered the core of librarianship business and the most respected job in a Serbian library. The advent of Internet and prevailing importance of electronic resources is creating changes that are ongoing. Following these changes and being on top of them is now considered to be the core and the fine art of librarianship. New technologies provide tools for metadata usage that has not been possible in the previous periods especially in the field of automation of digital data delivery. Metadata describing relations between digital objects are considered to be an important issue and preparations are in full blown phase to incorporate this additional aspect of metadata usage in Serbian libraries.

Overall situation in regards to metadata usage in Serbia today can be described as sketchy with different types of metadata used and a range of various purposes and ideas for metadata usage and even more ideas and initiatives for planning of future use of metadata. Presentation of this variety may be useful for anyone studying metadata since a range of historical usage can be juxtaposed by library types and content types leading to some interesting conclusions about general trends of librarianship practice development in Serbia and explanations on how metadata are being indicative or driving these trends. Also the idea of user orientation has been driven by contemplation of metadata usage in Serbian libraries. If one is creating metadata his or hers job is directly in relation to usage of the materials described by this metadata. Hence sooner or later the purpose and nature of metadata is brought into the focus of attention and soon user needs and expectations are more in the focus of librarians then they have been before. Lively discussions are often heard at librarianship conferences and meetings in Serbia on metadata usage and purpose of their creation sparking the dialogue on essence of librarianship industry and always bringing back the focus on users. This is perhaps the most important trend when one describes metadata usage in Serbia. Questions arising from discussing choices of metadata model, usage and production are important drivers for librarianship in Serbia and therefore need to be addressed frequently.

METADATA DESCRIBING PRINTED HOLDINGS OF SERBIAN LIBRARIES

Creation of electronic records for the printed items in Serbian libraries is affected by dual impact of historical and financial issues. Numerous editions printed before 1980 are still not described by electronic records, because to create those records scares work hours need to be devoted. Therefore most libraries in Serbia with large printed holdings have decided not to create electronic records for certain items until they are borrowed for the first time. Often large parts of the holdings are not used at all and this makes creation of electronic records not a high priority. In order to identify those items that are really used and therefore needs to be visible through OPAC this method was chosen by many libraries in Serbia (Popović-Bošković & Filipi-Matutinović, 2001). Some libraries in Serbia still do use card catalogues to describe their printed holdings. Some smaller libraries have no resources to implement OPAC (Online Public Access Catalogue) but the number of these is declining. Although still existent in Serbian libraries card catalogues have little practical value for users and exist only because of historical reasons. Therefore we will not describe metadata used via this venue. Instead we will describe only electronic records that describe printed holdings in Serbian libraries.

Electronic records describing printed holdings of libraries available to users thorough OPAC are almost always formatted and shaped in regards to library automation system they originate in. In Serbia two library automation systems prevail today, although a tiny fraction of libraries do use several other systems. Most libraries in Serbia use Cobiss automation system including three major libraries: National Library of Serbia, University library in Belgrade and the "Matica Srpska" library in Novi Sad (Stevanović, 2003). On the other hand some public libraries, mostly in northern Vojvodina region of the country do use Bisis system (Sabovljev, 2008). With this in mind one can conclude that electronic metadata created for printed holding description are mostly created by Cobiss system. Therefore we present a short review of this system and an extended description of metadata created in this system.

Cobiss (Cooperative Online Bibliographic System and Services) library automation system is a product of Institute of information science Izum from Maribor, Slovenia (COBISS.net, 2008). It is in use in all former republics of Yugoslavia except Croatia. It originated from Yugoslav era shared cataloguing system called Atlas, also an Izum product that was used across the country just before its breakup (Nogić, 2004). Cobiss is basically an organizational model that allows libraries to join into a uniform library information system with shared catalog, shared bibliographic database and local bibliographic databases of participating libraries (COBISS.net, 2008). Currently the system is going through a version upgrade that will reflect on metadata usage. Cobiss 3 is the third generation software for library automation and access to different databases and is implemented for use in Serbian libraries in 2012. Second generation of application software Cobiss 2 is still in use for shared cataloguing and reports software modules.

Cobiss system uses specific proprietary Comarc metadata model derived from Unimarc (Comarc/B Format za bibliografske podatke, 2009). The historic reason for this is the fact that in 1986 Unimarc was accepted as a standard for machine readable bibliographic data across former Yugoslavia. In the course of implementation of Unimarc in the Cobiss system at first original Unimarc was used. During time the need for additional fields and subfields appeared and Comarc/b format was developed. Today Comarc/b is used for metadata regarding bibliographic records, Comarc/a for normative data description and Comarc/h for describing collection status. All three are based on Unimarc format and when data are exchanged internationally libraries that do use Cobiss system operate with Unimarc. Conversion from Marc21 to Comarc is built in Z39.50 client implementation and conversion from Comarc to Marc21 is built in in Z39.50 server implementation.

In order to facilitate metadata creation Cobiss system offers interface that provide for easier input of certain most frequently used fields and subfields. These are in turn grouped for further ease of metadata creation for certain item types as follows: M – monographs, K – continuous sources, A – papers, etc. Fields that make up each of these are designated by three numbers and subfields by a letter or by a number. Data element that may be distinguished during the search is a subfield. In some instances fields and subfields can be repeated. Some fields do have indicators that define the way in which these fields will be presented in search results. Cobiss system is being used across former Yugoslav republics that use different alphabets. Because of this the system allows for metadata creation in different alphabets. The rules for creation of metadata in various alphabets and for their presentation are clearly defined (Grbić, 2004). As in Marc21 format fields are grouped in blocks (Network Development and MARC Standards Office, 2006). We present fields of both formats.

- **Comarc/b:**
  0XX: Identification Block
  1XX: Coded Information Block
  2XX: Descriptive Information Block
  3XX: Notes Block
  4XX: Linking Entry Block
  5XX: Related Title Block
  6XX: Subject Analysis Block
  7XX: Intellectual Responsibility Block
  8XX: International Use Block
  9XX: National Use Block
- **Marc21:**
  0XX: Control information, identification and classification numbers, etc.
  1XX: Main entries
  2XX: Titles and title paragraph (title, edition, imprint)
  3XX: Physical description, etc.
  4XX: Series statements
  5XX: Notes
  6XX: Subject access fields
  7XX: Added entries other than subject or series; linking fields
  8XX: Series added entries, holdings, etc.
  9XX: Reserved for local implementation

Cobiss system provides for two additional means of metadata creation. It allows for subject classification and Universal decimal classification scheme application. According to rules applied in the system for the defining the subject of a document subject heading is defined by one or more words that are most suited and accepted by local librarian community for describing the subject of the document (Grbić, n. d.). It is important to underline the difference that does exit in the system between keywords and subject headings defined in this way. Keywords might be arbitrary and copied from the title, abstract or the text itself while subject headings are defined by librarians and endorsed by local community of colleagues based on the document subject. Also subject headings are defined by rules endorsed by the National library of Serbia that adhere to international standards. For subject classification in Cobiss system one uses the block of fields with their subfields 6XX for accepted and 96X for new items. Fields in the range of 600 to 609 are structured and comprise of descriptors as follows:

600: Personal name used as subject
601: Corporate body name used as subject
602: Family name used as subject
605: Title used as subject
606: Topical name used as subject
607: Geographical name used as subject
608: Temporal subject heading
609: Form, genre or physical characteristics used as subject

Controlled subject headings only should be used in these fields. Field 610 is reserved for uncontrolled subjects that have no hierarchical structure. Libraries that currently use Cobiss system do not use controlled vocabularies. Usage of fields 600 to 609 is a kind of substitute for this. Historical reason for this is that all libraries using the system used to work with its previous version since 1989. That version also didn't require use of controlled vocabularies. Therefore certain tradition and needs have been created and these were met by Cobiss system in its current form. Some rules have been accepted though by all libraries using the system. Abbreviations are written in capital letters, numbers in Arabic numerals except when written along the dignitaries' names when they are written in roman numerals. Subject headings in fields 600-609 need to start with a capital letter, while those in the field 610 need not start with it. There are some issues that are still unresolved even in Serbia let alone among libraries from different ex-Yugoslavia countries. Academic libraries use Latin alphabet when creating subject headings while the National library of Serbia and most of the public libraries use Cyrillic alphabet for this purpose. Academic libraries tend to use more scientific oriented terms while public libraries use the most commonly used ones. In order to achieve unified approach libraries in Serbia need to work together to find the solution for a more convergent approach to subject headings creation.

Classification of documents in accordance with Universal decimal classification scheme is a part of usual metadata creation process in Serbian libraries that use Cobiss system (Lazarević, n. d.). Because of this the education of librarians in regards to this classification system is extensive both at undergraduate level of library information science studies in Serbia and in the course of the lifelong learning process in Serbian libraries. Udc number fits into 675 field of Cobiss system. This field can be repeated and its subfields are as follows:

- **$a:** Classification number according to Udc tables
- **$b:** Used for bibliographies production
- **$c:** Used for searching in the database
- **$s:** Used for statistical purposes

Numbers in the subfields $b, $c and $s are designated by the usage of normative tables. Although a lot of efforts are committed to creating Udc compliant classification for various documents in Serbian libraries the effects are not in relations to resources committed. Users rarely use this metadata to perform searching and libraries rarely use it for purposes of providing location on shelves for users according to this schema. Therefore on numerous occasions the mere purpose of providing this kind of metadata has been raised.

In the Cobiss system Comarc/B format is used for bibliographic data, Comarc /A format for authority data and Comarc /H format for holdings data. The first two formats are based on the Unimarc format; the third was developed entirely by Izum. For the international data exchange, Marc 21 format is used. Conversions are possible from Comarc format into the Marc 21 format and vice versa. Records are available in either the ISO 2709 structure (Marc 21, Comarc) or Xml (Dublin Core, Mods, Marc 21, Comarc). Bibliographic data can be exported from the Cobiss system in Marc 21 and Dublin Core.

For creating records for serial titles, the international ISSN database is used as the authority database. It is possible to download bibliographic records from WorldCat and from the Library of Congress Union Catalog. A special agreement between the Library Information Service and OCLC is required to download records from WorldCat.

The quality, uniformity and consistency of databases containing metadata in Cobiss system are provided in different ways: by authority control for personal names, by duplicates control, by Comarc program controls, by record editing, by introduction of local codes that provide uniformity of data within a library and above all by providing a systematic training for record creators and integrating the Comarc formats documentation into software.

During recent years subject of authority files for personal names have been a hot button topic in Serbian libraries. During the seventies, IFLA initiated development of international system of authority control. International rules have been designed to improve the quality of library services by ensuring during the search to find the required information quickly and efficiently regardless of the variation forms of the author's name in library catalogues and bibliographies worldwide. Various national bibliographic agencies have long standing experience on creating and maintaining library's authority files, but Serbia has only made the first step in preparing for development of such authority files (Plassard, 2010).

Cobiss system allows for creation and updating of authority file databases. As of May 2013 a comprehensive database of authority files is under construction by major libraries of Serbia collaboration effort and authority files for personal names database is in use. A specific system of parallel headings is employed in this database due to equal use of two alphabets, Cyrillic and Latin, in Serbian language. The challenge was to address the existence of parallel phonetic and etymological headings in Serbian libraries. The solution was found in the system that will allow for creation of pairs of name headings that present the same name in both alphabets (Kojevic, Dakic, & Nogic, 2011).

Cobiss system use Comarc/A format of machine readable record for description and exchange of authority files. This format is based on authority file format Unimarc/A (UNIMARC/ Authorities, 1991).

- **Format COMARC/A:**
  0XX: Identification block
  1XX: Coded information block
  2XX: Authorized access point block
  3XX: Notes block
  4XX: Variant access point block
  5XX: Related access point block
  6XX: Classification and entity history block
  7XX: Authorized access point in other language and/or script block
  8XX: Source information block
  9XX: National use block

Blocks of fields are identical as in Unimarc/A format, but some of the fields and subfields that make the blocks differ. Some fields and subfields are Unimarc/A identical and some are characteristic and developed specially to suit the needs of authority file records in Cobiss system structure.

Bisis is a library automation system used by many public libraries in Serbia. It is a product of Faculty of technical Sciences at University of Novi Sad that develops it since 1993 (Ilić-Kiš, 2007). It confirms to international standards for this kind of systems and allows for certain degree of interoperability with other systems especially since it uses Unimarc metadata standard. This system is specially designed for use in public libraries. Some additional enhancements have been installed in regards to multilingual features. Both Cyrillic and Latin alphabet are available in the system along with language support for Serbian Hungarian, Romanian, Slovakian, English and German. These features are especially important is in regards to multicultural environment of Vojodina, northern province of Serbia, where this system is mostly used

(Marković, 2005). Besides metadata creation according to Unimarc standard the system allows for automation of circulation in a library, shared cataloging system, OPAC and report creation. It is based on publicly available operating systems based on Linux and databases that does not require additional fees for licensing like SAP DB, MySQL and PostgreSQL. It may work also with all important operating systems Windows and Unix based and databases like Oracle, Microsoft SQL Server, IBM DB2 and Informix (Udicki, 2006). The usage of two different library automation systems in a relatively small library environment of Serbia does not foster collaboration among libraries and the nature of usage with public libraries using one system and academic and big libraries using the other one further creates problems in cooperation among different kind of libraries (Đukić, 2005). Therefore a more divergent course should be followed in future and metadata may be a way for achieving this Bisis system operates with Unimarc metadata model while Cobiss system operates with Comarc metadata model which is derived from Unimarc. Therefore a high level o f interoperability may be achieved in regards to metadata exchange which ground basis for further unification of two systems (Filipi-Matutinović, 2004).

METADATA DESCRIBING DIGITAL OBJECTS OF SERBIAN LIBRARIES

Digital materials are commonly available through library repositories and Web pages of libraries in Serbia. Academic libraries operate with newborn digital materials provided by big publishing companies e.g. scientific journals and e-books. Both public and academic libraries are engaged in digitization of cultural and scientific heritage. Both kind of digital materials require metadata so that users can more easily locate data they need. Libraries in Serbia depend on publishers to provide metadata and search tools for newborn digital materials. Some experiments do exist in regards to creating collections of area specific materials, mostly scientific ones, by using individualization of search environment usually labeled My library. Also tagging in Delicious environment is experimentally used for providing collections of newborn digital materials that correlates with specific interests of some user groups. Both activities are implemented at experimental level at University library in Belgrade.

Digitized materials are stored and available to users in repositories or via library Web sites. As an example of metadata usage in this area in Serbia we will describe with some detail digital repository of University of Belgrade hosted and operated by University library of Belgrade. In the course of realization of the TEMPUS project New Library Services at Western Balkan Universities a digital repository of University of Belgrade has started its operations as of September 2011. It is a PHAIDRA repository obtained through the project from a project partner University of Vienna. It primarily collects and stores for long term preservation doctoral thesis of University of Belgrade in pdf/a format, but it also provides infrastructure for long term preservation of other digital materials: pictures, audio and visual materials. Preferred file formats are pdf/a, tiff, jpg, avi, mpg2 and wav. In order to provide metadata for this diverse collection of digital materials Dublin Core based (Hillmann, 2005), (Coyle & Baker, 2009) metadata schema is employed. On the other hand for convenience of users who are uploading their digital materials in this repository there are only eight required fields that need to be filled in order to make a legitimate upload (Ciljevi i zadaci univerzitetskih repozitorija Zapadnog Balkana, 2010).

If a more elaborate metadata are needed there is a range of options available: EuroVoc, ACM – Computing Classification System, PACS – Physics and Astronomy Classification Scheme, Classification Scheme for Sciences of University of Belgrade PHAIDRA repository and keywords. Besides these a furthering of available classification schemas, thesauri and indexes is possible. Classification Scheme for Sciences of University of Belgrade PHAIDRA repository is a specific scheme created in University library in Belgrade in order to provide a more user oriented approach to creation of metadata describing digital resources. It is a hierarchical, general scheme of scientific fields in natural language. It has been developed on basis of Universal decimal classification scheme so that the automatic conversion between this system and the COBISS library automation system may be maintained. UDC scheme has not been appropriate because it is too elaborate in some fields and not enough descriptive in regards to newly developed scientific fields. Also for precise description of certain scientific fields long and elaborate string of numbers needs to be entered into the system which was deemed too user unfriendly for a digital repository and therefore a specific classification schema was needed (Grbić, Đurđulov, & Lazarević, 2011). Because of described downturns of UDC classification scheme for purposes of creation of new classification scheme for sciences two other existing schemes were used as a grounding basis: RVK - Regensburger Verbundklassifikation and ÖFOS - Österreichische Systematik der Wissenschaftszweige. RVK is a classification scheme developed at University of Regensburg in Germany in sixties and has been updated since. It is used by many academic libraries in Germany, Austria and Switzerland. ÖFOS is Austrian version of international UNESCO originated FOS – Fields of Science and Technology schema. This schema is also used by statistical bureau of Serbia but its 48 scientific fields were not enough for describing variety of materials that will be available in University of Belgrade digital repository. New schema has, besides being user oriented, two important elements: possibilities for metadata conversion so that metadata from the repository may be used in COBISS library automation system and conversion to FOS schema so that they can be used for national statistical purposes.

An important initiative dealing with metadata describing digital objects in Serbia is NCD – National Center for Digitization. NCD is a joint activity of several leading institutions in Serbia in the field of digitization gathered together by idea of coordinating digitization initiatives, idea exchange, and providing best practice based recommendations for other institutions in Serbia in this field (Butigan, n.d.). In the course of its operations NCD has provided two important recommendations regarding metadata describing digitized materials. Firstly it provided the recommendation for standardized description of movable cultural objects and secondly it provided the recommendation for standardized description of collections. The recommendation for standardized description of movable cultural objects was agreed upon in 2007 by NCD and national UNESCO digitization committee (Butigan, 2007). It was the first attempt to provide national standard for metadata creation in Serbia. This recommendation contains descriptions for single object and a collection made out of single objects and other collections. Metadata describing single objects are grouped into descriptive and administrative metadata. Descriptive metadata contain data on original object and administrative metadata contain data on digitization process. In order to bypass possible problems caused by parallel dual usage of Latina and Cyrillic alphabets recommendations insists on usage of Unicod fonts. The recommendation for standardized description of collections was agreed upon in 2011 by NCD member institutions and should represent a major contribution of NCD to national metadata creation practice and theory and also internationally since not many recommendations or standards for metadata describing collections exists. In the scope of this recommendation metadata are grouped as descriptive and administrative metadata. Descriptive metadata contain data on collection itself: name, author, contributor, proprietor, subject headings, description, timeline of collection existence, type, number of objects, links to other collections, etc. Administrative metadata contain data on digitization process: copyright, access rights, date of creation, creator, owner, etc. By providing these recommendation institutions joined in NCD hope to enhance metadata creation in a more unified manner. Also a more user oriented metadata may be a product of wider acceptance of these recommendations in Serbia in the future.

Important trend in creation of metadata describing digitized materials in Serbia is usage of internationally accepted metadata models driven by institutions' participation in international digitization and aggregation projects. Most of contemporary digitization initiatives in Europe are in relations with Europeana portal. Almost all of European Union funded multinational digitization initiatives are regarding this portal. Hence the importance of metadata model used in Europeana for all European libraries (Antonic, Mitrovic, & Sofronijevic, 2011). In Serbia in particular projects that have the aim of providing metadata for Europeana are especially potent drivers for creation of metadata that adhere to ESE – Europeana semantic elements and EDM – Europeana data model, metadata models used by Euorpeana (Europeana Semantic Elements Specification, 2011; Europeana Data Model primer, 2010). Several important libraries in Serbia has been involved in such projects or are currently involved. National library of Serbia has been one of the founding members of TEL - The European Library and was involved with several projects adding metadata to Europeana. During 2011 and 2012 University library in Belgrade was a partner in Europeana libraries project that brought digital materials from European academic libraries to Europeana. Thanks to this project University library got experience in creation of metadata in ESE metadata model and aggregation scheme of Europeana. Also, in January 2012 new metadata model was implemented – EDM (Europeana Data Model) (Sofronijevic, 2011). As of May 2013 University library in Belgrade is a partner in Europeana Newspapers project that aims to add newspaper materials to Europeana. In addition, the project addresses challenges particularly linked with digitized newspapers: use of refinement methods for OCR, OLR/article segmentation, and named entity recognition (NER), and page class recognition to enhance search and presentation functionalities for Europeana customers; quality evaluation for automatic refinement technologies; transformation of local metadata to the Europeana Data Model (EDM); metadata standardization in close collaboration with stakeholders from the public and private sector. Belgrade city library has also been involved in Europeana related project that aimed at bringing digital materials from public libraries to Europeana. All three institutions now have experience in creation of metadata in ESE metadata model and aggregation scheme of Euopeana which is important for providing better visibility for their digital contents. Being a hub of digitization activities in Europe Europeana is dynamicly developing and along with it its metadata model is changing in order to facilitate more rich structure and to be more user oriented. Also semantic elements are important for enriching user experience of Europeana and because of this EDM metadata model is primarily being introduced (Doerr, Gradmann, Hennicke, Isaac, Meghini, & van de Sompel, 2010). Its development and implementation is proved to be hard for some librarians since many ideas and concept contains have originated in computer sciences (Definition of the Europeana Data Model elements, 2011). Because of this it is important for libraries in Serbia to be in front rows of EDM implementation and that is what only international projects can provide for them.

Emergence of the semantic Web is perceived as an opportunity and a challenge in Serbian libraries. Implementation of technologies such as Resource Description Framework (RDF), Web Ontology Language (OWL), Simple Knowledge Organization System (SKOS) and Protocol and RDF Query Language (SPARQL) is difficult with scares resources and librarians need new skills and additional education in order to implement them. Because of this debate is open between management of big Serbian libraries on means to gain necessary resources and educate stuff in order for Serbian libraries to hop on a fast moving train of semantic Web. Plans for employment of a more ICT oriented stuff have been made and new curricula in LIS education and long life learning programs for employees are discussed. In parallel monitoring of new developments in related areas is intensive and workshops, lectures and experience exchange events are organized with participants coming from foreign libraries that are more advanced in this field. As of May 2013 collaborative effort is planned to lunch a working group consisting of metadata, ICT and library management experts that will propose project ideas, guidelines and other support for implementation of RDF, OWL, SKOS, SPARQL and other tools and technologies that ground basis for efficient creation of metadata compliant with semantic Web. Exiting experiences in usage of Extensible Markup Language (XML) for creation of metadata is an important starting point and therefore Serbian libraries participating in EU related projects that have experience with XML based metadata schema such as EDM will lead this initiative. First results in the form of proposals and national guidelines are expected by the end of 2013.

METADATA AS MEANS FOR AUTOMATION OF DIGITAL DATA DELIVERY FOR PATRONS IN SERBIAN LIBRARIES

Libraries often add items to their collections, both printed and digital. The important part about this is to make users aware of new data available to them (Hodge, 2004). Usually this is achieved by posting online news via library Website or more recently via Web 2.0 tools e.g. Twitter, Facebook. RSS feed is a tool to automate digital data delivery for patrons. The data delivered may be metadata describing new items in a collection. A large number of digital objects are being added to library collections on daily basis and even larger number becomes available for library users via Internet. Librarians need to make users aware of the new data available which is effective only if users are informed on new data available in the field of their interest. It might be a scientific area, cultural heritage related topic or pure entertainment. The principle is the same: in the flood of data users might process just those relevant to their interest. If the metadata is digested and prepared for them by librarians the higher are the chances of data actually being used and information created.

RSS is a family of Web feed formats used for syndicating content from blogs or Web pages. RSS is an XML file that summarizes information items and links to the information sources (Murgesan, 2007). It informs users of updates to blogs or Web sites they're interested in. RSS stands for Rich Site Summary or Real Simple Syndication. It is a type of XML document used to share news headlines and other Web pages. Any Web page with an RSS feed enables the user to track updates on that specific page in an automated manner through a single subscription, and without having to visit the page from time to time (Mishra, 2009). Yahoo Pipes is a software tool that allows for RSS feeds filtering and in this way optimization of several feeds to specific user's needs. Yahoo Pipes provides an interactive, Web-based way to manipulate information from the Web in order to create custom feeds and Web apps. Yahoo Pipes is a tool to create new pages by aggregating and filtering RSS feeds from different sources (791 Linked Data in Libraries, 2011). The RSS feed is displayed as a list of titles and optionally summaries. A click on a title displays the new one. Titles are updated automatically. A script in PHP or other language, builds the list each time the page is displayed by loading the RSS file and extracting the data from it (Sureau, 2011). RSS has become the standard data format for communicating news, updates or any other type of information that a company or individual wants to syndicate to a large audience. The name is an acronym that stands for Really Simple Syndication, which is an XML format that consists of designated elements that are consistent for all RSS feeds and conform to the XML 1.0 specification. These elements need to stay consistent to allow for a standardized data format that RSS aggregators can then consume (Hadlock, 2011). RSS materials and hence Yahoo Pipe provided materials have a structure. Each new material needs to have a title, URL and description. Besides these additional metadata on a certain material can be produced: author's name, date, type of material, source etc. These metadata allow for filtration of RSS data through Yahoo Pipe aggregator according to different criteria e.g. keyword search in title or description, desired date or date range, material type. These criteria may be chosen in accordance to desired outcome that should provide for users needs fulfillment.

As latecomers in regards to information and communication technologies librarians in Serbia had the chance to skip the phase of RSS implementation for aggregation of information only and skip right ahead to aggregation and filtering in order to provide specific data for certain user groups. Data from sources that are updated with low frequency are still just aggregated but the number of such sources diminishes daily since every data providing entity is in the race to provide as much data as possible and thus attract more users. Because of this filtering of those sources that are frequently updated is needed in order to provide effective set of subject specific data for patrons. Among Serbian libraries University library in Belgrade is a leader in this field implementing both RSS and additional tools for filtering existing RSS feeds from other data sources. Yahoo Pipes have been chosen for this because of ease of use that allow librarians that have no advanced ICT skills to implement filtering on RSS feeds for creation of subject specific data sets. Librarians have provided specific Yahoo Pipes made having certain user groups in mind regarding various scientific areas. Having this experience in mind University library in Belgrade's RSS feeds have been created with metadata designed to facilitate use of tools similar to Yahoo Pipes by other librarians or users that might filter out just a section of metadata provided by this library. Having opted for this strategy in creating metadata that describe new data available for users University library set an example for Serbian libraries on how to effectively provide users with data delivery automation.

CONCLUSION

The role and use of metadata is debated in Serbian libraries, but the common notion is that efficient and effective use of metadata is the key to success in contemporary librarianship. Metadata is perceived as a very important both in its role as a tool and as a venue for providing access to digital and printed library collections. Fast changing environment, technological one above others, dictates dynamic approach to technically related topic of metadata. Therefore debate is open in Serbian libraries on proper ways of implementation of various available models and tools for metadata development and use. Current Metadata usage in libraries of Serbia is diverse and provides for description of library collections and materials available at libraries for different user groups. Some instances of old fashioned usage can be still found with some smaller libraries still operating card catalogues and sometimes metadata are contemplated upon from the old fashion librarian centered position. On the other side of the scale some instances of up to date usage of metadata as EDM development can be noticed in bigger libraries. In the middle of this range most libraries in Serbia create metadata in line of their everyday work in order to provide descriptions of their collection available for users via OPAC in one of two library automation systems available in Serbian libraries.

Increasing importance of metadata in the world of semantic Web that emerges is properly understood and steps have been taken in big libraries in Serbia to prepare for transition to metadata compliant with demands for semantic correlation of digital objects and metadata that will allow for digital objects of collections of Serbian libraries to be effectively accessible and visible for users worldwide. Relatively high resources demands for achievement of this goal is a challenge for Serbian libraries, but the opportunities to be a part of the new brave world of semantic Web present a hope that needed resources will be provided by funding governmental bodies. Plans have been made, debate is open and librarians in Serbia are hopeful that their digital objects will be well described by metadata based on advanced technologies providing for semantic compatibility with emerging standards.

Librarians in Serbia are aware of importance of international access to their digital collections and the most important role metadata has for this, but they are also well aware of importance of keeping an eye on contemporary trends of usage in Serbia and users' needs and expectations in regards to both printed and digital collections and adjustments in metadata produced needed to meet these needs. Because of this not only that a contemporary landscape of metadata usage in libraries of Serbia is diverse it may become even more diverse and exciting in the future.

REFERENCES

Antonic, S., Mitrovic, J., & Sofronijevic, A. (2011). Fostering open access usage by creation of the library aggregator for Europeana: Project Europeana libraries. In *Proceedings of INFORUM 2011: 17th Conference on Professional Information Resources*. Prague. Retrieved from http://www.inforum.cz/pdf/2011/antonic-sanja.pdf.

Butigan, V. T. (2007). *Preporuka formata meta-podataka za objekte digitalizovane nacionalne baštine: (Pokretna kulturna dobra)*. Retrieved from http://www.ncd.matf.bg.ac.rs/?page=news&lang=sr&file=predlogStandardaMetadata.htm

Butigan, V. T. (n. d.). *Nacionalni centar za digitalizaciju*. Retrieved from http://www.nb.rs/view_file.php?file_id=625

Ciljevi i zadaci univerzitetskih repozitorija Zapadnog Balkana. (2010). Retrieved from http://www.westbulnet.com/AmplioCMS2/public/EnterPublic.cms2?langId=74&request_locale=sr_CS#menuId=1347

COBISS.net. (2008). *Platforma COBISS - Kooperativni online bibliografski sistem i servisi*. Retrieved from http://www.cobiss.net/platforma_cobiss-SR.htm

COMARC/B Format za bibliografske podatke. (2009). Maribor, Institut informacijskih znanosti.

Coyle, K. (2005). Understanding metadata and its purpose. *Journal of Academic Librarianship*, *31*(2). doi:10.1016/j.acalib.2004.12.010

Coyle, K., & Baker, T. (2009). *Guidelines for Dublin Core application profiles*. Retrieved from http://dublincore.org/documents/profile-guidelines/

Definition of the Europeana Data Model elements: Version 5.2.1. 2011. (2011). Retrieved from http://group.europeana.eu/c/document_library/get_file?uuid=aff89c92-b6ff-4373-a279-fc47b9af3af2&groupId=10605

Digital Media, J. I. S. C. (2010). *An introduction to metadata. Managing your digital resources*. Retrieved from.

Doerr, M., Gradmann, S., Hennicke, S., Isaac, A., Meghini, C., & van de Sompel, H. (2010). The Europeana Data Model. In *Proceedings of World Library and Information Congress: 76th IFLA General Conference and Assembly*. Gothenburg, Sweden. Retrieved from http://www.ifla.org/files/hq/papers/ifla76/149-doerr-en.pdf

Đukić, P. (2005). Razvoj bibliotečko-informacionog sistema u Srbiji: od Biblisa do Bisisa. *Pančevačko čitalište, 4*, 28-29.

Europeana Data Model primer. (2010). Retrieved from http://group.europeana.eu/c/document_library/get_file?uuid=718a3828-6468-4e94-a9e7-7945c55eec65&groupId=10605

Europeana Semantic Elements Specification: Version 3.4. 2011. (2011). Retrieved from http://version1.europeana.eu/c/document_library/get_file?uuid=77376831-67cf-4cff-a7a2-7718388eec1d&groupId=10128

Filipi-Matutinović, S. (2004). Bibliotečki sistemi i problemi njihovog povezivanja u Srbiji. *Glas biblioteke, 11*, 5-10.

Flynn, E. (2013). Open access metadata, catalogers, and vendors: The future of cataloging records. *Journal of Academic Librarianship, 39*, 29–31. doi:10.1016/j.acalib.2012.11.010

Good, J. (2002). *A gentle introduction to metadata*. Retrieved from http://www.language-archives.org/documents/gentle-intro.html

Grbić, B. (2004). Sadržinska obrada u sistemu COBISS. *Infoteka, 5*, 53-56. Retrieved from http://www.zbus.rs/cir/infoteka/spec2004/INFOTEKA_V_spec_Maj2004_53-56.pdf

Grbić, B. (n. d.). *Predmetna klasifikacija u sistemu COBISS*. Retrieved from http://www.zbus.rs/cir/pdf/prirucnici/predmetizacija_u_cobissu.pdf

Grbić, B., Đurđulov, J., & Lazarević, G. (2011). *Sadržinska obrada dokumenata u repozitorijumu Phaidra - metapodaci*. [Web seminar]. Retrieved from http://www.westbulnet.com/AmplioCMS2/public/EnterPublic.cms2?langId=74&request_locale=sr_CS#menuId=1569

Greenberg, J. (2005). *Understanding metadata and metadata schemes*. Retrieved from.

Hadlock, K. (2011). *The Anatomy of an RSS Feed*. Retrieved from http://www.webreference.com/authoring/languages/xml/rss/feeds/

Hillmann, D. (2005). *Using Dublin core*. Retrieved from http://dublincore.org/documents/usageguide/

Hodge, G. (2004). Metapodaci na lak način. *Glasnik Narodne biblioteke Srbije, 1*, 157-180. Retrieved from http://www.nb.rs/view_file.php?file_id=860

http://www.ils.unc.edu/mrc/pdf/greenberg05understanding.pdf

http://www.jiscdigitalmedia.ac.uk/crossmedia/advice/an-introduction-to-metadata

Ilić Kiš, I. (2007). Softverski bibliotečki sistem Bisis: Petnaest godina razvoja i usavršavanja. *Pančevačko čitalište, 6*, 34.

Khoo, M., & Hall, C. (2013). Managing metadata: Networks of practice, technological frames, and metadata work in a digital library. *Information and Organization, 23*, 81–106. doi:10.1016/j.infoandorg.2013.01.003

Kojevic, S., Dakic, N., & Nogic, B. (2011). Normativne datoteke ličnih imena. In Standardizacija i kvalitet bibliotečkih usluga (pp. 307-322). Belgrade: Bibliotekarsko drustvo Srbije.

Lazarević, G. (n. d.) *UDK u sistemu Cobiss*. Retrieved from http://www.zbus.rs/cir/pdf/prirucnici/UDK_u_sistemu_COBISS.pdf

791. *Linked Data in Libraries: Course Blog for SOIS UWM course 791: Linked Data in Libraries: Library Mashups, the Semantic Web and Web 2.0: Yahoo Pipes*. (2011). Retrieved from http://791linkeddata.blogspot.com/2011/03/yahoo-pipes.html

Marković, B. (2005). Programski paket BISIS: Iskustva Gradske biblioteke u Novom Sadu. *Pančevačko čitalište, 4*, 30-31.

Mishra, S. (2009). Really simple syndication. *STRIDE Handbook: E-Learning, 8*, 113-116. Retrieved from http://elf.westernsydneyinstitute.wikispaces.net/file/view/eLearning+STRIDE_Hb8_Full.pdf/114728879/eLearning%20STRIDE_Hb8_Full.pdf#page=120

Murugesan, S. (2007). Understanding Web 2.0. *IT Pro*, 34-41. Retrieved from http://hcotuk.etu.edu.tr/bil554/Understanding_web_2.pdf

National Information Standards Organization. (2004). *Understanding metadata*. Retrieved from http://www.niso.org/publications/press/UnderstandingMetadata.pdf

Network Development and MARC Standards Office. (2006). *Marc 21 – Format for bibliographic data*. Retrieved from http://www.loc.gov/marc/bibliographic/bdintro.html

Nogić, B. (2004). Uzajamni katalog. *Infoteka, 5*, 47-52. Retrieved from http://www.zbus.rs/cir/infoteka/spec2004/INFOTEKA_V_spec_Maj2004_47-52.pdf

Plassard, M. (2001). Authority control in an international environment. Retrieved from http://www.nii.ac.jp/publications/CJK-WS/2-1Plassard.pdf

Popović Bošković, G., & Filipi-Matutinović, S. (2001). Virtuelna biblioteka Srbije (VBS) - računarsko povezivanje biblioteka u Srbiji. *Infoteka, 2*, (1- 2), 57-79.

Sabovljev, D. (2008). Četvrta verzija sistema BISIS: Uključivanje u svetsku bibliotečku mrežu. *Pančevačko čitalište, 7*, 28-29.

Sadun, E. (2009). *Yahoo Pipes: getting started with custom RSS feeds*. Retrieved from http://arstechnica.com/web/guides/2009/03/yahoo-pipes-getting-started-with-custom-rss-feeds.ars

Shukair, G., Loutas, N., Peristeras, V., & Sklarss, S. (2013). Towards semantically interoperable metadata repositorics: Thc assct description metadata schema. *Computers in Industry, 64*, 10–18. doi:10.1016/j.compind.2012.09.003

Sofronijevic, A. (2011). Biblioteke Europeane: 24 evropske biblioteke i Univerzitetska biblioteka Svetozar Marković stvaraju bibliotečkiagregator za Europeanu. *Visokoškolske biblioteke, 1*. Retrieved from http://www.zbus.rs/cir/index.php?a=visoko skolske&b=cirilica&c=osam&d=jedan#2.

Stevanović, V. (2003). Virtuelna biblioteka Srbije. *Infoteka, 4*(1), 95–102.

Sureau, D. (2011). *RSS - Really simple syndication: Building and using an RSS feed*. Retrieved from http://www.xul.fr/en-xml-rss.html#overview

Udicki, V. (2006). BISIS godinu dana posle: Povratak u budućnost. *Pančevačko čitalište, 5*, 25.

UNIMARC/Authorities: Universal Format for Authorities. (1991). München: K. G. Saur.

Chapter 4
Social Networks and Employee Knowledge Sharing and Performance:
A Chinese Case Study of a State-Owned Enterprise

Jianping Peng
Sun Yat-sen University, China

Jing Quan
Salisbury University, USA

ABSTRACT

In this chapter, the authors investigate the correlation between characteristics of the four social networks and employee task and contextual performance. The chapter focuses on the degree centrality and betweenness centrality of the four social networks (Job Advisory, Work Discussion, Friendship and Email Networks) of a Chinese state-owned enterprise as well as the individual attributes of knowledge sharing behavior and IT capability. The findings of this research are 1) employee contextual performance is uncorrelated with the network characteristics; 2) it is significantly and positively correlated with knowledge sharing behavior, but significantly and negatively correlated with individual IT capability, and 3) task performance is correlated, both positively and negatively, with various network characteristics, but not with knowledge sharing behavior and individual IT capability. In addition to discussing the cultural dimension of these results, the authors draw theoretical and managerial implications based on our research framework and findings.

DOI: 10.4018/978-1-4666-4711-4.ch004

INTRODUCTION

Social networking has recently made significant strides into the corporate intranets, and employee social networks (ESNs) become increasingly valuable assets to organizations (Skeels & Grudin, 2009). The rise of ESNs has generated important research questions for both academia and practitioners. While researchers agree in general that ESNs have a positive effect on innovation and firm performance (Dyer et al., 1998; Dyer et al., 2000; Mower et al., 1996; Rowley et al., 2000; Vander et al., 2002; Wu et al., 2007), how they affect employee performance remains largely unanswered (Castilla, 2005). Studies on employee performance in the past have largely relied on the economics theory that assumes the rationality of human beings in economic agents' behavior. However, they fail to take into consideration the fact that the behavior can be influenced by their interactions with others in the social networks. Social network analysis (SNA) studies individual choices in the context of the social networks and assumes that personal behavior choices are influenced by networks with which they interact (Jackson, 2008). Based on social network analysis, this research proposes a new approach to studying individual employee performance by examining the influence of social network characteristics on employees. This approach can not only overcome some of the limitations of the conclusions derived from the economic theory, but also provide theoretical support for helping enterprises improve their employee social network structures, promote knowledge sharing, and improve employee performance.

Employee performance can be divided into task performance and contextual performance (Granovetter, 1973; Uzzi, 1997). Task performance can be understood as job performance, that is, employees complete the work specified in their job descriptions. Contextual performance refers to employees' pro-organizational behaviors, which are shown empirically to contribute to firm performance (Bormant et al., 1993). The current mainstream of empirical research on employee performance is done by using the individual attributes of employee data. We adopt a new approach by adding social network characteristics in our social network analysis model on performance. The network characteristics used in this study are the degree centrality and betweenness centrality, extracted from the workplace social networks. Also, we include two individual attributes of the employee knowledge sharing behavior and IT capability.

Although social network analysis has been applied to assess performance (Ahuja et al., 2003; Cross & Cummings, 2004; Soda & Zaheer, 2012; Sparrowe et al., 2001; Waber et al., 2010), integrating social network characteristics and individual attributes in the same model represents a novel approach. This research is a case study of an independent company of a large state-owned enterprise in China. Through the construction of the company's overall social networks and extraction of the individual network characteristics, we build a quantitative model to assess the relationships between social network characteristics, IT capability, knowledge sharing behavior, and performance. Based on the results, we articulate the theoretical and practical implications for advancing performance theory development, improving employee accomplishment, and enhancing a firm's core competitiveness.

LITERATURE REVIEW

Employee Performance

Orga (1986) proposes that performance assessment should pay attention to organizational citizenship, which represents individual behavior that is beneficial to the organization and is discretionary, not directly or explicitly recognized by the formal reward system. This is similar to the popular concept of conscientious dedication in the Chinese society, which puts a great emphasis on individual duties and responsibilities to their working units and the country. Campbell (1990) proposes another performance model to consider that members may exceed the scope of requirements specified by the job description to benefit organizations. Bormant et al. (1993) propose that job performance should be divided into the task performance and contextual performance. The task performance evaluates individual behaviors required by organizations or specific jobs, or, for the completion of the mandate in the job descriptions. The contextual performance evaluates individual psychological, social, and interpersonal behaviors that help to complete the work of the organization, including spontaneous behaviors, social behaviors, organizational commitment spirit, as well as voluntary acts outside the requirements of work. The organizational citizenship behaviors (Orga, 1986) can be considered as a subnet of contextual performance.

The contextual component in employee job performance has received extensive attentions from scholars. For example, in an experiment done by Motowidlo et al. (1994) three experts were invited to evaluate 421 aviation mechanics for their overall performance, task performance and contextual performance after a 90 day observation period. The task performance is measured by 14 items on a five-point scale, the contextual performance by 16 items on a five-point scale, and the overall performance by three items on a seven-point scale. The correlation analysis and stepwise regressions show that both task performance and contextual performance independently affect overall performance. Another study by Conway (1999) proposes that contextual and task performances contribute equally to overall performance.

Van Scotter and Motowidlo (1996) further divide contextual performance into interpersonal facilitation and job dedication. While contextual performance generally includes possessing interpersonal skills, maintaining good working relationships and helping others to complete work, interpersonal facilitation refers to behaviors conducive to achieving the organizational objectives; and these behaviors improve staff morale, encourage collaboration, and create an environment for better task performance. Job dedication focuses on self-disciplined behaviors, such as obeying the rules, working hard, and taking the initiative to solve work-related problems. In their empirical study (Van Scotter & Motowidlo, 1996), the managers of 975 aviation mechanics evaluated their task performance, interpersonal facilitation, job dedication, and overall performance. The results show that task performance and interpersonal facilitation greatly affect the overall performance and the two can be differentiated based on their contributions to the overall performance.

Social Network Analysis

Social network analysis (SNA) places the people in the context of the society and studies a person's behavior as a social being (Jackson, 2009). As a result, SNA avoids the "social isolation" assumption made in the economic theory. While retaining a person's free will, it places individuals in the context of social networks and analyzes their behaviors and interpersonal interactions. Social networks play a critical role in determining how organizations are run and whether individuals succeed in achieving their goals (Carley, Martin, & Hirshman, 2009).

SNA uses nodes and connections to describe social relationships. Nodes are the individual actors within the networks, and connections are the relationships between the actors. In a social network diagram, nodes are the points and connections are the lines. Two of the important measures in SNA metrics are degree centrality and betweenness centrality (Jackson, 2009). Degree refers to how many direct connections a node has. For example, in a network of n nodes, a node with degree n-1 is directly connected to all other nodes. This node is said to be central to the network. The ratio of the numbers of connections a node has to n-1 measures the degree centrality the node. Betweenness is a measure of importance of a node's position in a network. Nodes which bridge clusters of nodes have a higher value of betweenness, reflecting the influence a node has over the spread of information through the network (Brandes, 2001). Betweenness centrality is normally calculated as the fraction of shortest paths between pairs of nodes passing through the node of interest (Newman, 2005).

Social Network and Performance

Empirical research demonstrates that social network related factors have an effect on performance. For example, by analyzing 61 independent samples in literature, Stam, Arzlanian, and Elfring (2013) found that the social networks–performance link was positive and significant. Cross and Cummings (2004) find that individual performance in knowledge-intensive work is affected by both networks and ties in the organization, and betweenness centralities of information and cognition networks are positively related to individual performance. A field study of 190 employees in five diverse organizations by Sparrowe et al. (2001) shows that employees in the center of the advisory network have higher enthusiasm for work outside their own jobs and better job performance than those in the peripheral. As a result, the degree centrality of the advisory network has a positive impact on employee task and contextual performances. The empirical study by Ahuja et al. (2003) indicates that network centrality mediates the effects of the formal organization structure of the functional role and status on individual job performance. That is, status and performance are correlated with network centralities.

As the focuses of task performance and contextual performance are different, the impact of social networks on the two will differ as well. In an empirical study by Chen (2004) the degree centralities of advisory and emotion networks have positive influences on contextual performance. Liu (2008) finds that degree centralities of advisory and emotion networks in employee social networks have positive influences on both task performance and contextual performance. In addition, emotion networks positively influence task performance, but have different effects on the two dimensions of contextual performance. Emotion networks promote interpersonal behaviors while reducing work dedication. For example, Santarelli and Tran (2013) find that interaction of human capital and social capital displays a statistically significant positive correlation with performance.

In summary, the current social network analysis combines the centrality of social network structure characteristics and network types (emotion, information and advice networks) within the organization to study the impact of individual network positions on job performance (Yao, 2009).

RESEARCH HYPOTHESES

Our research anchors on the central issue of correlations of employee performance with network characteristics and individual attributes. The network characteristics are the degree centrality and betweenness centrality of the employee social networks. The individual attributes are knowledge sharing behavior and IT capability. And finally, performance includes both task and contextual performance.

Network Characteristics and Employee Task Performance

In its simplest form, a social network is a map of specified ties, such as friendship, between the nodes being studied. The nodes to which an individual is thus connected are the social contacts of that individual. Research shows that social networks have a positive impact on performance (Shaw, 1964; Robert et al., 1979; Baldwin, 1997; Cross & Cummings, 2003; Ahuja et al., 2003; Manju et al., 2003). More specifically, network centrality is identified as a key contributor to positive performance (Baldwin, 1997; Liu, 2008). Different positions in the organizational social networks entitle employees to different resources, information, support, and assistance. As a result, they can influence employees' task performance and contextual performance. Empirical studies (Cross et al., 2004; Sparrowe et al., 2001; Ahuja et al., 2003) have shown that person-to-person interactions and the network degree centrality are positively correlated with performance. Liu (2008) has empirically shown a positive relationship between the degree centralities of the advisory and the friendship networks and employee task performance.

Employee task performance measures how employees complete their assigned tasks. Those who are well respected in organizational social networks and have large influences on the behaviors of other employees are usually competent in their work. Otherwise, they cannot become the center of work discussion and advisory networks. In addition, working together generates emotions, and friendships among employees are more likely to form than among strangers. An employee's position in a friendship network reflects the person's prestige and influence among friends. This power of influence is strongly correlated with performance because the employee's actions will have an effect on other employees.

Hypothesis 1a: An employee's degree centrality of the social networks and employee task performance are positively correlated.

Hypothesis 1b: An employee's betweenness centrality of the social networks and employee contextual task performance are positively correlated.

Network Characteristics and Contextual Performance

The centers of social networks help to build better links with other members, and they possess an informal social influence (Brass & Burkhart, 1992). That is why it becomes a key measure of prestige and power in the structural analysis (Wasserman & Faust, 1994). Because the effective personal control can reduce the uncertainty, the person in the center position can improve the organization's environment than those who are in the peripheral.

Contextual performance is closely related to personality factors (Coleman, 1998; Salomon, 2000; Mohammed, 2002). Social networks formed by employees at work can promote mutual assistance and communication among friends, and hence, can promote trust and voluntary commitments to perform extra work. The network degree centrality and betweenness centrality are two of the important indicators of individual locations and connections in social networks. A person with a high level of network degree centrality and betweenness centrality tends to have high social status in the sociology perspective, is powerful in the organizational behavior perspective (Luo, 2010), and is greatly influential in the network. Those who have a high level of influence in the social networks must have a high level of personal dedication and willingness to help others. Otherwise, the colleagues will not recognize and respect their positions in the network. That is, employees with high degree and betweenness centralities are more likely to voluntarily help others and perform extra work. This leads to higher contextual performance.

Hypothesis 2a: An employee's degree centrality of the social networks and employee task performance are positively correlated.

Hypothesis 2b: An employee's betweenness centrality of the social networks and employee contextual performance are positively correlated.

Knowledge Sharing and Performance

Knowledge sharing is the dissemination of knowledge. Through various channels, employees exchange and share knowledge. Organizations often find that employees are reluctant and unwilling to voluntarily share knowledge (Wasko & Faraj, 2005). Senge (1997) uses the "learn" point of view to explain the knowledge sharing process. French (1959) considers that the main obstacle to knowledge sharing comes from the point of view of knowledge and power. Employees traditionally believe that knowledge is a source of power. Someone with the knowledge has the power to obtain available organizational resources and to receive promotions and raises more easily. Employees are more willing to share knowledge with others, if the sharing behavior gets them some rewards or promotions. Stevenson (1997) believes that knowledge sharing is a distribution of resources. The more trust managers place in subordinates, the more knowledge sharing will happen. This is consistent with the view that trust in virtual communities impacts knowledge sharing. Subramanian and Soh (2009) introduce inducement and opportunity mechanisms of knowledge management that are essential for promoting knowledge sharing among employees. In the inducement mechanism, both reward and power are two important enablers for knowledge sharing.

Although the relationship between knowledge sharing and job performance is theoretically supported, empirical research remains limited (Ismail & Yusof, 2009). One of the few existing studies is by Du et al. (2007), which finds that knowledge sharing is related to performance. In this study, we hypothesize that knowledge sharing and performance are positively correlated. We also empirically test the relationships. Davenport (1998) defines "knowledge sharing" as a voluntary act and distinguishes it from "reporting." While reporting is the information exchange behavior based on a certain set of rules, sharing implies a conscious behavior with the intention to help recipients. Hence, knowledge sharing and contextual performance are correlated. In addition, at the individual level, knowledge sharing allows workers to collaborate with others and this action enhances their skills. Knowledge sharing between individuals increases their competencies, and hence, improves their task performance (Sveiby, 2001).

Hypothesis 3a: An employee's knowledge sharing behavior and task performance are positively correlated.

Hypothesis 3b: An employee's knowledge sharing behavior and contextual performance are positively correlated.

Individual IT Capability and Performance

Information system is, in general, a socio-technical system in the organization. IT capabilities are one of the important organizational resources. Although IT capabilities are defined at the organizational level, we can consider them as the sum of individual IT capabilities. Based on the definition of enterprise IT capabilities (Tippins et al., 2003), we define individual IT capabilities as the abilities of the individual employees' understanding, and effective use, of enterprise information systems.

With the widespread applications of information technology in enterprises, the work and communication of employees are generally carried out with the help of computers. Many business processes in the workflow are controlled by information systems. The Internet and other virtual means of communication have made the exchange of ideas among employees much easier and have facilitated work consultations with colleagues.

The research on IT capabilities can be anchored on either personal or organizational levels. While most of the existing research is done at the organizational level, some (e. g. Bharadwaj, 2000) point out that it is the individual capabilities needed for IT applications that form the foundation for organizational IT capability, while the level of corporate IT applications has a direct impact on the IT capabilities of individual employees. Employees with strong IT capabilities can have more means at their disposal to work more efficiently and achieve higher task performance. In the meantime, they can take advantage of the IT capabilities they have to do more work in addition to their job requirements. This, in turn, improves their contextual performance.

Hypothesis 4a: An employee's IT capability and task performance are positively correlated.

Hypothesis 4b: An employee's IT capability and contextual performance are positively correlated.

DATA COLLECTION

To test the hypotheses above, we need to measure and compute the employees' contextual and task performances, their knowledge sharing behaviors and IT capabilities as well as their social network characteristics. Based on the existing literature, we adopt the measurement model proposed by Van Scotter and Motowidlo (1996) for employee contextual performance. Wang et al. (2003) translate this maturely established scale into Chinese and back to English and empirically test it. For the task performance, the data came from the scores based on the 360-degree assessment of the employee task performance conducted by the company. The employee task performance is the average of the three sets of evaluations: managers on employees, employees on employees, and employees on themselves. For knowledge sharing behaviors, we modify the measurement dimensions and scale by Senge (1997) to create seven measurement items. The items are tested using exploratory factor analysis (EFA) to create the formal measurement model. Finally, for employee IT capability, we adopt Peng's (2009) study, combined with the firm's demand for employee IT skills, to develop the scale for measurement. Again, the initial items are tested by EFA to create the final measurement model.

Based on the measurements developed above, two sets of data are collected. One set is the relational data reflecting the network characteristics of employees, such as the network degree centrality and betweenness centrality. The other set is the attributes of employee characteristics, such as the IT capability, knowledge sharing behaviors, contextual performance, and task performance.

The survey was conducted from October to December 2009 in an independent company of a large state-owned enterprise in China. The company, with five departments, is mainly engaged in providing maintenance and technical support for corporate computers and large mechanical, electrical and hydropower equipment. The questionnaire was reviewed and approved by the management. A cover letter on the company's letterhead stating the research purpose and the anonymity of the project asked the employees to voluntarily participant in the survey. At the annual meeting of the company, the questionnaire was distributed to all 124 employees, including managers, technicians, and front-line technical workers. After the department managers reviewed the relationship data provided by the employees, incomplete and inaccurate questionnaires were discarded, yielding 109 useful responses. Table 1 provides the age distribution and education levels of the respondents.

Table 1. Age and education level

Age	
30 or younger	32 (29%)
30 to 40	45 (41%)
40 to 50	26 (24%)
50 or older	6 (6%)
Education Level	
Graduate School	1 (1%)
Undergraduate	26 (24%)
3 year Professional School	43 (39%)
2 year Technical School or below	39 (36%)

We used SPSS and Amos7 to perform the reliability analysis and convergent validity analysis, respectively, for the returned questionnaires. The results show that the data has good reliability and validity (see Table 2).

The characteristics of employee social network are measured according to the concept of the social network scale proposed by Wasserman (1994). Our questionnaire asked employees to whom they often turned to for advice about work, with whom they often discussed work related problems, with whom they often chatted, and to whom they sent and from whom they received e-mails in the internal e-mail system provided by the company. Based on the responses, the organizational social network can be divided into the job advisory network, work discussion network, friendship network, and email network. Figure 1 and Figure 2 show the maps of the job advisory and work discussion networks based on the relationship matrices of the overall network generated by the UCINET application software.

QAP Tests of Overall Network Characteristics and Relationships

The UCINET software calculated and tested the overall network characteristics including the network density, the average path-length among employees in the network, and the cohesion factor. Based on the results, any differences between various social networks

Table 2. CFA results

	RA	X2	df	X2/df	RMSEA	NFI	CFI
Contextual Performance	.918	63.34	40	1.583	.074	.912	.965
Knowledge Sharing Behavior	.845	14.9	9	1.659	.078	.985	.965
IT Capability	.913	17.9	12	1.488	.067	.976	.992
Reference Value	**≥0.6**			**≤2**	**≤0.08**	**≥0.9**	**≥0.9**

Notes: RA=Reliability

Figure 1. Job advisory network

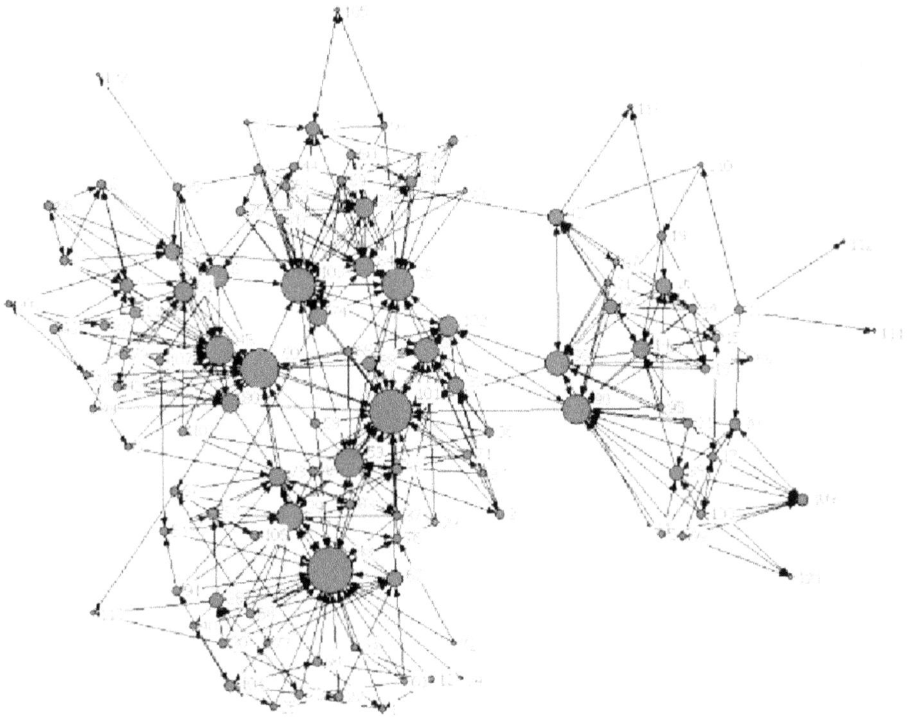

Figure 2. Work discussion network

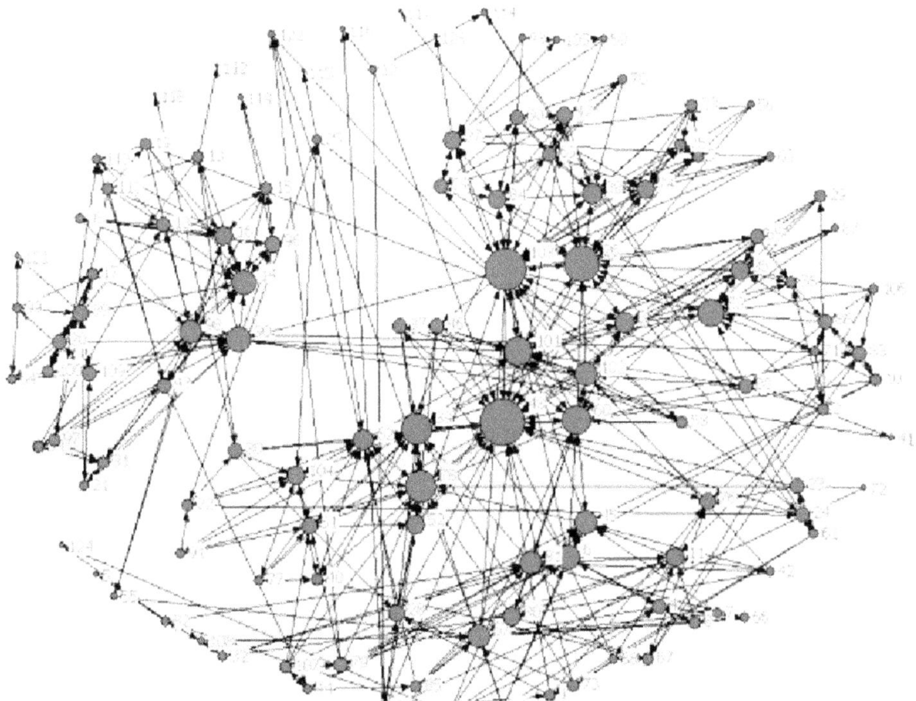

formed by the employees at work and their characteristics can be detected.

QAP (Quadratic Assignment Procedure) is the method that compares the value of each of corresponding paired elements in two or more square matrices. Specifically, it calculates the correlation between the original and transposed matrices to obtain the correlation coefficients and significance levels of different network relationships (Liu, 2009). Table 3 shows the results based on the QAP analysis of the four different networks in this study, Job Advisory Network (J), Work Discussion Network (W), Friendship Network (F) and Email Network (M). It shows that J and the other three networks (W, F, and M) are significantly related, W is significantly associated with F, and F is significantly related to M. The coefficient of correlation between J and F is the highest and significant, while W and M is not correlated.

The network densities of the employees are not high. This may be attributed to the company's nature of work and organizational structure. Employees in the same department generally had close relationship but they had infrequent contacts with people in the other departments. In the four social networks formed by the employees, the path for information transmission is an average of 3.03 individuals. This shows that a limited level of inter-department communication existed. In addition, the path for the e-mail network was only 1.77 individuals. This demonstrates that the company can more effectively communicate via the e-mail network than the social networks.

MODELS

Based on the literature, we extract the degree centrality and betweenness centrality as the employee network characteristics. Other variables in our study are employee performance, employee knowledge sharing behaviors, and employee IT capability. Employee performance is further divided into task performance and contextual performance. The correlation analysis of the variables is in Table 4. The results show that task performance is negatively correlated with the betweenness centrality of the Job Advisory Network. It is also negatively correlated with both the degree centrality and intermediate centrality of the Email Network. Contextual performance is positively correlated with the betweenness centralities of the Job Advisory Network, the Work Discussion Network, and the Email Network. The knowledge sharing behaviors of individual employees are positively correlated with both the network characteristics of the

Table 3. Network characteristics and relationships

	J	W	F	M
Network Density	.0268***	.0496***	.0422***	.0172***
Compactness	.119	.3	.278	.032
Average distance	3.6	3.214	3.546	1.77
Work Advisory Network (J)	1	-	-	-
Job Discussion Network (W)	.031***	1	-	-
Friendship Network (F)	.319**	.046***	1	-
Email Network (M)	.015*	.07	.017*	1

*** $p < .01$, ** $p < .05$.

Table 4. Correlation analysis

	TP	CP	KS	IT	JD	JB	WD	WB	FD	FB	MD	MB
TP	1	-	-	-	-	-	-	-	-	-	-	-
CP	-.002	1	-	-	-	-	-	-	-	-	-	-
KS	-.111	.477**	1	-	-	-	-	-	-	-	-	-
IT	-.144	-.005	.286**	1	-	-	-	-	-	-	-	-
JD	-.146	.239*	.299**	.159	1	-	-	-	-	-	-	-
JB	-.252**	.166	.261**	.138	.794**	1	-	-	-	-	-	-
WD	-.182	.194*	.261**	.196*	.912**	.675**	1	-	-	-	-	-
WB	-.079	.186	.235*	.104	.704**	.660**	.686**	1	-	-	-	-
FD	.041	.110	.152	.099	.720**	.547**	.747**	.474**	1	-	-	-
FB	.014	.029	-.062	.041	.514**	.384**	.470**	.469**	.525**	1	-	-
MD	-.297**	.222*	.265**	.336**	.704**	.486**	.642**	.416**	.509**	.402**	1	-
MB	-.261**	.157	.251**	.288**	.656**	.553**	.640**	.562**	.438**	.334**	.784**	1

Notes: TP = task performance. CP = contextual performance. KS = employee knowledge sharing behaviors. IT = employee IT capability. D = Degree centrality. B = Betweenness centrality. J = Job Advisory Network. W = Work Discussion Network. F = Friendship Network. M = Email Network

** p < .01, * p < .05 (2-tailed).

Job Advisory, the Job Discussion, and the Email Networks. The network characteristics of the four networks are highly correlated and significant.

Network Characteristics and Task Performance

The network characteristics of an individual reflect one's positions in the different social networks in relation to others. We examine the relationship between task performance and the individual network characteristics are shown in Table 5 and use the following model:

$$y = \alpha + \beta Z + \beta_{KS} KS + \beta_{IT} ITC + \gamma_1 x_1 + \gamma_2 x_2 + \gamma_3 x_3 + \varepsilon \quad (1)$$

where the dependent variable is the task performance, Z is the vector of degree and betweenness centralities of the four social net-

Table 5. Impact of network characteristics on task performance

Coefficient	Estimate
$\beta_{J\text{-}D}$	.931***
$\beta_{J\text{-}B}$	-.612***
$\beta_{W\text{-}D}$	-.812***
$\beta_{W\text{-}B}$	.244*
$\beta_{F\text{-}D}$	.460***
$\beta_{F\text{-}B}$	.005
$\beta_{M\text{-}D}$	-.444***
$\beta_{M\text{-}B}$	-
β_{KS}	-.031
β_{IT}	-.003
γ_1	-.065
γ_2	.086
γ_3	-.107
R^2	.373
F	3.73***

Notes: - dropped variable with VIF > 5
*** $p < .01$, ** $p < .05$.

works, and x1, x2 and x3 are the control variables for age, degree, and company tenure, respectively.

The degree centrality of the Job Advisory Network and the betweenness centrality of the Work Discussion Network are positively correlated with task performance, but the betweenness centrality of the Job Advisory Network and the degree centrality of the Work Discussion are negatively correlated with performance. We will explain these seemingly contradictive results in the discussion section.

The degree centrality of the Friendship Network is positively related to task performance. This suggests that a well-connected individual in the Friendship Network tends to have high task performance. However, the degree centrality of the Email Network is significantly but negatively correlated with task performance. The somewhat surprising result may be explained by the nature of the firm. The employees normally do not use emails, which are mainly used by the management to broadcast announcements. Too many emails burden and distract the employees and are adversely correlated with their task performance.

Individual IT capability and knowledge sharing behavior are not significant. In addition, neither are any of the control variables (age, degree, and company tenure).

In conclusion, our hypotheses 1a and 1b are partially supported and hypotheses 3a and 4a are rejected.

Network Characteristics and Contextual Performance

We replace the dependent variable in Model (1) with the contextual performance:

$$y = \alpha + \beta Z + \beta_{KS}KS + \beta_{IT}IT + \gamma_1 x_1 + \gamma_2 x_2 + \gamma_3 x_3 + \varepsilon \qquad (2)$$

The results in Table 6 show that none of the network characteristics is significant. Hence, both hypotheses 2a and 2b are rejected. Knowledge sharing is positively correlated with contextual performance. This is not surprising because knowledge sharing is a voluntary act that helps others to do their jobs better. This supports hypothesis 3b. Interestingly, IT capability is negatively related to the performance. This may be explained by the fact that contextual performance is a pro-organizational behavior and the altruistic act of helpfulness. Employees with a high IT capability can often work independently with minimum face-to-face interaction with other people. This reduces their contextual performance.

One of the possible explanations for the insignificance of the network characteristic may be that degree and betweenness centralities lack personality dimensions. Exten-

Table 6. Impact of network characteristics on contextual performance

Coefficient	Estimate
$\beta_{J\text{-}D}$	-
$\beta_{J\text{-}B}$	-.018
$\beta_{W\text{-}D}$	-.019
$\beta_{W\text{-}B}$	.117
$\beta_{F\text{-}D}$	-.038
$\beta_{F\text{-}B}$	-.008
$\beta_{M\text{-}D}$	.233
$\beta_{M\text{-}B}$	-.123
β_{KS}	.490***
β_{IT}	-.204*
γ_1	.086
γ_2	.092
γ_3	-.092
R^2	.294
F	3.33***

Notes: - dropped variable with VIF > 5
*** $p < .01$, ** $p < .05$.

sive research has found that personality and contextual performance are closely related (Motowidlo & Van Scotter, 1994; Coleman, 1998; Salomon, 2000; Van Scotter, 2000; Mohammed, 2002). Since personality is captured in employee knowledge sharing behaviors and IT capabilities, it is reasonable to find the significant correlations between them, but not between the network characteristic and contextual performance.

A similar result is found in a study by Shen and Wang (2004) of employees in China Post, a state owned enterprise. They surveyed the maintenance workers for the large electronic equipment used by China Post and found that the average score of contextual performance was 4.418 out of five with a standard deviation of 0.277. They concluded that the employees in the state owned firms usually evaluated themselves over-optimistically in order to gain more benefits. They found little correlation between social network characteristics and contextual performance.

DISCUSSION

We offer our explanations for the negative correlations between the betweenness centrality of the Job Advisory Network and the degree centrality of the Work Discussion Network and task performance by examining the dual aspects of network degree and betweenness centralities. The Advisory Network is constructed based on the relationship between an employee and the person who the employee would seek advice from before making decisions. The degree centrality reflects the degree of influence the employee has on others. Hence, it is expected that the degree of influence of the employee and the task performance are correlated. That is, influential employees in the network can use their own experience and knowledge to directly help and persuade others. This will gain recognition and respect from their peers and management and improve their task performance. The betweenness centrality reflects, however, the extent to which employees have control over the communication among others. The higher degree of control distracts an employee from performing the task and leads to lower performance. Our interviews showed that due to the different lines of work of the five departments in the company, inter-departmental communication is a rare occurrence, resulting in the emergence of a number of structural holes in the networks (see Figure 1). The persons with high betweenness centrality are normally department heads, because they need to focus on the inter-departmental communication. This leads them to spend more time to coordinate the inter-departmental communication. However, task performance is evaluated by the management based on completed work assignment. The effort and output gap results in the negative correlation between the betweenness centrality and task performance.

A culture dimension can be added to the explanation for the negative correlation between the degree centrality of the Advisory Network and task performance. The Chinese people are known for their insistence of "good face." A strong performer has a disincentive to offer opinions on the key issues consulted on the online discussion board, because if wrong, the person would lose "face." The unwillingness to participate actively in the network activities is manifested by the weak connection in the network.

The Work Discussion Network is constructed based on the question "with whom you frequently discuss work related issues." In reality, if one spends too much time on discussion boards, it will no doubt adversely affect the task performance. One with high degree centrality implies that he is over-involved in the discussions. This will cause distractions from the work and thereby unfavorably affect the person's task performance. Similarly, while email was found to be the most efficient way of communicating, the amount of emails was found to be negatively correlated with task performance. This suggests that companies should have balanced email and discussion board policies and guidelines in place to facilitate smooth communication as well as to endure a certain level of productivity.

Social network characteristics, in general, do not have significant correlations with contextual performance. Individual knowledge sharing behavior is the only variable that was positively correlated with contextual performance. The implication of this finding is twofold. First, future research on performance should delineate different dimensions related to performance. Moreover, the relationship between different knowledge sharing dimensions and performance is also interesting (Du et al., 2007). Second, such a connection between knowledge sharing behavior and contextual performance can be made explicit in an organization to encourage employees to share their knowledge and promote collaboration.

Further research should include other social network characteristics such as weak ties, structural holes, and network diversity. Stam, Arzlanian, and Elfring (2013) find that effect sizes of weak ties were smaller than those of structural holes. Similarly, Santarelli, and Tran (2013) also discover that benefits from weak ties outweigh those from strong ties on performance. Moreover, network diversity plays a very important role in enhancing performance (Stam, Arzlanian, & Elfring, 2013).

CONCLUSION

This Chinese case study is based on an independent company of a large state owned enterprise. We extract the degree centrality and betweenness centrality of the four social networks (Job Advisory Network, Work Discussion Network, Friendship Network and Email Network) and obtain individual attribute data on employee knowledge sharing behavior, IT capability and task and contextual performance. Our results show the various correlations between the network characteristics, individual knowledge sharing, IT capability, and performance.

This study adopts a new approach for evaluating performance by combining social network analysis and individual attributes. The traditional methods overlook the social aspect of employees' behavioral actions. Social network analysis is based on the assumption that actions of an individual are often not isolated, but interrelated to other members in the social networks in the workplace. The relationship ties formed between them are channels for transmission of information and reallocation of resources, and the structural network relationships determine opportunities and results of their actions (Lin, 2009). Combining individual attributes and the relational data can better explain the motivation of employees' behaviors and provide a new theoretical foundation for the design and development of firm human resource policies for evaluating employee performance. In addition, our results can help firms realize the effectiveness of social networks and their relationship with employee performance. Finally, our findings are particularly interesting to multinational companies (MNCs) doing business in China because our results show that cultural differences play a key role in the relationship between social network characteristics and performance. MNC managers should be sensitive to the cultural dimensions when evaluating Chinese worker performance.

The research is based on one Chinese state-owned company. To extend the applicability of the conclusions of this research, more data on various types of companies should be collected in the future. In addition, with a larger sample size, more robust statistical analysis can be performed to discern causal relationships between the independent variables (network characteristics, knowledge sharing, and IT capabilities) and performance as the dependent variable.

ACKNOWLEDGMENT

This study is partially supported by the National Natural Science Foundation of China under Grant Number 71072086 and by the Ministry of Education of China, Humanities and Social Sciences Grant: "Impacts of Social Network on Employee Knowledge Sharing and Innovation (No. 10YJA630124)."

REFERENCES

Abuja, G., & Carley, K. M. (2003). Individual centrality and performance in virtual R&D groups: An empirical study. *Management Science*, *49*(1), 21–38. doi:10.1287/mnsc.49.1.21.12756

Bharadwaj, A. S. (2000). A resource-based perspective on information technology capability and firm performance: An empirical investigation. *Management Information Systems Quarterly*, *24*(1), 169–196. doi:10.2307/3250983

Borman, W. C., & Motowidlo, S. J. (1993). Expanding the criterion domain to include elements of contextual performance. In N. Schmitt, & W. C. Bormaned (Eds.), *Personnel selection in organizations*. San Francisco: Jossey-Bass.

Brandes, U. (2001). A faster algorithm for betweenness centrality. *The Journal of Mathematical Sociology*, *25*, 163–177. doi:10.1080/0022250X.2001.9990249

Campbell, J. P. (1990). Modeling the performance prediction problem in industrial and organizational psychology. In M. D. Dunnette, & L. M. Hough (Eds.), *Handbook of industrial and organizational psychology*. Palo Alto, CA: Consulting Psychologists Press.

Carley, K. M., Martin, M. K., & Hirshman, B. (2009). The etiology of social change. *Topics in Cognitive Science*, *1*(4), 621–650. doi:10.1111/j.1756-8765.2009.01037.x

Castilla, E. J. (2005). Social networks and employee performance in a call center. *American Journal of Sociology*, *110*(5), 1243–1283.

Chen, R. (2004). *The formation and influence of social networks within the organization: Social capital perspective* (PhD Dissertation). Sun Yat-sen University, China.

Coleman, V. I. (1998). Investigation of the underlying structure of the contextual performance domain. *Dissertation Abstracts International: Section B: Science and Engineering.*, *58*(8-B), 4499.

Conway, J. M. (1999). Distinguishing contextual performance from task performance for managerial jobs. *The Journal of Applied Psychology*, *84*, 3–13. doi:10.1037/0021-9010.84.1.3

Cross, R., & Cummings, J. N. (2004). Tie and network correlates of individual performance in knowledge intensive work. *Academy of Management Journal*, *47*(6), 928–937. doi:10.2307/20159632

Du, R., Ai, S., & Ren, Y. (2007). Relationship between knowledge sharing and performance: A survey in Xi'an China. *Expert Systems with Applications*, *32*(1), 38–46. doi:10.1016/j.eswa.2005.11.001

French, J. R. P., & Raven, B. (1959). The bases of social power. In D. Cartwright (Ed.), *Studies in social power*. Ann Arbor, MI: University of Michigan.

Ismail, M. B., & Yusof, Z. M. (2009). The relationship between knowledge sharing, employee performance and service delivery in public sector organisations: A theoretical framework. *Public Sector ICT Management Review*, *3*(1), 37–45.

Jackson, M. O. (2008). *Social and economic networks*. Princeton, NJ: Princeton University Press.

Luo, J. (2005). *Social network analysis notes*. Beijing, China: Social Sciences Academic Press.

Luo, J., Zheng, M., & Xie, Z. (2007). Social capital impact on knowledge sharing within the practical community. *Jiangxi Social Sciences*, *3*, 131–141.

Mohammed, S., Mathieu, J. E., & Barlett, A. L. (2002). Technical administrative task performance, leadership task performance, and contextual performance: Considering the influence of team and task related composition variables. *Journal of Organizational Behavior*, *23*(7), 795–814. doi:10.1002/job.169

Motowidlo, S. J., & Van Scotter, J. R. (1994). Evidence that task performance should be distinguished from contextual performance. *The Journal of Applied Psychology*, *79*, 475–480. doi:10.1037/0021-9010.79.4.475

Newman, M. E. J. (2005). A measure of betweenness centrality based on random walks. *Social Networks*, *27*, 39–54. doi:10.1016/j.socnet.2004.11.009

Peng, J. (2009). Comparative analysis of the key factors on IT application in Chinese and foreign enterprises. *Business Economics and Management*, *8*, 30–35.

Salomon, L. M. (2000). The impact of personality variables on different facets of contextual performance. *Dissertation Abstracts International. B, The Sciences and Engineering*, *61*(6-B), 3313.

Santarelli, E., & Tran, H. T. (2013). The interplay of human and social capital in shaping entrepreneurial performance: The case of Vietnam. *Small Business Economics*, *40*(2), 435–458. doi:10.1007/s11187-012-9427-y

Senge, P. (1997). Sharing knowledge. *Leadership Excellence*, *14*(11), 17–18.

Skeels, M. M., & Grudin, J. (2009). When social networks cross boundaries: A case study of workplace use of Facebook and LinkedIn. *GROUP '09 Proceedings of the ACM 2009 International Conference on Supporting Group Work*. Sanibel Island, Florida.

Soda, G., & Zaheer, A. (2012). A network perspective on organizational architecture: Performance effects of the interplay of formal and informal organization. *Strategic Management Journal*, *33*(6), 751–771. doi:10.1002/smj.1966

Sparrowe, R. T., Liden, R. C., Wayne, S. J., & Kraimer, M. L. (2001). Social networks and the performance of individuals and groups. *Academy of Management Journal*, *44*(2), 316–325. doi:10.2307/3069458

Stam, W., Arzlanian, S., & Elfring, T. (2013). Social capital of entrepreneurs and small firm performance: A meta-analysis of contextual and methodological moderators. *Journal of Business Venturing*.

Stevenson, M. A. (1997). *The antecedents and consequences of interpersonal trust in mixed-motive dyadic negotiation* (Doctoral Dissertation). The Ohio State University, OH.

Subramanian, A. M., & Soh, P. H. (2009). Contributing knowledge to knowledge repositories: Dual role of inducement and opportunity factors. *Information Resources Management Journal*, *22*(1), 45–62. doi:10.4018/irmj.2009010103

Sveiby, K. E. (2001). A knowledge-based theory of the firm to guide in strategy formulation. *Journal of Intellectual Capital*, *2*(4), 344–358. doi:10.1108/14691930110409651

Uzzi, B. (1997). Social structure and competition in interfirm networks: The paradox of embeddedness. *Administrative Science Quarterly*, *42*(1), 35–67. doi:10.2307/2393808

Van Scotter, J. R. (1999). *Impact of autonomy on task performance, interpersonal facilitation, job dedication, and their relationships with overall performance.* Paper presented at the 1999 SIOP Conference, Atlanta, GA.

Van Scotter, J. R., & Motowidlo, S. J. (1996). Interpersonal facilitation and job dedication as separate facets of contextual performance. *The Journal of Applied Psychology*, *81*, 525–531. doi:10.1037/0021-9010.81.5.525

Waber, B. N., Olguin, O. D., Kim, T., & Pentland, A. (2010). Productivity through coffee breaks: Changing social networks by changing break structure. Retrieved from http://ssrn.com/abstract=1586375

Wang, H., Li, X., & Luo, S. (2003). The validation of two-factor model about task performance and contextual performance. *China Management Science*, *8*, 79–84.

Wasko, M. M., & Faraj, S. (2005). Why should I share? Examining social capital and knowledge contribution in electronic networks of practice. *Management Information Systems Quarterly*, *29*(1), 35–57.

Wasserman, S., & Faust, K. (1994). *Social network analysis: Methods and applications*. Cambridge, UK: Cambridge University Press. doi:10.1017/CBO9780511815478

Wellman, B., & Berkowitz, S. D. (Eds.). (1988). *Social structures: A network approach*. Cambridge, UK: Cambridge University Press.

Yao, J. (2009). Relationship-structure effect of dual social network on the mechanism of job performance-the empirical analysis on real estate sales industry in N City. *Soft*, *23*(3), 134–139.

APPENDIX

Questionnaire

Part 1: Demographic Background

1. Department:_____________ Title:__________________
2. Total years working:_______ Years with this company:_______ Gender: ☐ M ☐ F
3. Age: ☐ 30 or younger ☐ 30-35 ☐ 36-40 ☐ 41-45 ☐ 46 or older
4. Education:☐ Middle School ☐ High/ Secondary technical school ☐Technical school ☐ College ☐ Graduate School

Part 2: IT capability, Collaboration and Knowledge Sharing

1. Your familiarity with office automatic system:
   ☐ Very Inexperienced ☐ Inexperienced ☐ Somewhat Experienced
   ☐ Experienced ☐ Very Experienced
2. Your familiarity with Word:
   ☐ Very Inexperienced ☐ Inexperienced ☐ Somewhat Experienced
   ☐ Experienced ☐ Very Experienced
3. Your familiarity with Excel:
   ☐ Very Inexperienced ☐ Inexperienced ☐ Somewhat Experienced
   ☐ Experienced ☐ Very Experienced
4. Your familiarity with Powerpoint:
   ☐ Very Inexperienced ☐ Inexperienced ☐ Somewhat Experienced
   ☐ Experienced ☐ Very Experienced
5. Your familiarity with Access:
   ☐ Very Inexperienced ☐ Inexperienced ☐ Somewhat Experienced
   ☐ Experienced ☐ Very Experienced
6. Your familiarity with Windows OS:
   ☐ Very Inexperienced ☐ Inexperienced ☐ Somewhat Experienced
   ☐ Experienced ☐ Very Experienced
7. Your familiarity with Computer Hardware:
   ☐ Very Inexperienced ☐ Inexperienced ☐ Somewhat Experienced
   ☐ Experienced ☐ Very Experienced
8. You usually use what tools to communicate at work (select all that apply):
   A. Telephone/cellphone
   B. Office automatic (OA) system
   C. Email
   D. QQ
   E. MSN
   F. FeXing
   G. Other:_______

9. How many hours do you spend on the Internet or Intranet?
   A. None
   B. less than 1
   C. 1-2
   D. 3-4
   E. 5-6
   F. 7 or more
10. Indicate the degree to which you agree with the statements – 1. Disagree 2. Somewhat Disagree 3. Neutral 4. Somewhat Agree 5. Agree

	1	2	3	4	5
1. You will praise colleagues for their success	☐	☐	☐	☐	☐
2. You will support and encourage colleagues when they face family difficulties	☐	☐	☐	☐	☐
3. When a practice that may affect colleagues, I will inform them in advance	☐	☐	☐	☐	☐
4. .I only talk about things that are beneficial to colleagues and teams	☐	☐	☐	☐	☐
5. I would encourage others to overcome interpersonal obstacles and to get along	☐	☐	☐	☐	☐
6. I treat others fairly	☐	☐	☐	☐	☐
7. I take the initiative to help others	☐	☐	☐	☐	☐
8. I will work overtime to ensure the on time completion of tasks	☐	☐	☐	☐	☐
9. I pay attention to the important details of my work	☐	☐	☐	☐	☐
10. I Work extra hard	☐	☐	☐	☐	☐
11. I seek challenging work	☐	☐	☐	☐	☐
12. I am self disciplined	☐	☐	☐	☐	☐
13. I take the initiative to solve problems at work	☐	☐	☐	☐	☐
14. I persistently overcome the difficulties in completing tasks	☐	☐	☐	☐	☐
15. I take the initiative to do difficult tasks with enthusiasm	☐	☐	☐	☐	☐
16. I am satisfied with the interpersonal relationships and working environment	☐	☐	☐	☐	☐
17. I am very satisfied with my job	☐	☐	☐	☐	☐
18. I am very satisfied with the pay	☐	☐	☐	☐	☐
19. I am very satisfied with my career	☐	☐	☐	☐	☐
20. I am very satisfied with my work assignment	☐	☐	☐	☐	☐
21. I often provide to others: documentation, manuals, technical reports, methods, models and other internal organization documents	☐	☐	☐	☐	☐
22. I often provide to others: the corporate self-regulatory rules and work performance standards, for example: the staff code of conduct, guidelines and other corporate business strategy.	☐	☐	☐	☐	☐
23. I often provide to others: the knowledge gained from the mass media (for example, Web sites, news, magazines, radio, etc.) the article reported the gained.	☐	☐	☐	☐	☐
24. I often provide to others: the places to retrieve knowledge; For example, a person asks you about certain knowledge, although you can not directly answer his question, you know where he can find the knowledge he needs, such as which department file cabinet has the needed file, which database has the needed program, and so on.	☐	☐	☐	☐	☐

continued on following page

	1	2	3	4	5
25. I often provide to others: who has the body of knowledge; For example, someone asks you about certain knowledge, although you can not directly answer his question, you know someone he can ask to find it, such as who is the PLC electrical control expert, who is a computer expert, and who is a database expert, etc.	☐	☐	☐	☐	☐
26. I often provide to others: my own specialized work experience and professional knowledge from working in this company and the other companies I worked prior	☐	☐	☐	☐	☐
27. I often provide to others: the specialized knowledge or skills acquired from the internal education and training or some refresher courses. (eg, computer technology, electrical technology, hydropower equipment maintenance, etc.)	☐	☐	☐	☐	☐

11. Please fill in the name of the colleagues you often or frequent contact with in the different scenarios.

Name / **Scenario**	**Please fill in five or more names of the specific employees**
With whom do you often discuss job-related matters?	
At work, before making important decisions, to whom do you usually turn for consultation?	
For work related problems, from whom do you usually seek help?	
If facing the setbacks at work or difficult times from the boss, to whom do you normally share your grievances?	
With whom do you usually chat?	
When something private comes up, to whom do you usually turn for talks or help?	
After work, with whom do you normally do recreational activities?	

Chapter 5
Semiotics is Fundamental Science

Mihai Nadin
Institute for Research in Anticipatory Systems, University of Texas at Dallas, USA & Hanse Institute for Advanced Study, Germany

ABSTRACT

There is no way to acquire, store, and disseminate knowledge other than semiotically. Yet semiotics is hardly acknowledged in science, and not at all as science. Were it not for the fame of a few writers (Barthes, Derrida, and especially Eco), associated more with the semiotics of culture, few would even know that such a knowledge domain exists. In the age of computers, genetics, and networks—all of underlying semiotic condition—semiotics would at best qualify as pertinent to an obscure past, but insignificant for current endeavors. Gnoseologically, there is little to gain from acknowledging the shortcomings of semiotics. Epistemologically, quite a bit is at stake in grounding semiotics among the fundamental sciences. For this to come about, new interrogations become necessary: Why knowledge? What is knowledge? What kind of knowledge? How is knowledge acquired? One way or another, the answer will acknowledge semiotic processes as a necessary factor. The perspective advanced in this chapter relies on an understanding of the living, and, in particular, of the human being, that ascertains anticipation as definitory. The future is made part of the present via semiotic processes. This is significant because in the age of neurons, suggestive of brain activity and of attempts to emulate it, to distinguish between knowledge supporting human activity, embodied in new technologies, and knowledge essential to the unfolding of the living becomes very difficult.

1. PRELIMINARIES

The largely accepted foundation of semiotics as a "sign" discipline explains its accomplishments. But it explains even more the inadequacy of semiotics in affirming itself as a fundamental science. Indeed, being captive to a recursive model, embodied in the sign definition, affects its own credibility as a specific knowledge domain. Those active in physics, and even chemistry, economics, and cognitive science, know that they cannot practice these

DOI: 10.4018/978-1-4666-4711-4.ch005

disciplines without mathematics. Of course, language descriptions, such as those utilized for science in its philosophic phase (Aristotle, Plato, Galen, Ptolomy, Bacon, Occam) are an alternative, but only to a certain extent.

The semiotics of the beginnings of science were pretty much disguised as philosophy (Copernicus, Galileo, Leibniz, Descartes, even Kant). The separation of the sciences from philosophy is marked by the constitution of scientific languages: subsets of so-called natural language. Semiotics followed suit, and attempts were made, especially by Peirce, to define a semiotic language. Within this attempt, the sign consolidated its center-stage position. The necessity of scientific languages corresponds to the desire to transform descriptions of reality (such as geography, astronomy, geology, hydrology, etc.) into conceptual tools for operating on models. Moreover, these tools would have to inform activities for making tools that can be used to change reality.

Semiotics has a different knowledge domain. It does not actually deal in changing reality, but in supporting the acquisition of knowledge based upon which human action takes place. It is in this role that semiotics is fundamental. There is a degree of necessity that explains the body of knowledge of particular disciplines. Geography requires specific tools and methods for describing the world in its permanent change. Astronomy and, for that matter, geology and hydrology are by necessity a cognitive reflection of the reality they capture or try to affect. For semiotics to reach the same level of necessity, it would have to reflect the characteristics of the knowing subject, not, as with the sciences, of the known object. Only when semiotics acquires the same degree of necessity as the sciences, but in respect to the process of knowledge acquisition, will conditions be created for complementing the obsession with depth (specialized knowledge) with an understanding of breadth, corresponding to an integrated view of the world. This will further consolidate its condition as fundamental science.

Many attempts have been made to write a history (or histories) of semiotics: biographies of semioticians, history of semantics, history of symptomatology, anthologies of texts relevant to semiotics, and the like. Few would argue against the perception that we have much better histories of semiotics (and semioticians) than contributions to semiotics as such. What can be learned from the ambitious projects of the past is that semiotic concerns can be identified along the entire history of human activity. This is what prompted some authors (in particular, Eco, 1976; as well as Lotman, 1990) to consider culture as the subject matter of semiotics. Initially, semiotic activity was difficult to distinguish from actions and activities related to survival. Over time, semiotic concerns (especially related to language) constituted a distinct awareness of what is needed to succeed in what we do and, furthermore, what it takes to be successful.

Since our aim is the grounding of semiotics in the human activity of knowledge acquisition, we shall examine the variety of angles from which its domain knowledge was defined. In parallel to the criticism of conceptions that have led to the unsatisfactory condition of semiotics in our time, we will submit a hypothesis regarding a foundation different from that resulting from an agenda of inquiry limited to the sign. Finally, we will argue that the semiotics of semiotics (embodied in, for instance, in the organizations dedicated to its further development and in the teaching of semiotics) deserves more attention, given the significance of "organized labor" to the success of the endeavor. We will affirm the grounding of semiotics in the dynamics of phenomena characteristic of the threshold of complexity associated with the living. A more specific grounding, in *anticipation* as a characteristic of the living, will be suggested, as well.

It does not suffice to ascertain that the living, by its nature, is complex. Therefore, in order to make a clear distinction, we define complexity in connection to the criterion of decidability that Gödel (1931) introduced. Accordingly, a complex system cannot be fully and consistently described. All other systems (those that can be unequivocally specified) qualify either as simple or, at most, complicated.

Within this view, complexity is not a matter of scale. Moreover, it does not accept degrees (the empty formula of "higher complexity" and the like). Since the living is characterized by complexity, it follows that any formal representation, including the modeling of the natural system, can be only a reduction. However, in line with Gödel's original subject of inquiry (consistency and completeness, the description of natural numbers), it also follows that formal means, which the human being constructs in the process of acquiring knowledge, can themselves reach complexity. Such formal means, which Gödel defined in the strictest known manner, are as undecidable as the living itself. It is quite reasonable to assume that semiotics, understood in its broadest sense, is itself undecidable. This probably applies to all fundamental sciences. Short of providing the formal proof here, it suffices to say that semiotic entities, such as new sciences, continue to multiply as the semiotic activity itself expands.

Complex systems being undecidable, their dynamics is only partially subject to predictive, probability-based descriptions: expectation, forecast, prediction, etc. Indeed, representations of the living are not the outcome of deterministic processes, but rather of interactions that involve randomness, as well as non-deterministic processes. Nobody can predict the next scientific breakthrough, the next creative work of art, the next breakdown of markets, or the next revolution. Predictions are nothing but an extension from a description of a past or current state to a future state conceived within a law-based understanding of phenomena. But not everything in reality is subject to law. (We shall return to these observations.)

The non-living is subject to prediction. Indeed, the knowledge acquired over time and expressed in scientific laws supports a broad spectrum of successful predictive activities: the entire exploration of outer space is based on such activities; so are the most common uses of machines (cars, TV sets, computers, refrigerators, etc.). The laws of physics and chemistry underlie such practical endeavors. Prediction applied to the living, in the form of medical assessments, for example, corresponds to the misguided notion that since the laws of physics apply to everything material, they apply just as well to life. Some are successful, some are not.

To affirm that the decidability threshold, in Gödel's sense, is embodied in semiotic descriptions means that the living is fundamentally not the domain of quantified physical and chemical processes, but the domain of meaning. Meanings do not have to be consistent.

2. TO REMEMBER IS TO EMBODY THE MEMORY OF EXPERIENCE

Regardless of which semiotic perspective (language-based, logic-based, informational, etc.) the various groups of semioticians have adopted, it should not be too difficult to settle on some very simple preliminary observations regarding what is of semiotic significance in the self-making of humankind. Furthermore, we can easily agree that prediction, as an expression of understanding the dynamics of the physical world, has led to the affirmation of humanity's dominant role in nature. This is a technology-dominated nature within which the human being exercises a controlling power. To refer to the human being's domination over the rest of the living realm might not be politically correct, but it describes a matter of fact. The associated fact is the role of semiotics. We seek meaning in natural and other phenomena. Awareness of the semiotic nature of human activity is implicit in science and in the humanities. Nevertheless, semiotics empowered the human being to the detriment of the rest of reality, in the sense that human interpretation of the various representations of the world guides human action.

We might not like such a pronouncement, just as many would not like to see how semiotics contributes to dictatorships (Hitler's, Stalin's, the North Korean and Saudi dynasties, etc.). It will cost a lot, in terms of knowledge and awareness, to ignore the victims of the "friendly fire" that caused so much "collateral damage" (in either "hot" or "cold" wars). Indeed, the dominating position of reductionist-deterministic theories prompted not only successes (the Industrial Revolution, for instance), but also serious damage to the environment and to human nature.

Be this as it may, we don't really need an agreement on what the subject of semiotics is, or what a sign is, in order to realize that the underlying element of any human interaction, as well as interaction with the world, is semiotic in nature. Interactions take place through an intermediary. Signs or not, semiotics is about the *in-between*, about *mediation*, about guessing what others do, how nature will behave. It is about dealing with the re-presented, the image, the word, the smell, the tactility. They are re-presentations. Of course, they can be re-presented in turn (the name of an odor is quite different from what it smells like). Two human beings touching each other transcend the physical act. In addition to the immediate, material, energetic aspect, the gesture entails a sense of duration, immaterial suggestions, something that eventually will give it meaning. It is a selection (who/what is touched) in a given situation (context). And it prompts a continuation.

But there is more to this preliminary observation. Just as a detail, to be further discussed, the following observation from brain imaging: The three most developed active brain regions—one in the prefrontal cortex, one in the parietal and temporal cortices—are specifically dedicated to the task of understanding the goings-on of other people's minds (Mitchell et al., 2008)—reading someone else's mind (identifying patterns of brain activation associated with different things). This in itself suggests semiotic activity related to anticipation, in the sense of a pre-understanding of the other via representations. Actions, our own and of others, are "internalized," i.e., understood and represented in terms of what neurobiology calls "mental states." So are intentions. In this respect, Gallese (2001) wrote about mind-reading and associated this faculty with mirror neurons. From this perspective, the semiotics of intentions, desires, and beliefs no longer relies on representations embodied in cognitive states, i.e., successive phenomena eventually expressed in choices, decisions, or actions. There is no sign to be identified in this context.

It would be presumptuous, to say the least, to rehash here the detailed account of how the human species defined itself, in its own making, through the qualifier *zoon semiotikon* (Nadin, 1997), i.e., semiotic animal. Felix Hausdorff, concerned that his reputation as a mathematician would suffer, published, under the pseudonym Paul Mongré, a text entitled *Sant' Ilario. Thoughts from Zarathustra's Landscape* (1897). A short quote illustrates the idea:

The human being is a semiotic animal; his humanness consists of the fact that instead of a natural expression of his needs and gratification, he acquired a conventional, symbolic language that is understandable only through the intermediary of signs. He pays in nominal values, in paper, while the animal in real, direct values [...] The animal acts in Yes and No. The human being says Yes and No and thus attains his happiness or unhappiness abstractly and bathetically. Ratio and oratio are a tremendous simplification of life. . . . (p. 7). (Translation, mine)

Through semiotic means (mainly representations), grounded in anticipatory processes (attainment of happiness, for instance), individuals aggregate physical and cognitive capabilities in their effort. Indeed, group efforts make possible accomplishments that the individual could not obtain. Obviously, this perspective is much more comprehensive than the foundation of semiotics on the confusing notion of the sign. In what I described above, there is no sign to identify, rather a process of understanding, of reciprocal "reading" and "interpreting," of "coordination." The decisive aspect is the process; the representation is the unfolding of the process defining cognitive states. This view has the added advantage of explaining, though indirectly, the major cause why semiotics as the discipline of signs continues to remain more a promise than the "universal science" that Morris (1938) chose to qualify it.

A discipline dependent upon a concept (on which no agreement is possible) is much less productive than a discipline associated with activities: What do semioticians do? If we know what they do, we know what it is—provided that we do not fall in a circular manner of reasoning.

3. TO DESCRIBE IS TO MAKE LANGUAGE

Every instance of acknowledging change is at the same time an instance of making up the language to describe what change brings about. We have access to a large body of shared knowledge on the evolution of humankind, in particular on the role of various forms of interaction among individuals and within communities. Also documented is the interaction between the human being and the rest of the world. This knowledge is available, in shared language (speech, writing, images, etc.), for persons seeking an understanding of semiotics in connection to practical activities. Mathematics is in the same situation. Let us recall only that geometry originates in activities related to sharing space, and eventually to laying claim to portions of the surroundings, to ownership and exchange, to production and market processes. There are no triangles in the world, as there are no numbers in the world, or lines. To measure a surface, i.e., to introduce a scale, is related to practical tasks. Such tasks become more creative as improved means for qualifying the characteristics of the area are conceived and deployed. To measure is to facilitate the substitution of the real (the measured entity) with the measurement, i.e., re-presentation of what is measured. Of course, no measurement replicates the measured in its entirety! To travel, to orient oneself, to navigate are all "children of geometry," extended from the immediacy of one's place to its representation.

This is where semiotics shows up. The experiences of watching stars and of observing repetitive patterns in the environment translate into constructs, which are integrated in patterns of activity. Rosen (1985, p. 201) took note of "shepherds [who] idly trace out a scorpion in the stars. . ." (the subject of interest being "relations among components").

He also brought up the issue of observation: "Early man . . . could see the rotation of the Earth every evening just by watching the sky" (p. 201). In the spirit of Hausdorff's definition of the semiotic animal, Rosen's suggestion is that inference from observations to comprehension is not automatic: An early observer "could not understand what he was seeing," as "we have been unable to understand what every organism is telling us," (p. 201). The "language" in which phenomena (astronomic or biological) "talk" to the human being is that of semiotics. The human being constructs its "vocabulary" and "grammar." We make our language as we make and remake ourselves. This applies to our entire knowledge, from the most concrete to the most abstract.

Mathematics, in its more comprehensive condition as an expression of abstract knowledge, is expressed as a description of the changing world. Descriptions, such as points, lines, and intersections, and formal entities, such as circle, square, volume, etc. are part of mathematical language. It is expressed numerically, e.g., in proportions, which means analytically, through observations of how things change or remain the same over time. It can as well be expressed synthetically, that is, how we would like to change what is given into something else that we can describe as a goal (using numbers, drawings, diagrams, etc.). The language of mathematics, of logic, of chemistry, of physiology, of genetics, of physics, for example, are constructs. In the attempt to describe something, we make the language necessary for the task. The language consists of an alphabet and of rules for operating on the "words," "sentences," and "texts" we generate. The most intuitive example is that of the digital computer: an alphabet of two letters, and Boolean logic. "Utterances" in this language are precise, but not necessarily expressive.

4. FORMING THE THOUGHT

Informed by mathematics, or by any other science, we gain an intuitive understanding of how humans, in making themselves, also make their comprehension of the world part of their own reality. The perspective from which we observe reality is itself definitory for what we "see" and "hear," for our perceptions, and for our reasoning. The fact that we see and hear "before" we actually see or hear corresponds to the "predictive" component of visual or sound perception. The fact that each action is based on pre-actions corresponds to the anticipatory nature of human dynamics. This should help in realizing that the foundation of semiotics is, in the final analysis, a matter of the angle from which we examine its relevance: Semiotics is consubstantial with living and self-awareness.

The hypothesis we shall address is that the definition upon the ill-defined notion of the sign is the major reason why semiotics remains more a promise than an effective theory. The failure of semiotics is semiotic: the representation of its object of inquiry through the entity called sign—regardless how defined—is relatively deceptive. It is as though someone were to establish mathematics around the notion of the number (we would need at least operations in order to reach from numbers to arithmetic); or the notion of an integral, or the notion of sets. Indeed, there have been mathematicians who have tried to do just that. Those attempts are at best documented in the fact that there is number theory (with exceptional accomplishments), integral calculus, and set theory (actually more than one). But none defines mathematics and its goals. They illustrate various mathematical perspectives and document the multi-facetedness of human abstract thinking. Mathematics transcends numbers and seeks higher levels of generality and abstraction.

If we focus on the sign, we can at most define a subset of semiotics: sign theory, around classical definitions (as those of Saussure, Peirce, Hjelmslev, for example). But semiotics as such is more than these; and it is something else. It is the awareness of change captured in representations. In terms of its meaning, it is the actions it informs. A noise in the woods can mean danger, or nothing at all consequential. Interaction being the definitory characteristic of the living, and semiotics its underlying condition, we could identify as subfields of interest the variety of forms of interaction, or even the variety of semiotic means through which interactions take place. Alternatively, to make interactions the subject of semiotics (as Sadowski, 2010, attempted) will also not do because interactions—subject of psychology and sociology—are means towards a goal. Goals and activities are dynamically connected. Activities integrate actions. Actions are associated with representations. What is left out is the meaning, because the reference of representations is itself changing and eludes capture within the sign.

What is semiotics?" not unlike "What is mathematics?" or for that matter "What is chemistry, biology, or philosophy?" are abbreviated inquiries. In order to define something, we actually differentiate. Semiotics is not mathematics. It does not advance a view of the world, but it provides mathematics with some of what it needs to arrive at a view of the world—with a language. Mathematicians do not operate on pieces of land, or on stones (which mathematics might describe in terms of their characteristics), or on brains, on cells, etc. They produce and operate on *representations*, on semiotic entities conjured by the need to replace the real with a description, and to infer from it to the meaning of the process they describe. The goal of the mathematicians' activity, involving thinking, intuition, sensory and motoric characteristics, emotions, etc., is abstraction. Their *activity* focuses on very concrete semiotic entities that define a specific language: topology, algebra, category theory, etc. Mathemeticians are after the truth of phenomena. A mathematical proof is nothing other than the confirmations of a precise description of reality.

Among many others, Nietzsche (cf. Colli & Montinari, 1975, p. 3) observed that "Our writing tools are also working, forming our thoughts." As we program the world, we reprogram ourselves: Taylor's assembly line "reprogrammed" the worker; so do word and image processing programs; so do political programs, and the programs assumed by organizations and publications. Computation-based mathematics reshapes mathematics. It gives mathematics a new condition: outcome of a deterministic machine. The predictive component in visual and aural perception reflects the fact that we acquire data from the world, but also produce our own data (Nadin, 2003). Associated with meaning, data becomes information.

5. ALL REPRESENTATIONS ARE INCOMPLETE

To represent is a fundamental human activity. To express is to represent within the context of interaction. The fact that there is a connection between how some state (e.g., pain) is expressed (through a scream) and what it expresses is a late realization in a domain eventually defined as cognition. The relation between *what* (surprise, for example, can also lead to a scream) is expressed and *how* expression (wide-open eyes) becomes representation (i.e., presentation of whatever prompts the expression) is yet another cognitive step. And one more: There is a relation between what is represented (e.g., fear) and the means of representation; they can vary from moving away from the cause of the fear to descriptions in words, images, etc. As already suggested above, to represent is to present one's self as a living entity interacting with other living entities (human or non-human). Representation is the path towards what cognitive science describes as generalizations and abstractions. In the representation in Figure 1, a stadium was chosen as an example: It can be described in words, it can be photographed or videotaped; memorabilia connected to the experience of being at the stadium can evoke the experience.

Among the most common representations are those used in mathematics (the so-called symbols, such as the numbers, the variables, operations among numbers, the equal sign, the integral sign, etc.). Similar, and often the same, are the representations used in physics. Partially, the language of mathematics undergirds descriptions of physical phenomena. Chemistry, genetics, computer science, artificial intelligence, and artificial life also utilize representations. Sometimes they extend into the culture: the table of elements (whcrc, for instance, Au stands for gold, H for hydrogen, C for Carbon) is an example. So are the representations of astronomy, meteorology, and geography. To understand a map (city, country, trail, etc.) for the purpose of navigation is to be aware of a language that includes scale and other conventions (e.g., a red cross stands for a hospital), and even codes e.g., (highways are represented differently than are country roads).

These examples focus more on visual notations. But there are sounds or sequences of

Figure 1. The subset of possible partial representations (text description, mathematical description, video or film, visualization, etc.). The aggregate of all possible representations cannot capture dynamic reality. All representations are subject-dependent.

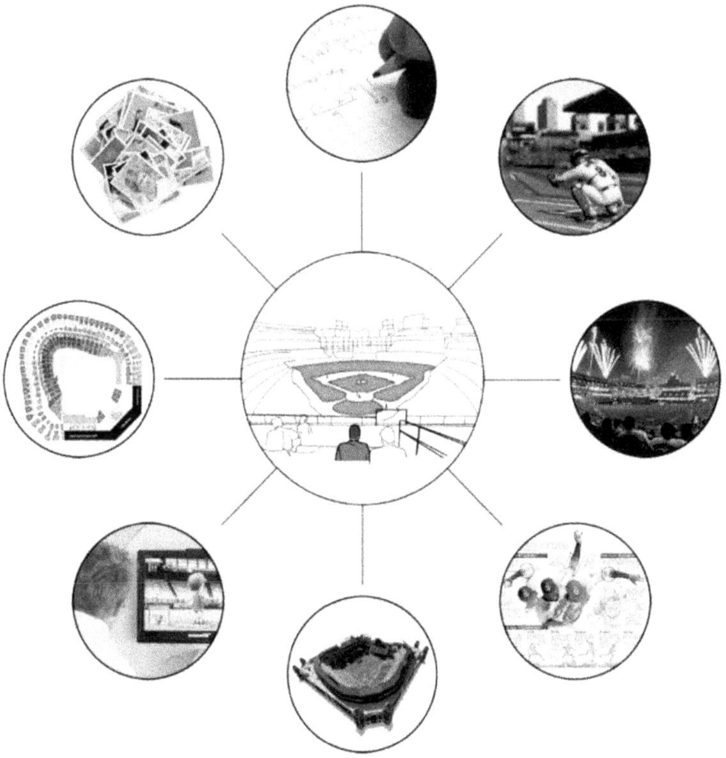

sounds that perform the same function: they re-present. Actually, sound representations precede visual representations. Imitating the sound of a dangerous animal is an example that comes easily to mind; likewise for imitating sounds with the aim of enticing (such as bringing a bird or animal within reach).

It is within natural interactions where the awareness of re-presentation, as a means for knowing, finds its origins. Indeed, in nature, smell, sound, and marks left are indicative not only of presence (immediacy), but also of what was (some animal just passed through) or what is coming. In this respect, re-presentations embody awareness of past, present, and future, as well as proximity or remoteness (the distant howl of an animal, the flapping of wings, the buzz of an insect, the distant thunder). Nature continuously "makes" new representations: changes in behavior of plants and animals, changes in the genetic code, for instance. The awareness of what representations stand for is acquired through interactions. Without doubt, sexuality (i.e., reproductive drive) is probably dominant for the longest stretch in the history leading to current representations. As a matter of record: The vector of change over time (along the path of evolution) is from direct interactions to representation-based interactions, and currently to interactions limited to representations, or representations of representations. This is what defines the human being's cognitive path: from being an outcome of natural dynamics and part of nature, to becoming an engineer of a dynamics subordinated to human goals. Semiotic awareness, which instantiates metacognition (knowing what we know) is nothing other than the realization that acting upon representations enhances the outcome of human activity. The rest of the living realm does not reach metacognition.

Between the marks left by living entities in the environment of their existence and the notations of mathematicians, chemistry, physics, genetics, etc., the difference is between awareness of the immediate (in time and space) and predictive capabilities. No other form of the living has acquired such capabilities, notwithstanding anticipatory characteristics of the living. The subject will come up again.

Representations, usually called "symbols" (Cassirer, 1923-1929), are present in the respective knowledge domains where they are generated, not as semiotic entities, but as notations. The integral sign ∫ stands for a limit of sums. It represents the operation (e.g., calculate an area, a volume). The human being "reads" nature as a "language" expression, and, in the process of knowing, generates new representations. Let us recall Lewis Mumford's observations: No computer can make a new symbol out of its own resources," (1967, p. 29), in order to, once again, point to semiotics as consubstantial with human activity.

The abbreviated inquiries invoked earlier—What is semiotics? What is mathematics? What is chemistry?—are relevant because behind them are explicit questions: What, i.e., which specific form of human activity, do they stand for? What do they mediate? What semiotics, or mathematics, or chemistry, stands for has the following meaning: What are their specific pragmatic justifications? What can you do with them? We have just seen that awareness of re-presentation is augmented over time, through learning. We have also seen that this awareness is not the specific domain knowledge of the sciences.

From the perspective of knowledge, the following needs to be stated: If we could aggregate all representations we would still not capture the reality in its infinite level of detail; nor could we capture dynamics in its open-endedness (not to say without affecting it). The living unfolds beyond our epistemological boundaries. We are part of it. Our change is part of a broader change, which, again, influences our own. The sequence is infinite. Therefore every representation contains the observed and the observer. If the representation is only a sign, dynamics is left out.

Without exception, in every form of the living, the body is represented in the "brain," i.e., in the cortex (no matter how simple such a cortex for more rudimentary entities). For something to take place, muscles are engaged, otherwise, there is just no expression anywhere. This is even more so the case with the human being. The representation of different parts of the human body in the primary somatosensory cortex is a very clear example of the role of representation processes. Representations in the somatosensory cortex change as the individual's activity, translated in muscle engagement, changes. They facilitate preparation for future activities; they predate decisions and activities. They are in anticipation of change. In this particular expression, we can identify the process of representation of the body in the cortex as a semiotic process: the change in reality becomes a change in the representation of reality. The semiotics of the process is pragmatically driven (that is, it depends on what we do). Think about the new fascination with text messaging and how the fingers involved are represented in the cortex. Semiotics understood in this vein returns knowledge regarding how technology empowers as it reshapes our cognitive condition at the same time. While in the last 60 years the brain has not changed in any significant way, the human being's cognitive condition has undergone deep changes, expressed in the higher sensory threshold, decreasing attention span, and multi-tasking abilities, for example. "The human brain has not changed at the anatomical level, but now it works differently," (Togo & Cantelmi, 2012).

6. THE GNOSEOLOGICAL CONDITION OF SEMIOTICS

Knowledge is pursued in many ways (including some more than doubtful). The hope is that knowledge will assist the human being in performing better in a fast-changing world. The reference to knowledge is always in respect to the human being animated by the practical need to know in order to succeed, or at least to improve efficiency of effort under specific circumstances (context). Thus, "What is semiotics?" translates as "What defines and distinguishes human interactions from all other known forms of interaction? Indeed, the interaction of chemical elements (i.e., chemical reaction) is different from that of two individuals. Obviously, some chemistry is involved; however, the interaction characteristic of the living is not reducible to chemistry. "Mind reading" is not *abracadabra*; it is not picking up some mysterious or real waves (electro or whatever); it is not second-guessing the biochemistry of neuronal processes. It is modeling in one's own mind what others are planning, what goals they set for themselves. In some way, this involves adaptive percept-action processes.

Physical interaction at the atomic level is quite different from that at the molecular and macroscopic levels, and even more different at the scale of the universe. As exciting as it is in its variety and precision, the physical interaction of masses (as in Newton's laws of mechanics) does not explain aggregation, e.g., the behavior of crowds, or the "wisdom of crowds." In the end, "What is semiotics?" means not so much to define its concepts (sign, sign processes, meaning, expression, etc.) as it means to address the question of whether whatever semiotics is, does it correspond to all there is, or only to a well-defined aspect of reality. Neither mathematics, nor chemistry, nor any other knowledge domain encompass all there is. Their specific knowledge domain is not reducible to others. If the same holds true for semiotics, the specific knowledge domain would have to correspond to a well-defined aspect of reality. It is obvious, but worth repeating, that semiotics (not unlike mathematics, chemistry, physics, etc.) is a human product, a large construct subject to our own evaluation of its significance (the level of metacognition). The significance of physics or mathematics can be quantified. The significance of semiotics is subject to meaning awareness (or lack thereof).

Before there was mathematics, or chemistry, or physics, there was an activity through which individuals did something (e.g., kept records using knots, mixed substances with the aim of making new ones, used a lever). In this activity, they constituted themselves as mathematicians, chemists, or physicists; and were recognized as such by others (even before there was a label for activities qualifying, in retrospect, as mathematics, chemistry, physics, etc.).

Returning to mathematics: Is the integrating view of the world it facilitates exclusively a human-generated representation of gnoseological intent and finality? Or can we identify a mathematics of plants or animals, of physical processes (such as lightning, earthquakes, the formation of snowflakes)? Does nature "make" mathematics? The fact that mathematics describes the "geometry" of plants, the movement of fish in water, and volcanic activity cannot be automatically translated as "plants are geometricians," or "fish are analysis experts," or "volcanoes are topologists." Rather, watching reality through the lenses of mathematics, we identify characteristics that can be described in a language (or several) that applies not to one specific flower or leaf, not to one specific fish or swarm, not to one volcano, but to all activity, regardless where it takes place. The generality of mathematical descriptions, moreover mathematical abstraction, is what defines the outcome of the activity through which some individuals identify themselves as mathematicians (professional or amateur).

For the sake of clarity: Nature does not make mathematics, as it does not make semiotics. Anthropomorphism is convenient—"the language of plants," the "symbols of nature"—but confusing. Only with awareness of the activity is it epistemologically legitimized. There are no signs of nature. The marks left, the odors, and the sounds are natural expressions consubstantial with what they express (an animal in heat smells differently, behaves differently, even sounds different). There are no semiotic processes of nature: Interrelations are not of semiotic intent, but of existential significance. There are, however, human constructed models for understanding nature. Some of them belong to biology, zoology, botany, etc.; others to cognitive science. The same observation applies to machines: There is no semiotics in the functioning of a machine. It is made of parts assembled in such a way that it turns an input into a desired (or not) output. An artificial muscle can do the same. The human being projects semiotics into interaction with machines. Of course, there are signals, best expressed through values defining the physical process (e.g., electrons traveling along circuits). But to confuse signal—physical level—and sign—semiotic level—means to make semiotics irrelevant. Too many well-intended researchers operate in the space of ill-defined entities.

In the more recent infatuation with predictions (of political, economic, sports, meteorological events, for example), the word "signal" describes meaningful data, i.e., relevant information as opposed to noise. This shift in semantics cannot be ignored, especially since the complex networks discipline (Newman,

2003), almost synonymous with large data sets processing, has become very fashionable. Facing the difficulties of handling huge amounts of data afforded by large set of sensors of all kinds (e.g., for weather prediction, economic cycles, elections) integrated in networks, scientists also distinguish between signal—data that is significant to what they are looking for—and noise, which Shannon defined in connection to data transmission over communication channels. Obviously, signal in this sense is different from what is discussed from the semiotic perspective: signals in machines, signals in nature. Since pragmatics is decisive, it is too late to reach a consensus with the new complex networks scientists for the proper terminology. In fact, what they call "signal" is nothing other than information, i.e., meaningful data (Nadin, 2011). Interestingly enough, the scientists of complex networks realize that there is a deterministic component to their effort (establishing the inventory of the network), and a non-deterministic component: to understand the meaning of connections.

7. WHO IS A SEMIOTICIAN?

Is there some generality, or level of abstraction, that can define the identity of a semiotician? Or are we all, regardless of what we do, semioticians, given that interaction, characteristic of all the living, cannot be avoided. Moreover, given that we all indulge in representations and act upon representations, does this not qualify us even more as semioticians? Given that we all interpret everything—regardless of the adequacy of our interpretations—does this make everyone (including their dogs and cats; Sheldrake, 2011) semioticians? The entire domain of the living is one of expression and interaction that seems to embody semiotics in action. Mental states are associated with neuronal activity. The physics and biochemistry, and the thermodynamics for this activity form one aspect. The other aspect is the understanding of each instance of the process, of the aggregate state to which it leads. However, there is a distinction between the activity and awareness of its taking place, of its consequences. Based on knowledge from different disciplines (biology, genetics, neuroscience, etc.), the following statement can be made: Semiotics at the genetic level, semiotics at the molecular level, and semiotics at the cell level, in association with the particular forms of information processes, are human constructs that serve as prerequisites for explaining the viability of the living as such. Along this understanding, which rejects the realism of biosemiotics (where symbols are as real as chemical elements or as electrons), it can be ascertained that bottom-up and top-down semiotic processes define life as semiosis. This definition is as legitimate as that of life as information process, or as a thermodynamic process. Awareness of semiotic process is not characteristic of genes or molecules; neither is information awareness located where our knowledge states that information processes take place. Awareness (of semiotics, or of information processes) corresponds to the meta-level, not to the object level. This distinction seems to escape the biosemioticians' understanding of semiotics, or that of various information theory practitioners (e.g., neural networks scientists, AI researchers).

What can we learn about semiotics by examining the world? First and foremost, that interaction, as a characteristic of the living, is extremely rich, and ubiquitous. Second, and not least important, life being change, interactions not only trigger change, but they themselves are subject to change. Observation yields evidence that some interactions seem more patterned than others (and accordingly predictable). Take the interaction between a newborn (human, animal) and parent. There is a definite pattern of nurturing and protection—although there are also cases of filial cannibalism (eating one's young, as do some fish, bank voles, house finches, polar bears). These patterns correspond to representations of the present and future, i.e., they are connected to anticipatory processes (underlying evolution). Or take sexual interactions (a long gamut, extended well beyond evolutionary advantage in the life of human beings); or interactions between the living and the dying. The epistemological condition of semiotics derives from the fact that life would continue even if there were no semioticians to ever observe it and report on what they "see" as they focus on interactions, or on the constructs we call signs or sign processes. The existence of life, or the making of life, does not depend on adding semiotic ingredients to the combination of whatever might be necessary to make it. For that matter, it does not depend on adding mathematics or physics or chemistry to the formula. The physical has past and present imprinted on it; the living, the future, in anticipation of which it unfolds. The awareness resulting from a semiotic perspective leads to the distinction made above. Indeed, in the absence of representations, the future could not be expressed, and life would cease. The hypothesis that representation is a necessary, but probably not sufficient, condition for life can be experimentally verified.

8. COHERENCE

But things are not so simple as a cookbook for life. The mathematics for the cookbook is important in defining quantities and sequences in time (for example: first bring water to a boil, add ingredients in a certain order, simmer). The semiotics is relevant not so much for cooking for oneself, but in supporting preparation of the meal for others. This is what representations do when they are passed along in the organism. Cells "work" for each other; a cell's state depends on the states of the adjacent or remote cells. The organism is the expression of all that is needed in terms of means of interaction to make possible an aggregated whole of a nature different from that of its components. It is on account of complexity that this aggregation takes place and lasts as long as what we call *life*. However: Complexity is not the outcome of aggregation.

Expressed differently, semiotics is relevant for "engineering" interactions: recipes are the "shorthand" of cooking. They carry explicit instructions and implicit rules, that is, assumptions of shared experiences. Semiotics embodies the sharing, but does not substitute for the experience. The informational level corresponds to "fueling" the process, providing the energy. Taken literally, the simplest, as well as the most elaborate, recipe is disappointing. There is always something expected from those who will try it out. No recipe is or can be complete. The possibility to discover on your own what cannot be encapsulated in words, numbers, procedures, or images opens up the process of self-discovery. In this sense, semiotics is relevant for dealing with the question of what the future will bring: you beat egg yolk and oil together, and instead of getting mayonnaise, the ingredients start to separate. What now? At the level of the living, life, not mayonnaise, is continuously made. At the end of the life cycle, the ingredients separate, the semiotics disappears, information degrades. Semiotics encodes in generating representations, and decodes in interpreting representations. These are distinct practical functions otherwise inconceivable. Encode means as much as semiotic operations performed on representations. Let's say: Make a Morse Code-based equivalent. *Decode* means the reverse. Machines encode in such a manner that decoding always retrieves the original. In the living, there is no guarantee that the encoded will be retrieved. Quite often, we find a different "encoded" reality: Semiotic processes are non-deterministic.

9. LAW AND HISTORY; GESTALT

It comes as no surprise to anyone that interactions can be mathematically (or genetically) described. But mathematical descriptions (or genetic, as well) can only incompletely characterize them. More precisely: the mathematics of interactions is, after all, the description of assumed or proven laws of interaction. In this respect, law is a repetitive pattern. Physical phenomena are acceptably described in mathematical descriptions called laws. This is what Windelband (1894) defined as the *nomothetic* (derived from *nomothé* in Plato's *Cratylus*, 360 BCE). The same cannot be said of living interactions, even if we acknowledge repetitive patterns. No living entity is identical with another. The living is infinitely diverse. Therefore, semiotics could qualify as the attempt to acknowledge diversity unfolding over time as the background for meaning, not for scientific truth. This is what Windelband defined as the *idiographic*. Remember the primitive man watching the sky and not knowing the "truth" he was seeing (Earth's rotation). Organisms, while not devoid of truth (corresponding to their materiality), are rather expressions of meaning. Representations can be meaningful or meaningless. They are perceived as one or the other in a given context.

With meaning as its focus, semiotics will not be in the position to say what is needed to make something—as chemistry and physics do, with the help of mathematics—but rather to identify what meaning it might have in the infinite sequence of interactions in which representations will be involved. This applies to making rudimentary tools, simple machines, computer programs, or artificial or synthetic entities. Semiotic knowledge is about meaning as process. And this implies that changing a machine is very different from changing the brain. Inadequate semiotics led to the metaphor of "hardwired" functions in the brain. There is no such thing. The brain adapts. Activities change our mind: We become what we think, what we do. We are our semiotics. This is why the cognitive condition of information-age individuals changed as much as it has.

10. ON THE POSSIBILITY OF INTERACTIONS

The fact that signs—better yet, representations—are involved in interactions is an observation that needs no further argument. Being entities that stand for other entities, signs might be considered as agents of interaction. Evidently, with the notion of agency we introduce a new expectation for the understanding of signs. They are not to be conceived as "containers" of representation, but rather as intelligent entities. Signs are "alive," interacting with each other, self-reproducing as the context requires. Consequently, one might be inclined to see interaction processes mirrored into sign processes—or what Peirce called semiosis. But interactions are more than sign processes. Better yet: sign processes describe only the meaning of interactions, but not the energy processes undergirding them. This needs elaboration, since the question arises: What does "ONLY the meaning of interactions" mean? Is something missing?

11. VITALISM IS DEAD. BUT THE PHYSICAL AND THE LIVING ARE STILL DIFFERENT

When vitalism, as the doctrine of the *élan vital* (which some equate with the soul) was debunked, the questions of causality associated with the realization that the biosphere is not reducible to the physical were simply brushed aside. Over time, every scientist claiming that the living and non-living have a different dynamics was eliminated from the list of potential Nobel Prize nominees (and avoided). In recent years, this has started to change. For whatever it is worth, Stewart Kauffman (2012, and Giuseppe Longo, quite in agreement with him) managed a breakthrough. You can ascertain that the evolution of the biosphere has no entailment laws, and this will not expel you from science. Moreover, a large number of scientists from many different fields—the chemist Gunter von Kiedrowski, mathematician Giuseppe Longo, quantum physicist Gabor Vattori, and others in computer science, molecular biology, among other fields—enlisted their expertise in dealing with issues pertinent to what life is, how life is expressed, how life emerges. The major meeting at CERN (May 2011), not necessarily a vitalist address, defined a research agenda not yet matched by similar efforts in the USA (although he NASA Astrobiology Institute is looking for signs of life in the universe at a price of 40 million dollars in grants).

The pressing question is, of course, the beginning of life (pretty much in the spirit of the beginning of the universe, an acceptable inquiry even for those fanatically opposed to a distinction between the living and the non-living). While this is not the place to enter the dialog on the beginning of life, let it be noted that semiotic considerations are an expression of awareness. To the extent that there is no life on Mars (still a subject of inquiry), there is no Martian semiotics. But there are semiotic questions, rooted in the living on Earth, that can be formulated in respect to Mars (or any other planet).

To describe interactions pertinent to non-living matter (the physical) is way easier than to describe interactions in the living, or among living entities. For such descriptions we rely on the physics of phenomena—different at the nano-level in comparison to the scale of reality or to the cosmic scale. Quantum mechanics contributed decisive details to our understanding of physical interactions (for instance, in evincing the entanglements of phenomena at the quantum level of matter). Focusing on signs caused semiotics to miss its broader claim to legitimacy: to provide not only descriptions of the meaning of interactions, but also knowledge regarding the meaning of the outcome of interactions, the future. When the outcome can be derived from scientific laws, we infer from the past to the future. Statistical distribution and associated probabilities describe the level of our understanding of all that is needed for physical entities to change. When the outcome is as unique as the living interaction itself, we first need to acknowledge that the living is driven by goals—which is not the case with the physical, where, at best, we recognize attractors: the "teleology" of dynamic systems. Therefore, we infer not only from the past, but also from the future, as projection of the goals, or understandings of goals pursued by others. Possibilities describe the level of our understanding of what is necessary for living entities to change, i.e., to adapt to change. This is the domain of anticipation, from which semiotics ultimately originates. (In addition to my arguments, Nadin, 1991, on this subject, see Hoffmeyer, 2008). Therefore, semiotics should be more than the repository of meaning associated with interaction components.

As information theory—based on the encompassing view that all there is, is subject to energy change—emerged (Shannon & Weaver, 1949), it took away from semiotics even the appearance of legitimacy. Why bother with semiotics, with sign processes, in particular (and all that terminology pertinent to sign typology), when you can focus on energy? Energy is observable, measurable, and easy to use in describing information processes understood as the prerequisite for communication. Information is more adequate than semiotics for conceiving new communication processes, which, incidentally, were also iterative processes. But there is also a plus side to what Shannon suggested: Information theory made it so much more clear than any speculative approach that semiotics should focus on meaning and significance rather than on truth.

Over time, semiotics attracted not only praise, but also heavy criticism. In general, lack of empirical evidence for some interpretations remains an issue. The obscurity of the jargon turned semiotics into an elitist endeavor. Structuralist semiotics (still dominant) fully evades questions of semiotic synthesis and the interpretant process. Too often, semiotics settled on synchronic aspects, a-historic at best (only Marxist semioticians take historicity seriously, but at times to the detriment of understanding semiotic structures). Closer to our time, semiotics has been criticized for turning everything into a sign, such semioticians forgetting that if everything is a sign, nothing is a sign. In one of his famous letters to Lady Welby, Peirce writes:

It has never been in my power to study anything—mathematics, chemistry, comparative anatomy, psychology, phonetics, economics, the history of science, whist, men and women, wine, metrology—except as a study of semiotics (Peirce, 1953, p. 32).

The message here is that semiotics is inclusive, and that it should not be arbitrarily fragmented. He does not bring up a semiotics of mathematics, chemistry, comparative anatomy, etc. because it is nonsensical to dilute the "study of semiotics" into partial semiotics. Those who do so deny semiotics its comprehensive perspective.

Parallel to this recognition is the need to assess meaning in such a manner that it becomes relevant to human activity. So far, methods have been developed for the experimental sciences: those based on proof, i.e., the expectation of confirmation and generalization. But there is nothing similar in respect to meaning, not even the realization that generalization is not possible; or that semiotic knowledge is not subject to proof, rather to an inquiry of its singularity. The nomothetic comprises positivism; the *idiographic* is the foundation of the constructivist understanding of the world (cf. Piaget, 1955; von Foerster, 1981).

Of course, the question of whether one can identify semiotic processes within the living cannot be ignored. Biosemioticians are given to the model of "semiotics" at work at all levels of the living. Their position (called "realism in philosophy") deserves closer scrutiny. Let's be clear: If their assumption is correct, the beginning of life is the beginning of semiotics (in implicit form). I have reasons to argue (and shall return to this) that this is not the case, and that semiotics, like other means of knowledge acquisition, expression, and dissemination is a human construct.

12. PROOF AND INFERENCE

Mathematicians would claim that their proofs are absolute. Indeed, they make the criterion of falsifiability (Popper, 1934/1959) one of their methods: Let's assume, *ad absurdum*, that parallels meet. If they do, then what? No scientific ascertainment can be proven to the same level of certainty as the mathematical, because it is a projection of the mind. By extension, this applies to computer science and its many related developments, in the sense that automated mathematics is still mathematics. (Mathematicians themselves realize that in the future, mathematical proofs will be based on computation.) Science lives from observation; it involves experiment and justifies itself through the outcome. If the experiment fails, the science subject to testing fails. That particular observation is not absolute in every respect. Let us name some conditions that affect the outcome of experiments: selection (what is observed, what is ignored); evaluation (degrees of error); expression (how we turn the observation, i.e., data, into knowledge). Experiments are always reductions. To reproduce an experiment is to confirm the reduction, not exactly the claim of broader knowledge. The outcome might be disappointing in respect to the goal pursued: for example, the various drugs that have failed after being tested and approved. But the outcome might, as well, prove significant in respect to other goals: drugs that are dangerous in some cases prove useful in treating different ailments: thalidomide for arthritic inflammations, mouth and throat sores in HIV patients; botox for treating constricted muscles.

Failed scientific proofs prompt many fundamental reassessments. Compare the scientific theory of action at distance before Newton and after Newton's foundations of physics; compare Newton's view to Einstein's; and compare Einstein's science to quantum entanglement. Compare the views of biology prior to the theory of evolution, or to the discovery of the genetic code. Given the epistemological condition of mathematics, new evidence is not in the jargon of mathematics. A new mathematical concept or theorem is evidence. Probably more than science, mathematics is art. It is idiographic, not nomothetic knowledge. As we know from Turing and Gödel, it cannot be derived through machine operations (Hilbert's challenge). If there is a cause for mathematics, it is the never-ending questioning of the world appropriated by the mind at the most concrete level: its representation. The outcome is abstraction. This is what informed Hausdorff (alias Paul Mongré) as he described human nature. There is, of course, right and wrong in mathematics, as there is right and wrong in art. But neither a Beethoven symphony nor Fermat's conjecture (proven or not) is meant as a hypothesis to be experimentally confirmed. Each has an identity, i.e., a semiotic condition. Each establishes its own reality, and allows for further elaborations. Not to have heard Beethoven's symphonies or not to have understood Fermat's law does not cause bridges to collapse, or airplanes to miss their destinations.

13. SEMIOTICS IS NOT A DISCIPLINE OF PROOFS

Not even Peirce, obsessed with establishing semiotics as a logic of vagueness (Nadin, 1980, 1983) produced proofs. In physics, the same cause is associated with the same effect (in a given context). Take the example of thalidomide first used as a sedative, which led to birth defects ("thalidomide babies") when pregnant women took it. Now consider the reverse: the medicine is used for alleviating painful skin conditions and several types of cancer. The semiotics behind symptomatology concerns the ambiguous nature of disease in the living. The ambiguity of disease is reflected in the ambiguity of representations associated with disease. Better doctors are still "artists," which is not the case with software programs that analyze test results. Diagnosis is semiotics, i.e., representation and interpretation of symptoms. They are both art and science. Machine diagnosis is information processing at work. Human diagnosis is the unity of information and meaning.

When mathematicians, or logicians, translate semiotic considerations into mathematical descriptions, they do not prove the semiotics, but the mathematics used. For example, Marty (1990) provided the proof that, based on Peirce's definition of the sign and his categories, there can indeed be only ten classes of complete signs. But this brilliant proof was a contribution to the mathematics of category theory. Goguen's brilliant algebraic semiotics (1999) is in the same situation. "In this setting [i.e., user interface considered as representation, our note], representations appear as mappings, or morphisms . . . which should preserve as much structure as possible."

My own attempts at proving that signs are relationally defined as fuzzy automata (Nadin, 1977) are more a contribution to automata theory than to semiotics. No semiotician ever cared about these attempts; none took such proofs to mean anything in examining signs in action, or in understanding semiotics. For their art, which is the art of semiotic interpretation, the mathematical proof is of no relevance. The same holds true for the classes of signs. There are no such signs as *iconic*, *symbolic*, or *indexical*. These are types of representation. But to deal with the ten classes that Peirce advanced is cumbersome, to say the least.

14. ONE REDUCTION TOO MUCH

This preliminary discussion deals with how we might define a foundation of semiotics that is not around a formal concept—the sign. Since the concept is subject to so many different interpretations, none more justifiable than another, we need to avoid it. The goal is to make the reader aware of why even the most enthusiastic semioticians end up questioning the legitimacy of their pursuit. Before further elaborating a new foundation for semiotics, let us survey the semiotic scene. Let's be clear: It is not because semioticians (of all stripe) come from different perspectives, and use different definitions, that semiotics does not emerge as a coherent approach. They surrendered their inquiries to a discipline that cannot succeed in its current form. Semiotics as a sign-focused endeavor promises more than it can deliver. The subject of semiotics does not yet have a well-defined correlate in reality, in respect to which one could infer from its statements to their legitimacy and significance. It is circular by its own definition: Signs report on signs. Only because we can practice semiotics, or put on the hat that qualifies someone as semiotician (professor or not), does not justify semiotics as something more than quackery. Can semiotics have a defined correlate in reality? Can it transcend the speculative condition that made it into a discourse of convenience spiked with technical terminology? (Jack Solomon, 1988, argued that its own principles disqualify it from having universal validity.)

Everyone in the more affluent part of the world knows that society can afford supporting the unemployed, or helping people without insurance, or providing for self-proclaimed artists. But this by-product of prosperity, and the general trend to support everything and anything, cannot justify semiotics more than the obsession with gold once justified alchemy, or the obsession with cheap oil justifies wars in our time. The model of life emerging from a "lucky" combination of chemical elements belongs to the same family. (The obsession with this model does not fade away (Longo *et al.*, 2013) In order to earn its legitimacy, semiotics (i.e., semioticians) has to define itself in relation to a compelling aspect of the living, something in whose absence life itself—at least in the form we experience it—would not be possible. If this sounds like a very high-order test of validity, those readers not willing to take it are free to remain insignificant, whether they call themselves semioticians or something else. With the demotion of Aristotelian inspired *vitalism*, life was declared to be like everything else, moreover, nothing except like a machine (Descartes, *Discourse de la méthode,* 1637; de la Mettrie, *L'homme machine*, 1748). As our science evolved, the "knowledge chickens" came home to roost: We pay an epistemologically unbearable price for having adopted the machine as the general prototype of reality. The semiotic animal is not reducible to a machine (even though signs, in Peirce's definition, are reducible to fuzzy automata; cf. Figure 2). And sign processes, i.e., semioses, are not machine-like, but rather life-like: difficult to fathom (not to say, predict). Science in the echo-chamber of determinism can only confirm a poor form of causality, instead of uncovering the richness of causal processes.

15. INSIGNIFICANCE IS THE RESULT OF FAILED PRAGMATICS

The reader who still opens any of today's publications on semiotics—journals, proceedings, even books—often has cause to wonder: Is semiotics an exercise in futility? A speculative discourse? Authors of articles, conference papers, books, and other publications will probably present arguments like:

- There is a peer-review process in place that legitimizes their efforts;
- The situation in semiotics is not different from that in any other knowledge domain;
- There are no evaluation criteria to help distinguish the "wheat" from the "chaff." In the democratic model of science (semiotics and other fields), "Anything goes."

Each argument deserves attention. Some disciplines are focused on relevant aspects of science, humanities, and current technology. They define vectors of societal interest. It does not take too much effort to identify the life sciences as a field in the forefront of research and education; or, for better or worse, computer science, in its variety of directions. Nanotechnology is yet another such field. It originated in physics, (which, in its classic form, became less relevant) only in order to ascertain its own reason for being well beyond anyone's expectations. Some readers might recall the time when scientists (Smalley, 2001) claimed that nanotechnology would not work, despite the scientific enthusiasm of the majority of scientists in the field. In the meanwhile, nanotechnology has prompted spectacular developments that effected change in medicine and led to the conception of new materials and processes. Computer science met nanotechnology at the moment Moore's law, promising the doubling of computer

Figure 2. Sign and fuzzy automata

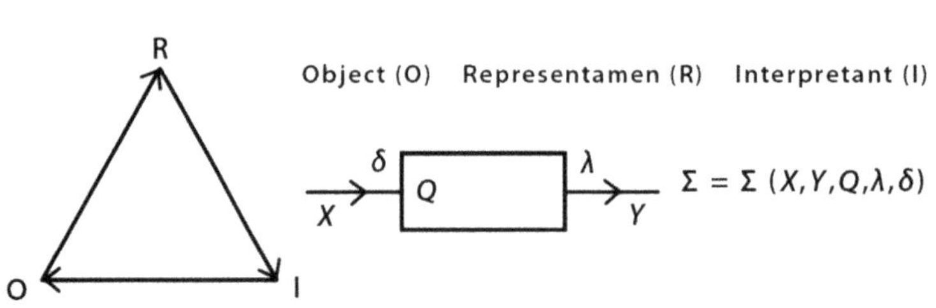

performance every eighteen months, reached its physical limits.

Besides semiotics, many other disciplines (including traditional philosophy) live merely in the cultural discourse of the day, or in the past. More precisely, they live in a parasitic state, justifying themselves through arcane requirements, such as the famous American declaration: "We need to give students a liberal arts education" (a domain in which semiotics is often based). They do not even understand what "liberal arts" or "humanities" means today: Using Twitter and the iPhone, or reading the Constitution? Being on social media or reading the "Great Books"? These are questions of a semiotic nature.

16. EMBODIED IN DEAD STRUCTURES

Semiotics as it is practiced, even by dedicated scholars, certainly does not qualify as fundamental science or as groundbreaking, no matter how generous we want to be. Rather, it illustrates what happens to a discipline in which its practitioners, most of them in search of an academic identity—a placeholder of sorts—regurgitate good and bad from a past of promise and hopes never realized. Ignore the fact that the quality of writing is sometimes questionable. What strikes the possible reader is the feeling that semiotics deals more with its own questions than with questions relevant to science, philosophy, or to today's world. Even when some subjects of current interest come up—such as the self-defined niche of bio-semiotics (cf. Uexküll, 1934, 2010; Barbieri, 2007)—they are more a pretext for revisiting obscure terminology or for resuscitating theories dead on arrival.

Very little has been clarified regarding the questions articulated in the context of a new beginning for semiotics. On behalf of the first congress in semiotics (Milan, 1974), Umberto Eco (1975) wrote (in the Preface to the Proceedings) about a "fundamental" and an "archeological" task. The first would be the justification for the existence of semiotics; the second, to derive from its past a unified methodology and, if possible, a unified objective. In short: What justifies the existence of semiotics? What are its objectives? What is its methodology? These questions are still open (and avoided).The only significant aspect is that, despite their irrelevance, events such as conferences, symposia, and congresses continue to take place. However, this is the time of new opportunity for semiotics to make its case as a viable discipline and to confirm its necessity. But for this to come about, the never challenged understanding that semiotics is a theory of the sign deserves to be discussed—and debunked, if possible.

Why is semiotics, with very few exceptions, in such a lamentable condition today? This is a scientific question. Concerning the "Why?" of the position I take: The attempt to redefine its foundation is intended as an invitation to everyone dedicated to semiotics, not to its occasional visitors. In the absence of fundamental research, for which nobody seems to have patience and dedication, semiotics has been monetized in applications that promised public success. The broader questions of the significance of semiotics to the acquisition, expression, and dissemination of knowledge are not fundable—and not really welcome by publishers. The semiotics of fashion is apparently more lucrative than the semiotic processes involved in the modeling of the world, or the semioisis of cognitive processes. Fundamental research might be shunned, but without it, not only semiotics will face further degradation into journalistic or essayistic discourse.

17. LOST OPPORTUNITIES

The most captivating mathematics (a subject I place in the humanities), the most brilliant attempts to understand language, the most dedicated effort to understand the human condition—these are themes impossible to even conceive of without acknowledging their semiotic condition. Take only the still not concluded attempts to prove Fermat's Theorem (most recently Colin McClarty, 2013). Fundamentally, the approach extends deep into the notion of representation. The very elaborate mathematical apparatus, at a level of abstraction that mathematics never reached before, makes the whole enterprise semiotically very relevant. The entire discussion that accompanied the presentation of the proof, expressions of doubt, commentaries, and attempts to explain the proof are *par excellence* all subjects for semiotics. The subject is interpretation, the "bread and butter" of semiotics, *its raison d'être*. A question that begs the attention of semioticians is, "How far from the initial mathematical statement (Fermat's Theorem) can the proof take place?" That is, how far can the representation of representation of representation, and so on extend the semiotic process before it becomes incoherent or incomprehensible?

Fermat's short message in Latin ("Cubem autem in duos cubos, etc.") on his copy of a translation of Diophantus' *Arithmetica* (3rd century CE) is a theorem represented in words, i.e., in a "natural" language (Figure 3). It is relatively easy to interpret. Later (1637), this theorem was "translated" into mathematical formulae. Fermat's Last Theorem states that no nontrivial integer solutions exist for the equation:

$$a^n + b^n = c^n$$

if n is an integer greater than 2.

One did not need to know Latin, but had to be familiar with mathematical symbols in order to understand. And now, over 370 years later, after computation changed the way we think, mathematicians say that in order to prove Fermat's Theorem, we would have to prove a conjecture (Taniyama-Shimura Conjecture) that deals with elliptic curves. Understanding in this case implies specialized knowledge. Mathematicians are still not united in fully accepting the proof produced by Andrew Wiles (1995)—a brilliant piece of mathematics, regardless of its relation to Fermat. Chances are that no other discipline besides semiotics can assist in giving meaning to the effort.

As suggested, semiotics is a knowledge domain different from mathematics. Within this knowledge domain, the mathematical question concerns what in Peirce's semiotics is defined as the *interpretant process*. Fermat's description in Latin was unequivocal; the translation into mathematical symbolism is also unambiguous. The mathematical proof is

Figure 3. Fermat's Theorem in Latin

OBSERVATIO DOMINI PETRI DE FERMAT.

CVbum autem in duos cubos, aut quadratoquadratum in duos quadratoquadratos & generaliter nullam in infinitum vltra quadratum poteſtatem in duos eiuſdem nominis ſas eſt diuidere cuius rei demonſtrationem mirabilem ſane detexi. Hanc marginis exiguitas non caperet.

so far removed from the simplicity of the Theorem that one can question the semiosis: from simple to exceedingly complicated. Under which circumstances is such a semiosis (i.e., epistemology) justified? McClarty argues that since Fermat's Theorem is about numbers, we should probably be able to prove it just by limiting ourselves to numbers. But this goes well beyond Fermat; it transcends mathematics. It becomes an issue of relevance because many semiotically based activities (such as genetics, visualizations, sonification, virtual reality, ALife, synthetic life) pertinent to the acquisition of knowledge in our age tend to evolve into complicated operations not always directly connected to what is represented. This is an issue of meta-knowledge. If knowledge acquisition, expression, and communication are indeed semiotically based, then this would be the moment to produce a semiotic foundation for meta-knowledge.

Would Charles Sanders Peirce, given his very broad scientific horizon, have missed the opportunity to approach the subject? Probably not. By the way: as Einstein produced his ground-breaking theory, Cassirer (1923) found it appropriate to offer an interpretation informed by his semiotics. In other words, there is proof that semiotics can do better than indulge in useless speculative language games, as it does in our time.

This all suggests that specialization—such as in the mathematics required to produce the proof, or the mathematics that Einstein mastered—is a necessary condition for the progress of science. But not sufficient! Specialists—and there are more and more of them—ought to relate their discoveries to other fields, to build bridges. For this they need the interface of semiotics as an integral part of their way of thinking, as a technique of expression, and as a communication guide, but also as an integrative procedure. Within the cell, as a significant biological entity, there is chemistry, physics, genetics, and there are exchanges of data, and even of information (interpreted data). To examine only one aspect is to miss the fact that the cell *integrates* all these levels. Reductionism, so fruitful in examining physical reality, is deadly when applied to the living. Of course, the reduction to signs is no less damaging, especially in view of the fact that life is identified as an open-ended dynamic process within and open system.

We are experiencing various attempts to integrate computation, genetics, anthropology, philosophy, and more into understanding how language emerged and diversified. Never before has language—in its general sense, not only as the language we speak—been as central to research as it is today. Hausdorff, the mathematician who understood the semiotic nature of the human being, predicted this development. And since semiotics has, more often than not, been understood as the semiotics of language, it would be only natural to expect semioticians of all stripes to get involved in it. Genetics is, in fact, the study of DNA "expression," of a particular kind of language defining the narrative and the associated stories that make up the "texts" and "books" of life. Or, as we shall argue, the narrative and the associated stories defining the unfolding of life over time. "Sentences" of a genetic nature identify not only criminals in a court of law, but also genetic mechanisms related to our health. Would Ferdinand de Saussure have missed the chance to collaborate with researchers who uncover the first "language genes"? Would Hjelmslev? No one expects semioticians to clarify the relation between brain activity and language. Brain imaging opened access to cerebral activity. But language is not necessarily housed in the brain, or only in the brain. There are motoric aspects to it, as there is a powerful sensorial component. Natural language is the most ubiquitous medium of interaction. It is involved in knowledge acquisition, in its expression, communication, and validation. Semiotics, if founded not around the sign concept—quite counter-intuitive when it comes to language (Where is the sign: the alphabet, the word, the sentence?)—but with the understanding of the interactions languages make possible, would contribute more than descriptions, usually of no consequence to anyone, and *post facto* explanations.

18. DOWNLOADING THINKING

The monkey that Miguel Nicolelis (2001) used in order to "download" the thinking that goes on while we play games does not qualify as an example for using language. The monkey initially acted upon the joystick in order to score. But once it noticed that it was sufficient to think about what it wanted to do, it chose the economy and speed of thinking. Are downloaded streams of data describing brain processes (such as those involved in the monkey's thinking) made up of signs? Do the components of such strings stand for some represented entity? Obviously not. This is data to be validated in action, that is, to obtain its meaning in the action performed. The semiotics is implicit in the observation that thinking and acting upon representations can be connected. The monkey condition in the experiment is not equivalent to what we call the human condition. There is no metacognition to speak of. But humans play entire games of chess in their mind, not by necessarily moving pieces on a chessboard. The monkey would qualify for semiotic awareness if it could play in its mind. With the same technology, Nicolelis used, we could get access to it (Figure 4).

As speculative as the notion of the human condition is, we have finally arrived at the juncture at which very good dynamic models can be conceived, constructed, and tested. Mental causation (richer than determinism), free will, and the neural substratum of consciousness are no longer only subjects of speculation (Tse, 2013). We obtain access to data specific to each, even if in the process of doing so we affect them (given the extreme sensitivity of the cortex).

Figure 4. Experiments with primates conditioned to behave like human beings are actually demonstrations

The underlying element of our interrogations is actually what Hausdorff defined as the *zoon semiotikon*, and what Cassirer defined as *animal symbolicum*. Hausdorff, a distinguished mathematician, could have defined the human being as "mathematical animal," but to him the qualifier "semiotic" meant a more general, more encompassing level. Cassirer was a philosopher; to him, generating symbols seemed more relevant than generating new philosophies. Before Hausdorff, and before Cassirer, many other scholars in the humanities considered the qualifier "semiotic" as co-extensive of being human. (Some extended it to animals, as well.) Leibniz, with his *miroirs vivants de l'universe*, inspired Cassirer's definition of the symbol and his attempt to define the human condition in semiotic terms. The active role of the Russian and Czech semioticians in explaining the role of language in the making of humankind, and Roland Barthes' subtle analysis of language and culture, are convincing arguments that would not have failed to be in the forefront of the semiotic research associated with the current attempts to define the human condition. (For more on the subject, see Nadin, 1986, p. 163.) They would have, I suspect, joined the scientists who are trying to obtain access to thinking.

The subject ought to be understood as broadly as possible. This means that within the realm of the living, there is a whole gamut—from the mono-cell to *homo faber*—of representations to consider. Is there anything that qualifies as semiotically relevant across the various forms of the living? As already stated in the preliminaries, interaction is probably the most obvious aspect. At a closer look, the making of the living consists of integrated interactions—from the level of the cell to that of organisms. At all these levels, representations are exchanged. Therefore, semiotic processes appear as a characteristic of the whole (organism), but also as one among organisms (same or different). Semioticians are not invited to become biologists, rather to engage biological knowledge (acquired in specific experiments) in order to generalize the notion of semiotic process. That which lives is defined not only by the physics, chemistry, or energy of the process, but also by the various representations exchanged and the ability to interpret them. There was interactivity in every previous stage of evolution, as well as in cultural definition. Interactivity implied interpretation—the outcome depended on it—but never at the scale at which society makes semiotic-based interactions its major form of activity.

Society hopes to have the guidance of science, in particular semiotics, in giving meaning to data processing. This guidance could help avoid costly consequences—such as those experienced in recent years: terrorism, technological errors, speculation, various forms of addiction, etc. Success and failure depend decisively more upon interpretation than upon the amount of data. An infinite amount of data cannot compensate for an error in interpretation. Machines are, by many orders of magnitude, better in processing information, but not really better than humans in interpreting it. They can handle way more data than the people who build them; but quantity does not automatically lead to improved comprehension. In a changing context, interpretation becomes consubstantial with dynamics. Machines do not change; humans (the living) change.

The major themes in the sciences beg no less for the contribution of semiotics. Computation is, for all practical purposes, semiotics at work in information processing. Artificial intelligence, in its many flavors, cannot be conceived without integrating semiotic concepts in its concrete implementations. The new forms of computation—genetic, quantum, DNA, etc.—are all forms of semiotic processes. So are neural networks, modeled on the brain. More specifically: No information process (e.g., computer, sensor-based information harvesting, intelligent agents-based activities) is possible without representation. Representation is the definitory subject of semiotics. While electrons move through circuits, and while logic is emulated in hardware (circuits performing logical operations), operations on representations are the prerequisite for any information processing. The variety of representations (for which Peirce delivered the types, i.e., indexical, iconic, symbolic) and their specific dynamics are superficially understood, if at all. The entire focus on the living, which affects the academic landscape, and human activity in general, is ultimately a focus on the semiotic processes implicit in mechanisms of life. It suffices to check out the major research directions in order to discover that we are getting better at understanding the object level—cells or membrane biochemistry, for example—and in describing the associated representational level. To realize the unity between the informational and the semiotic is a major scientific challenge.

Let us be clear: Representation is not reducible to the entity we call "sign," regardless of how it is defined. Signs are media for representation, like letters in the alphabet are media for words, sentences, texts. The process we call "representation" cannot be reduced to one or several signs (cf. Figure 2). Just for the sake of the parallel mentioned earlier, we can say that the definition of semiotics based on the sign is at least as unsatisfactory as a definition of mathematics would be if it were based on numbers alone, or of chemistry based on elements, or of biology based on cells, or of linguistics-based on the alphabet. Representation would have to be further defined as a process, uniting data (measurable) and meaning (result of interpretation), that is, allowing access to information. It is in this condition that representation proves to be significant for the understanding of the living, of mathematics (a specific form of human activity), of science, of the arts, of communication, and of interaction. Despite this peculiarity, semioticians are so removed from the major scientific and humanistic themes of the day that they don't even know that this is their greatest chance—ever! The entire stem cell debate could have taken a different path had competent semioticians contributed to an understanding of stem cell "semiosis" and the relation to the broader issues of creativity. The new focus on the brain (the brain-mapping initiative) is yet another opportunity.

19. INTERACTION IS (ALMOST) ALWAYS SEMIOTIC

I will conclude this compressed exposition by stating that technology is shaped by questions that, at first glance, impress as being semiotic in nature. Technological artifacts of all kind—from games to virtual reality labs, in which new materials are conceived—rely on various types of semiotic entities, on representations in the first places, and their interpretation. They make sense, and can become a relevant subject of inquiry, only as new "languages of interaction." In the virtual reality cave (a notion inspired by Plato's understanding of knowledge), the interaction is semiotic. The global scale of life (reflected in the global economy) makes an integrative approach necessary. In our time, we need a semiotic theory based on acknowledging diversity, while simultaneously providing means of expression, communication, and signification that pertain to the new scale of human activity.

It does not suffice to sing hymns of praise to the global economy of higher profits, or to deplore its consequences for those who rarely enjoy its advantages. Semiotics could facilitate a better understanding of the choices we have in the global economy. The GPS facility, accessible worldwide, is the first global embodiment of semiotics in action. I do not, of course, expect semioticians to start writing articles on what kind of a sign a GPS indicator is, but rather to contribute semiotic concepts that will make the language of the system so much easier to understand and use. When GPS data will seamlessly integrate in what we do—drive, visit new places, connect to others, for example—that is, when it becomes part of our language, semiotics could support a concrete accomplishment. Hopefully, semioticians will be able to understand this opportunity. In the absence of such a development, technology will continue to deliver solutions to problems that are none, but that become part of our life. In absence of semiotic awareness, hacking, cyberterrorism, and identity theft are nothing but the result of greedy technological advances.

On this note, a simple observation: Brain imaging revealed that taxi drivers in some of the big cities (London was the first address researched), difficult to navigate, developed in the process measurable new faculties Indeed, the plasticity of the brains of those who navigate under the influence of GPS data changes (not always for the better). Of course, these changes are semiotic in nature: Understanding of representations and the ability to match goals and means (a request such as "Get me to Piccadilly in the shortest time," involves quite a number of parameters) are semiotic processes. The emergence of GPS-based navigation might lead to the loss of some faculties. (The same have a tougher time working with maps or following verbal instructions.) Semioticians should be aware of the fact that the world before maps and the world after maps became available are very different realities.

As technology evolves, more and more automated systems guide our navigation—in libraries, on the worldwide Web, in air travel, on high-speed trains, on highways and toll roads, for example. Aaron Koblin (2008-present) documented this process in visualizations of extreme semiotic significance. So did Albert-László Barabási (see examples from their work in Figures 5 a, b, c). If Google, where Koblin currently works, had been the invention of semioticians, I could not find today's state of semiotics deplorable. But it was not. Neither was Barabási's mathematical work inspired by semiotics, but by networks. And if the Worldwide Web, through which many publications (including a few of semiotic interest) are presented, had involved the least participation of semiotics, we would have had a Web that is not syntactically driven. The inventor of the Web (Berners-Lee, 1998) is still dreaming of a semantic stage.

On this note, a statement of principle: For me, personally, only a pragmatically driven Web makes real sense. Indeed, as a medium of interaction, the worldwide Web will become significant when new forms of activity will become possible. There are some modest beginnings: designers working on the same project in a cooperative manner; the new possibilities offered by the so-called 3D printing. Spectacular innovations are almost regular occurrences. Moreover, medicine practiced over networks is a new experience promising not only remote diagnosis and surgery, but also the interaction of experts involved in understanding the uniqueness of the patients. The new 3D printing technology could deliver artificial skin for grafts performed after an accident.

While the GPS actually changes the nature of our relation to space, and indirectly to time, its semiotics is a legitimate question waiting to be addressed because it involves a new semiotic condition for the human being. The military purpose of the orientation system is spectacularly transcended by rich semioses that, strangely enough, emerged without any input from semioticians. Koblin's work is only one example among many. If today semiotics were to contribute to a semantic Web, we would avoid the many errors that have affected the growth of the Web into the monster it is now. We find data on the Web, to the extent of overwhelming the user, but we do not really find information, and almost never meaning. If this is not a challenging semiotic project, then I don't know of any. The Google Glass project is an attempt to integrate semiotics (of seeing and hearing, in particular) in the new "embodiment" (i.e., glasses) of computation that the company makes possible.

Figure 5. a, b) Aaron Koblin: flight pattern and air traffic paths Atlanta, c) Albert Laslo Barabasi: social networks in Canberra

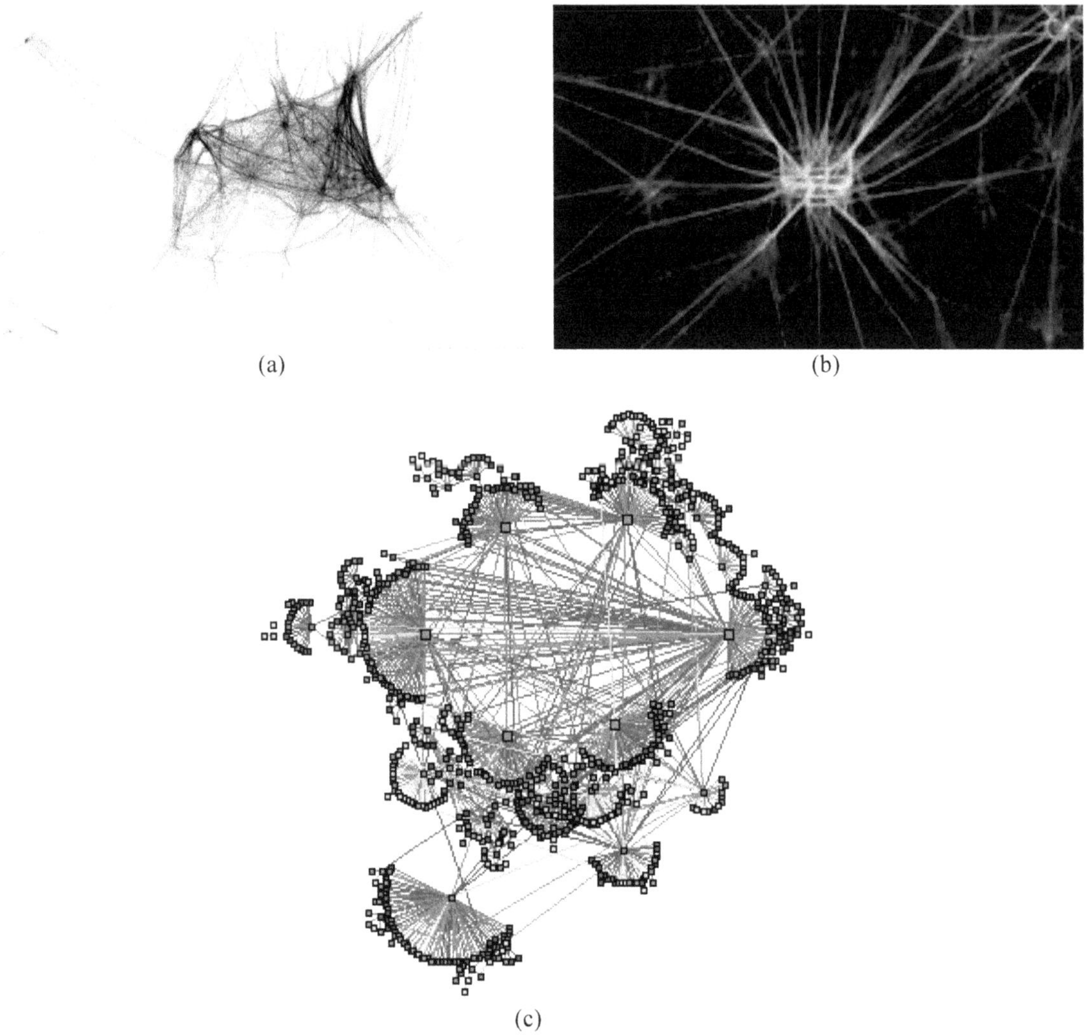

Yes, there is semiotics at work in the activity of Luc Steels, Stevan Harnad, and Juyan Weng. João Queiroz and Angelo Loula (the latter two initiated a new journal in semiotics) pursue a promising agenda. And yes, in the AI domain, there is a definite awareness of the semiotic component of intelligence. Tony Belpaeme and Angelo Cangelosi come to mind in this vein. But the work of such researchers is not presented at semiotics meetings and congresses or in the regular semiotics publications.

Obviously, this short account is not exhaustive, and it is less systematic than it would be in a different context. The intention is only to suggest that semiotics has a very fertile ground to cultivate, if semioticians care to work at it, or if professionals from other disciplines pay more attention to semiotics. It is not too late! In a different context (Nadin, 2005, 2011), I brought up *The Semiotic Engineering of Human-Computer Interaction*, a book written by a computer science professor (trained as a linguist), Clarisse Sieckenius de Souza (2005), who "spread" the semiotic word in the HCI community. We have here an example of an applied understanding of semiotics informed by the desire to advance issues of interaction—to make it into a foundation for new forms of engineering. It is modest proof, if anyone needed more proof, that so much can be done, provided that semiotics competence guides the effort. Aware of this characterization of her book (which semioticians managed to ignore), she recently wrote to me by e-mail: "Having studied semiotics does make a difference [...] I have the impression...that HCI professionals and students educated in North America tend to have a 'What is in it for me?' approach. [...] As you know, the answer is, 'a whole new world, but it will take a lot of critical thinking to get it.' "

20. SEMIOTICS HAS MORE HISTORY THAN CURRENCY

The first Congress of the International Association of Semiotic Studies justified the need for a historic account as a step in defining its methodology. Semiotics has had more than one chance in history to make its case, and to make useful and sensible contributions. Semiotic "seeds" were planted early in all known cultures. But as is always the case with history, you find in the past what you are looking for. And attention was focused on spoken language and the sign more than on representation. Before the Greek word *simeiotika* was acknowledged, there was the Hebrew *oth* for sign: the Hebrew Torah makes reference to the lights in the firmament, Shabbat, the mark of Cain, the rainbow, the token of the covenant, all covering a broad understanding of the sign ("And this shall be a sign to you . . ."). Avicenna's work on prophethood can be mentioned in the same vein (cf. Al-Akiti, 2004).

The intention underlying these signs is pragmatic, guiding human activities that aided in establishing a stable body of knowledge: the sign as a mark of genuineness, of authenticity, of promise. The same pragmatic propensity is obvious in the Chinese, the Indian, and the Arabic infatuation with the sign. In Western Europe, the sign emerged also in a context of an applied understanding: means of orientation, symptoms as a prerequisite for diagnosis. It was only very late—probably after Locke (1690)—that questions related to the way in which the mind operates prompted a focus on the sign as a means for understanding and sharing. With Lambert (1764), questions concerning the connection between thinking and things were articulated. But these were questions of representation pertinent to cognition, not sign-based considerations.

21. SYNCHRONY – DIACHRONY: A DISTINCTION OF PRAGMATIC RELEVANCE

We cannot avoid the general observation that semiotic awareness led to more than one attempt to define its knowledge domain and its specific methods. Still, so it seems, each start was relatively short-lived. The generically defined "ancient times" had such a start, with works such as Plato's *Sophistes* (*The Sophist*, 360 BCE), Aristotles' *Poetica* (350 BCE), and the Stoics, mentioned in almost every account of history. It is worth mentioning that Sextus Empiricus (*in Adversus Mathematicos*, VIII) took note of the fact that the distinction between what is signified, what signifies, and the object informs early attempts to understand semiotics as focused on the verb "to introduce" (something). The object and the signifier are material; the signified (*lekton*) is not, but it can only be right (adequate) or not (inadequate). Indian Buddhism and Brahmanism, the Christian infatuation with signs (St. Augustine's *De Doctrina Cristiana*, 397 CE, and St. Anselm's *Monologion*, 1075-1076; see Hopkins, 1986), and Avicenna's explorations in medicine and theology remain documentary repositories of the many questions posed by two very simple questions: How can something in the world be "duplicated" in the mind? Take note: the question is not about signs, but about re-presentation. Moreover, once we think about it (the reality duplicated in the mind), can we know it (or assume that what we know corresponds to reality)? Or does knowing actually involve a practical activity with a desired outcome?

Edward O. Wilson (1984) came up with a provocative statement of significance to semiotics: "Scientists do not discover in order to know, they know in order to discover." The inversion of purpose (the causality) points to opportunity. Reading classical texts (such as those mentioned above)—and very few semioticians care to do that—reveals that the sign was only the trigger of the interactions it made possible, not associated with their meaning, and even less with their significance. From the beginning, the fascination was with semiotic knowledge, that is, what we learn from observing interactions, and how these are subject to betterment. It is not the history that is important here, but rather the attempt to understand the need for semiotics—if a need indeed exists. The premise guiding this effort is *pragmatic relevance*: If semiotics does not make a difference, as mathematics, chemistry, and physics do, why bother with it? After the rather modest beginning of semiotic inquiry, the interest in formulating semiotic questions diminished. However, the still controversial "Middle Ages" were yet another start. The works of Roscelin (who introduced extreme nominalism); Guillaume de Champeaux (who maintained that universals exist independent of names), and Abélard (on logic) stand as examples for the enthusiasm of those seeking in semiotics answers to the many challenges of those times. Let's be clear: The fundamental opposition between nominalism and realism is a test case. If things are only names, semiotics would be in charge of the world. If, alternatively, the world, in its manifold materiality, were to look at names and call them a poor attempt at describing it, semiotics would be useless. Jean de Salisbury (*Metalogicon*) suggested that abstractions are not related to signs and take the role of names and naming. It is a fascinating journey to read Occam, William of Shyreswood, Lambert d'Auxerre, and Roger Bacon, first and foremost because their questions, extended to the domain of rationality, will inspire the third attempt at restarting semiotics in the classical age. To put it succinctly, it was not much more successful than the previous beginning. Hobbes (*Leviathan*, 1651) the *Logique de Port Royal*, (or *The Art of Thinking*, 1662) John Locke (the forms of reasoning and *The Division of Sciences*, 1690), and foremost, Leibniz (symbolic and mathematical thought, 1672-1696) are precursors of the modern rebirth associated with de Saussure and Peirce.

Important, even for those disinclined to seek guidance in works of the past, is the distinction between language associated with convention or law (*nomoi*)—such as programming languages—or with nature (*phusei*)—such as the genetic code. Nobody expects today's semioticians to become historians. But in the absence of a broader understanding of our concepts, we will continue to explore, blindfolded, new continents (of thought and action). I do not doubt that Saussure and Peirce are valid references, but I suggest that Hermann Paul's (1880/1970) *diachrony* is far more conducive to understanding the specific dynamics of languages. This is only one example. Nikolai Sergeyevitch Trubetzkoy (1939/1969) might be another, as is Louis Hjelmslev (1943).

22. TAROT CARD READING IS NOT (YET) AN ACADEMIC DISCIPLINE

But it might become one. Universities are teaching square dancing, how to have an orgasm, mixed marriage (and techniques for politically correct divorce), for example. And since education is by its nature one of the most involved semiotics activities, it is fair to state that semiotics can take credit (or blame) for the MOOCs, but also for the degradation of teaching and learning into entertainment. The context is the modern rebirth of semiotics. It actually legitimized what others were doing within their respective disciplines: philologists, structuralists, scholars in literary theory, morphology. Many fascinating ideas were advanced, and it seemed that a promising new age began. But the effort remained focused on the sign, since everything—sex, food, art, elections, and nanoscience, for instance—could be interpreted as signs. Once a new territory was defined, many moved into it, while actually continuing to do what they had done before. This is not unusual. The most recent example is the morphing of mathematicians and physicists into computer scientists. It took a while until the "new science" (if "new" can be justified in having Leibniz as the final reference) settled into its "language" and "methods." But in the case of semiotics, those who have run over the border and sought "political asylum" in the "free country" of semiotics actually remain faithful ("captive" would be a more accurate descriptor) to their old questions and methods.

More precisely, semiotics enrolled itself in the service of a perspective of reality that ignores fundamental distinctions—such as those between the living and the non-living (*physis*)—within reality. It adopted determinism and became an instrument for its further consolidation, against the evidence that dynamics, i.e., change, is non-deterministic

Semiotics became the stage for literary critics, art historians, confused structuralists, and even for some linguists, mathematicians, and sociologists. Some philosophers also ventured on the stage. Before too late, we had the semiotics of feminism, multiculturalism, human rights, sexuality, food, and even the semiotics of wine; we had gay and lesbian semiotics, environmental semiotics, and even global warming or sustainability semiotics. *But no semiotics!* Anticipation, on account of which semiotics was legitimized as a new perspective of change, was discarded. Semiotics in this form became a critical discourse of convenience for everything opportunistic. Philosophy, in its classical form, could have performed the same without the heavy terminology that alienated even those who were convinced that semiotics is a legitimate endeavor. While all the subjects—and there are way more than what is listed—are, of course, relevant within the broader context of culture and civilization, the qualifier semiotic at most justified the opportunistic take around the sign as identifier, but did not essentially contribute anything constructive.

Most relevant is the estrangement of semiotics from medicine, where at least some of its necessity, in the form of diagnostics, was established. Aligned with all disciplines looking at humans (and animals and plants) as having the sameness that physical entities have (all electrons are the same, after all), it ended up as a useless exercise. In reality, there are no identical patients; labels define a spectrum, not a precise condition. What's good for one patient can be lethal for another. If semiotics had accounted for this uniqueness, and for an understanding of health or disease as process, medicine would have continued to practice it. Since it did not, physics ("Let's weigh the patient, measure blood pressure, height, etc.") and chemistry ("Let's check the composition of blood, urine, stool, etc.") took its place. Human beings become machines to be repaired. The consequence of this failure of semiotics cannot be deplored enough.

23. THERE IS MORE TO INTERACTION THAN LANGUAGE

Preoccupation with what is called *natural language* affected the focus on the sign. It informed the reading of past attempts in semiotics in such a manner that what actually lies behind the sign is cast aside, never really recognized. All this rendered the notion of sign captive to an ideology that dominated semiotics from its beginnings. Simply stated, this ideology is *logocratic*. That is, it ascertains that every sign can be reduced to a language sign; moreover, that any interaction is language dependent. Since language is the dominant medium of formalization and abstraction, one can understand why this ideology went unchallenged until Charles Sanders Peirce, and later, Cassirer. Roland Barthes thematized the totalitarian nature of this language. Totalitarian regimes rely upon the authority of language in order to consolidate their power. Even the sciences (physics, mathematics, chemistry, etc.) can at times consolidate their "power" through the "languages" they cultivate, to the detriment of alternative understandings in their object domain. Computer science and genetics fully illustrate this thought. The echo-chamber effect is based on pressure exercised through language.

Attempts were made within semiotics to challenge the logocratic model. For instance, some scholars tried to advance semiotic notions connected to human activity; others (inspired by Jakob von Uexküll, 1884-1944, as author of theoretical biology; cf. 1934/2010) reached beyond the human being into the larger domain of nature. But within semiotics itself, dominated by scholars who fled language studies, such attempts were at best tolerated, but never taken as a scientific challenge. If, finally, semiotics could in our days free itself from the obsession with sign-based language as object of its inquiry, it could help debunk quite a number of dogmatic positions. Or at least it could become a guide for maintaining meaningful dialog, among those who acknowledge images, sounds, smell, and tactility as relevant to interactions.

Even though some historical references have been provided, this is not the place to rewrite the history of semiotics (in which very convincing work was already done). We are not so short of histories as we are short of better semiotics. Here an attempt has been made to point to a development that explains the linguistic bent of even some of the best works produced at the end of the last century. The brilliant literary accomplishments of the French School, as well as the powerful arguments of the Russian-Prague formalists and the Soviet school, and even the German and American elaborations of the 1980s and 1990s are pretty much driven by the same implicit understanding that natural language is paradigmatic, and that a sign-focused semiotics could further consolidate this position. We will not be able to escape the deadly embrace of this limited understanding unless and until semioticians establish a fresh perspective. Language is only one among the many semiotic entities involved in representation, expression, and communication.

They should at least acknowledge that language is not always language. This is important because even though languages are structurally different, we have generalized from the Indo-European languages to the new languages of programming. In doing so, we miss the opportunity to take advantage of the characteristics of other cultures. Moreover, we have generalized from Indo-European language to images, sounds, and other expressive means, although their semiotic conditions are different. If the logocratic model is problematic in the first place, it becomes even more so when it generalizes on account of a particular language experience instead of integrating as many as possible (corresponding to the richness of human activities unfolding in various contexts). However, at the periphery—i.e., exactly that part of the world that was ignored by Western semiotics—semiotic awareness "outside the box" developed quite convincingly and semiotics gained in significance. Of course, the periphery was "colonized;" English is the *lingua franca*, and semiotics was imported like so many West-based intellectual endeavors. But recently, awareness of language and logic characteristics of practical experiences not reducible to those of western civilization started to inform alternative understandings.

Let me explain: French (as an example of western language and logic) and Japanese (as an example of a very different language and logic) are difficult to reconcile. Thinking in German is quite different from thinking in Chinese. And so is the phonetic writing of many western languages different from the synthetic Korean alphabet. Let's face it: the most interesting semiotics today seems to evolve in China, Korea, Japan, and India. The latter is the recipient of most of Western outsourcing, which is often semiotic work by the way: translations, word processing, scanning, record keeping, programming, etc. While the sign is not discarded, the focus of such a work is rather on broader semiotic entities (text, narrative, game, etc.). This suggests, indirectly, an interest in issues of representation, which are not affected by differences in languages and the associated differences in logic (from the 2-valued Aristotelian logic to the Oriental multi-valued logical systems). If only Baumgarten's sketchy semiotics, which is part of his attempt to provide a foundation for aesthetics (*Aesthetica*, 1750), were to be considered, semioticians would at least, instead of generalizing from the language-defined sign, seek a broader understanding of the sign as such, as Peirce attempted. Such an understanding will in the end have to translate into the most important dimcnsion of the sciences: predictive power. We are pretty advanced in the predictive aspects of the physical world; we are still at a loss in regard to predictive aspects of living processes. Let it be noticed that the logographically driven semiotics focused on the sign could at best deliver explanations for semiotic processes concluded (characteristic of the physical reality). Analytical performance characterizes this attempt. But it could not serve, even in the best of cases, as knowledge on whose basis future semiotic processes could be envisaged or, for that matter, designed, tested, and validated as means to support human activity. A semiotics running after, instead of leading to desired semiotic processes cannot serve as a bridge among sciences, and even less as an innovative field of human activity.

These lines are only an indirect argument in favor of more semiotics of the visual, the aural, or of multimedia, of learning from the differences in various languages, and of discovering the underlying shared elements of such languages. Whether we like it or not, language ceased being the dominant means of knowledge acquisition, just as it ceased being the exclusive means of knowledge dissemination. Representations in expressions other than in language are the rule, not the exception. Moreover, representation, in its broad sense, shapes human interaction to the extent that it renders the semiotics of natural language an exercise in speculative rhetoric.

The fact that means of representation are simultaneously constitutive of our own thinking and acting is not yet reflected in the semiotic elaborations of our time. To visualize or to sonify is to acquire a cognitive identity different from that of individuals talking about or writing about the same subject. Some researchers, unfortunately ignoring each other, rushed to establish a computational semiotics, and even cognitive semiotics, not realizing that the fashionable qualifiers "computational" and "cognitive" mean, after all, a semiotics of semiotics. What semiotics does not need is a new way of packaging the worn-out speculations resulting from the ceremonial of an old-fashioned dance around the sign—the elusive princess at a ball where everyone seems blessed with eternal oblivion.

Since computational semiotics was mentioned (cf. Stephan, 1996; Rieger, 1997, 2003; Gudwin & Queiroz, 2005) it is appropriate to ask whether such a discipline is possible. The broad agreement that knowledge is expressed more and more in computational form could translate into a well-defined goal: express semiotic knowledge computationally. As such, the goal deserves attention because even though deterministic machines are inadequate for capturing nondeterministic processes, we can work towards conceiving new forms of processing that either mimic the living or even integrate the living (hybrid computation). Computational semiotics (making reference to Dmitri Pospelov and Eugene Pendergraft, to James Albus, to "language games" behind which Wittgenstein is suspected, to Luis Rocha and Cliff Joslyn, and even to Leonid Perlovsky and his intelligent target tracker) is more than looking for justification for AI research, or for some computer-based terminology associated with signs. It would be encouraging to engage those interested in foundational aspects of semiotics in a computational effort. One possible result could be a semiotic engine conceived as a procedure for generating representations and for supporting interpretation processes. But this is already a methodological direction, probably more significant within the broader context of human activity in our days.

We do not want to eliminate the possibility of computer-based generation of representations. Even if such representations would facilitate limited forms of knowledge acquisition and expression, there is no need to downplay their use. However, if machine-generated representations were to trigger the claim of replacing the living processes leading to comprehensive dynamic representations of a changing world, we would face a real danger. In representing something, the living simultaneously re-presents itself. This contributes to the knowledge the outlook and the sense of future derived through human representations. Each representation, after all, embodies anticipation. Machines, regardless of their level of sophistication, do not anticipate.

24. IS THERE A SEMIOTIC METHOD?

What defines the semiotic method? Concepts, whether semiotic or not, are a projection of our own reality. The environment (the world in which the living is identified) embodies matter in an infinite variety of expression. The dynamics of the world results from energy-related processes, themselves of infinite variety. There is change, including our own; there is the rate of change, testifying to an acceleration related to improved performance. This, of course, does not necessarily lead to better understanding of what and why we do what we do. There is also failure. The broader the scale of human endeavors, the bigger the scale at which we experience failure. Failure as much as success testifies to the adequacy of knowledge. For all practical purposes, a powerful earthquake and a massive tsunami are of a scale comparable to a nuclear power plant breakdown (and its many consequences).

Knowledge of natural phenomena as much as awareness of the limits of our knowledge as it applies to what we conceive are related.

Nature is becoming more and more what human beings are doing to it (sometimes responsibly, many times not). For the living, regardless of its scale and kind, the following holds true: we are what we do! The human being acquired awareness of this condition; as we moved farther away from the rest of nature this awareness informed new forms of expressing human identity. We are currently experiencing the computational condition of research and activity. The role of representations within this condition has changed considerably.

Among other things, humans observe nature (while being part of it) more through the deployment of computational means. And they attempt to change the world according to needs they have, desires they form, goals they express, capabilities they acquire. In this encompassing process of the human-being's continuous self-making, humans are semiotic animals, able to operate not only on what is available (from stones, tree branches, edible vegetation, to swiftly running rivers and combustible matter), but also on representations of what the world actually is. Computation is representation driven. This ability is acquired, tested, and continuously changing. To operate on representations is to transcend the immediate, the present. Only *the zoon semiotikon* (and similarly the *animal symbolicum*) has an awareness of the future in the sense that they can affect the dynamics of existence. Only through the intermediary of semiotic processes of representation do human beings free themselves from the immediate.

25. SEMIOTICS IS ABOUT MEANING

The living takes in the world as *representation*. Representations are a prerequisite for natural or artificial reproduction. The sperm and the egg to be fertilized are embodied representations of the particular male and female; so is the stem cell, unfolding under complex anticipatory dynamics. Computer programs "translate" algorithms—describing a course of action for reaching a well-defined goal—into operations on representations. Computer viruses, probably more than other successful programs, illustrate artificial reproduction as it results from a dynamics associated with predefined operations. The reverse engineered Stuxnet is a good introduction to the subject. Adaptive characteristics of the living and adaptive mechanisms in the world of machines, as different as they are, correspond to two different modalities for generating representations appropriate to changing contexts of existence or functioning. In adaptive processes, the living experiences information processes and semiotic processes. Information processes correspond to energy- and matter-related aspects of the living. Semiotic processes correspond to meaning. They are embodied in the narrative of life, unfolding along a timeline, and expressed in its many associated stories.

This is an opportunity, as good as any, to spell out the alternative to the semiotics focused on the sign. I suggest that, instead of the atomistic view of a sign obsessed with semiotics, we adopt a dynamic view, of events succeeding in time. The notion that each event—such as perceiving an image, hearing a sound, experiencing a texture, etc.—is "made up" of signs is less important than the determination to integrate successive experiences. Narration is a historic record:

event1, event2, event3. . . .

Influenced by information processing, some would call it a time series:

$S_1\ S_2\ S_3$. . . .

In this view, the series is made up of succeeding signs. While each event is relevant, the focus is on the integrated series, more precisely, on its meaning. But more on a narration-based semiotics in the concluding part of this study.

Space and time are constitutive representations. Furthermore, it is epistemologically suicidal not to realize that concepts, which are representations, help to both describe and constitute the world. We perceive the world empowered (when not blinded) by our thinking and supported (when not handicapped) by artificially extended perceptions. We "see" today much, much more than what we see; we "hear" today much more than what our ears bring to us. But in the end, we never escape the epistemological circularity of our perspectives. This applies to mathematics as it does to semiotics. For people focused on a sign-centered semiotics, a sign definition is as adequate as we can make it adequate. But it is a construct, always subject to questioning, as Sadowski (2010) recently questioned Peirce's definition, or as I (Nadin, 1983) questioned Saussure's definition (notwithstanding the relevance of his linguistic contributions, cf. Bouissac, 2010). Something else is at stake: not the adequacy of sign-based semiotic concepts, but the ability to support, to guide practical experiences.

The first integrated VLSI (i.e., integrated circuits), celebrated as one of the major accomplishments in the technology of the last 50 years, was a project in applied physics. Today, we integrate millions of transistors in a chip, or achieve technological performance in myriad ways; physics and awareness of the characteristics of the living fuse into a new perspective. But after all is said and done, the entire effort is focused on *representations*—of arithmetic, calculus, geometry, physics, etc. No doubt, the chip remains a magnificent outcome of mathematics, physics, chemistry, and technology, i.e., engineering. But what is "condensed" on the chip is knowledge—representations, not signs, expressed in digital form. Ultimately, this knowledge is representation of all we know about arithmetic, calculus, geometry, etc., of what we know about graphics, color, form, shape, etc. The most recent (and probably soon-to be improved upon) 3DS game player from Nintendo makes 3D representation on a 2D monitor (no goggles needed) possible. The victory of information processing (implementation of the binocular parallax) is associated with a semiotic accomplishment: the meaning of 3D in situations of search, hiding, exploring realistic representations of landscapes, etc. Playing hide-and-go-seek involves our individual characteristics, our ad hoc knowledge pertinent to hiding and seeking. Playing an MMOG (massively multi-player online game) involves embodied knowledge. If this knowledge reflects the reductionist-deterministic view of the world, the game will be a good simulation of this perspective—but not a new perspective of our own being, of our condition as semiotic animals. This is a world of action-reaction. Playing with others, located around the world, via the medium of the game recovers anticipation. This is a victory for semiotics, even if semioticians have to date missed the meaning of such innovative applications.

26. IN THE AGE OF GAMIFICATION

The most fascinating semiotic applications of recent years came not from semioticians, but from the people who practice semiotics without knowing they do so. To talk about military applications (supported by public money, of course) would require an expertise I do not have. To repeat: *Semiotics is fundamental science*. The entire genome project is an example of semiotics in the forefront (even if not carried out by semioticians). Virtual reality, that is, computing representations that recreate aspects of the real world, is applied semiotics. In a virtual reality application for someone who wants to learn how to juggle more than three or four balls at a time, the action pertains to the representation, not to real balls. The glove senses "representation" of balls; speed can be adjusted, and gravity itself is re-presented, made subject to the individual's control. (Figure 6) Not only *Nike* and *MacDonald's*, but also the whole branding craze is semiotic in nature. Lawyers engage semiotics in defining the nature of patents (Jones, 2013). Politics—the practice of gaining access to power—involves itself in semiotics, and elections are won (or lost) on account of the appropriate (or inappropriate) semiotics. This is an example of *gamification*—make everything a game, stimulate new forms of interactions, use reward mechanisms to stimulate performance (Figure 6). Indeed, if still images are acceptable representations of a world changing slowly, film images are a next step: keep a record of change as it takes place. However, if interactions are of interest, games are a good medium for representing them. All of the above, and much more, is semiotics at work without the involvement of semiotics.

But what are semioticians doing? The old soup of psychoanalytic extraction is warmed up again and again; literary criticism is disguised as semiotic analysis; structuralist considerations are rewritten in semiotic jargon; linguistic terminology is madc to appear semiotic. Semiotics became part of the jargon of intellectual property lawyers because, of course, a bit of exotic vocabulary could make an impression in the courts. Since patents became a source of profit to be adjudicated by judges who can barely understand the science (or the speculation) behind them. Semiotics is brought up as a "social science" arbiter. To forever analyze popular culture (after Barthes and Eco exhausted the theme), film, music, new media, and video games might lead to texts published by editors as clueless as the writers, but not to the knowledge that society has the legitimate right to expect from semiotics. Books on the semiotics of games will never replace the experience of the game itself, or of conceiving the game. On a constructive note, here is a suggestion in the spirit of the time: Let us open a "Story Lab" where semiotics can be practiced in generating new stories, corresponding to the fast

Figure 6. Learning how to drive (or fly, or navigate, etc.) by using games (embodied in simulators). Reality is represented, realistic control elements serve for training and evaluation.

dynamics of the present. Instead of continuing the impotent discourse on narrativity (without understanding the difference between narration and story), we could build upon the knowledge pertinent to how brains react to stories (Pollack, 2013; Stephens *et al.*, 2011). And let us provide semiotic methods for the human interactions of the future, not attempts to explain what these interactions were.

Conditions were not ideal in the "good old days" of the semiotic revival of the early 1970s (or earlier). But the questions asked were inciting. I still hold to the notion (Peircean, by the way) that without an ethics of terminology, each of us will be talking about something (the sign, let's say) and understanding something else. The best example is the use of the word "sign," and the tendency to substitute "symbol" for "sign" (or *vice versa*). For this ethics to emerge, we also need an encompassing semiotic culture: more people who read primary sources, not approximate derivations, and more people with *original* ideas who actually read what has already been written on the topic—and give credit where credit is due. Yes, there used to be more quality scholarship, despite the absence of Google or Wikipedia—sources of generalized mediocrity—which some believe substitute for true research effort. Society could not afford, as it does in our days, to fund mediocrity. Without the realization of the need for scholarship, well-intended newcomers will rediscover "continents" that were already explored, and consequently miss their chance to contribute fresh thoughts.

Mediocrity corresponds to a new semiotic condition of the human being: Within shorter cycles of change, and under the inescapable pressure of faster dynamics, there is no room left for depth. Humankind is shaping itself as a species of shallow enterprise, a breadth-focused existence, contributing spectacularly to its own end (within a perspective of time that makes the end still far away).

In various attempts at making up "specialized" semiotics—of music, law, sex, and so on and so on—mostly left in some state of indeterminacy, well-intentioned authors decided to use the concept of the sign in order to deal with particular objects of their interest. Obviously, someone can take a ruler to measure how long a carrot is, or how short a mouse's nose. Appropriateness of perspective, and thus of qualifiers for a certain action or tool, is a methodological prerequisite for any scientific endeavor. Philosophy is not measured in gallons; a work of art is not reducible to the number of knots in the canvas; music is not the map of sound frequencies. The sign, well- or ill-defined, can be the identifier of choice for pragmatic reasons: How well does the STOP sign perform its function? Of course, when the car is fully automated (that is, when it navigates autonomously, as in the self-driving car almost at the implementations stage), the sign as such becomes obsolete. How appropriate are the various components of a sign such as a logo in a corporate identity "language"? Of course (again) when the life of a corporation is no longer than the life of its only product, identity is consumed. Why is a certain selection made (color, shape, rhythm) in the attempt to establish conventions for communication purposes, or within a culture? Such choices will change as fast as anything does in our time. Sonification promises to make representations more powerful by addressing hearing, the most "natural of human senses. The fact that meaning, not sound, is the purpose of representation often escapes the understanding of the newly minted sonificators.

It is undisputed that semiotics integrates the concept of the representation through something called a sign (or, previously, a symbol). It is less evident that semiotics is not reducible to signs, or to the formal relation among signs (what is called syntax). Those who do not realize this irreducibility might at times generalize in a manner not beneficial to semiotics. The best example is that of semioticians forcing their contrived terminology on hot domains of knowledge. *Biosemiotics* (cf. Barbieri, 2007) is such a domain; and many self-delusional attempts have been made to find semiotics in biology, instead of first asking the question of how semiotics might be relevant to advancing biology. The grounding of semiotics in biology will not justify it more than its grounding in sign theory. What counts is that biological processes are defined by representation, consisting of both informational and semiotic processes. This could be important to semioticians, but only after they find out what this means. However, more important than the syntax of life is life itself, a narration that encompasses semiotics and pragmatics. We are all our narration. Its aggregate defines the species in a certain span of time Its deviations in stories (disease, accident, birth and death, etc.) are far more conducive to knowledge than inventories of signs.

27. NARRATION AND STORY

The most intuitive description of the *narrative* is the following: the record of a sequence of events as they succeed in time. The word (from the Latin *narrare*) means to recount. It suggests that a record of succeeding events in time, a time series, describes what individuals or groups accomplish and how. Therefore, each narrative adds up to knowledge, at least in the sense of documenting successful and less successful activities.

The simplest way to organize our own experiences is to take note of how they succeed, one after the other, along the timeline of our own existence. This inspired Gelernter (1991) to generate the *flowing stream*: the sequence of every electronic document—mail, photo, draft, URL, notes, etc.—in the order of their reception (or in the order of their generation). It seems a simple idea, but in fact it was the innovation that changed the naturc of data management in the broadest sense possible.

A record of succeeding experiences allows us to see what these experiences have in common, and what distinguishes them. It is a conduit towards understanding them. The most telling narratives are those we experience naturally: the succession of day and night, of seasons; the succession of plant life, of animal behavior in the environment, of celestial bodies (sun, moon, stars, etc.). The succession of our activities is relevant: some we choose, others are imposed upon us by the nature of our activity.

With the exception of Windelband (1915), almost no one has tried to define the distinction between narrative knowledge, corresponding to a historic record of change (*idiographic*), and scientific knowledge (*nomothetic*), corresponding to our attempts to describe how reality works. (Psychoanalysis tried to hijack the concepts, but the attempt remained unsuccessful.) The idiographic captures patterns of events; the nomothetic focuses on scientific law. Of course, those who accept the religion of determinism would like to transform the uniqueness of experience captured in the narration into laws, thus opening the avenue towards automating whatever we do. To a certain extent, such attempts have succeeded: all tools are an expression of this preoccupation. In our age of digital descriptions and digital machines (which actually are programs), more progress in this direction is made. A concise formulation of the attempt described above is: to transform the art of doing things into the science and technology of performing.

Thesis 1: Narration is a record of change.

Let's take a closer look at narration. For the sake of illustration shown in Box 1: On September 11, 2001, two airplanes flew into the Twin Towers in lower Manhattan and destroyed them. One airplane hit and damaged the Pentagon; a fourth plane crashed southeast of Pittsburgh. Of course, you can consider any other record of successive events. Temporality defines the condition of the narration: something happened after something else.

7:59: American Airlines Flight 11, departs 14 minutes late from Logan International Airport in Boston for Los Angeles International Airport

8:14: Aircraft is hijacked

8:14: United Airlines Flight 175, departs from Logan International Airport in Boston for Los Angeles International Airport.

8:20: American Airlines Flight 77 departs from Washington Dulles International Airport for Los Angeles International Airport.

8:42: United Airlines Flight 93 takes off from Newark International Airport bound for San Francisco International Airport, following a 40-minute delay due to congested runways. 8:42 to 8:46 (approx.): Flight 175 is hijacked.

8:46:30: Flight 11 crashes at roughly 466 mph (790 km/h or 219m/s or 425 knots) into the north face of the North Tower (1 WTC) of the World Trade Center, between floors 93 and 99.

8:50 to 8:54 (approx.): Hijacking begins on Flight 77.

9:03:02: Flight 175 crashes at about 590 mph (950 km/h, 264 m/s or 513 knots) into the south face of the South Tower (2 WTC) of the World Trade Center, between floors 77 and 85.

9:28: Hijackers storm the cockpit on Flight 93 and take over the flight. The entry of the hijackers is overheard by flight controllers at Cleveland.

9:37:46: Flight 77 crashes into the western side of the Pentagon at 530 mph (853 km/h, 237 m/s, or 460 knots) and starts a violent fire.

9:58:59: The South Tower of the World Trade Center collapses 56 minutes after the impact of Flight 175.

10:03:11: United Airlines Flight 93 is crashed by its hijackers and passengers at 583 mph (926 km/h, 272 m/s, or 509 knots), due to fighting in the cockpit 80 miles (129 km) southeast of Pittsburgh in Somerset County, Pennsylvania

5:20:27: The penthouse on top of 7 World Trade Center crumbles apart, only about 6 seconds before the entire building would begin to collapse.

5:20:33: 7 World Trade Center, a 47-story building, collapses.

Consider everything that the events of 9/11 changed. The world after the 9/11 narration is different from the world before September 11, 2001.

The following are interpretations of the narration (Box 2), i.e., stories, and I would refrain from validating or discarding any of them.

Box 1.

7:59 8:14 8:14 8:20 8:42 8:46:30 8:50 9:03:02 9:28 9:37:46 9:58:59 10:03:11 5:20:27 5:20:33

Box 2.

9/10,12:45	9/11, 16:45	9/11, 6:45	9/11, 8:17	9/11, 8:20	9/11, 8:40	9/11, 9:49	9/20-23, 2011

On September 10, at 12:45: Willie Brown, mayor of San Francisco, gets a call from his airport security advising him to be cautious about air travel on September 11.

September 11: Two hours before the first airplane takes off, 2 workers at the instant messaging company ODIGO receive warning messages about the attack to take place.

September 11, 8:17: Passenger Daniel Lewin, from a top secret Israeli anit-terrorist unit is either stabbed or shot to death.

September 11, 8:20: Transponder signal stops transmitting identification for AA flight 14

September 11, 8:40: Nasty and Duff, code names for 2 F-15 pilots from the 102nd Fighter Wing of the Otis Air Force Base National Guard in Falmouth, scramble after UA flight 175.

September 11, 9:49: F16 from Langley AFB reaches Washington to perform Combat Air Patrol. It took them 19 minutes for a flight that should have lasted 7 minutes.

September 20-23, 2001: "Five of the alleged hijackers have emerged, alive, innocent and astonished to see their names and photographs appearing on satellite television. ... The hijackers were using stolen identities, and investigators are studying the possibility that the entire suicide squad consisted of impostors." [quote from *London Times*, 9/20/01, see also BBC]. Yet these same individuals are later officially established as the 9/11 hijackers in the 2004 9/11 Commission Report.

The second timeline is an excerpt. Actually, a great amount of variations is available, in full detail, on the world-wide Web. The reader should take note of the following:

1. The timeframe is extended in order to suggest prior knowledge of the attacks.
2. Unrelated information is added.
3. Data is provided on events (such as the assassination of a passenger) to which nobody had access.
4. It is intimated that actions to avoid or mitigate the situation are delayed.

Of course, all kinds of hypotheses ("The government did it." "The buildings were blown up intentionally." "The secret services engineered the attacks," and much more along this line) made it into the public arena (and continue to engender more stories). In short: The narration (historic record) is interpreted and becomes an open-ended story-generating machine.

Thesis 2: Story is an open-ended process of interpreting narration.

Change characteristic of the living (from conception to birth, maturity, and death), and change of the physical world (mountains change, stones are "polished" by wind and water, oceans undergo cycles of ebb and flow, etc.) can be recorded. Depending upon the resolution (how fine the grain of our distinctions) of our observations, the various narratives of change constitute a body of knowledge on whose basis science advances and technology is produced. In this sense, narrations are data sequences about change over intervals. Given the open-ended nature of reality, the data is always incomplete. Moreover, the data is not associated with meaning. It only reports on changes (at minute 8:46 on 9/11, the Towers were still intact; seconds later, the South Tower is hit), not on the context (terrorism in the contemporary world). The interpretation confers meaning, and puts the events in context.

As interpretations, stories are contextual. In storytelling (memories, memoirs, fictional works, among many kinds of interpretations), data is associated with meaning. Quite often, intentionality takes over: moralizing, alerting to danger, making false statements, debunking false statements, etc. Narrations are intention-free. Stories are driven by goals, that is, by intentions.

Thesis 3: Narrations are representations of change.

Without entering into details, let us take note of the fact that objects $\{o_1, o_2, \ldots\}$, natural or man-made, processes $\{p_1, p_2 \ldots\}$, natural or artificial, attributes $\{a_1, a_2, \ldots\}$ of objects or processes, can be described in many ways. They can be named (labeled, as the terminology of cognitive science suggests), measured, depicted in drawings, photographed, videotaped, filmed, turned into sounds, animations, games, etc. Words can be used (and made up if necessary) to explain what they are. These are all substitutes for something else, i.e., *representations* of the real in its materiality.

The structure of language corresponds to the same perception. It is sequential in the way in which existence itself is sequential. The sequentiality of narration corresponds to an understanding of time as durations between successive states of the narrated change.

Thesis 4: Stories are interpretations of the narration of change.

To interpret a narration means no more or less than the attempt to reconstitute the represented from the representation. Succeeding events and their representation are, of course, not the same. Therefore, the "reconstitution" of reality from the representation is not so simple as remaking an image in a puzzle. A person's picture is a representation; the "remaking" of the person is always partial: memories of how the person behaved, moved around, spoke, are part of the interpretation. Reconstitution of the represented from a time series (a scientific method currently in use) can acknowledge the time sequence, confirming it, or challenging it. Interpretation of a narration can take many paths. One, for instance, is the ever more intrusive data-mining. The sequence associated with patterns of behavior (the store one visits, time of visit, how long the shopping lasts, the number of items on the shopping list, payment modality, etc.) becomes a profile. Data is associated with meaning: to shop at Kmart indicates an economic status different from that of shoppers at high-end boutiques in Manhattan or Hollywood. All kinds of inferences are made from consumer patterns; and new information is dumped on the individual in order to affect changes in behavior. There are, of course, many other profiles that can be derived from the narration representing human behavior.

In contrast to data-mining, stories are interpretations of a different nature. Indeed, the sequence "Queen dies, then King dies" (a simple narration) can easily lead to a story: Queen dies because the King was unfaithful; King dies because Queen poisoned him (or had someone do it), or cursed him. In the story, data is associated with meaning corresponding to the context. Stories often challenge the sequence: first, second, third, etc. are sometimes reshuffled in the story (third becomes first, or second, etc.). Data-mining is data driven; stories are meaning processes.

Through stories, information is associated with meaning (Nadin, 2011) in view of the intentions of the storyteller (or the story-generating machine). The information regarding the falling apple (or the falling of anything: stones, meteorites, individuals, etc.) reveals the meaning of the physical laws, in particular the law of gravity. But it can, as well, associate the narrative to a story different in its condition from the one expressed in the theory of gravity: poetic, dramatic, religious, metaphysical. Kings fall from power, leaves float in the wind (slow falling), the fall of Rome marked the beginning of the "Dark Ages" (whose meaning is disputed by many); people who fall on account of faith lost need help to get up and get on with life; fallen angels come to earth to redeem themselves; and so on. Some are subject to confirmation through experiment; others, being unique, are not. Richard Feynman, recalling the passing away of his first wife, noticed the clock that stopped at the time recorded on his wife's death certificate. The narration prompted the physicist, a self-declared atheist, to produce a scientific story: elimination of mystery, poetry, religion, etc. He knew that he had fixed the clock, and that it might stop if moved. But similar narrations—the clock that stops exactly with the last breath of a dear person, or of some celebrity—populate culture and foster storytelling in many variations.

Thesis 5: The clock of narration and the clock of interpretation are different.

The clock of narration corresponds to the rhythm of events in the physical world (see the timeline of the 9/11 events, above). The clock of interpretation projects into the physical world rhythms characteristic of the change in the living, in particular, rhythms associated with interpretation (all the stories about the same event). When we react to something, the reaction time affects performance. When we imagine things in thc future, we have the convenience of controlling the rhythm of time. Indeed, as events unfold in time, the gravity-based machine that measures the interval corresponding to the movement of celestial bodies—the clock—serves as a reference. This is the meaning of the data delivered by clocks. The living is affected by intervals in the environment of existence; but the living also introduces its own rhythms into reality. Saccadic movements, the foundation of sight, have a rhythm different from the heartbeat and neuronal connections. Birds in flight or the slow fall of leaves are other examples of particular time scales; the heartbeat of animals is extremely varied.

Time characteristic of life is not reducible to intervals. As a matter of fact, there is no proof that time scales uniformly. In other words, time at universe scale, where we refer to phenomena that happened way in the past (even millions of years ago), and time at the nanoscale, where we refer to very fast interactions, might be different in more ways than order of magnitude. The narration of phenomena from the remote past—let's say star explosions—and the narration of current phenomena of extreme dynamics (such as fermentative metabolism, and earthquakes) are different to the extent that they appear to us as associated with different realities (Lara *et al.*, 2009). Being a record of change, each narration is a representation of the dynamics of reality. Each interpretation of a narration is a story: the meaning we associate with the information on record. A faster clock, such as the clock of interpretations, is what it takes to evaluate the possible consequences of the phenomena on record in the narration. In other words, the future itself is nothing but the outcome of a faster clock. As a virtual reality, this future depends on the rate of change expressed by the clock. We refer to possible futures—plural!—because we can build clocks with various speeds: from very slow to extremely fast. Each such clock allows us to investigate the future *not as a probability*, but *as possibilities* (often negating probabilities). This is where innovation takes place. If the information in the narration is continuously subjected to interpretations from the future, facilitated by the faster clock, its meaning becomes *anticipation*. Therefore, a foundation of semiotics that reflects the nature of the living can only be grounded in the anticipatory processes definitory of the living.

28. SEMIOTICS IS ABOUT THE MEANING OF CHANGE

In Section 25, meaning was identified as the outcome of semiotics. In the same section, a semiotics emancipated from the sign and focused on narration was suggested as an alternative. The following will specify the thought. Moreover, the suggestion that semiotics is consubstantial with anticipation, as the definitory characteristic of the living, will be pursued.

At each level of the living, from the monocell to the human being (so far the most elaborate form of the living) we distinguish the sensorial, the cognitive, and the motoric. Knowledge is accumulated with the help of the senses, with the contribution of the brain, or in association with the motoric. Metabolism, reproduction, and self-repair are expressions of the interaction between the individual and the world. The fact that science has focused all it takes to qualify something as "alive" has consequences for our understanding of ourselves and of the environment in which we live.

The descriptive, analytical approach of the past is transcended in the present of synthetic science. All kinds of sensors, mimicking the senses, are designed and fabricated with the aim of facilitating new forms of perception. Neurons are the next to go on line. Since Pitts and McCulloch (1943), they were mathematically described, and more recently embodied in silicon, carbon nanotubes, and other materials. As far as the motoric is concerned, even more daring projects are carried out by those seeking to emulate muscles, joints, and cartilage. There is so much to fix and so much to replace.

In this study, an argument was made along the line of questioning the tendency to boil down all phenomena to the Cartesian reductionist-deterministic understanding of reality (Nadin, 2010). More precisely, we need to make distinctions: synthetic neurons are representations of living neurons. As such, synthetic neurons facilitate knowledge acquisition based on the reduction

Living → Neurons → Deterministic Aspects → Dynamics of Synthetic Neurons

Thus, it is intrinsically ascertained that the dynamics of the living, i.e., the variety of processes through which the living is expressed, is identical, or at least significantly equivalent, to the dynamics of the synthetic; moreover, that this dynamics can be represented by deterministic processes (some non-linear in nature).

Empirical evidence strongly contradicts this viewpoint. A neuron extracted from the whole represented by a living entity is quite different from the neurons in action as the living entity interacts with the world. Within the wholeness of the living entity, neurons are further integrated in the sensorial perception and the motoric. It is a never-ending back-and-forth through which each neuron is continuously "remade." Actually, what we call neurons, or sensors, or muscles are continuously evolving organic entities.

But let us not restrict the discussion to the neuron. Rather, let us examine the more encompassing modeling issue. Robert Rosen's model is adopted in what follows. Regardless of the position we adopt in respect to the synthetic (or artificial), it is not so much an expression of knowledge about what is synthesized as if is an attempt at modeling.

In what Louie (2007) entitled "A Rosen Etymology," a distinction is made between physical science pertaining to entities purely physical in nature (i.e., non-living), and biology, pertaining to organisms. In 2003, Louie presented Robert Rosen's a modelling relation between two systems, shown in Figure 7 (Louie, 2009).

A modeling relation between two systems, such as the natural system N and a formal system F, has F as a model of N if and only if the diagram commutes:

$$c = \delta \circ i \circ e$$

Without going into further details (involving the mathematics appropriate to describing the modeling process), let us take note of the fact that the dynamics of the natural system is represented in the final system. All our operations on the representation reflect our own condition. Change in N takes place along a series of intervals (what is called a "timeline"). Therefore, we need to assure that in the formal system the representations are coherent with the time series of the dynamics of the natural system. One more necessary condition: Changes in natural system ought to be reflected (encoded) in the formal system.

From this simple diagram, once can easily infer that a model is supposed to reflect the wholeness of the natural system represented. A synthetic neuron (sensor, muscle, etc.) does not fulfill the conditions of a modeling relation. In fact, when coupled to the natural, the synthetic changes the condition of the natural. Indeed, a knee replacement (a pretty standard surgical procedure) changes the organism. The hybrid new entity has different characteristics. From a semiotic perspective, the following are the consequences:

1. Modelling is part of the pragmatics of knowledge acquisition.
2. There is no effective procedure for distinguishing between the observed and the observer.

With all these in mind, it is easy to infer that a modeling relation implies semiotics in encoding and decoding between the system N and the formal system F. The nature of representations that make up the formal system depends upon the precise activity through which

Figure 7. Rosen's modelling relation

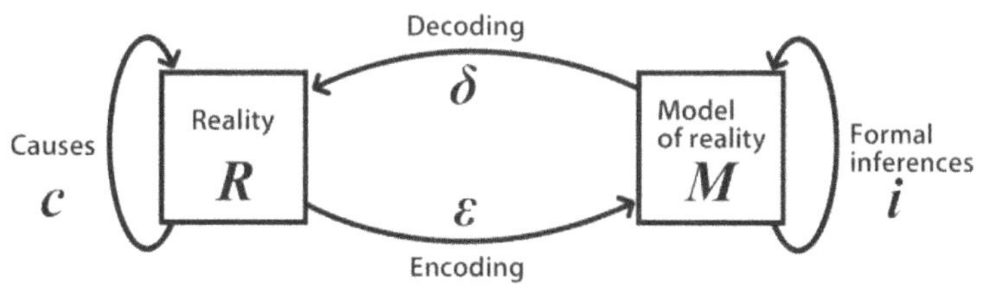

the final system is established. This activity is ultimately determined by the purpose of the representation. Aesthetic modeling (expressed in the formalism of art, literature, design, music, etc.) is definitely of a nature different from that of mathematical and computational modelling. Within each formal system, inferential entailments ars possible. Each results in a different form of knowledge. Indeed, there is knowledge about the world in art, as there is also in physics, chemistry, philosophy, etc. In the final analysis, representation implies interpretation, i.e., the purposeful attempt to derive new knowledge about the represented from operations on the representation.

These preliminaries could be conducive to a new understanding of semiotics only if they set a methodological framework for understanding the possibility of and necessity for the discipline. As with science and every other form of human activity, semiotics is grounded in the awareness of change.

CONCLUSION

The day when scholars and students of semiotics become the hottest commodity in the labor market and are traded like neurosurgeons, high-performance programmers, footballs players, movie stars, or animators, we will all know that semiotics finally made it. Currently, semiotics is of marginal interest, at most, in academia. Nobody hires semioticians. I am convinced that this can change. If semiotics changes But for this change to come about, everyone involved in semiotics will have to think in a different way, to redefine their goals. Semioticians need the patience and dedication necessary for working on foundational aspects, starting with defining the specific domain knowledge and the appropriate methodology. And they need to define a research agenda for semiotics above and beyond the speculative. A semiotics that has narration as its defining subject will be able to approach change much better than a sign-obsessed semiotics.

ACKNOWLEDGMENT

Sometimes we owe it to publishers that we revisit our work, go deeper where we initially only scratched the surface, and refine our arguments. This study is an example of how the publisher stimulated the effort. After many occasions of fighting publishers, I want to express my gratitude for their initiative.

REFERENCES

Al-Akiti, A. (2004). The three properties of prophethood in certain works of Avicenna and al-Ghazali. In J. McGinnis & D.C. Reisman, (Eds.), *Interpreting Avicenna: Science and philosophy in medieval Islam—Proceedings of the 2nd Conference of the Avicenna Study Group* (Islamic philosophy, theology and science: Texts and studies). Aristotle. (350 BCE). *Poetics*. (S. H. Butcher, Trans.). Retrieved March 31, 2011 from http://classics.mit.edu/Aristotle/poetics.html

Arnauld, A., & Nicole, P. (1662). The art of thinking. Port-Royal logic. New York: Bobbs-Merrill. (1964).

Astrobiology, 9(10), 979-987. doi:10.1089/ast.2009.0384.

Augustine. (397). *De doctrina cristiana*, I-III.

Barbieri, M. (Ed.). (2007). *Introduction to biosemiotics: The new biological synthesis*. Heidelberg, Germany: Springer. doi:10.1007/1-4020-4814-9

Baumgarten, A. G. (1750). *Aesthetica*. Frankfurt-an-der-Oder [Kley]. *Impens., I*, C.

Berners-Lee, T. (1998). *Semantic Web roadmap*. Retrieved on March 31, 2011 from http://www.w3.org/DesignIssues/Semantic.html

Cassirer, E. (1923). *Zur Einstein'sche Relativitätstheorie* [Substance and Function and Einstein's Theory of Relativity]. (W. C. Swabey, & M. C. Swabey, Trans.). Chicago: Open Court Publishing Co.

Cassirer, E. (1955). *(1923-1929). Philosophy of symbolic forms* (R. Manheim, Trans.). New Haven, CT: Yale University Press.

Chen, I. A., Roberts, R. W., & Szostak, J. W. (2004). The emergence of competition between model protocells. *Science, 3*(305), 1474–1476. doi:10.1126/science.1100757 PMID:15353806

Eco, U. (1975). Preface. In S. Chapman, U. Eco, & J.-M. Klinkenberg (Eds.), *A semiotic landscape/Panorama sémiotique* (pp. v–vii). The Hague, The Netherlands: Mouton.

Eco, U. (1976). *A theory of semiotics (Advances in Semiotics)*. Bloomington, IN: Indiana University Press.

Gallese, V. (2001). The shared manifold hypothesis. From mirror neurons to empathy. *Journal of Consciousness Studies, 8*(5-7), 33.

Gelernter. (1991). *Mirror worlds: Or: The day software puts the universe in a shoebox...How it will happen and what it will mean.* New York: Oxford University Press.

Gödel, K. (1931). Über formal unentscheidbare Sätze der Principia Mathematica und verwandter Systeme I [On Formally Undecidable Propositions of Principia Mathematica and Related Systems I]. *Monatshefte für Mathematik, 38*, 173–198. doi:10.1007/BF01700692

Goguen, J. (1999). An introduction to algebraic semiotics, with application to user interface design. In C. L. Nehaniv (Ed.), *Computation for metaphors, analogy, and agents* (Vol. 1562, pp. 242–291). Lecture Notes in Computer Science Berlin, Heidelberg, New York: Springer. doi:10.1007/3-540-48834-0_15

Gudwin, R., & Queiroz, J. (2005). Towards an introduction to computational semiotics. In *Proceedings of the 2005 IEEE International Conference on Integration of Knowledge Intensive Multi-Agent Systems* – KIMAS'05, (pp. 393-398).Waltham, MA.

Hjelmslev, L. (1943). *Prolegomena to a theory of language*. Baltimore: Indiana University Publications in Anthropology and Linguistics.

Hobbes, T. (1651). *Leviathan*. London: Andrew Cooke.

Hoffmeyer, J. (Ed.). (2008). *A legacy for living systems. Gregory Bateson as precursor to biosemiotics*. Berlin, Heidelberg, New York: Springer.

Hopkins, J. (1986). *A new, interpretive translation of St. Anselm's Monologion and Proslogion*. Minneapolis, MN: A.J. Banning Press.

Hordijk, W., Hein, J., & Steel, M. (2010). Autocatalytic sets and the origin of life. *Entropy*, *12*(7), 1733–1742. doi:10.3390/e12071733

Jones, P. (2013, March 15). Supplement: Using semiotics to identify patent-eligible software. *Groklaw*. Retrieved April 2, 2013, from http://www.groklaw.net/article.php?story=20130314152416723#topics

Kauffman, S. (2011). *The end of a physics worldview: Heraclitus and the watershed of life*. Paper presented at NECSI & MIT/ESD Seminar. Retrieved November 20, 2011, from http://vimeo.com/30875984

Kauffman, S., & Longo, G. (2011). *No law entails the evolution of the biosphere*. Paper presented at Computational Systems Biology, Tampere University of Technology, Finland. Retrieved November 11, 2011, from http://csb.cs.tut.fi/no_law_entails_the_evolution_of_the_biosphere.php

Koblin, A. (2008-present). Aaron Koblin website: Information. Retrieved on April 1, 2011 from http://www.aaronkoblin.com/info.html

Lambert, J. H. (1764). *Neues Organon oder Gedanken über die Erforschung und Bezeichnung des Wahren und dessen Unterscheidung vom Irrtum und Schein*. Leipzig, Germany: Johann Wendler.

Leibniz, G. W. (1672-1696). *Mathematical, Scientific, and technical correspondence* (6 vol.). Hannover, Germany: Leibniz-Archiv Hannover.

Locke, J. (1690*). Of the division of the sciences: An essay concerning human understanding*. Chapt. XXI. Retrieved from http://www3.nd.edu/~afreddos/courses/439/locke0421.htm

Longo, G., Montévil, M., & Kauffman, S. (2012). No entailing laws, but enablement in the evolution of the biosphere. In T. Soule & J. H. Moore (Eds.), *Genetic and Evolutionary Computation Conference, GECCO '12, Philadelphia, PA, Companion Material Proceedings*, (pp. 1379-1392). New York: ACM.

Longo, L. M., Jihun, L., & Blaber, M. (2013). Simplified protein design biased for prebiotic amino acids yields a foldable, halophilic protein. In *Proceedings of the National Academy of Sciences*, (pp. 2135-2139).

Lotman, J. M. (1990). *Universe of the mind: A semiotic theory of culture* (A. Shukman, Trans.). Bloomington, IN: Indiana University Press.

Louie, A. H. (2007). A Rosen etymology. *Chemistry & Biodiversity*, *4*, 2296–2314. doi:10.1002/cbdv.200790188 PMID:17955478

Louie, A. H. (2009). *More than life itself: A synthetic continuation in relational biology (Categories)*. Frankfurt, Germany: Ontos Verlag. doi:10.1515/9783110321944

Luisi, P. L. (2003). Autopoiesis: A review and a reappraisal. *Naturwissenschaften, 90*, 49–59. PMID:12590297

Mansy, S. S., Schrum, J. P., Krishnamurthy, M., Tobé, S., Treco, D. A., & Szostak, J. W. (2008). Template-directed synthesis of a genetic polymer in a model protocell. *Nature, 454*, 122–125. doi:10.1038/nature07018 PMID:18528332

Marty, R. (1990). *L'Algèbre des Signes: Essai de Sémiotique Scientifique d'après Charles Sanders Peirce (Foundations of Semiotics, 24)*. Amsterdam, The Netherlands: J. Benjamins Publishing Co. doi:10.1075/fos.24

Maurer, S. E., Deamer, D. W., Boncella, J. M., & Monnard, P.-A. (2009). Chemical evolution of amphiphiles: Glycerol monoacyl derivatives stabilize plausible prebiotic membranes.

McClarty, C. (2013). Fermat's last theorem and more can be proved more simply. Retrieved April 2, 2013, from http://www.rdmag.com/news/2013/03/fermat%E2%80%99s-last-theorem-and-more-can-be-proved-more-simply.

McCulloch, W., & Pitts, W. (1943). A logical calculus of the ideas immanent in nervous activity. *The Bulletin of Mathematical Biophysics, 7*, 115–133. doi:10.1007/BF02478259

Mitchell, T. M., Shinkareva, S. V., Carlson, A., Chang, K. M., Malave, V. I., Mason, R. A., & Just, M. A. (2008). Predicting human brain activity associated with the meanings of nouns. *Science, 320*(4), 1191–1195. doi:10.1126/science.1152876 PMID:18511683

Mongré, P. (F. Hausdorff). (1897). Sant' Ilario. Thoughts from Zarathustra's landscape. Leipzig, Germany: C.G. Nauman.

Mumford, L. (1967). *The myth of the machine: Technics and human development*. New York: Harcourt, Brace Iovanovich.

Nadin, M. (1977). Sign and fuzzy automata. *Semiosis, 1*(5), 19–26.

Nadin, M. (1980). The logic of vagueness and the category of synechism. *The Monist, 63*(3). doi:10.5840/monist198063326

Nadin, M. (1983). The logic of vagueness and the category of synechism. In E. Freeman (Ed.), *The relevance of Charles Peirce* (pp. 154–166). La Salle, IL: The Monist.

Nadin, M. (1991). *Mind—Anticipation and chaos (Milestones in research and discovery)*. Stuttgart/Zurich, Switzerland: Belser.

Nadin, M. (2003). *Anticipation – The end is where we start from*. Basel, Switzerland: Lars Müller Verlag.

Nadin, M. (2005). *E-mail exchange with Clarisse Sieckenius de Souza*.

Nadin, M. (2010). Anticipation and the artificial. Aesthetics, ethics and synthetic life. *AI & Society – Computer Science,* (special issue: *Ethics and Aesthetics of Technologies*), 103-118.

Nadin, M. (2011). Information and semiotics processes. The semiotics of computation (review article). *Cybernetics & Human Knowing, 18*(1-2), 153–175.

Namani, T., & Deamer, D. W. (2008). Stability of model membranes in extreme environments. *Origins of Life and Evolution of the Biosphere, 38*(4), 329–341. doi:10.1007/s11084-008-9131-8 PMID:18560991

Nayak, A., Takeo, O., Tsuruoka, T., Terabe, K., Hasegawa, T., Gimzewski, J. K., & Aono, M. (2012). Controlling the synaptic plasticity of a Cu_2S gap-type atomic switch. *Advanced Functional Materials, 22*(17), 3606–3613. doi:10.1002/adfm.201200640

Nessi, M., & Nordberg, M. (September, 2011). *Collaborative effort as an engine for developing strategic capabilities and innovation: Insights from the ATLAS Project at CERN* (Keynote address at the SKM Symposium, Linz).

Newman, M. E. J. (2003). The structure and function of complex networks. *SIAM Review*, *45*, 167–256. doi:10.1137/S003614450342480

Nicolelis, M. A. L., & Shuler, M. (2001). Thalamocortical and corticocortical interactions in the somatosensory system. In M. A.L. Nicolelis (Ed.), Advances in neural population coding (Progress in Brain Research, vol. 130), (pp. 89-110). Amsterdam, The Netherlands: Elsevier Science.

Nietzsche, F. (1975). In G. Colli & Montinari (Eds.), Kritische Gesamtausgabe Briefwechsel. Berlin: Walter de Gruyter.

Paul, H. (1970). *Principles of the History of Language* (H. A. Strong, Trans.). College Park, MD: McGrath Publishing Company. (Original work published 1880)

Peirce, C. S. (1953). *Letters to Lady Welby* (I.C. Lieb, Ed.). New Haven, CT: Whitlock. Plato. (360 BCE). *Cratylus*. (B. Jowett, Trans.). Retrieved on April 10, 2011 from http://classics.mit.edu/Plato/cratylus.html

Piaget, J. (1955). *The child's construction of reality*. London: Routledge and Kegan Paul.

Plato. (360 BCE). *Sophist*. (B. Jowett, Trans.). Retrieved on April 10, 2011 from http://classics.mit.edu/Plato/sophist.html

Pohorille, A., Schweighofer, K., & Wilson, M. A. (2005). The origin and early evolution of membrane channels. *Astrobiology*, *5*(1), 1–17. doi:10.1089/ast.2005.5.1 PMID:15711166

Pollack, J. (2013). *In defense of the liberal arts: Judah Pollack at TEDxWhitehorse*. Retrieved March 28, 2013from http://www.youtube.com/watch?v=OfTCW-IV8tg

Popper, K. R. (1934/1959). *The Logic of Scientific Discovery*. London: Routledge.

Rieger, B. B. (1997). Computational semiotics and fuzzy linguistics. On meaning constitution and soft categories. In A. Meystel (Ed.), *A learning perspective: International Conference on Intelligent Systems and Semiotics (ISAS-97)* (pp. 541-551).Washington, DC: NIST.

Rieger, B. B. (2003). Semiotic cognitive information processing: Learning to understand discourse. A systemic model of meaning constitution. In R. Kühn et al. (Eds.), *Adaptivity and learning. An interdisciplinary debate* (pp. 347–403). Berlin, Heidelberg, New York: Springer. doi:10.1007/978-3-662-05594-6_24

Rosen, R. (1985). Organisms as causality systems which are not machines: An essay on the nature of complexity. In R. Rosen (Ed.), *Rosen: Theoretical biology and complexity* (pp. 165–203). Orlando, New York, London: Academic Press. doi:10.1016/B978-0-12-597280-2.50008-8

Sadowski, P. (2010). *Towards systems semiotics: Some remarks and (hopefully useful) definitions*. Retrieved March 16, 2011 from http://www.semioticon.com/semiotix/2010/03/towards-systems-semiotics-some-remarks-and-hopefully-useful-definitions/

Shannon, C. E., & Weaver, W. (1949). *The mathematical theory of communication*. Urbana, Chicago, London: University of Illinois Press.

Sheldrake, R. (2011). *Dogs that know when their owners are coming home: And other unexplained powers of animals* (2nd ed.). New York: Crown.

Sieckenius de Souza, C. (2005). *The semiotic engineering of human-computer interaction.* Cambridge, MA: MIT Press.

Smalley, R. E. (2001, September). Of chemistry, love and nanobots (Nanofallacies). *Scientific American, 2001*, 76–77. doi:10.1038/scientificamerican0901-76

Solomon, J. (1988). *The signs of our time. Semiotics: The hidden messages of environments, objects, and cultural images.* Los Angeles: Jeremy C. Tarcher.

Stephan, P. (1996). Auf dem Weg zu Computational Semiotics. In D. Dotzler (Ed.), *Computer als Faszination* (p. 209). Frankfurt, Germany: CAF Verlag.

Stephens, G. J., Osborne, L. C., & Bialek, W. (2011). Searching for simplicity in the analysis of neurons and behavior. *Proceedings of the National Academy of Sciences of the United States of America, 107*(32), 14425–14430. doi:10.1073/pnas.1008662107 PMID:21383186

Tanoue, R., Higuchi, R., Enoki, N., Miyasato, Y., Uemura, S., & Kimizuka, N. … Kunitake, M. (2011). Thermodynamically controlled self-assembly of covalent nanoarchitectures in acqueous solution. *ACS Nano*. doi: doi:10.1021/nn200393q PMID:21480643

Thomas, J. A., & Rana, F. R. (2007). The Influence of environmental conditions, lipid composition, and phase behavior on the origin of cell membranes. *Origins of Life and Evolution of the Biosphere, 37*(4), 267–285. doi:10.1007/s11084-007-9065-6 PMID:17361322

Togo, M. B., & Cantelmi, T. (2012). *Technoliquidity*. Retrieved April 4, 2013, from http://www.upi.com/Science_News/Technology/2012/12/15/Technology-has-spawned-new-brain/UPI-71421355602808/

Trubetzkoy, N. S. (1939/1969). *Principles of Phonology* (C. Baltaxe, Trans.). Berkeley, CA: University of California Press.

Tse, P. U. (2013). *The neural basis of free will. Criterial causation.* Cambridge, MA: The MIT Press. doi:10.7551/mitpress/9780262019101.001.0001

von Foerster, H. (1981). *Observing systems.* Seaside, CA: Intersystems Publications.

von Kiedrowski, G., & Patzke, V. (2008). Self-replication and autocatalysis. In S. Rasmussen, M. A. Bedau, L. Chen, D. Deamer, D. C. Krakauer, & P. F. Stadler (Eds.), *Protocells: Bridging nonliving and living matter* (pp. 200–316). Boston: MIT Press.

von Uexküll, J. (2010). *A foray into the worlds of animals and humans* (J. D. O'Niell, Trans.). Minneapolis, London: University of Minneapolis Press. (Original work published 1934)

Wilson, E. O. (1984). *Biophilia: The human bond with other species.* Cambridge, MA: Harvard University Press.

Windelband, W. (1894). *Geschicthte und Naturwissenschaft, Präludien. Aufsätze und Reden zur Philosophie und ihrer Geschichte (History and Natural Science. Speech of the Rector of the University of Straßburg)* (pp. 136–160). Tubingen, Germany: J.C.B. Mohr.

Chapter 6
One Year Forward: The 2013 Update to the E-Readers and E-Books in Public Libraries Survey

James Hutter
Westbury Memorial Public Library, USA

ABSTRACT

With the prevalence of affordable e-Readers in the consumer marketplace and library users increasingly having access to lendable e-Books from their local library institutions, library administrators continue to have difficulty in determining the immediate and long term effect of these technologies on their organizations. This chapter attempts to provide administrators with a brief overview of the current e-Reader and e-Book technology landscape and describe trends and issues. To help Administrators better understand their library users' experiences and expectations with e-Readers and e-Books, the researcher conducted a survey of 70 individuals. This survey is a follow-up to 2012's E-Readers & E-Books in Public Libraries: Measuring Library Patron Expectations research project. Using the same survey questions, format and potential respondent pool, One Year Forward demonstrates that patrons are increasingly demanding access to e-Books and e-Readers. Library patrons are finding these services more easy to use than in the past. Users clearly see value in these services both now and in the future. The results of this research project should be difficult for any library administrator to ignore.

INTRODUCTION

Few technologies have had as profound an impact on public libraries as the adoption of affordable e-Readers and e-Books. Like all disruptive technologies, e-Books and e-Readers have had a mixed reception by public library Administrators and other library professionals. This has been especially true over the last few years while the e-Book and e-Reader marketplace has been in flux. Many see the huge benefits that these technologies offer, such as portability, ease of use and remote access to materials. Others see potential problems,

DOI: 10.4018/978-1-4666-4711-4.ch006

such as increased costs, legal issues pertaining to lending and the possible reduction of physical materials in the library.

One Year Forward is an attempt by the researcher to bring library Administrators up-to-date on the changes in the e-Reader and e-Book landscape. The marketplace for both e-Readers and e-Books has altered incredibly in the months since the *e-Readers & e-Books In Public Libraries* research project was undertaken. Library Administrators should absolutely be aware of these events and how those changes have affected the experiences and expectations of public library users. To help Administrators recognize the needs of their users, a survey is another key component of this report. Over the course of several weeks, 70 individuals were asked about their experience with e-Books and e-Readers. The results of this survey should further cement the notion that library users are increasingly demanding these types of services from their local institutions.

SURVEY OF RELATED LITERATURE

For the last few years, it has been hard to read any library-related publication, journal or trade magazine without seeing mention of the term e-Book or e-Reader. For many professionals in the field, these technologies have seemingly sprung from nowhere and have suddenly plopped themselves into the world of public libraries. In reality, this is far from the truth. E-books have co-existed with both public and academic libraries for quite some time. Public and academic libraries have experimented with the loaning of e-Books to library users for the last decade and have met with varying degrees of success.

The main cause for the newly apparent prevalence of e-Books and e-Readers is the extremely low cost of these technologies. Major manufacturers, such as Sony, Apple, Amazon and Barnes and Noble have been able to lower production costs of their e-Readers and tablets, thus making them affordable and more readably accessible to consumers. Over the last few years, ownership of technology items, such as tablets and e-Readers, has continued to increase rapidly. An often cited Pew Research Center poll that was published in 2012 revealed that the percentage of Adults that owned either of these two items had jumped from 18% to 29% (Buckely, 2013). At this rate, it will not be long before the majority of patrons that use public libraries own either a tablet, e-Reader or both. As such, there will be even more demand for materials that can be used on these devices. Already, some statistics demonstrate that demand for e-Books and other materials, such as downloadable audiobooks is hitting record levels. Public libraries, over the last year, have seen a huge rise in the amount of circulations of their e-Books. Of particular note is that during the 2012 holiday season, transactions were especially high. Some library systems broke single-day circulation records around the Christmas holiday, when most "dramatic growth occurred among users of iPad, Kindle Fire, and Android devices" (Enis, 2013). For 2013, public libraries should expect increased demand for their downloadable services, particularly after consumer devices experience another inevitable price drop.

Many libraries or library consortia have witnessed this increased demand and have tried to accommodate it. However, some changes in the marketplace have caused them to pause and re-assess how much budgetary commitment they can make towards supplying e-Books to their users. Approximately 12 months ago, much anger from public library professionals was directed at major publishers for their adoption of new pricing models for loanable e-Books, for the destruction model of loanable e-Books and also for the reluctance to allow their materials to be lent at all. Some publishers instituted a rule stating that particular books could only circulate a certain number of times before they had to be re-purchased. Just when libraries were getting somewhat comfortable with the systems they implemented to provide e-Books to users, pricing changes instituted by publishers forced libraries to rethink what they would and could offer.

One of the best examples of these pricing changes occurred last year. In 2012, Random House produced shock waves in the world of libraries when it announced that it was going to greatly increase pricing for its lendable e-Books. For example, titles that cost $28 were increased to $84. Another publisher, Hachette, doubled the prices of titles that were on their backlist (Harris, 2013). Much of the reasoning behind this price jump has to do with the longevity of digital titles. Publishers are still worried that libraries will be spending less to replace "worn out" or physically damaged titles, since digital titles cannot degrade from usage. With the advent of e-Books, many library Administrators thought that the digital format and lack of manufacturing cost would greatly lower the cost of e-Books. Instead, exactly the opposite has occurred.

The ongoing e-Book pricing issues that currently surround public libraries can be summed up excellently by Jamie LaRue. Libraries are always going to be trying to buy the content that their patrons desire. As long as content is being created by authors, pushed by publishers and wanted by patrons, public libraries will be attempting to secure that material. The chief problem is that many libraries are facing declining budgets. Publishers continue to increase the number of formats that materials are available in, such as hard cover, paperback, large print, audio book and now e-Book. While e-Books are increasing in popularity, publishers have chosen to greatly inflate the cost of a typical e-Book that is available for lending to libraries. Libraries can't "keep pouring more money into an ever smaller number of titles in an ever greater variety of containers" (LaRue, 2012). At some point, it is inevitable that libraries will have to select one format to focus on and pour their budgetary resources into supporting it. The day when libraries will have to decide whether or not to focus a large portion of their acquisitions budget on e-Books is approaching extremely rapidly.

There have been many developments in the complex relationship between public libraries, e-Book publishers and e-Reader manufacturers in the last 12-18 months. While many in the field term this relationship as experiencing "friction," others have been less charitable in their descriptions of the current situation. As with the introduction of any new technologies, libraries and content creators have struggled over pricing models that protect both of their interests. The "friction" that currently exists in the world of public libraries today seems to be a product of that delicate balancing act.

With the issue of pricing, availability and ownership legality coming to a head, it was becoming more clear that only one organization could step in and attempt to start a constructive dialogue between publishers and public libraries. Last year, the American Library Association (ALA) made attempts to reach out to the largest publishers and find some middle ground between both parties. Recognizing that there was still much confusion in the marketplace regarding e-Books, ALA President Maureen Sullivan met with the Association of American Publishers. "Publishers, libraries, and other entities have worked together for centuries. Given the obvious value of libraries to publishers, it simply does not add up that any publisher would continue to lock out libraries," were the thoughts offered by Maureen Sullivan on the current situation

(ALA, 2012). Her meetings were described as being frank and it appears they did generate some good will between the parties involved.

ALA knows that now is the critical time to be discussing these issues. While reporting on the outcome of the meeting between ALA and the Association of American Publishers, Maureen Sullivan noted that 76% of public libraries now offer e-Books. That percentage is double the reported percentage from five years ago. Additionally, Sullivan noted that 39% of libraries currently circulate e-Readers (ALA, 2012). It is apparent that the only way to remove this friction between publishers and libraries was for libraries to reach out to publishers and ask them to lay out their concerns regarding e-Books and e-Book lending in public libraries. Luckily, it seems that having a dialogue has lessened some of publisher concerns and has demonstrated a good faith effort by libraries to respect publisher and author interests.

Last year also saw another notable event take place in regards to publishers and their views on public library e-Book downloading services. When one major publisher, Penguin, dropped support for the download service OverDrive, many in the library field felt that this was a hugely significant turn of events and a possible sign that other publishers may follow suit. However, librarians may have reacted too quickly or had miscalculated Penguin's intentions. In June of 2012, Penguin decided to partner with 3M and launch a pilot project involving the New York Public Library and Brooklyn Public Library. Penguin felt comfortable working with an established library vendor and was then willing to make their titles available on a downloading platform. Bringing a publisher "back into the fold" was certainly a big public relations coup for 3M, who have been working to establish their Cloud Library platform (Enis, 2012b). Again, this may be a sign that publishers feel that their needs are not being properly met by download service vendors. If vendors, such as 3M, can make assurances about pricing and protections against piracy of e-Books, then publishers may be more willing to take part in these services.

At the start of 2013, libraries were finally starting to see tensions ease between themselves and publishers. In January, Macmillan was the latest publisher to wade into the realm of lendable e-Books. They decided to work with OverDrive, Axis 360 and 3M. The pricing model that they decided to implement was to have titles cost $25 each and, once purchased, "each title will be available for two years, or 52 circulations, whichever comes first" (Macmillan announces library lending pilot, 2013). Particularly worth noting was CEO John Sargent's feeling that "'we do not expect it will heavily impact our retail sales over time'" (Macmillan announces library lending pilot, 2013). This is one of the few instances of a publisher CEO coming forward and stating the lending model can co-exist with the retail model of e-Books. This was a comforting development for libraries and the positive attitudes displayed by the CEO of Macmillan will likely impact the attitudes of other publishing houses.

One of the most prominent complaints about the current crop of downloading services that are available to public libraries is that they are too difficult for the lay person to use. Reports of patrons being frustrated with these services is common and many potential users may decline to use these downloading services if they run into technical difficulties. Responding to criticisms about the "ease of use" for its e-Book downloading service, companies such as 3M have strived to make the downloading experience much easier for library users. In the Baltimore County Public Library, 3M worked to integrate their downloading service into the library's catalog system. Merging the physical collection with the digital collection in the online catalog made it easier for patrons to find the titles they desire. 3M is working to make sure that "this application programming interface (API) suite has the ability to meld with other ILS platforms," which should be promising news for library systems throughout the country (Enis, 2013). Anything that will streamline the user's downloading experience is greatly welcomed by libraries.

Recently, new downloading services have entered the market, with the effects of increasing competition and keeping costs down. In June of 2012, a new competitor entered the e-Book download service market, Bibliotheca. The major selling points being promoted by Bibliotheca included an open source model for the actual aggregation service and a focus on the ease-of-use aspect for library users. Of particular note about Bibliotheca's entry into the lendable e-Book market is the fact that they made publishers and their needs a primary focus. As a way of diffusing tension and animosity in the marketplace, Bibliotheca felt that a new approach was needed and that listening to publisher's needs and concerns could benefit libraries in the long run. According to the head of content and publisher relations for Bibliotheca, Jordana Vincent, "'Publishers are happy to have Bibliotheca ask them what they want. They appreciate the opportunity to give their opinion and not be told how their books will be sold and delivered'" (Polanka, 2012). It is this approach that may lead to an eventual reconciliation between public libraries and publishers. Bibliotheca has also implemented a technology developed by the Douglas County Libraries download service to give some incentive to publishers to sell e-Books to public libraries. Bibliotheca will add a "buy now" link in the aggregator so that library users can choose to purchase a title that may be currently checked out or unavailable (Polanka, 2012a).

One of the most interesting approaches that public libraries have undertaken in 2012 to provide lendable e-Books was to create their own downloading system for their users. One library system, Harris County Public Library (HCPL), decided to launch their own content server that would host e-Books that the library system had purchased from self-published authors. The library system implemented an Adobe Content Server and modeled their distribution system on the one pioneered by Colorado's Douglas County Libraries (DCL). In this instance, the HCPL has decided to offer this service alongside their current OverDrive offerings. This "homebrew" system gives them far greater control over ownership of the e-Book collection. It also allows much room for growth in the future. It is not without difficulties, though. The roll-out had posed challenges to the library system's IT staff. HCPL had also experienced difficulty in the acquisitions aspect of this project. Staff had to reach out to small publishers and individual authors in order to properly negotiate contract terms for the purchasing and lending of e-Book titles (Enis, 2012a).

As with each passing year, 2012 showed continued growth in the trend of public libraries purchasing and loaning e-Readers to their users. Public libraries had started purchasing and circulating e-Readers for a variety of reasons. Devices such as the Barnes and Noble Nook Simple Touch, Nook HD or an Amazon Kindle Fire HD were being acquired by public libraries for training purposes. These devices were given to staff so that they could become familiar with the devices and be able to assist patrons that needed help properly using them. Many of these devices were compatible with popular downloading services, so it made sense for the staff to become acquainted with them, should library users need help borrowing e-Book titles.

The use of loanable e-Readers pre-loaded with popular titles continues to grow as well. Libraries are purchasing a major consumer brand of e-Reader, such as the Barnes and Noble Nook or Amazon Kindle, loading it with titles that their users have requested, and then circulating them. There are two different methods being utilized in this form of lending. In some instances, libraries are using their own download services to put titles onto these devices. This is a special, catered form of lending. Patrons may request certain titles be loaded on these devices beforehand and then, once ready, the e-Readers are loaned out to that user.

Another method of lending is based around the practice of a library purchasing popular copies of an e-Book title from a vendor, such as Barnes & Noble or Amazon, and then loaning out the device. The use of a download service, like OverDrive, is not incorporated in this process. This form of lending is becoming increasingly popular. However, there are still some outstanding issues with this form of lending that remain somewhat unresolved in 2013. In terms of the legality of lending copyrighted materials on these devices to patrons, many library professionals are recommending that public libraries proceed with caution when implementing these lending services. As of right now, it seems that "online bookstores are aware that libraries are lending out devices loaded with content, but they do not have official statements on library lending programs" (Polanka, 2012b). It is also being recommended that libraries talk to their legal counsel before implementing a lending program that depends upon purchasing titles from online e-Book sellers and utilizing loanable e-Readers.

A legal development that recently took place, one which all libraries should be cognizant of, is the legal ruling that e-Readers which are lent to patrons must be accessible by users who are blind. This recent legal requirement occurred in August of 2012 and originated in a lawsuit against the Sacramento California Library Authority. This library consortium had been one of the first to loan pre-loaded e-Readers to their users. A lawsuit against the library consortium eventually resulted in a settlement between that library system and the United States Justice Department. Under that settlement, the Sacramento California Library Authority agreed to stop purchasing non-accessible e-Readers and would purchase 18 e-Readers that would support text-to-speech interpretation of e-Book titles (Polanka, 2012). Currently, only Apple iOS devices, such as the iPad, seem to have full text-to-speech support. The Amazon Kindle HD only has limited text-to-speech support (Amazon, 2013). The Barnes and Noble Nook HD has text-to-speech support, though it appears that the software that provides this functionality is still in BETA status (Hoffelder, 2012).

The recent legal issues surrounding accessibility rules will also cause publishers to change some of their practices. In the past, some publishers have actively disabled the text-to-speech capability for e-Books that they have released. One example of this is Lawrence Lessig's Creative Commons licensed e-Book. In the future, publishers will, most likely, try to ensure that e-Books support this functionality to minimize legal liability (Yelton, 2012). For the time being, it seems that public libraries are being cautious about the devices they are purchasing for lending. They want to make sure that the devices and e-Books that they do decide to purchase will offer full text-to-speech compatibility, thus ensuring they are in full legal compliance with the recent U.S. Justice Department ruling.

THE 2013 RESEARCH INSTRUMENT

While a review of literature detailing the current conditions of the e-Book and e-Reader landscape is helpful for library Administrators, getting actual feedback from library users can be even more valuable. In 2012, the *e-Readers & e-Books In Public Libraries: Measuring Library Patron Expectations* research project incorporated use of a survey to poll library users and determine their feelings and expectations in regards to e-Books and e-Readers. The research instrument in 2012 was created with simplicity and brevity in mind. Questions asked of library users were broken into two groupings. The first section asked if patrons had borrowed an e-Reader or e-Book from their library, asked about ease-of-use and for reasons why they may not have borrowed one. The second section of the research instrument asked patrons, through use of a Likert Scale, to detail the value that they placed upon e-Books and e-Readers. It also asked them to determine the value that libraries and library Administrators should place upon e-Books and e-Readers.

For the purposes of the 2013 survey, the researcher made every effort to keep all research conditions as similar as possible. When creating the 2013 survey, no modifications were made to the language, descriptions, layout or configuration of the survey. When launching the 2013 survey, the researcher made sure to target the same populations of users. The researcher dispatched the survey URL link to the same e-mail announcement list as in 2012. The researcher also secured permission to set up a link to the 2013 survey in the same medium-sized public library computer lab as 2012. These steps were taken to ensure that direct comparisons between the 2012 and 2013 survey results could be made with a high degree of confidence.

Presented in Table 1 is a portion of the questions in the survey.

LAST YEAR'S SURVEY RESULTS: A BRIEF RECAP

In 2012's *E-Readers and E-Books in Public Libraries* survey (Hutter, 2012), library user sentiments and experiences with these technologies were made quite clear. Having utilized a popular library-oriented e-mail announcement list to share a link to 2012's survey and prominently displaying that same link on the starting page of a medium-sized public library's computer lab, results were gathered from a pool of approximately 85 respondents.

In 2012, *77% of survey participants had yet to borrow an e-Reader*, such as a Barnes and Noble Nook or Amazon Kindle, from their local public library. Notably, of those respondents, *57.4% had made it clear that they would be interested in borrowing an e-Reader from their local library if they had the opportunity to do so*. A portion of the respondents at that time had no desire to borrow an e-Reader from the local library. The survey results had gathered two main reasons why this was the case. Many library users already owned an e-Reader device for personal use, so there was no reason for them to borrow a device from the library. A smaller portion of users had personally preferred the tactile feel of a physical book in their hands and had no desire to utilize an e-Reader.

Of users that had borrowed an e-Reader device from the library, *a staggering 94.4% had found that device easy to use*. This confirmed the notion that consumer-grade e-Readers had become easy enough for most library users and those users experienced minimal frustration with those devices. To library Administrators, this should have been a clear indication

Table 1. Survey questions

1. Have you ever borrowed an e-Reader (such as a Nook or Kindle) from a public library?				
Yes No				
a. If not, would you consider borrowing an e-Reader from a public library?				
Yes No				
b. If no, please state why:				
c. If yes, did you find the device easy to use?				
Yes No				
2. Have you ever borrowed an e-Book (from a service such as OverDrive) from a public library?				
Yes No				
a. If not, would you consider borrowing an e-Book from a public library?				
Yes No				
b. If no, please state why:				
c. If yes, did you find the borrowing service easy to use?				
Yes No				
3. Overall, what value do you personally place upon e-Readers?				
Lowest Value				Highest Value
1	2	3	4	5
4. Overall, how much focus should your public library place upon e-Reader services in the future?				
Lowest Value				Highest Value
1	2	3	4	5
5. Overall, what value do you personally place upon e-Books?				
Lowest Value				Highest Value
1	2	3	4	5

that e-Reader manufacturers had engineered e-Readers that were no longer bulky or complicated to use. Library users were confidently reporting that they were indeed comfortable with major brand e-Readers.

Moving on to the subject of borrowing e-Books from public libraries, respondents were also rather clear about their experiences and preferences. Library users were discovering that their local libraries were lending e-Books for use. In the pool of survey participants, *60% had reported borrowing an e-Book from their public library*. Of the portion of users that had never borrowed an e-Book before, *87.1% stated that they would certainly borrow an e-Book from their local library if they had the chance to do so*. With only 4 respondents, it was not conclusively clear why certain library users would avoid borrowing an e-Book from their local library. The responses offered indicated that these particular users either did not own a required device or preferred to have a physical book for reading.

The 2012 survey provided some enlightenment into the area of e-Book borrowing services and the perceived difficulties that users were facing when using download services such as OverDrive. In the original survey, *72.3% of users indicated that they found borrowing services such as OverDrive easy to use*. A significant portion of users, *27.7%, still had difficulty*, yet this number was lower than what the researcher had expected.

The second major section of the 2012 survey presented participants with a Likert Scale that asked them to place value upon different aspects of e-Readers, e-Books and their relationship to library users and libraries themselves. The Likert Scale was the same format for every question. The scale consisted of 5 rankings, starting with 1, which represented least value, and 5, which represented highest value.

Last year, survey participants were asked "Overall, what value do you personally place upon e-Readers?" and the response was rather clear. For this question, the Likert Scale values of 3, 4 and 5 had the most responses, approximately 19 to 22 responses for each. Of the total pool of participants that took part in that question, *only 19.5% gave a value of less than 3* for their response. *Values of 3 or higher represented 80.6% of the scoring*. It was clear that individuals personally placed a high value upon e-Readers as a technology.

Scoring was similar for other questions posed to participants using the Likert Scale. When asked "how much focus should your public library place upon e-Reader services in the future," (Figure 1) respondents made it adequately clear that they saw e-Reader technology as being an important focus for libraries in the future. *On the Likert Scale, 93.6% of respondents scored this question*

Figure 1. 2012 survey result showing value library users believe libraries should place upon e-Reader services in the future

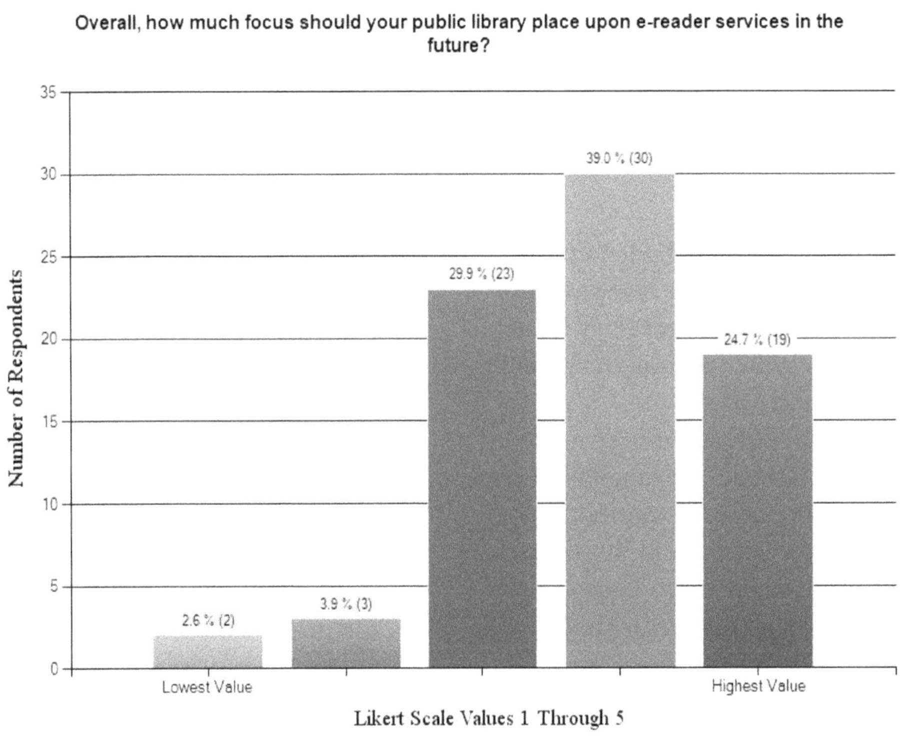

with a value of 3 or higher. Just a mere 6.4% of respondents felt that e-Reader services should be a minor concern of libraries.

When asked, "Overall, what value do you personally place upon e-Books," (Figure 2) 80.8% of respondents chose the values of either 3, 4 or 5. *The highest value, 5, was chosen by 31.5% of the respondents.* Participants in this survey felt that e-Books were vitally important to them and it was this response that should have been of particular note to library Administrators.

The 2012 survey was rather clear in its findings. Public library users were well aware of the introduction of both e-Books and e-Readers into the consumer marketplace. They were familiar with the e-Book format and thought it was highly important to both themselves and public libraries. For those users that did not have e-Readers, they wished their libraries would offer them to borrow. It seemed only a minority of users preferred usage of physical books over that of an e-Book. Users that owned e-Readers had been able to utilize downloading services to borrow books and they had not found these services difficult to use. This sentiment ran counter to what many professionals in the library field had personally believed. Overall, the findings were quite revealing.

THE 2013 SURVEY RESULTS: REPORT AND ANALYSIS

The 2013 survey was open to participants for several weeks and garnered 70 responses from individuals. While some of the results were consistent with findings from the previous year, some areas showed significant differences. When asked if patrons "had ever borrowed an e-Reader (such as a Nook or Kindle)

Figure 2. 2012 survey result showing value library users personally place upon e-books

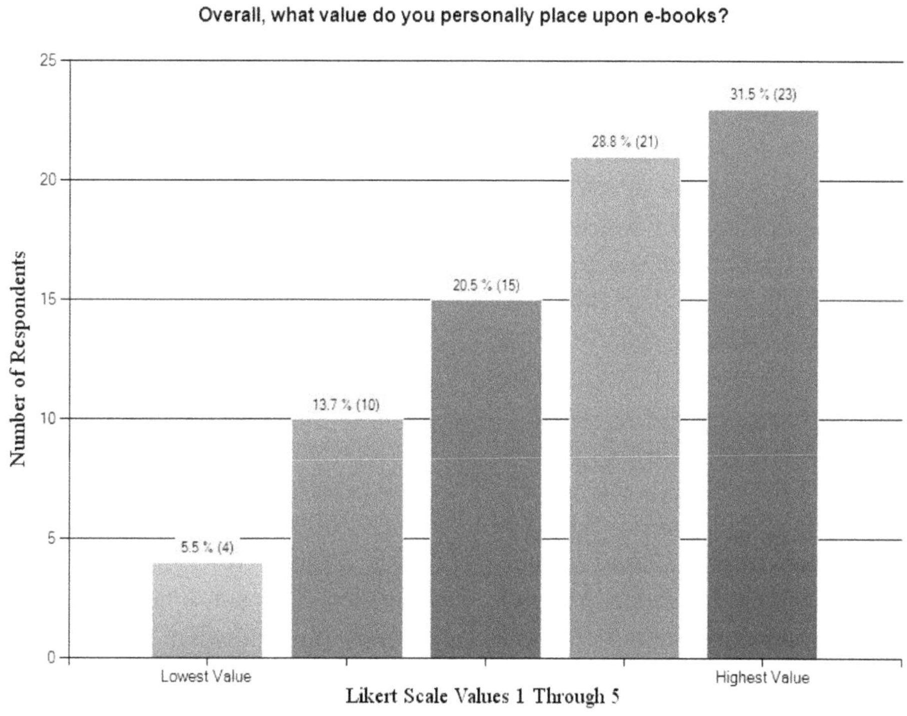

from a public library," *66.7% of respondents indicated that they had not*. This result is down from the 77% of respondents that had indicated that they had not borrowed devices in 2012. This *drop of over 10%* indicates that either more users now have access to lendable e-Readers or that libraries have done more to advertise these services to their users.

Users that had not borrowed an e-Reader from their public library were asked if they would consider doing so. Here, the response from participants indicated that *65.1% of them would borrow an e-Reader from their public library*. This is a significant jump from the 57.4% of individuals that indicated interest in borrowing an e-Reader in 2012. Of the users who stated that they were not interested in borrowing an e-Reader, their reasons for doing so were very similar to the responses received in 2012. Of the 14 users that provided reasons for not borrowing an e-Reader, the responses collected mostly stated that users already owned a device and had no need to borrow one. Four of the responses stated that they had no interest in using an e-Reader device and that they preferred use of a physical book.

Library patrons that had borrowed an e-Reader from their library were asked if they found the device easy to use. Here, astonishingly, the 22 total respondents all indicated that they found the device easy to use. *This was a 100% survey result.* This was up from the 94.4% result that occurred in the 2012 survey. It is clear that users are reporting that they are having almost no difficulty in using these devices.

Moving on to questions about e-Book borrowing in libraries, the results were equally informative. When asked if patrons had ever borrowed an e-Book from a public library, *65.6% of the respondents indicated that they had*. This result was an increase from the 60% reported in 2012. For patrons that had not borrowed an e-Book from a public library, *85% of the respondents indicated that they would consider doing so*. This result was down slightly from the 87.1% that indicated they would consider borrowing an e-Book in 2012. Only four respondents provided reasons why they would not consider borrowing an e-Book. The reasons listed included not owning an e-Reader or preferring to have a physical book, similar to the reasons listed in 2012.

Ease-of-use was measured in the next survey question. Patrons who had borrowed e-Books from their libraries were asked if they found the borrowing service easy to use. Of the respondents, *73.2% found the download service to be easy*. This result is remarkably close to the 72.3% result found in the 2012 survey.

The second section of the survey consisted of a Likert Scale scoring system for survey participants to convey their feelings and expectations about e-Books and e-Readers in public libraries. Scores ranged from 1 to 5, with a score of 1 representing "Lowest Value" and a score of 5 representing "Highest Value."

When asked "Overall, what value do you personally place upon e-Readers," (Figure 3) the highest amount of respondents, 20, gave a score of 5. *Exactly 80% of the respondents scored this question as a 3 or higher*. The 20% that scored this question with a score of less than 3 provided a result that was nearly identical to the 19.5% that also scored it less than 3 in 2012.

Respondents were then asked to place value upon the question of "how much focus should your public library place upon e-Reader services in the future?" (Figure 4). *This resulted in the highest number of respondents, 37.3% of them, answering with a value of 5*. Exactly zero respondents scored this question with a 1. The total percentage that scored this question with a value of 3 or higher represented 86.4% of the respondents. Compared with last year's 6.4% of respondents

Figure 3. 2013 survey result showing value library users place upon e-readers

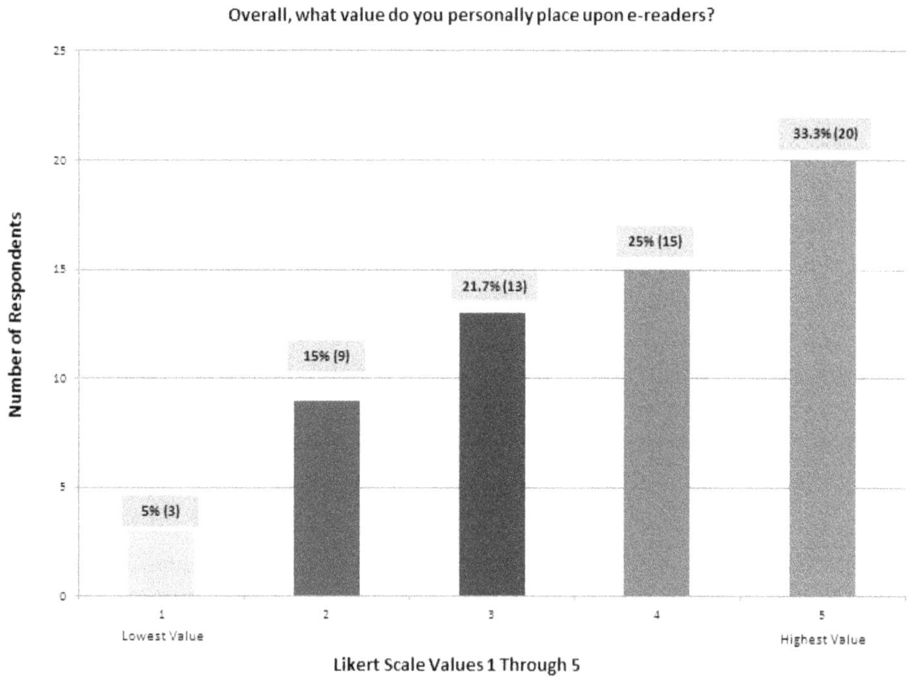

Figure 4. 2013 survey result showing value library users feel libraries should place upon e-readers services in the future

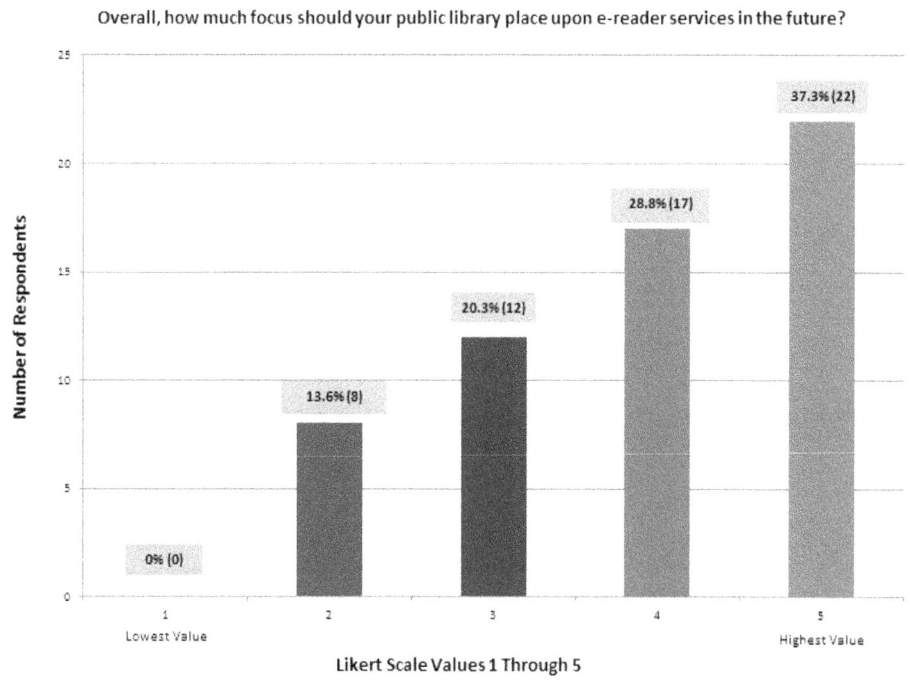

that scored this question with less than 3, the 2013 result actually saw the number grow to 13.6% of respondents, which is worth noting. One possibility for this change in percentage could be due to more users having their own personal e-Reader devices.

Next, Likert Scale questions focused on respondents' feelings about e-Books. When asked the question, "What value do you personally place upon e-Books," (Figure 5) *85.7% of participants chose a score of 3 or higher.* Only 14.3% of respondents scored this question with a value lower than 3. Last year, 80.8% of participants scored this question with a value of 3 or higher, so it would appear that patrons personally value e-Books more than they did last year.

When patrons were asked "How much focus should your library place upon e-Book services in the future," (Figure 6) participants overwhelmingly chose high values. The values of 4 and 5 were tied with 21 votes each, representing a 37.5% score for both of those values. *In total, 91.1% of the participants scored this question with a value of 3 or higher.*

CONCLUSION

While there are still many unanswered questions for library Administrators about how their relationship with e-Books, e-Readers and publishers may change over the coming months, one thing is certainly clear. Library users want to borrow both e-Books and e-Readers from their public libraries. Library users see e-Books and e-Readers as being important technologies and want to see libraries continue to focus on those technologies in the future. When comparing the results of this year's *e-Readers & e-Books In Public Libraries* survey to last year's, it is apparent that even more library users have borrowed

Figure 5. 2013 survey result showing value library users place upon e-books

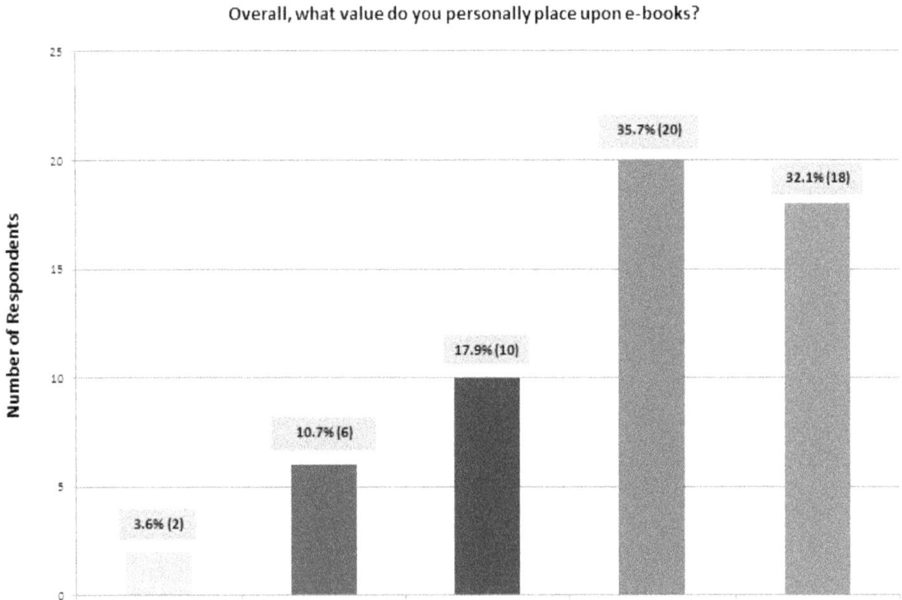

Figure 6. 2013 survey result showing value library users feel libraries should place upon e-book services in the future

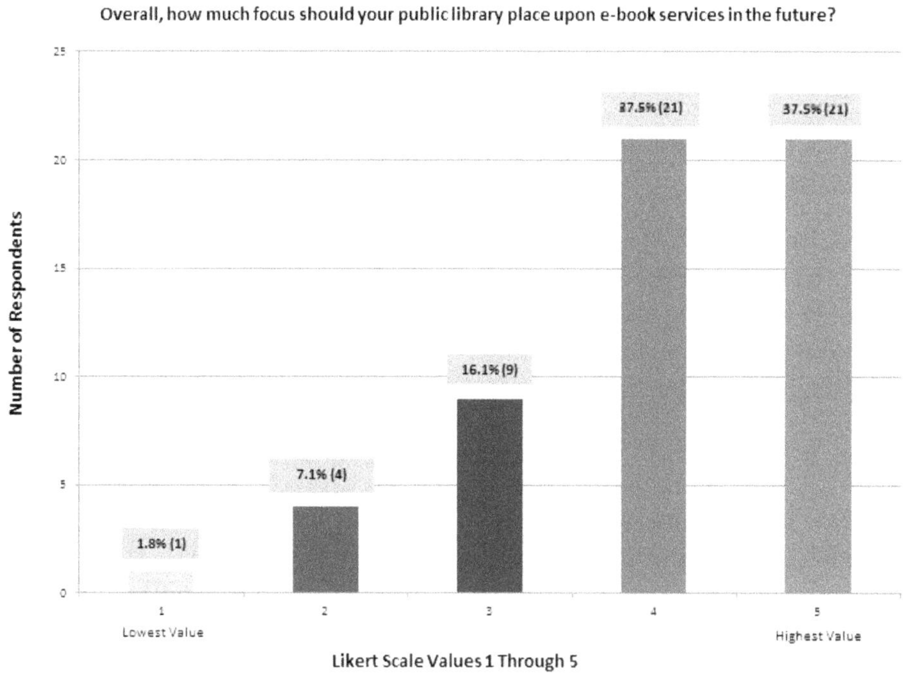

e-Books and e-Readers from their local libraries. When library users have had to use either e-Readers or e-Book downloading services, they found them easy to use. Once again, this seems to dispel the notion that these services are clumsy or difficult. Like last year, users who have not borrowed an e-Reader from their local library cite the fact that they already own one as their main reason. A small amount of users still prefer the feel of a physical book. For 2013 and even 2014, Administrators must strive to meet the needs of their library users. Hopefully, the *e-Readers & e-Books in Public Libraries* research project will help them to decide where they should direct their focus.

REFERENCES

ALA. (2012). Publishers talk ebooks. *American Libraries*, *43*(11-12), 10.

Amazon. (2013). Reading on Kindle Fire HD 7". Retrieved from http://www.amazon.com/gp/help/customer/display.html?nodeId=201009460

Buckley, M. J., & Johnson, M. M. (2013). The why's and how's of integrating academic ebooks: Since ebooks are getting used, it makes sense to ensure that the library provides a full range of functionality to give library users as many options as possible. *Computers in Libraries*, *33*(1), 9.

Enis, M. (2012a). Harris County PL to test DCL ebook model. *Library Journal*, *137*(16), 16.

Enis, M. (2012b). 3M makes its presence felt: An ebook platform with easy setup, use, and ILS integration. *Library Journal*, *137*(17), 42.

Enis, M. (2013). Overdrive, 3M debut ebook developments. *Library Journal*, *138*(2), 16.

Harris, C. (2013). Ebooks 2013: New leasing models, cheaper devices, more content. *School Library Journal*, *59*(1), 16.

Hoffelder, N. (2012, November 17). Did you know the new Nook HD has text-to-speech? Retrieved from http://www.the-digital-reader.com/2012/11/17/did-you-know-the-new-nook-hd-has-text-to-speech

Hutter, J. (2012). E-Readers & E-Books in public libraries: Measuring library patron expectations. *International Journal of Digital Library Systems*, *3*(2), 48–59. doi:10.4018/jdls.2012040105

LaRue, J. (2012). All hat, no cattle: A call for libraries to transform before it's too late. *Library Journal*, *137*(13), 32.

Macmillan announces library lending pilot. (2013). *Library Journal, 138*(4), 12.

Polanka, S. (2012a). Bibliotheca spices up the library ebook market. *Online*, *36*(5), 54.

Polanka, S. (2012b). Lending e-Readers: Legal? Ethical? Practical? *Online*, *36*(6), 54.

Yelton, A. (2012). The ethics of ebooks: A founding member of Unglue.it ponders the soul of librarianship. *Library Journal*, *137*(15), 30.

Chapter 7
Open Source vs. Proprietary Collaborative Virtual Learning Environments

Apostolos Mavridis
Aristotle University of Thessaloniki, Greece

Andreas Konstantinidis
Centre for Technology-Enhanced Learning, King's College London, England

Thrasyvoulos Tsiatsos
Aristotle University of Thessaloniki, Greece

ABSTRACT

This chapter is an evaluation of the efficiency of 3D Collaborative Virtual Learning Environments to facilitate the implementation of collaborative learning activities. Firstly, there is a presentation of the state of the art regarding open source as well as proprietary platforms. Afterwards, the use of a case study reveals issues concerning the suitability of open source Collaborative Virtual Learning Environments, rationalizing the choice of executing a collaborative learning scenario in Second Life. The specific scenario is then presented culminating in evaluation results related to the appropriateness of Second Life with regards to its technical and pedagogical affordances. Finally, students' suggestions and reactions towards such a novel didactical approach are discussed.

INTRODUCTION

Educational research (e.g., Vygotsky, 1962) has led to several theories, such as those of constructivism and social learning. Vygotsky, who is the main supporter of social learning theories, states in the basic principles of his theory that "learning and developing is a social, collaborative activity."

Collaborative Learning is rooted in Vygotsky's views regarding the social side of learning and as a general term is used for the

DOI: 10.4018/978-1-4666-4711-4.ch007

description of educational practices based on the simultaneous cognitive and mental effort of multiple students or/and educators. Students share a common goal, depend on each other and they are mutually responsible for their success or failure.

Several studies (i.e., Dillenbourg, Baker, Blaye, & O'Malley, 1996; Bruckman & Hudson, 2001; Karantzas et al., 2013), have proven that collaborative learning is more effective in specific educational situations in comparison to other teaching methods (e.g., competitive or personalized learning). In particular, it seems collaborative activities centered on a cognitive goal and guided and supported by experts, result in the more meaningful and efficient acquisition of knowledge.

Collaborative efforts among students result in a higher degree of accomplishment by all participants as opposed to individual, competitive systems in which many students are left behind (Slavin & Tanner, 1979). Through collaborative learning, students can be stimulated to negotiate information such as abstract, ill-defined and not easily accessible knowledge and open-ended problems. According to Gokhale (1995) collaborative learning is a beneficial method for the enhancement of critical thinking and improvement of problem solving skills. Also, collaboration enables the discussion of complex problems from different perspectives and supports learners in the elaboration, explanation and evaluation of information in order to re- and co-construct new knowledge or to solve problems (Veerman & Veldhuis-Diermanse, 2001).

The application of collaborative learning is usually hampered by the lack of motivation and engagement of learners which can be attributed to the absence of interactivity and challenge. Failing to stimulate learners, makes the collaborative experience unattractive and discourages progress. To counter this issue our main purpose is to exploit the advantages of Collaborative Virtual Environments (CVEs).

A CVE is a 2D or 3D space where students can communicate and interact with others, with agents, or with virtual objects. The purpose for students is to acquire knowledge through the sharing of ideas in the context of achieving a common goal. The architecture of CVEs is usually based on distributed and interconnected computer systems. Access to CVEs is by no means limited to desktop devices (Churchill, Snowdon, & Munro, 2001), but might well include mobile or wearable devices (Reitmayr & Schmalstieg, 2001), public kiosks, etc.

Studying the problems in the application of collaborative learning in conjunction with its pedagogical benefits, we can surmise that the most important factor in designing a CVE is the catering for immersion. Immersion happens through four processes of engagement: interest, involvement, imagination and interaction (Burbules, 2004). For the digital generation, these four aspects are to some extent shaped by their engagement with technology and the media. Therefore, educators seeking to create interesting and enjoyable learning conditions in order to attract and retain student attention will have to learn from what makes those environments so appealing to contemporary students.

Compared to tools supporting traditional teaching methods, CVEs have many advantages (Bruckman & Hudson, 2001; Dalgarno & Lee, 2010). In addition to supporting real time distance learning, advantages can vary from student motivation and amusement to the simplification of the development of cognitive models from complicated or abstract material. CVEs let users experience environments, which, for reasons of time, distance, scale, and safety, would not otherwise be available, especially to those with disabilities (Muller

& Koubek, 2002; Moore, Cheng, McGrath, & Powell, 2005).

In addition, CVEs could be useful for supporting Complex Learning approaches. According to Guglielman and Vettraino (2007), "Complex learning represents the hybridization of environments, languages and interaction in a learning community composed of the whole world wide web" (p. 1). The contribution of a CVE to this hybridization is the support of distance learning and collaboration services along with traditional lectures in a class of students.

This paper focuses on a specific category of CVEs that aims to support Collaborative Learning. We call these environments Collaborative Virtual Learning Environments (CVLEs). According to Bouras and Tsiatsos (2006), a CVLE can be defined as an environment in which:

- The users participating have different roles and privileges.
- The educational interactions in the environment transform the simple virtual space into a communication space.
- The information in the environment is represented in multiple ways, which can vary from simple text to three dimensional (3D) graphics.
- Students are not passive users but they can interact with each other and with the virtual environment.
- The system that supports the environment integrates multiple technologies.
- The possibility of implementing multiple learning scenarios is supported.
- Recognizable elements from the real world are visualized.

Depending on the instructional methods employed, CVLEs can support constructivist learning, in terms of distributed and situated learning (Dieterle & Clarke, 2006). A virtual learning environment can distribute knowledge and cognition among various artifacts (such as tools and virtual objects), students (for example when collaborating to solve a problem, or when performing an experiment) (Perkins, 1992), and symbols. It introduces new possibilities for scientific thinking and representational methods through the avatar's existence in the virtual space. In other words, students learn while associating with other novice or experienced participants of the learning community (Barab & Duffy, 1998; Zhao & Kuh, 2004).

However, regarding CVLEs, there are many issues to be resolved. For example, many practitioners and researchers have concluded that totally free, unguided or unstructured collaboration does not necessarily result in productive activity or learning (Kreijns, Kirschner, & Jochems, 2003; Kobbe et al., 2007). Also, students perform better in a virtual environment with guided exploration, independent from their learning style (Zaharias, Andreou, & Vosinakis, 2010). This is a result that highlights the consequence of virtual world design decisions on learning outcomes.

Other main issues include:

- The selection of a suitable CVLE among the wide range of CVLE platforms. One of the strongest arguments against the use of virtual reality for education is that the software and equipment require technical expertise and skills beyond that of most teachers (Winn, 2002).
- The design of a CVLE on top of the selected process. Designing a Computer Supported Collaborative Learning (CSCL) environment is not just a matter of taking a technological tool, an instructional approach supporting collaboration and an approach to studying its effects and putting them all to-

gether. The challenges to instructional designers are creating motivating goals and tasks for students to perform and choosing educational topics and concepts where the 3D visualization and simulation have clear advantages compared to traditional presentation formats such as slides, articles and diagrams (Prasolova-Førland, 2008).

- The organization of an effective evaluation process not only to uncover usability and functional problems but also to assess the potentiality of CVLEs to support collaborative learning scenarios. At present a systematic approach to the design of CSCL environments is missing (Strijbos, Kirschner, & Martens, 2004). More research is required on the relationship between a theoretical framework and the educational design of a CSCL setting.

The main goal of this paper is to examine whether it is possible to implement traditional collaborative learning activities in a 3D CVLE by evaluating the issues that hinder collaboration. These issues are usually related to the functional and pedagogical characteristics of 3D CVLEs, which foster collaboration among students. In addition, we are investigating the suitability, in terms of functionality and usability, of multiuser 3D platforms for supporting the completion of a collaborative project by postgraduate and undergraduate students. Second Life and OpenSim are the multiuser 3D platforms on which the case studies took place.

Initially, this paper presents some open source and proprietary CVLEs and then analyzes the problems encountered in trying to implement a collaborative activity through their utilization. These problems rationalize our attempt to implement the collaborative activity in the Second Life platform. Afterwards, we discuss the design of our collaborative e-learning environment within the chosen platform, we proceed to present its evaluation. Conclusions and future work are presented in the final section.

3D COLLABORATIVE VIRTUAL LEARNING ENVIRONMENTS

In this section we present the state of the art in 3D collaborative virtual learning environments. The presented CVLEs were chosen based on their popularity, proven educational and collaborative value (e.g., Bedford, Birkedal, Erhard, Graff, & Hempel, 2006; Ang & Wang, 2006), respective user testimonials and support of the generic features and advantages of current systems. Specific selection criteria for a 3D CVLE can be found in Tsiatsos, Konstantinidis, and Pomportsis (2009).

- **Active Worlds:** Active Worlds (http://www.activeworlds.com) is an interactive virtual world platform based on client-server architecture. A user connects to the virtual world using a suitable client provided free and having similar features to a Web browser. There is also the ability for users to host their own virtual worlds in their own facilities using the "World Server." The educational capabilities of Active Worlds have been explored by a learning community known as Active Worlds Educational Universe (AWEDU) which provides educators, students, educational institutions and individual programs with the Active Worlds technology. Nevertheless the use of the features offered by the community is not free of charge but is accompanied by annual costs that are related to the type of use. Institutions already using Active

Worlds include the Boston Museum of Science, the San Jose Tech Museum of Innovation, the NASA Ames Research Laboratory and many others.

- **Croquet/Open Cobalt:** Croquet (http://opencroquet.org) is an open source cross platform 3D environment designed for rich interaction and simulation, with a combination of powerful graphics and multi-user collaborations (McCahill, 2004). The development of Croquet stopped in 2007 and all continued development of the technology has taken place under a new project called Open Cobalt (http://opencobalt.org). The Open Cobalt is still in early development stage, offering some features, but with the existence of several bugs. Open Cobalt makes it possible for schools and other organizations to freely set up their own networks of public and private 3D virtual workspace. This is possible through the peer to peer architecture of the system that enables different users to hyperlink their virtual worlds via 3D portals to form a large distributed network of interconnected collaboration spaces.
- **Second Life:** Second Life is the most popular platform of virtual worlds which when first introduced was mainly used as means of social networking. Second Life is based on a network of thousands of servers which create an interconnected grid of virtual worlds. Users can connect to Second Life by installing on their personal computer one of the several available clients. In Second Life, educators can create real time interactive activities for the support of experiential, project-based and community service-based learning (Bedford, Birkedal, Erhard, Graff, & Hempel, 2006). Nevertheless, its use for educational purposes is not for free because firstly there is no offered possibility to install the server of Second Life in a private server infrastructure and secondly because creating permanent objects in Second Life requires owning virtual land. As mentioned before a CVE should feature recognizable elements from the real word, thus many companies, institutions and non-profit groups have setup virtual counterparts in the world of Second Life.
- **OpenSim:** OpenSim (http://opensimulator.org) can be regarded as an open source alternative to Second Life. OpenSim has the same architecture with Second Life but with the difference that allows the installation of the server on a personal machine. This allows the creation of virtual environments without any charge and without any restrictions. The modeling tools and the scripting language are the same as the ones in Second Life. In particular, the creation of objects made with the in-world 3D modeling tool and the functionality is imparted to the objects using the Linden Scripting Language. OpenSim offers the possibility of creating a network of virtual worlds as the server can run either in standalone or grid mode. This means that different servers running in entirely separate machines can communicate with each other offering this way a collaboration feature that can be used for educational purposes.
- **Open Wonderland:** Open Wonderland (http://openwonderland.org) is an open source toolkit for creating collaborative 3D virtual worlds based on Java technology which implies that there is great interoperability but also some limitations regarding the response

speed. Like most of the virtual world platforms, so the Open Wonderland is based on client-server architecture. Therefore, the creation of a virtual environment requires installation of the server and connection to the virtual world through the Open Wonderland client. Creating and editing objects in Open Wonderland is an easy process, but this is not true for adding functionality τo this objects as there is no support for any in-world scripting language. All functionality can be deployed only in server level by configuring and then building the server.

- **Pivote:** Pivote (http://www.pivote.info) is not exactly a virtual world platform but an authoring system which can assist in educational activities through the creation of courseware independent of the virtual world. The key point of Pivote is that all the structure and information content of an exercise is stored on the Web, not in the virtual world. Pivote uses the HTTP protocol to transfer into the virtual world data that have been created in the Web environment. Therefore, since structure and content are separate, similar exercises with varying degrees of scaffolding, help and support can be facilitated.

The success, in terms of the very large user base, of these environments (for example in 2008, within sixty days 1.437.910 users had entered Second Life (Beard, Wilson, Morra, & Keelan, 2009)) is not difficult to explain: the freedom given to users to express themselves, to experiment, to configure their representation and to develop a kind of social life in the artificial environment have shown to be highly desirable (Herman, Coombe, & Lewis, 2006).

However, with regards to the comparison between open source and proprietary CVLEs, the main issue seems to be the cost of implementing a learning activity. There is no charge for creating a virtual learning world in an open source CVLE, whereas in proprietary software a fee is required in order to use a virtual space or some necessary features for the process.

According to Vosinakis, Koutsabasis, and Zaharias (2011), the main reasons for setting up a learning environment in OpenSim, instead of Second Life are:

- **Visualization and Functionality:** There are no differences in graphics quality (both platforms use the same client), with OpenSim supporting most of the functionality of Second Life.
- **Cost:** Besides the cost for owing private land, Second Life places a charge for every image uploaded. On the other hand a limitless number of images can be uploaded in OpenSim at no cost.
- **Data Recording:** Using OpenSim all voice sessions can be recorded directly from the server. This would not be possible in Second Life, which allows only for the recording of public discussions at close range.

Furthermore, open source 3D CVLEs are almost completely configurable and enable tuning and improvement. In an open source 3D CVLE users can create, import and customize an unlimited number of virtual objects. Moreover, there is no restriction on the number of users who gain access to a virtual world. Theoretically they can be unlimited but in practice they are limited by the hardware and software infrastructure which hosts the virtual world as well as the ability of the 3D CVLE as software to efficiently exploit the resources of a system.

FIRST CASE STUDY - OPENSIM

Based on previous research (i.e., Konstantinidis, Tsiatsos, Terzidou, & Pomportsis, 2010; Tsiatsos, Konstantinidis, & Pomportsis, 2009) which assessed and compared the characteristics of state of the art open source CVLEs, OpenSim has been selected in order to examine its ability in supporting collaborative learning activities. The overall objective was to see whether environments such as this have gained the necessary maturity in order to allow for the implementation of effective collaborative activities. Meanwhile, our design objective included researching how the four aspects of immersion (i.e., interest, involvement, imagination and interaction) could be effectively utilized to transform a learning space into a learning place.

Learning spaces are spaces where creativity, problem solving, communication, collaboration, experimentation, and inquiry can happen. On the other hand, a learning place is a socially or subjectively meaningful space. As virtual spaces become familiar and significant, they become virtual places.

Design and Evaluation

The evaluation of OpenSim was carried out through two case studies. Seven postgraduate students (four female and three male students) participated in the first case study, using OpenSim as part of the course "Virtual Learning Environments," taught during the spring semester of the second year, of the postgraduate studies program at an Informatics Department in Greece. Ten undergraduate students (seven female and three male students) participated in the second case study for an activity carried out in the context of the course "Communications Management" taught during the winter semester of the second year, of the undergraduate studies program at the Faculty of Management of a University in Ukraine.

The participants of both case studies participated in a familiarization session where they could interact with the environment, communicate with other users and build objects. Afterwards they followed a collaborative scenario and created a presentation on a specific subject. In the first case study, the students were divided into two groups (i.e., one group with four students and one group with three students), while in the second case study the students formed three groups (i.e., one group with four students and two groups with three students). After the formation of the groups each student had to use the features of OpenSim in order to collaborate with his/her teammates and create the presentation. At the end of the activity, students answered a questionnaire about the functionality of OpenSim, potential problems and the collaboration among them.

The first case study had a slight differentiation and included the use of SLoodle in which users would present the deliverables they had been asked to prepare. The use of SLoodle was not proven to be very effective and eventually there was a problem in compatibility with OpenSim. Furthermore, all the students of both case studies experienced sound problems that made the activities very difficult as the students had to use text chat to present their work.

According to the questionnaires answered by the students, the failure to use voice chat hindered the collaborative activity process. Another issue was the responsiveness of OpenSim. When the virtual space filled with virtual objects then the response from the server where OpenSim was installed was too slow for the students to work with ease. The problem was not due to the speed of the network connection as the activity took place in a local network and there was plenty of free bandwidth (10 Gbps symmetric connection). We also used powerful computers for the OpenSim server and clients. Moreover, in the second case study where there were more participants than the first one, the OpenSim server stopped working three times and the operating system displayed a crash report with the message "OpenSim.exe has encountered a problem and needs to close." This forced all participants to log out, wait a few minutes to restore the operation of OpenSim and then log back in to continue the activity. The time that OpenSim server stopped working, only less than half of the system resources were in use making obvious that OpenSim could not effectively utilize the available resources.

In light of the aforementioned problems, the next move was the use of a proprietary 3D CVLE. The following section presents the application of a collaborative learning activity in Second Life and discusses the differences regarding efficiency between this activity and the one in the open source CVLE.

SECOND CASE STUDY: SECOND LIFE

This section presents the methodology of the evaluation, carried out at our Informatics Department, with the participation of undergraduate students in a virtual collaborative learning environment implemented in the Second Life platform.

Design and Evaluation

The main goal of our evaluation was to determine whether Second Life overcomes the problems of the open source CVLEs, thus making it more suitable for the implementation of collaborative learning activities. The evaluation methodology we applied in our case study comprised of two phases. At the first phase the students have been familiarized with the virtual world, the means of communication and the use and building of virtual objects. During the second phase the educational scenario has been implemented, (as described in detail in the corresponding subsection, titled "Phase 2").

Subjects of the experiment were ten undergraduate students (i.e., consisting of eight male and two female students) attending the "Multimedia Systems" course of the undergraduate program of studies in Informatics at our university. It would be unsafe to assume that the characteristics of this specific group of students correspond to the general student population of this level, we can however comment on the homogeneity of our subjects. In order to assess the previous experience of our subjects to online collaboration, the students have completed specific questionnaires. According to the results, the majority of the subjects in the group were experienced in collaborating online through 2D interfaces. On the contrary, the majority of students were inexperienced in the use of 3D virtual environments for either education or entertainment.

With regards to the educational design we took into consideration that the term "learning space" denotes the idea of movement, activity and the possibility of discovering meaningful connections between the elements found within the environment. However, it does not capture the distinctive ways in which people can make a learning space familiar, turning it into a learning place. It is often the quality of a shared space that plays a crucial role in its development into a place.

A space becomes a place when we build into it enduring structures (Burbules, 2004). Architectures transform not only a space but the patterns of activity for those who occupy them. These patterns can be viewed along five polarities: a) movement – stasis, b) interaction

– isolation, c) publicity – privacy, d) visibility – hiddenness, and e) enclosure – exclusion.

Phase 1

The goals of the first phase were to: a) allow students to familiarize themselves with the capabilities of the platform, and with the available collaboration and communication tools, b) gather information regarding students' previous experience, c) organize the students into pairs, d) gather first impressions and usability requirements and e) evaluate the previous experience of the users.

To gather the required information regarding students' previous experience, students answered a pre-test questionnaire which inquired about facts such as previous experience with 3D CVLEs.

In order to give students the chance to familiarize themselves with the virtual world, we created a special training corridor (Figure 1) where students passed through various stages of training.

To achieve this, we placed presentation boards in every room of the corridor where students could watch video tutorials about a specific subject. First, students learn about communication in Second Life using voice and text chat. Next, there is a maze where students have to learn to navigate and fly in the environment, with the guidance of an assistant. Afterwards, the video tutorial shows students how to use the camera of the environment independently of avatar movement. The next room related to avatar appearance in Second Life, since the students would have to wear specific clothes differentiating the collaboration pairs. The last room was about creating objects in Second Life and how students can use them in order to achieve application sharing functionality in the virtual world.

After the familiarization session, students were divided into pairs, because in the next phase they would work collaboratively in order to achieve the specified goals of the educational scenario.

Figure 1. Three replications of the training corridor

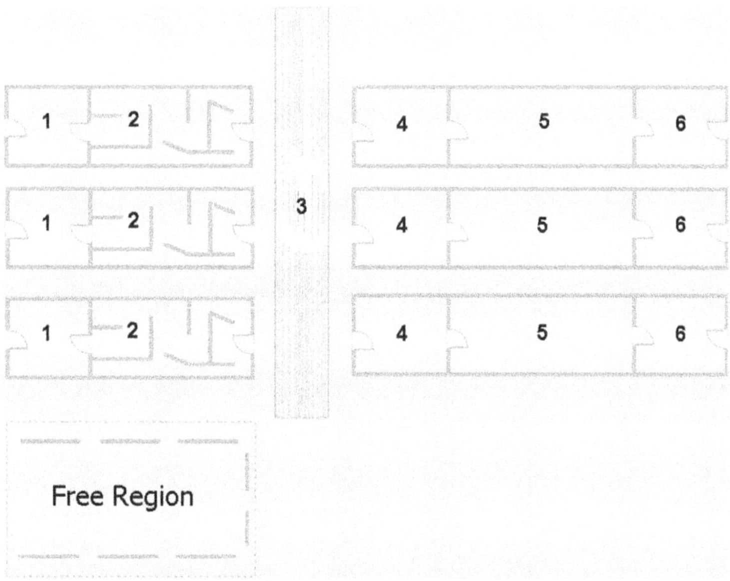

Phase 2

The goals of the second phase included: a) the specialization of students in specific tasks, b) the gathering of requirements concerning usability, communication and pedagogy, and c) the support of collaboration between pairs of students in order to answer specific worksheets.

In order to implement the second phase we created a special classroom which included a central place for discussion and smaller collaboration rooms for each pair of students (Figure 2). Also, it contained a library where students could access information from relative Websites which were linked to virtual objects. Finally, there was a room with lockers, where students could obtain clothes which could be used to differentiate the collaborating teams. This had emerged as a need from previous evaluations in open source CVLEs.

A worksheet was assigned to each pair of students which contained questions related to the course under which the activity took place. The worksheet could be collected by the students from the special library that was created to serve this purpose, but they also had the opportunity to see the worksheet from the Web browser in every room (Figure 3).

The presentation board in the central room contained the work requirements for the students. Searching for answers to the questions in the worksheets required use of the Web browsers which existed in each collaboration room. The members of the pairs of students exchanged views with each other through VoIP and by using Second Life notes. If necessary, they also had the opportunity to utilize application sharing, in order to facilitate collaboration. The whole process was supported by four assistants.

After completing the assigned task, each pair had to present the information they had retrieved. The presentations took place in the central area of the classroom where there was a presentation board in which the assistants had loaded the projects of all pairs of students on a Moodle environment.

At the end of this final phase of the scenario, each student had to answer an online questionnaire recording his/her experience and suggestions.

Figure 2. The central classroom area and the collaboration rooms

Figure 3. Students using the built-in Web browser to search the Internet for information

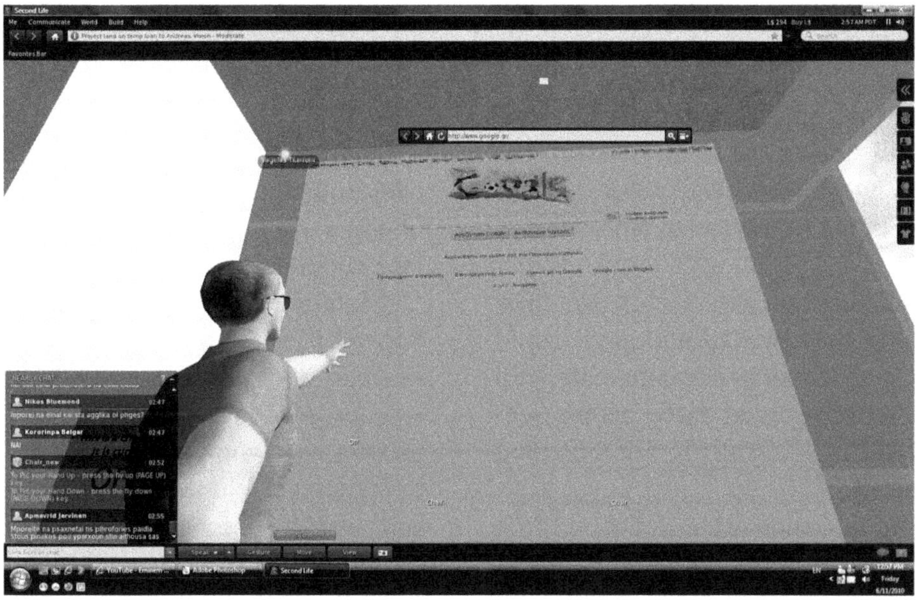

RESULTS

This section presents the evaluation results as revealed by analyzing the questionnaires submitted by the participating students. Furthermore, we discuss and compare these results in order to derive to conclusions.

Despite some obvious advantages of open source CVLEs, as mentioned in a previous section, the problems described above led us to implement a collaborative activity in Second Life. It had become obvious that the restrictions which existed in open source CVLEs would not allow the implementation of a collaborative activity in an efficient manner. Therefore, we tend to agree almost in everything with Vosinakis, Koutsabasis, and Zaharias (2011), regarding the problematic issues encountered within the OpenSim platform:

- Collaboration is hindered when there is a lack of voice communication.
- Lack of familiarity with 3D virtual environments, led to users focusing more on mastering the user interface and less on concentrating on the assigned collaborative task.
- Lack of 2D functions and embedded shareable applications obstructed the scenario.

Second Life is one of the most popular virtual worlds and provides an opportunity to use simulation in a safe environment to enhance experiential learning, allowing individuals to practice skills, try new ideas, and learn from their mistakes.

The implementation of the collaborative learning activity in Second Life gave us the opportunity to overcome some serious issues, which hindered the collaboration between the students in previous attempts. In Second Life, there were no problems in voice chat communication. That was very important since it was described by students in previous activities as a necessary feature.

The problems we had encountered, concerning system response time in OpenSim, were completely resolved. This gave students the opportunity to interact with each other and with the virtual objects without problems. Each pair of students had at its disposal special clothes, which were very useful as it was easy for everyone to recognize who belongs to which pair.

In general, the students could change their appearance as they wanted and users could now also use gestures to communicate with each other, utilizing either those that the Second Life platform inherently had or those that we had created.

In general, it seemed that in Second Life there were no usability and functionality problems and more importantly, there were no problems that hindered the collaboration among students, which was the main point we wanted to investigate.

Students were asked to comment on the general advantages and disadvantages of using 3D CVLEs for collaboration. The most important advantages of this pedagogical approach were considered to be spatial and temporal flexibility, innovation and originality of method (e.g., 83% of students entered the environment out of the educational process in order to simply explore the new environment) and the provision of enhanced communication and collaboration tools. On the other hand, disadvantages included lack of face to face interaction, increased technological dependency and the learning overhead imposed by the new tools.

With regard to other collaboration methods, the Second Life 3D CVLE is competing against more traditional approaches of 2D VLEs (or Learning/Content Management Systems) and core face to face interactions. Based on questionnaire results, Second Life is considered the most interesting (73%) and entertaining (80%) approach, incorporating the best collaboration tools (66%). On the other hand, it is also acknowledged as the least effective, direct and useful approach to collaboration. Thus, it becomes apparent that 3D CVLEs cannot compete with a traditional learning environment but they can assist the educational process in case of blended learning or when it is impossible to carry out a face to face collaborative activity.

Moreover, students commented that the Second Life platform hindered their ability to share information sources with their colleagues, and thus obstructed the collaboration process as a whole. Other issues, mentioned by students, included lack of desktop sharing and average graphics quality. Furthermore, the absence of a user friendly control scheme hindered the efficient use of the inventory system, as well as the appearance editing mechanism. Finally, a bug in the platform allowed the sound from video playback to be heard irrespectively of distance from the source, confusing and disorienting users.

Despite complications, students judged several aspects of the platform positively. According to the evaluation results, students enjoyed the 3D environment, finding it an interesting and immersive experience. One student commented that: "...it makes you want to stay online longer." Furthermore, students considered the Second Life collaboration process easier and more relaxing than a teleconference, taking pleasure in the feeling of presence of their peers.

Finally, with regard to specific functionality, students found the ability to move their camera independently of the avatar very useful and commented on the value of multiple communication channels: "…I could ask questions without interrupting." The majority of students were enthusiastic regarding the possible future use of the Second Life platform for collaborative activities, lectures and socializing.

Recommendations for future implementations are the following:

- **Application Sharing through the Built-In Browser:** Most students believe that application sharing through the Second Life environment would enhance its collaboration capabilities, simplifying the scenario execution.
- **Extended Periods of Familiarization and Collaboration Sessions:** Users had limited time in which to familiarize themselves with the interface and complete the collaborative scenario. The majority of students believe that the educational process would benefit if the virtual environment was run in parallel, but not concurrently, to the face to face sessions, in consistency with the context and content of the course. It seems people who work together over a series of sessions develop what has been termed a "collaborative working relation" (Baker, 2010), as they progressively share more extensive mutual knowledge and an enhanced ability to coordinate.
- **Increased Publicity with the Goal of Attracting more Students and Defining a Virtual Social Space:** Contemporary students are already skilled users of social software and Web 2.0 tools. Modern pedagogy, through 3D CVLEs, should exploit these abilities, by altering the context, medium and evaluation criteria of educational material.

CONCLUSION AND FUTURE WORK

Researchers have proven both the effectiveness of collaborative learning as an educational practice and the use of computers in aiding the acquisition of higher level cognitive and problem solving abilities. Combining the two, CVLEs exhibit many advantages compared to traditional teaching methods, including student motivation and the experience of unique environments.

This paper does not argue the superiority of the technological over the traditional face-to-face approach. Each domain has its own unique qualities and advantages. For this reason we did not focus on the matter of "Which is better?" but on "What is the distinct capability of 3D CVLEs to support immersive learning experiences?"

However, not all CVLEs are suitable for carrying out educational activities. There are problems both in terms of function and support of collaboration among learners. Dickey (2010) compared Second Life with Active Worlds, in a case study that did not include collaboration, and derived to the conclusion that both environments offered similar, as well as different, affordances and constraints. The main goal of this paper was to examine whether it is possible to implement collaborative learning activities in a 3D CVLE by evaluating some issues that hinder collaboration. This was accomplished within the context of comparing open source CVLEs to proprietary software.

The implementation of collaborative activities in open source CVLEs was not very effective and resulted in significant problems that prevented collaboration among students. The evaluation of the activity in OpenSim revealed that most of the students were left unsatisfied with the platform. The sound problems didn't allow students to collaborate efficiently as it was very difficult to communicate with each other and present work using only text chat. Also, delayed system response time made navigating the environment a complicated task. It should be noted that OpenSim does not have any installed service for voice chat but uses the Freeswitch voice server (http://www.freeswitch.org) as an external service that is connected in a certain way with the main server of OpenSim. Therefore sound problems are not caused by the OpenSim server which is responsible for the graphics but by the Freeswitch server which is used for voice chat.

Based on the above observations, our next attempt was to implement a collaborative learning activity in Second Life. The use of Second Life gave us the opportunity to overcome previous problems, which hindered collaboration between students.

The functionality and capabilities of Second Life allowed us to transform the virtual learning spaces we designed into meaningful virtual learning places by guiding the dynamics of interest, involvement, imagination, and interaction in ways that are judged to be educationally productive. Through this approach, the learning space becomes immersive and the students are engaged, actively relating to the subject-matter, seeing and feeling its importance.

The evaluation showed that the students worked without encountering any serious problems and without restrictions from the environment. Everyone submitted the deliverables which had been requested within the time frame that was set.

As a final conclusion, it becomes apparent that open source CVLEs are not mature enough yet to accommodate collaborative activities and allow educators to utilize them effectively. There are several problems seeking solution. For example, bad system responsiveness due to the use of a different data transmission protocol disappointed students and the lack of voice chat hampered communications. A quick and easy solution to the sound problems would be the utilization of a standalone voice chat application (e.g. Skype) that runs in parallel with the virtual world's server and client. However, this complicates the collaborative process and ruins immersion. There are many other issues that also need to be addressed, including the avatar's appearance editor, navigation and orientation.

Future work will include the attempt to resolve the issues identified during assessment. An interesting attempt would be the use of the Vivox voice service instead of Freeswitch. The Vivox service is the one used by Second Life for voice chat communication between users. This service is not for free but a short time ago Vivox gave the opportunity to OpenSim users to sample their service by submitting an application of interest. Unfortunately, this option recently became unavailable and could not be tested in this study.

The resolution of problems regarding open source CVLEs would allow them to highlight their advantages over proprietary software and make them more competitive in the facilitation of collaborative learning activities. Furthermore, future work can focus on developing approaches and designs which make learning spaces immersive, since immersion is an essential educational resource which can facilitate engagement and motivation for active student learning.

REFERENCES

Ang, K. H., & Wang, Q. (2006, December). A case study of engaging primary school students in learning science by using Active Worlds. In *Proceedings of the First International LAMS Conference* (pp. 5-14).

Baker, M. (2010). Relations between two qualities of collaborative dialogue: Knowledge co-elaboration and affective regulation. *Analysing the quality of collaboration in task-oriented computer-mediated interactions* (Workshop at the 9th International Conference on the Design of Cooperative Systems), Aix-en-Provence, France.

Barab, S. A., & Duffy, T. (1998). From practice fields to communities of practice. *Learning, 1*, 1–33.

Beard, L., Wilson, K., Morra, D., & Keelan, J. (2009). A survey of health-related activities on Second Life. *Journal of Medical Internet Research, 11*(2), e17. doi:10.2196/jmir.1192 PMID:19632971

Bedford, C., Birkedal, R., Erhard, J., Graff, J., & Hempel, C. (2006). Second Life as an educational environment: A student perspective. In *Proceedings of the First Second Life Education Workshop*, (pp. 25-27). San Francisco, CA.

Bouras, C., & Tsiatsos, T. (2006). Educational virtual environments: Design rationale and architecture. *International Journal of Multimedia Tools and Applications, 29*(2), 153–173. doi:10.1007/s11042-006-0005-7

Bruckman, A., & Hudson, J. M. (2001). Disinhibition in a CSCL Environment. In Proceedings of Computer Support for Collaborative Learning (CSCL), Maastricht, Netherlands (pp. 629-630). Boulder, CO.

Burbules, N. C. (2004). Rethinking the virtual. *Learning, 1*(2).

Churchill, E., Snowdon, D., & Munro, A. (2001). *Collaborative virtual environments: Digital places and spaces for interaction.* London: Springer-Verlag, London Limited. doi:10.1007/978-1-4471-0685-2

Dalgarno, B., & Lee, M. J. (2010). What are the learning affordances of 3-D virtual environments? *British Journal of Educational Technology, 41*(1), 10–32. doi:10.1111/j.1467-8535.2009.01038.x

Dickey, M. D. (2010). The pragmatics of virtual worlds for K-12 educators: Investigating the affordances and constraints of Active Worlds and Second Life with K-12 in-service teachers. *Educational Technology Research and Development, 59*(1), 1–20. doi:10.1007/s11423-010-9163-4

Dieterle, E., & Clarke, J. (2006). Multi-user virtual environments for teaching and learning. *Idea*, (c), 1-11.

Dillenbourg, P., Baker, M., Blaye, A., & O'Malley, C. (1996). The evolution of research on collaborative learning. In E. Spada, & P. Reiman (Eds.), *Learning in humans and machine: Towards an interdisciplinary learning science* (pp. 189–211). Oxford, UK: Elsevier.

Gokhale, A. A. (1995). Collaborative learning enhances critical thinking. *Journal of Technology Education, 7*(1).

Guglielman, E., & Vettraino, L. (2007). *Complex learning: A new approach for the age of knowledge.* Retrieved from http://www.scribd.com/doc/20062038/Complex-Learning

Herman, H., Coombe, R. J., & Lewis, K. (2006). Your Second Life? *Cultural Studies, 20*(2-3), 184–210. doi:10.1080/09502380500495684

Karantzas, G. C., Avery, M. R., Macfarlane, S., Mussap, A., Tooley, G., Hazelwood, Z., & Fitness, J. (2013). Enhancing critical analysis and problem-solving skills in undergraduate psychology: An evaluation of a collaborative learning and problem-based learning approach. *Australian Journal of Psychology*, *65*(1), 38–45. doi:10.1111/ajpy.12009

Kobbe, L., Weinberger, A., Dillenbourg, P., Harrer, A., Hämäläinen, R., Häkkinen, P., & Fischer, F. (2007). Specifying computer-supported collaboration scripts. *International Journal of Computer-Supported Collaborative Learning*, *2*(2-3), 211–224. doi:10.1007/s11412-007-9014-4

Konstantinidis, A., Tsiatsos, T., Terzidou, T., & Pomportsis, A. (2010). Fostering collaborative learning in Second Life: Metaphors and affordances. *Computers & Education*, *55*(2), 603–615. doi:10.1016/j.compedu.2010.02.021

Kreijns, K., Kirschner, P. A., & Jochems, W. (2003). Identifying the pitfalls of social interaction in computer-supported collaborative learning environments: A review of the research. *Computers in Human Behavior*, *19*(3), 335–353. doi:10.1016/S0747-5632(02)00057-2

McCahill, M. (2004). *Design for an extensible croquet-based framework to deliver a persistent, unified, massively multi-user and self organizing virtual environment.* Paper presented at Second Conference on Creating, Connecting and Collaborating through Computing, Kyoto, Japan.

Moore, D., Cheng, Y., McGrath, P., & Powell, N. J. (2005). Collaborative virtual environment technology for people with autism. *Focus on Autism and Other Developmental Disabilities*, *20*(4), 231–243. doi:10.1177/10883576050200040501

Muller, K., & Koubek, A. (2002). Collaborative and virtual environments for learning. In ACM SIG Proceedings, New Orleans, Louisiana.

Perkins, D. N. (1992). *Smart schools: Better thinking and learning for every child.* New York: Free Press.

Prasolova-Førland, E. (2008). Analyzing place metaphors in 3D educational collaborative virtual environments. *Computers in Human Behavior*, *24*(2), 185–204. doi:10.1016/j.chb.2007.01.009

Reitmayr, G., & Schmalstieg, D. (2001). Mobile collaborative augmented reality. In *IEEE and ACM International Symposium on Augmented Reality, 2001. Proceedings* (pp. 114-123). IEEE.

Slavin, R. E., & Tanner, A. M. (1979). Effects of cooperative reward structures and individual accountability on productivity and learning. *The Journal of Educational Research*, 294–298.

Strijbos, J. W., Kirschner, P. A., & Martens, R. L. (2004). *What we know about CSCL: And Implementing it in higher education.* Norwell, MA: Kluwer Academic Publishers. doi:10.1007/1-4020-7921-4

Tsiatsos, T., Konstantinidis, A., & Pomportsis, A. (2009). Collaborative educational virtual environments evaluation: The case of Croquet. Paper presented at *Workshop on Intelligent and Innovative Support for Collaborative Learning Activities (WIISCOLA), Computer Supported Collaborative Learning (CSCL09)*, Rhodes, Greece.

Veerman, A., & Veldhuis-Diermanse, E. (2001). Collaborative learning through computer-mediated communication in academic education. In P. Dillenbourg, A. Eurelings, & K. Hakkarainen (Eds.), *European perspectives on computer-supported collaborative learning: Proceedings of the 1st European Conference on Computer-Supported Collaborative Learning* (pp. 625-632). Maastricht: Maastricht University.

Vosinakis, S., Koutsabasis, P., & Zaharias, P. (2011). An exploratory study of problem-based learning in virtual worlds. *VS-GAMES, 11*.

Vygotsky, L. S. (1962). *Thought and language*. Cambridge, MA: MIT Press. doi:10.1037/11193-000

Winn, W. (2002). Current trends in educational technology research: The study of learning environments. *Educational Psychology Review*, *14*(3), 331–351. doi:10.1023/A:1016068530070

Zaharias, P., Andreou, I., & Vosinakis, S. (2010). Educational virtual worlds, learning styles and learning effectiveness: An empirical investigation. In A. Jimoyiannis (ed.), *Proceedings of the 7th Pan-Hellenic Conference with International Participation ICT in Education*, (pp.1-6). University of Peloponnese, Korinthos, Greece.

Zhao, C. M., & Kuh, G. D. (2004). Adding value: Learning communities and student engagement. *Research in Higher Education*, *45*(2), 115–138. doi:10.1023/B:RIHE.0000015692.88534.de

Chapter 8
An Integrated Notation for Business Process Models

Giorgio Bruno
Politecnico di Torino, Italy

ABSTRACT

Since business processes may address complex behavioral requirements resulting from the integration of several items, i.e. tasks, business entities (also called artifacts), control flow rules and data flow rules, they need notations able to accommodate several viewpoints. This chapter proposes a notation, ARTS, aimed at integrating the traditional activity-oriented viewpoint and the artifact-oriented one. The major benefits are the unification of the control flow and the data flow and a clear representation of the choices to be carried out by the participants. The basic features are illustrated with the help of three versions of a simplified hiring process. This chapter also deals with the structure of work lists, which are the major interface between the participants and their tasks. The organization of the work lists leverages the artifacts to emphasize human choices; for this reason, the traditional linear structure is replaced with a network one, which shows the artifacts along with their states, correlations and valid options.

INTRODUCTION

A business process is a standard way of organizing work in a business context. It consists of a number of tasks designed to produce a product or service (Rummler & Brache, 1995). Business processes cross functional boundaries in that they involve members of different departments; common examples are developing a new product, ordering goods from a supplier, and processing and paying an insurance claim (Davenport & Short, 1990).

Over the last years, various notations have been proposed to define business processes; they differ in the viewpoint adopted (Bruno, 2011). Probably, the most popular viewpoint is the activity-centric one, whose standard representative is BPMN (Business Process Model and Notation) (OMG-BPMN, 2011). It considers business processes essentially as

DOI: 10.4018/978-1-4666-4711-4.ch008

orchestrators of operational activities, which encompass human tasks and automated ones (Weske, 2007). The former are carried out by the participants in the process with the help of graphical interfaces, while the latter are implemented by services. Orchestration is achieved by means of control-flow elements which enforce rigid precedence relationships: a business process is like a master distributing the work to the participants in the process.

In recent years, the notion of Process-Aware Information System (Dumas, van der Aalst, & ter Hofstede, 2005), which advocates a tighter integration between the areas of information systems and business processes, has brought about a shift of interest from the activity-centric perspective to the artifact-centric one. The latter emphasizes the identification of the key business entities (called artifacts) and of their life cycles, which show how the artifacts evolve over time through the execution of the tasks. The major benefit is the right level of granularity, which facilitates communication among the stakeholders and helps them focus on the primary purposes of the business (Chao et al., 2009). In this chapter, terms artifact and business entity (or simply entity) will be used interchangeably.

The major criticism raised against the activity-centric approach is the emphasis placed on the tasks and the control-flow elements, while the artifacts are not considered as first-class citizens. As a matter of fact, the data flow in the activity-centric approach is based on process variables and there is no automatic mapping between artifacts and process variables. Moreover, this perspective seems to be more suitable for automated processes than for human-centric ones, as it lacks an adequate representation of the situations in which the choice among different courses of action depends on a human decision. The artifact-centric approach has the potential for coping with such issues owing to the emphasis placed on the artifacts on which human decisions are grounded. This approach, however, is not free from critical aspects; in particular, the handling of tasks operating on two or more artifacts calls for some form of coordination of their life cycles.

In order to overcome the above mentioned issues, this chapter proposes a notation, named ARTS (ARtifacts and TAsks), which integrates tasks and artifacts and emphasizes human choices. In a nutshell, ARTS follows the case handling approach (van der Aalst, Weske, & Grünbauer, 2005) and therefore the goal of a business process is to define the life cycle of a specific entity type, called primary entity type. When a primary entity is generated, a new instance of the process governing its life cycle is started, and the primary entity follows the path which is determined by the tasks defined in the process. However, a process is not required to manage a single entity in that other entities may be produced during its execution; these entities are linked to the primary entity and are called subordinate entities. It often happens that subordinate entities have their own life cycle and then the process may be in charge of a number of life cycles.

ARTS emphasizes the representation of choices, which may be divided into three categories: task selection, entity selection, and mixed selection. Task selection takes place when a business entity turns out to be the input entity of two or more tasks and the tasks have no additional input entities. Selecting a task means deciding what to do with the input entity and often implies the choice of a course of action. Entity selection is carried out by tasks taking their inputs from one or more sources; such tasks are called matching tasks. The choice of the inputs may depend on a human decision or may be subjected to a selection rule. When the input entities of a matching task are also input entities of other tasks, entity selection and task selection are intertwined: such situations are called mixed choices. In fact, the execution of a matching task implies both the selection of the input entities and the exclusion of the other tasks that could operate on these entities.

During the execution of a business process, the human tasks are assigned to the appropriate participants through their work lists. The content of the work lists depends on the notation adopted for the representation of the business processes. With ARTS, the organization of the work lists relies on artifacts to emphasize human choices.

This chapter is organized as follows. First it presents background information and gives an overview of ARTS; then it illustrates the basic features and the representation of human choices with the help of three versions of a simplified hiring process. It continues with the description of the structure of work lists and then ends with the conclusion.

BACKGROUND

ARTS is intended for knowledge-intensive processes (Marjanovic & Freeze, 2011), i.e., processes calling for some degree of creativity and adaptation to specific circumstances (Alvesson, 2004). What distinguishes knowledge-intensive processes from routines is that the participants are not considered as mere resources needed to carry out tasks which are not automatable; on the contrary, their involvement is required at a higher level where they may take decisions which affect the control flow.

Enhancing flexibility in the control flow is an important issue and several approaches have been proposed (Nurcan, 2008). BPMN provides ad hoc sub-processes, whose tasks may be carried out in any number and order as decided by their performers. If this solution is deemed too flexible, the introduction of constraints is needed. With Declare (van der Aalst, Pesic, & Schonenberg, 2009), any task of an ad hoc sub-process may be performed as long as the mandatory constraints are not violated; with the Business Process Constraint Network approach (Lu, Sadiq, & Governatori, 2009), process variants may be built at run-time. However, those approaches lack a clear representation of choices in terms of links between the entities to be chosen and the tasks to be performed.

The complementary aspects of business processes and information systems are emphasized by the notion of Process-Aware Information System (Dumas, van der Aalst, & ter Hofstede, 2005). A process is meant to take care of a specific business entity (e.g. an insurance claim), called the process case (van der Aalst, Weske, & Grünbauer, 2005): the process evolution depends on the state of the case and not only on the tasks performed (Künzle & Reichert, 2009).

In the artifact-centric approach, there are three major issues to cope with, i.e., structure, dynamics and coordination (Hull, 2008). Structure is about the properties (attributes and associations) of the artifacts involved, dynamics encompass the artifact life cycles, and coordination is concerned with the synchronization of the life cycles. Such issues are dealt with in various ways, ranging from separate models to holistic ones.

The Guard-Stage-Milestone (GSM) approach (Hull, 2011) is a holistic technique: the major building blocks are the artifacts, which contain informational aspects (i.e. attributes and associations), life cycles and coordination items (events and rules). The drawback is the difficulty of understanding the propagation of the events between the life cycles.

In PHILharmonicFlows (Künzle & Reichert, 2011), structure, dynamics and coordination are separate. The structural model shows the types of the artifacts involved along with their attributes and relationships. Life cycles are called micro processes; when an entity is generated, the corresponding micro process is started. The interactions between micro processes are defined with a coordination mechanism based on macro processes, which consist of macro steps and macro transitions. A macro step is associated with an artifact type and a particular state of its life cycle. A macro transition activates an output macro step only when the artifacts collected in the input macro steps satisfy certain conditions, which are related to the structure of the artifacts (in particular to the associations). The drawback is that the life-cycle states which need to be coordinated have to be repeated in the macro processes.

With the Proclets framework (Mans et al., 2010), the life cycles are defined in separate building blocks, called Proclets: they are equipped with ports through which they can send and receive messages. The drawback is to address coordination with notions, such as messages and send/receive operations, which are too close to the programming domain.

In ArtiNet (Kucukoguz & Su, 2011) and Chant (Bruno, 2012), the life cycles are integrated in a single model and coordination is obtained with transitions operating on two or more artifacts. Models are monolithic in that they are based on Petri nets where places represent life-cycle states.

In other approaches, where the relationships between the artifact types are explicitly defined, coordination takes advantage of them, in particular of hierarchical relationships. Hierarchical structures, such as those related to physical systems, are addressed by COREPRO (Müller, Reichert, & Herbst, 2007), which provides specific means to achieve mutual synchronization between the state of a compound object and those of its components. The technique presented by Küster, Ryndina, and Gall (2007) is aimed at automatically generating a process model from the entity life cycles provided that the synchronization points are manually identified beforehand.

In ARTS, dynamics and coordination are addressed in a single model, called process model. A process model is accompanied by an information model showing the types of the artifacts along with their attributes and relationships. The pre-conditions and the post-conditions that declaratively express the constraints and the effects of the tasks are based on the structure of entities provided by the information model.

It is common opinion that business process models and rule languages have several contact points, since both are aimed at defining organizational policies (zur Muehlen & Indulska, 2010). Rules may be used to define a number of conditions and constraints (Goedertier, Haesen, & Vanthienen, 2008) as well as precedence relationships between tasks (Pesic & van der Aalst, 2006). Pre/post-conditions in ARTS are rules written in a simplified version of OCL (OMG-OCL, 2010).

ARTS pays particular attention to the practical implications of process models, i.e., to their impact on work lists. Work lists are widely used to organize personal work (Riss, Rickayzen, Maus, & van der Aalst, 2005): they are fed by tasks generated by their owners (Bellotti et al., 2004) and may also include tasks automatically produced from emails (Grebner & Riss, 2008). Through task delegation, the members of a team can assign tasks of their work lists to each other, and this allows informal collaborative processes to take place (Stoitsev, Scheidl, & Spahn, 2007). In ARTS, work lists are centered on artifacts so as to support the three kinds of choice mentioned in the introduction.

INTRODUCTION TO ARTS

The purpose of ARTS is to provide a tight integration between the activity-centric approach and the artifact-centric one, while taking into account human-centric issues such as the representation of situations where the choice among different courses of action depends on a human decision.

This section illustrates the basic features of ARTS: the representation of processes, the kinds of tasks, and the information flow.

ARTS follows the case handling approach and therefore the goal of a business process is to define the evolution over time, i.e., the life cycle of a specific entity type, called primary entity type. Business processes and primary entity types are then linked by a biunivocal relationship. When a primary entity is generated, a new instance of the process governing its life cycle is started, and the primary entity follows the path which is determined by the tasks defined in the process. However, a process is not required to manage a single entity in that other entities may be produced during its execution; these entities are linked to the primary entity, and are called subordinate entities. It often happens that subordinate entities have their own life cycle and then the process may be in charge of a number of life cycles.

The units of work of a business process are defined by means of tasks, which may be performed automatically or may need human intervention: the former are called automated tasks and the latter human tasks. People participating in a process are called participants and are distinguished according to the role they play. A human task is assigned to one role, but several participants may play the same role; it is then necessary to determine whether any participant playing the role required is entitled to perform the task or a specific participant is needed. The task performer is generic in the first case, and specific in the second one.

A business process model defines an ordering of tasks which will be carried out by a support system called process management systems (PMS). A PMS is in charge of making the automated tasks performed, and of assigning the human tasks to the appropriate participants by adding entries to their work lists. Such tasks are called process-driven. There are other two kinds of human tasks, referred to as participant-driven and process-enabled. The former are carried out by participants when they want to; they are usually started from a menu appearing in the workspace of the participant. In general, the purpose of a participant-driven task is the generation of a primary entity and, as a consequence, the instantiation of the corresponding process. A process-enabled task allows the performer to participate in a process that is already running: the task usually results in the generation of a subordinate entity.

A process may handle entities of different types and then it is essential to show which entities the tasks are in charge of. Tasks exchange entities with the process: they receive input entities through the input flows and provide output entities through the output flows. A flow may be direct or indirect: direct flows are direct connections between tasks, while indirect ones are based on data stores.

Direct flows have a label and a weight: the label is the name of the type of the entities passing along the link and the weight is the number of entities issued by a single performance of the source task. A data store has one or more input flows and one or more output flows; the entities passing along the flows have the same type and then the type name is the first label of the data store. An indirect flow between tasks means that the source task has an output flow directed to a data store which provides an input flow to the destination task.

The basic features introduced so far are illustrated in the process fragment shown in

Figure 1. This process, named HandleApplication, will be analyzed in the next section. Its purpose is to handle the life cycle of the primary entity, an application, and those of its subordinate entities.

The basic graphical conventions for proccss models are as follows. Tasks are represented by rectangular icons with their names written inside. Human tasks show the role required close to the task icon. Data stores have two labels: the first is the name of the type of the entities that the data store may contain, and the second is the name of the stage that the data store represents in the life cycle of the entities.

Task enterApplication is not part of the process, which actually starts from task assign. In fact, it is a participant-driven task that generates the primary entity, and then it brings about the instantiation of the process. Such

Figure 1. Basic features

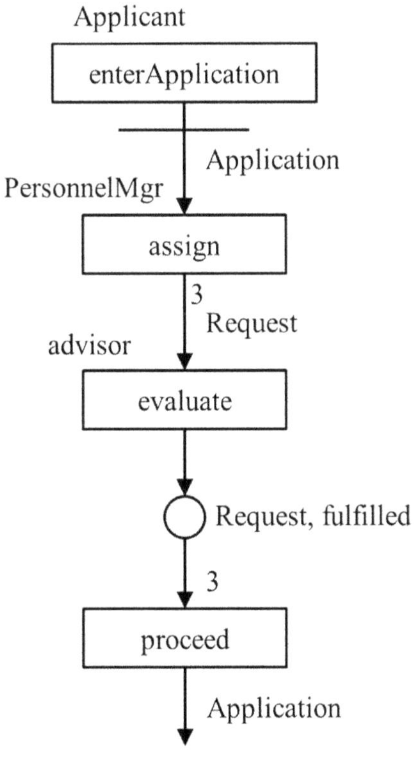

tasks are called starting tasks. The small bar crossing the output flow separates the starting task from the process. The starting task may be omitted; it is shown to give a more comprehensive picture of the process. Task enterApplication may be performed by any applicant: when the role is indicated with the role name with the initial in upper case, any member of the role may perform the task. If, instead, the initial is written in lower case, a specific member is required as will be illustrated in the next section.

The direct flow from task enterApplication to task assign implies a direct cause-effect relation between the tasks: each performance of the first brings about an assignment of the second. A new entry will then added to the work list of the personnel manager. The direct flow from task assign to task evaluate has a weight greater than one; each performance of the first task causes as many assignments of the second task as the weight of the flow. Therefore, for each of the three requests produced by task assign, an assignment of task evaluate will be generated. As will be explained in the next section, the three assignments of task evaluate are directed to three different advisors.

The data store between task evaluate and task proceed indicates that the cause-effect relation between them is an indirect one. Task proceed needs three requests but task evaluate produces one at a time. In general, if a task needs more than one input entity, it is fed from one or more input data stores.

The purpose of a task is described in its behavioral requirements, which consist of the intended effects on the underlying information system and of the constraints that limit its execution. The effects and the constraints are expressed declaratively by means of post-conditions and pre-conditions, respectively; they are based on the structure of the input and output entities. For this reason, an information model showing the types of the entities involved along with their attributes and relationships is needed. This issue is discussed in the next section.

BASIC FEATURES

This section explains the relations between process models and information ones, the use of mandatory properties and of associative attributes, the identification of the performer of human tasks, and the synchronization among a number of life cycles. It does so with the help of the first version of the hiring process, named HandleApplication; the process model and the related information model are shown in Figure 2.

The description of the process is as follows. The process enables applicants to apply for a job at a certain company. The job types for which there are a number of vacant posts have been published previously on the company Website. Applicants are assumed to register with the company before submitting their applications. Each application has to be

Figure 2. The model of process HandleApplication

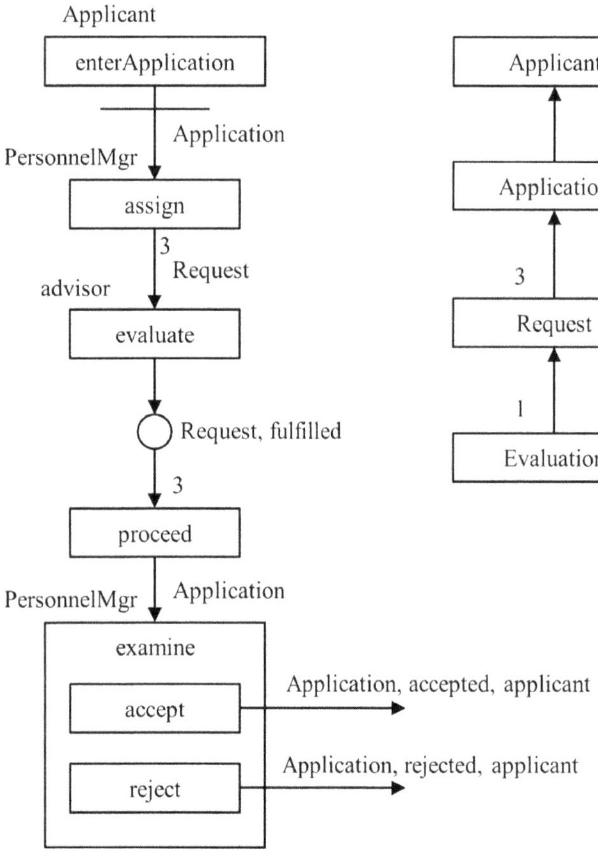

Post-conditions
enterApplication: new Application.
assign: new 3 Request as requests, requests.advisor distinct, requests.advisor in application.jobType.advisors.
evaluate: new Evaluation.

evaluated by three advisors who are selected from among those suitable for the job type referred to by the application; for this reason, the personnel manager issues three requests for evaluation directed to three different advisors. When the evaluations have been collected, the personnel manager decides whether to accept or reject the application, and the applicant is notified of the decision.

In general, a process is in charge of several entities, which may be divided into two groups, i.e., managed entities and contextual ones, on the basis of their impact on the process. The managed entities are those generated in the course of the process; they include the primary entity and the subordinate ones. On the contrary, the contextual entities already exist before the execution of the process and provide its context. The context of process HandleApplication consists of the job types, the advisors, the associations between the job types and the advisors, and the applicants. The applications are the primary entities while the requests for evaluation and the evaluations are the subordinate ones.

The information model is similar to a Unified Modeling Language (UML) class model (OMG-UML, 2011), but, in addition, it provides mandatory properties: they denote the attributes and relationships which must be set when a new entity is generated. Such properties simplify the writing of post-conditions and pre-conditions as explained in this section.

Task enterApplication is the starting task: in fact, it generates the primary entity, which causes the instantiation of the process. It may be performed by any applicant. The effects of the task are indicated by the post-condition "new Application;" operator "new" asserts that a number of new entities of the type specified will exist after the execution of the task. If the multiplicity is 1, it is omitted.

In general, when a new entity is generated, a number of attributes and associations with other entities have to be set; they are called mandatory properties and are emphasized in the information model as follows. Mandatory attributes are qualified with an exclamation mark while mandatory associations are represented by oriented relationships: the source entity type denotes the entities for which the associations are mandatory.

An application needs to be related to a job type and to the applicant entity representing its performer; for this reason, the information model shows relationships Applicant-Application and Application-JobType as mandatory. The name of a relationship is obtained from the names of the types involved (if there are no other relationships between the same pair of types) in alphabetic order.

The post-condition "new Application" does not explicitly indicate the partners of the mandatory associations. In such cases, the partners that may not be determined implicitly from the context of the task are assumed to be selected by the performer during the execution of the task. In general, the context of a task includes the input entities, the entity representing the performer of the task (referred to as the performer entity), and the primary entity of the process instance. In this case, since the task has no input entities and is not part of the process, the context only includes the performer entity, which is an applicant entity and then matches the requirements of relationship Applicant-Application. The other partner, i.e. a job type will be selected by the performer from among those available.

Task assign makes the personnel manager issue three requests for evaluation for the input application. Its post-condition is made up of three parts separated by commas. The first part "new 3 Requests as requests" specifies that 3 new requests will exist at the completion of the task, and it also introduces a name, i.e. requests to denote the newly generated requests. This name is used in the subsequent parts of the post-condition. The expressions in the last two parts place constraints on the requests as follows: the requests have to refer to distinct advisors and the advisors have to be chosen from among those related to the job type indicated in the application. The expressions are based on associative attributes.

Associative attributes denote the entities associated with a given entity and their names are inferred from the relationships in the information model. The general rule is that the associative attributes take the name of the entity type they refer to, in the singular form or in the plural one (with the initial in lower case) depending on the cardinality of the relationship. Within a post-condition, the associative attributes refer to the entities in the current scope and may be chained. The current scope includes the input entities of the task, the primary entity and those entities, such as the requests, which are generated as an effect of the task. In particular, term "requests.advisor" denotes the advisors associated with the requests and "application.jobType.advisors" the advisors associated with the job type connected to the application. The primary entity is indicated by its type name with the initial in lower case, e.g. application.

Task evaluate operates on a single request and produces an evaluation. The performer is a specific one as the role name with the initial in lower case is used. The specificity is determined by a connection, either direct or indirect, between the role type and the type of the input entity. In this chapter, it is assumed that if there is no direct connection, there is one and only one path consisting of mandatory relationships from the type of the input entity to the role type. The performer of task evaluate is identified by means of the associative attribute request.advisor, which represents a direct connection based on relationship Advisor-Request; an example of indirect connection will be shown in the next section. Although the result of the task is a new evaluation, the output entity is the input one. The label of the output flow is the first label of the output data store and is identical to the label of the input flow; when an input flow and an output one have identical labels, it is assumed that the input entity is also the one emitted.

The requests are subordinate entities but they, too, have a life cycle. They are produced by task assign, dealt with by task evaluate and then collected in the data store, where they stay until they are taken by task proceed. The data store represents a stage; its name, i.e. fulfilled expresses what it means for an entity to be in that stage.

Task proceed is an automated task as there is no role name associated with it. Its purpose is to synchronize the life cycles of the three requests as indicated by the weight associated with the input flow. It is a particular case of matching task, in that all the input entities come from the same data store; in addition, the content of the entities is irrelevant as only their number matters.

Macro task examine indicates a task selection for the personnel manager. Task selection takes place when an entity turns out to be the input entity of two or more tasks and the tasks have no additional input entities. The graphical representation consists of a box containing the competing tasks; such compound process elements are also called macro tasks.

The output flows of tasks accept and reject represent notifications, i.e., communication sent to the intended recipients. A notification has three labels: the type of the entity which is the payload of the notification, the meaning of the notification, e.g. accepted, and the recipient. The recipient is equivalent to a specific performer and is identified with the same rules; in this case the applicant to be notified is the one represented by the applicant entity directly connected to the application.

CHOICES

This section focuses on the representation of the three categories of choices, i.e. task selection, entity selection, and mixed selection, mentioned in the introduction.

The second version of the hiring process, called HandleJobAnnouncement and shown in Figure 3, presents an automatic task selection applied to the primary entity, a human task selection applied to a collection of subordinate entities and a process-enabled task. The description of the process is as follows.

The process enables the department directors of a certain company to make job announcements when they need to fill some vacancies. A job announcement is the primary entity: it includes the number of posts available (attribute nPosts) and the deadline for the submission of the applications (attribute d). The first step of the process is to automatically publish the job announcement on the company Website. Then, applicants are entitled to enter applications provided that they do so before the deadline. When the deadline expires, the process checks whether there are applications or not: if there are, it makes the applications evaluated by the personnel manager; if there are not, it notifies the director that the announcement has been unsuccessful. The number of applications that the personnel manager may accept has to be not greater than the number of vacant posts; the other applications are rejected. Each applicant is notified of the result.

Figure 3. The model of process HandleJobAnnouncement

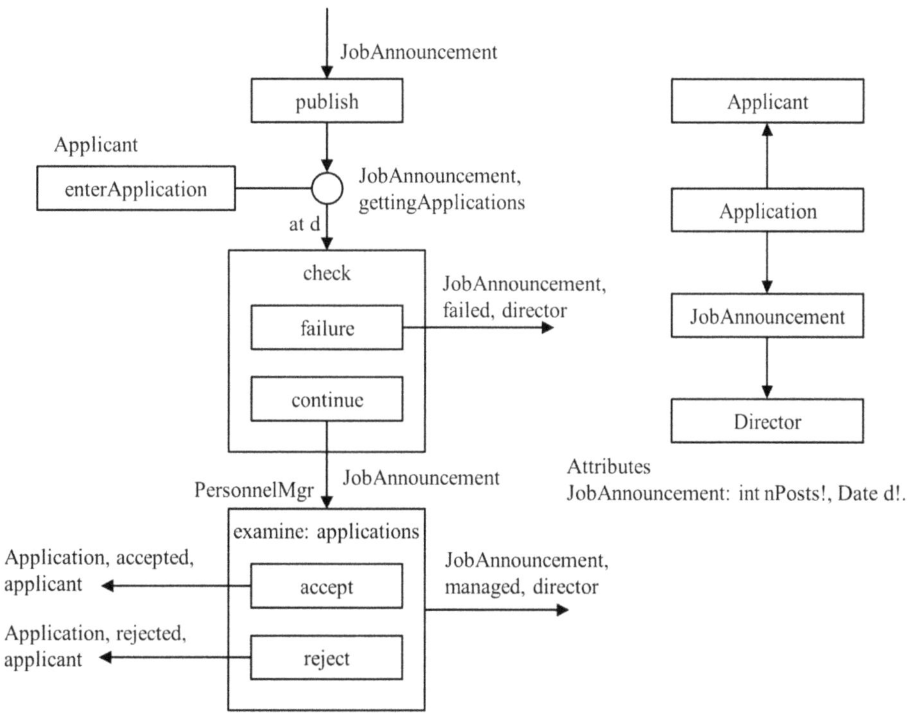

Post-conditions
enterApplication: new Application.
accept: ne <= jobAnnouncement.nPosts.
Pre-conditions
failure: N(jobAnnouncement.applications) == 0.

The starting task is not shown. The first task, "publish," is an automated task. There are no details about its effects and then the post-condition is omitted. The job announcement is put in a data store in that it does trigger no immediate task. A data store represents a stage in the life cycle of the entities it contains. An entity remains in a data store until an output task is ready to remove it; during its stay in the data store, tasks that do not remove it may be performed.

The stage name of the data store in Figure 3 is gettingApplications in that applicants may enter applications for the job announcement as long as the announcement is in that stage. Task enterApplication is a process-enabled task. Its post-condition indicates that the effect is the introduction of a new application: due to the mandatory relationships of type Application, the new entity will be connected to the performer entity and to the job announcement, both of which are part of the context of the task. The input flow is undirected (it has no arrow) because the same job announcement may be referred to (in read-only mode) in several performances of the task: as a matter of fact, several applicants may apply for the same job at the same time. The task has no output flow in that the newly generated application is not an event of interest for the process. The process removes the job announcement from the data store when the deadline expires, and passes it to macro task check. The removal is determined by the timing constraint "at d," which is the inscription on the output flow; d is a mandatory attribute of the job announcement.

Macro task check implies an automatic choice between tasks failure and continue. The choice is based on the pre-condition of task failure: if it is true, the task is performed, otherwise the other task is carried out. The pre-condition "N (jobAnnouncement.applications) == 0" is true if the number of applications related to the job announcement is zero; the system operator N gets a collection of entities and returns the number of its elements. The output flow of task failure is a notification to the director who issued the job announcement.

Task continue passes the job announcement to macro task examine, which enables the personnel manager to evaluate each application and then to accept or reject it. This is a case of human task selection whose purpose is the handling of a collection of entities related to the input entity of the macro task. The collection is indicated by an associative attribute, such as applications, of the input entity, written after the macro task name and separated by a colon. The execution of each task brings about a notification to the applicant. When all the applications have been processed, the output entity of the macro task is emitted: this is a notification for the director who made the job announcement. There is a limit on the number of executions of task accept: it is established by the system attribute ne (number of executions) appearing in the post-condition, and its value is the number of vacant posts.

Mixed selection is illustrated in the third version of the hiring process, named HandleHiringCampaign and shown in Figure 4. The description of the process is as follows. The primary entity is a hiring campaign; its major attribute is the end date. The campaign is initially open and will automatically be closed at the end date. As long as the campaign is open, department directors may enter job announcements and applicants may enter applications. The job of the personnel manager is to match an announcement and an application; the details of the matching rule are left undefined. The result of the match is a hiring proposal which is communicated to the parties involved. Moreover, the personnel manager may reject announcements and applications at their discretion, and the parties are informed.

Figure 4. The model of process HandleHiringCampaign

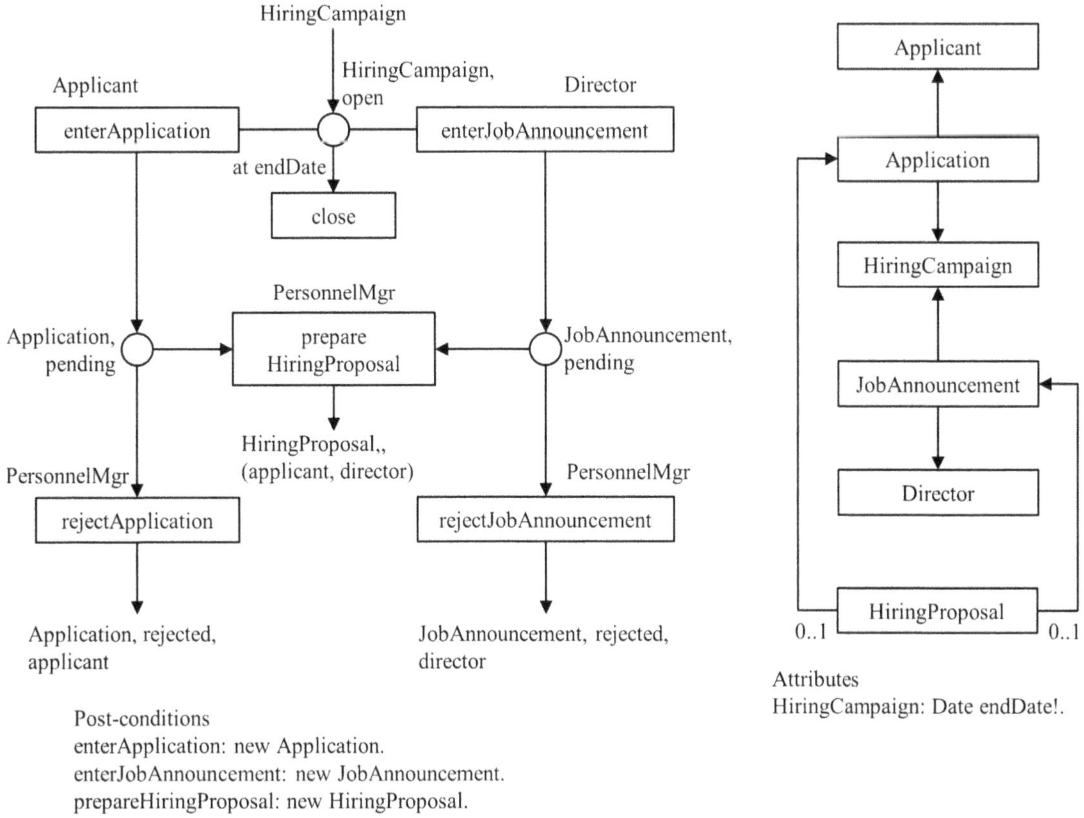

Tasks enterApplication and enterJobAnnouncement are process-enabled tasks. Job announcements and applications are put into two data stores and stay there until they are rejected or they are combined to form a hiring proposal. Task prepareHiringProposal is a matching task in that it combines input entities taken from different data stores. In a matching task, the selection of the input entities may be under the responsibility of the performer or may be made automatically if the task is an automated one; in the latter case a selection rule is needed. The post-condition indicates that the result of task prepareHiringProposal is the generation of a new hiring proposal: due to the mandatory relationships of type HiringProposal, the new entity will be connected to the two input entities, which are part of the context of the task. Both the applicant of the application selected and the director of the job announcement selected will be notified of the result. The applicant entity and the director one are indirectly connected to the hiring proposal through paths consisting of mandatory relationships; these paths are HiringProposal-Application-Applicant and HiringProposal-JobAnnouncement-Director, respectively.

When the input entities of a matching task are also input entities of other tasks, entity selection and task selection are intertwined: such situations are called mixed selections. In fact, both the applications and the job announcements may be handled with two competing tasks: the applications with tasks rejectApplication and prepareHiringProposal, and the job announcements with tasks rejectJobAnnouncement and prepareHiringProposal.

WORK LISTS

Human tasks are units of work to be performed by the users of the information system on the basis of their roles. They may be divided into three major categories, participant-driven tasks, process-enabled tasks and process-driven ones. The tasks in the first two categories are carried out on the initiative of the users, although some form of restriction may be applied. On the contrary, process-driven tasks are automatically assigned to the intended performers through their work lists. The content of the work lists depends on the notation adopted for the representation of the business processes. In an activity-centric notation, such as BPMN, there is no direct information on the business entities acted on by the tasks; in fact, the process variables are the source of the inputs and the destination of the outputs of the tasks, and there is no automatic mapping between business entities and process variables. The entries of the work lists follow the simple pattern "task-name info" where info stands for information taken from the task inputs. By clicking an entry, a participant may perform the corresponding task through the graphical interface provided by the implementation.

If the notation, such as ARTS, shows both the tasks and the entities handled by the tasks, the organization of the work lists may leverage the entities to emphasize human choices. A linear structure is then replaced with a two-level one as shown in Figure 5.

This work list belongs to the personnel manager and includes a number of entries related to the three processes examined in the

Figure 5. An example of work list

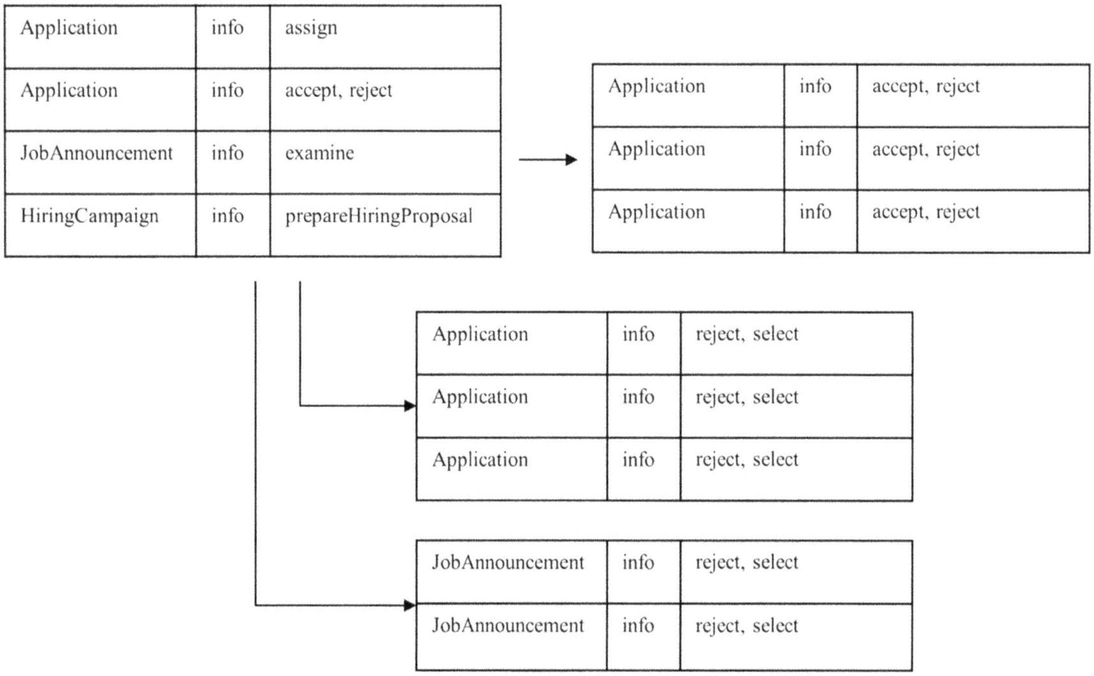

previous sections. It is organized in two columns, the left referring to primary entities and the right to subordinate entities. Entries are made up of three parts, which show the type name, some information about the entity and the options available. The content of the second part is not detailed and only the generic term "info" appears.

The first two entries refer to process HandleApplication shown in Figure 2. The first entry denotes a simple task, assign, and the second one a macro task consisting of two options, accept and reject. If, for example, the personnel manager clicks the accept option, the graphical interface of task accept appears and enables the performer to work on the application.

The remaining two entries involve subordinate entities. The third entry refers to process HandleJobAnnouncement shown in Figure 3 and corresponds to macro task examine. It is assumed that the current job announcement has got three applications: for each of them, the options available are accept and reject. The primary entry is then connected to a list of secondary entries. The personnel manager clicks an option for each application so as to perform the corresponding task; however, the number of acceptances cannot be greater than the number of vacant posts. When all the applications have been handled, the output flow of macro task examine is emitted.

The fourth entry refers to process HandleHiringCampaign shown in Figure 4, and deals with a mixed selection. There are two secondary lists, which present the job announcements and the applications contained in the input data stores of task prepareHiringProposal. If the personnel manager clicks the reject option, they perform the corresponding task and then the entry disappears. With the select option, they may match an application and a job announcement. First they select the two entities to be combined and then click the primary entry: at this time they can perform task prepareHiringProposal.

CONCLUSION

This chapter has proposed a notation, ARTS, aimed at integrating the traditional activity-oriented viewpoint and the artifact-oriented one. The major benefits are the unification of the control flow and the data flow and a clear representation of the choices to be carried out by the participants.

Models based on ARTS are conceptual models: in addition to helping analysts understand the problem under consideration, they facilitate communication between analysts and developers. To this end, process models are supplemented with information models which show the structure of the entities involved.

Most implementations of business processes follow a workflow approach in that they result in the distribution of task assignments to participants through work lists. The entries of the work lists follow the simple pattern "task-name info" where info stands for information taken from the task inputs. By clicking an entry, a participant may perform the corresponding task through the graphical interface provided by the implementation. This approach tends to consider participants as mere resources: they are needed to carry out tasks which are not automatable and are not supposed to autonomously select the tasks to perform. While this way of working may be appropriate for routine processes, in knowledge-intensive processes, participants are expected to make choices so as to affect the control flow of the business process. In this case, the organization of work lists need to be deeply revised.

The content of work lists is influenced by the notation adopted. If the notation, such as ARTS, shows both the tasks and the entities handled by the tasks, the organization of the work lists may leverage the entities to emphasize human choices. One of the challenges is the identification of the most expressive technique to help participants work in this way. This chapter has described a solution in which the traditional linear structure is replaced with a network one showing the artifacts along with their states, correlations and valid options.

Current work is dedicated to the implementation of the notation. Two solutions are being compared: one is meant to automatically generate BPMN representations so as to take advantage of existing open-software process management systems, and the other is aimed at providing a specific execution environment based on ECA (Event Condition Action) rules.

REFERENCES

Alvesson, M. (2004). *Knowledge work and knowledge-intensive firms*. Oxford, UK: Oxford University Press.

Bellotti, V., Dalal, B., Good, N., Flynn, P., Bobrow, D. G., & Ducheneaut, N. (2004). What a to-do: Studies of task management towards the design of a personal task list manager. In *Proceedings of SIGCHI Conference on Human Factors in Computing Systems* (pp. 735-742). New York: ACM.

Bruno, G. (2011). Agility and process agility: ho$w do they relate to each other? In M. M. Cruz-Cunha, & J. Varajão (Eds.), *E-business managerial aspects, solutions and case studies* (pp. 71–89). Hershey, PA: Information Science Publishing.

Bruno, G. (2012). Lecture Notes in Computer Science: Vol. 7447. *Combining information and activities in business processes* (pp. 481–488). Heidelberg, Germany: Springer. doi:10.1007/978-3-642-32597-7_43

Chao, T. et al. (2009). Lecture Notes in Computer Science: Vol. 5701. *Artifact-based transformation of IBM Global Financing* (pp. 261–277). Heidelberg, Germany: Springer.

Davenport, T. H., & Short, J. E. (1990). The new industrial engineering: information technology and business process redesign. *Sloan Management Review*, (Summer): 11–27.

Dumas, M., van der Aalst, W. M. P., & ter Hofstede, A. H. M. (2005). *Process-aware information systems: Bridging people and software through process technology*. New York: Wiley. doi:10.1002/0471741442

Goedertier, S., Haesen, R., & Vanthienen, J. (2008). Rule-based business process modelling and enactment. *International Journal of Business Process Integration and Management*, *3*, 194–207. doi:10.1504/IJBPIM.2008.023219

Grebner, O., & Riss, U. (2008). Implicit metadata generation on the semantic desktop using task management as example. In *Conference on Formal Ontologies Meet Industry* (pp.33-44). Amsterdam, The Netherlands: IOS Press.

Hull, R. (2008). Lecture Notes in Computer Science: Vol. 5332. *Artifact-centric business process models: Brief survey of research results and challenges* (pp. 1152–1163). Heidelberg, Germany: Springer. doi:10.1007/978-3-540-88873-4_17

Hull, R. et al. (2011). Lecture Notes in Computer Science: Vol. 6551. *Introducing the guard-stage-milestone approach for specifying business entity lifecycles* (pp. 1–24). Heidelberg, Germany: Springer. doi:10.1007/978-3-642-19589-1_1

Kucukoguz, E., & Su, J. (2011). Lecture Notes in Computer Science: Vol. 6551. *On lifecycle constraints of artifact-centric workflows* (pp. 71–85). Heidelberg, Germany: Springer.

Künzle, V., & Reichert, M. (2009). Towards object-aware process management systems: Issues, challenges, benefits. In *Lecture Notes in Business Information Processing, 29* (pp. 197–210). Heidelberg, Germany: Springer. doi:10.1007/978-3-642-01862-6_17

Künzle, V., & Reichert, M. (2011). PHILharmonicFlows: Towards a framework for object-aware process management. *Journal of Software Maintenance and Evolution: Research and Practice*, *23*(4), 205–244. doi:10.1002/smr.524

Küster, J. M., Ryndina, K., & Gall, H. (2007). Lecture Notes in Computer Science: Vol. 4714. *Generation of business process models for object life cycle compliance* (pp. 165–181). Heidelberg, Germany: Springer. doi:10.1007/978-3-540-75183-0_13

Lu, R., Sadiq, S., & Governatori, G. (2009). On managing business processes variants. *Data & Knowledge Engineering*, *68*(7), 642–664. doi:10.1016/j.datak.2009.02.009

Mans, R. S. et al. (2010). Proclets in healthcare. *Journal of Biomedical Informatics*, *43*(4), 632–649. doi:10.1016/j.jbi.2010.03.010 PMID:20359548

Marjanovic, O., & Freeze, R. D. (2011). Knowledge intensive business processes: Theoretical foundations and research challenges. In *Proceedings of the IEEE 44th Hawaii International Conference on System Sciences*. New York: IEEE Press.

Müller, D., Reichert, M., & Herbst, J. (2007). Lecture Notes in Computer Science: Vol. 4803. *Data-driven modeling and coordination of large process structures* (pp. 131–149). Heidelberg, Germany: Springer. doi:10.1007/978-3-540-76848-7_10

Nurcan, S. (2008). A survey on the flexibility requirements related to business processes and modeling artifacts. In *Proceedings of the IEEE 41st Hawaii International Conference on System Sciences*. New York: IEEE Press.

OMG-BPMN. (2011). *Business process model and notation*, V.2.0. Retrieved March 13, 2013, from http://www.omg.org/spec/BPMN/

OMG-OCL. (2010). *Object constraint language*, V.2.3.1. Retrieved March 13, 2013, from http://www.omg.org/spec/OCL/

OMG-UML. (2011). *Unified modeling language*, V.2.4. Retrieved March 13, 2013, from http://www.omg.org/spec/UML/2.4

Pesic, M., & van der Aalst, W. M. P. (2006). Lecture Notes in Computer Science: Vol. 4103. *A declarative approach for flexible business processes management* (pp. 169–180). Heidelberg, Germany: Springer. doi:10.1007/11837862_18

Riss, U. V., Rickayzen, A., Maus, H., & van der Aalst, W. M. P. (2005). Challenges for business process and task management. *Journal of Universal Knowledge Management*, *0*(2), 77–100.

Rummler, G. A., & Brache, A. P. (1995). *Improving performance: How to manage the white space on the organizational chart*. San Francisco: Jossey-Bass.

Stoitsev, T., Scheidl, S., & Spahn, M. (2007). A framework for light-weight composition and management of ad-hoc business processes. In *Lecture Notes in Business Information Processing, 4849* (pp. 213–226). Heidelberg, Germany: Springer. doi:10.1007/978-3-540-77222-4_17

van der Aalst, W. M. P., Pesic, M., & Schonenberg, H. (2009). Declarative workflows: Balancing between flexibility and support. *Computer Science -. Research for Development*, *23*(2), 99–113.

van der Aalst, W. M. P., Weske, M., & Grünbauer, D. (2005). Case handling: A new paradigm for business process support. *Data & Knowledge Engineering*, *53*(2), 129–162. doi:10.1016/j.datak.2004.07.003

Weske, M. (2007). *Business process management - Concepts, languages, architectures*. Berlin: Springer.

zur Muehlen, M., & Indulska, M. (2010). Modeling languages for business processes and business rules: A representational analysis. *Information Systems*, *35*, 379–390. doi:10.1016/j.is.2009.02.006

Chapter 9
The Impact of the Relationship between Gardner's Multiple Intelligence and Kolb's Learning Style

Tse-Kian Neo
Multimedia University, Malaysia

Sahar Sabbaghan
Multimedia University, Malaysia

ABSTRACT

In a diverse work environment, it is important to have diverse leaders, managers, and people with different talents and intelligence in order to deal with different problems. In this case, each individual can know their own strength and weakness, and know which position works best for them. The concept of learning styles is used to describe individual differences in the way people learn. According to Kolb (1984), each person has a unique way to absorb and process experiences and information. He has identified four statistically prevalent learning styles- diverging, assimilating, converging, and accommodating. On the other hand, Gardner's Multiple Intelligence Theory is very helpful to recognize that people have differing aptitude in different subject areas. This chapter documents a study in which the participants consisted of 153 bachelor students of Management from the Multimedia University of Malaysia. They were given two questionnaires, one for Kolb's learning style and other for Gardner's Multiple Intelligence inventory and a correlation was conducted. The results showed that there was a significant relationship between Kolb's Learning Style and Multiple Intelligence. The relationship could be seen particularly in Abstract Conceptualization (AC) and Multiple Intelligences which were Nature, kinesthetic, music, word, interpersonal, and picture. The results also indicated that the majority of the participants are between AC and AE which means they are convergers. Having the right information for companies can be beneficial since knowing how their employees learn can lead to a diverse workplace that would have significant results on organizational structure, planning, development, and operation.

DOI: 10.4018/978-1-4666-4711-4.ch009

INTRODUCTION

Learning to learn is a competence of which has great universal value. Knowledge is crucial for continual improvements to existing products and services and for radically innovative measures. Each individual needs to master this ability so that they can adjust to the constant changes in the working environment (Kessels, 2001).Due to the fact that knowledge productivity has become more crucial to the survival of most organizations, there is more stress on how one can learn faster and more productively. Organizations spend billions on training their employees every year according to *Training* magazine's 2012 Industry Report which found that the training budget has grown to 58.5 billion (Freifeld, n. d.).

Research by Warmerdam and van den Berg (1992) confirm the increasing importance of knowledge-based work. Simple, routine and low-level functions are decreasing, while complex high-level functions are increasing. Organizing educational provisions that promote learning to increase the knowledge productivity of individuals and teams have become part of the day to day business policy. Organizations are more aware about the importance of learning and on their way to promote it in every way possible. According to Kessels (1996), there are seven critical learning functions. The first one is the professional knowledge which is closely related to the organization's core competencies. This is due to the fact that professional knowledge is what the work is related to and all objectives are drawn to it. It can be both implicit and explicit knowledge and it can be transferred, codified and shared throughout the organization. The second and third functions are problem solving and reflecting which is learning to deal and identify new problems, Argyris 's double loop learning is a good example of questioning the existing values and therefore proceeding to consider other solutions and ideas. This tends to bring new visions and creativity. The fourth learning function is the communication skills which is foundation of how knowledge is transferred from one individual to another. Good communication skills help knowledge sharing and provide an environment where employees can be friendlier and work more effectively. The fifth function is self regulation of motivation which is the personal interest of learning. According to Pink (2010), people are motivated, when their job is challenging and they learn from it, he later states that intrinsic motivation is a powerful tool to get employees to go that extra mile. Personal interest is very much linked to inspiration, passion and sense-making (De Leenheer, 2004). The sixth learning function is the creative turmoil, According to Senge (1992) distance between vision and reality is the source of creative tension as distance makes it necessary to take action in order to come closer to the objective. A certain degree of chaos, disorder or even failure may prevent complacency, and could stimulate organizations to stretch beyond their strategic focus. Creative chaos can stimulate individuals to fundamentally change their ways of thinking and create new knowledge. The last function is peace and stability which is the need to reflect, learn and share. It gives the opportunity to assess one's performance and effectiveness. Peace and stability gives the certainty and the time which is required for specialization and improvement (Lakerveld, 2005). The learning functions peace & stability and creative turmoil may seem to be conflicting; however, they are supposed to balance one another.

Learning therefore, leads to better thinkers, vision, and personal mastery which is defined by Senge (1990, p.141), is "the discipline of personal growth and learning." It is a motivating factor for people who have high personal mastery skills to step towards their desired goals. Personal mastery according to Senge (1990) is recognized in several ways:

- They have a special sense of purpose or a calling.
- They accurately assess their current reality; in particular, they quickly recognize inaccurate assumptions.
- They are skilled at using creative tension to inspire their forward progress.
- They see change as opportunity.
- They are deeply inquisitive.
- They place a high priority on personal connections without giving up their individuality.
- They are systemic thinkers, that is, they see themselves as one part in a larger system.

Developing personal mastery is a lifelong process, in order for that process to begin, one must be ready to learn. In order for learning to happen, each individual must understand one's own learning style. The concept of learning styles is used to describe individual differences in the way people learn. One must understand the individuality of learners and the need to raise awareness their learning style. Therefore, different students may prefer different learning environments, learning modalities and the all exhibit unique strengths, talents and/or weaknesses. If we are to be successful in leading our learners through the task of learning, we must provide a variety of learning approaches so that these differences can be recognized and provided for in a learning environment. It helps them understand their learning styles, and thus "make transitions to higher levels of personal and cognitive functioning." (Knox, 1986, p.117). There have been many different approaches to measuring and identifying different types of learning styles, each of them having their merits and drawbacks. However, an amalgamation or blending of these concepts is probably more effective than any other approach.

According to Kolb (1984), each person has a unique way to absorb and process experiences and information. He argues that development in learning sophistication results from the integration of the dual dialectics of the learning process, i.e., conceptualizing or experiencing. Learning theory defines as "the process whereby knowledge is created through the transformation of experience(Kolb, 1984). The learning model portrays two dialectically related models of grasping experiences-Concrete Experience(CE) and abstract Conceptualization(AC) and two dialectically related modes of transforming experience-Reflective Observation (RO) and Active Experimentation(AE). Individual learning styles are determined by an individual's preferred way of resolving these two dialectics, favoring one mode over the other.

KOLB'S LEARNING STYLE

The Learning Style Inventory and the Four Basic learning Styles

In 1971, David Kolb developed The Learning Style Inventory (LSI) to assess individual learning styles (Figure 1). While individuals tested on the LSI show many different patterns of scores, research on the instrument has identified four statistically prevalent learning styles- diverging, assimilating, converging, and accommodating. The following summary of the four basic learning styles is based on both research and clinical observation of these patterns of LSI scores (Kolb, 1984).

Figure 1. Kolb's learning styles

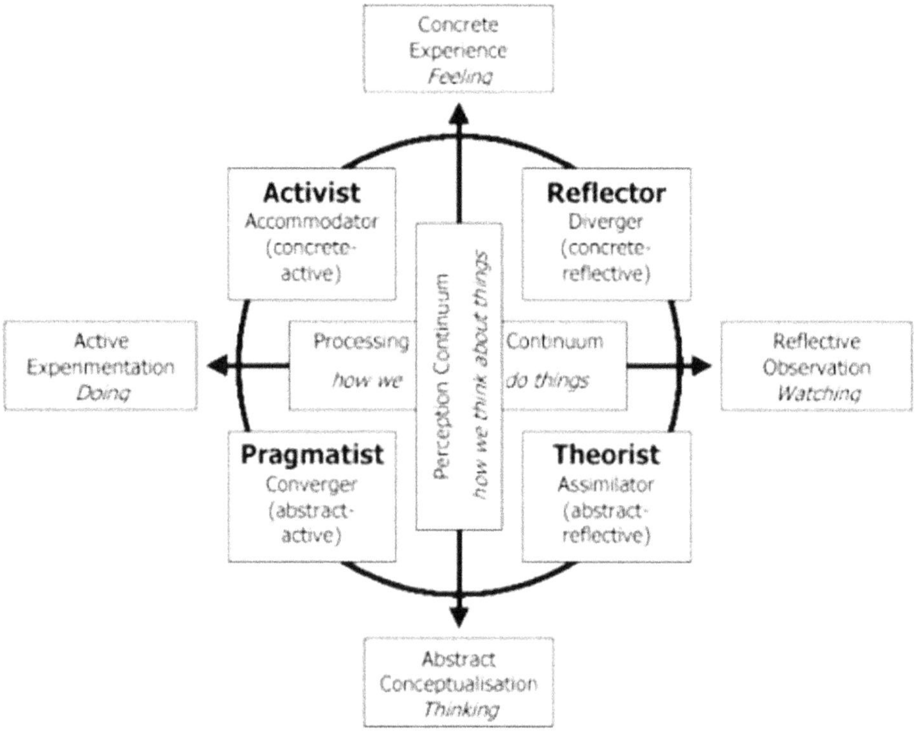

Diverging

The diverging style's dominant learning abilities are concrete experience and reflective observation. People with this learning style our best at viewing concrete situations from many different points of view. It is labelled "Diverging" because a person with it performs better in situations that call for generation of ideas, such as " brainstorming" session. People with a diverging learning style have broad cultural interests and like to gather information. Research shows that they are interested in people, tend to be imaginative and emotional, had broad cultural interests, and tend to specialize in the arts. In formal learning situations, people with the diverging style prefer to working groups, listening with an open mind and receiving personalized feedback.

Assimilating

The Assimilating style's dominant learning abilities are abstract conceptualization (AC) and reflective observation (RO). People with this learning style our best at understanding of a wide range of information and putting into concise, logical form. Individuals with an assimilating style are less focused on people and more interested in ideas and abstract concepts. Generally, people with this style find it more important that a theory have logical soundness than practical value. The assimilating learning style is important for effectiveness in information in a science careers. In formal learning situations, people with this style prefer reading, lectures, exploring analytical models, and having time to think things through.

Converging

The converging style's dominant learning abilities to be abstract conceptualization (AC) and active and experimentation (AE). People with this learning style are best at finding practical uses for ideas and theories. They have the ability to solve problems and make decisions based on finding solutions to questions or problems. Individuals with a converging learning style prefer to deal with technical tasks and problems rather than with social issues and interpersonal issues. In formal learning situations, people with the style prefer to experiment with new ideas, simulations, laboratory assignments, and practical applications.

Accommodating

The accommodating style's dominant learning abilities are concrete experience(CE) and active experimentation(AE), people with this learning style how the ability to learn from primarily "hand-on" experience. They enjoy carrying out plans and involving themselves in new and challenging experiences. Their tendency may be to act on "gut" feelings rather than on logical analysis. In solving problems, individuals with an accommodating learning style rely more heavily on people for information and then on their own technical analysis. This learning style is important for effectiveness in action oriented careers. In formal learning situations, people with the accommodating learning style prefer to work with others to get assignments done, to set goals, to do field work and to test out different approaches to completing a project.

MULTIPLE INTELLIGENCE

Multiple Intelligence Theory has been very helpful to recognize that people have different aptitudes in different subject areas. It is believed that each person possesses all eight of the intelligences, but to a different degree which can be developed with adequate instruction and training (Gardner, 1993).

Gardner advocates that there are at least eight intelligences which need to be considered:

1. **Linguistic:** The potential to use language, as used in reading, writing, telling stories, memorizing dates, and thinking in words.
2. **Logical-Mathematical:** The potential for understanding cause and effect and for manipulating numbers, quantities, and operations, as used in math, reasoning, logic, problem solving, and recognizing patterns.
3. **Spatial:** The potential for representing the spatial world internally in one's mind as used in reading maps and charts, drawing, solving mazes and puzzles, imagining and visualizing.
4. **Kinesthetic:** The potential for using one's whole body or parts of the body, as used in athletics, dancing, acting, crafting, and using tools.
5. **Musical:** The potential for thinking in music; for hearing, recognizing, and remembering patterns, as used in singing, identifying sounds, and in remembering melodies and rhythms.
6. **Interpersonal:** The potential for working with others, as used in understanding people, leading and organizing others, communicating, resolving conflicts, and selling.

7. **Intrapersonal:** The potential for understanding ourselves, as used in understanding self, recognizing one's own strengths and weaknesses, and setting personal goals.
8. **Naturalistic:** The potential for discriminating among plants, animals, rocks, and the world around us, as used in understanding nature, making distinctions, identifying flora and fauna.

Even though Gardner's multiple intelligences theory has been applied to the field of education, multiple intelligences can go much further and be used in business and other fields. Although research on multiple intelligence and leadership is still rather new, there are important implications to grasping the true relationship between multiple intelligences and leadership effectiveness (Friday, Friday-Stroud, Green, & Hill, 2006). Leaders with different intelligences may be able to deal with different approaches to promote the productivity of the organization. The theory of Multiple Intelligences has significant implications for leader effectiveness, leader selection and development. As globalisation has spread, leaders of organizations are required to have many attributes, showcasing "effective leadership skills, talents and abilities" (Wilson & Mujtaba, 2007, p. 1), these include "a sense of global sensitivity, cultural fluency, technological literacy and entrepreneurial flair." Wilson and Mujtaba (2007) suggest that the success of organizations is increased when effective leadership is present, particularly in different organizations where they may have different leadership expectations. Wilson and Mujtaba (2007) were then able to identify the relationships in a faculty between four domains of multiple intelligences. Once results were acquired, they then analysed the impact of Gardner's multiple intelligences on "leadership selection, training and development". Hoffman and Frost (2006), in a study in the Business Management domain, focussed on the dimensions of transformational leadership and the impact of emotional, social, and cognitive intelligences. Their findings indicated that using the multiple intelligences framework is a useful method to predict transformational leadership, and the effect that leaders will have on others. More recently, Riggio, Murphy, and Pirozzolo (2013) have stated that the incorporation of multiple intelligences constructs into existing leadership theories will improve the understanding of effective leadership, and that the possession of multiple forms of intelligence is important for effective leadership. Their research also stated that multiple intelligences have important implications for both the selection and training of future leaders.

METHOD

In the study, the participants consisted of 153 bachelor students of Management of Multimedia University of Malaysia. All participants were provided with a thorough explanation of the research, and its purposes, and how the findings would be valuable to the field of teaching and training. All participants were free to leave the project at any time, and incentives were not provided for their participation.

The participants in this study were given two questionnaires, one was Kolb's Learning Style Inventory and the other was the Multiple Intelligence Development Scale(MIDAS) which was administered to find one of eight dominant intelligence of the learner. It should be noted that, the scores were processed according to the MIDAS instruction Manual. In addition, the scores were tested on the skewness, in order to determine the normality of the data.

It is important to note that in order to encourage the students to answer with more care, they were told that the results of the test will have an impact on their final class grade.

Testing the Null Hypothesis

In order to investigate the relationship between Kolb's Learning Styles and the Multiple Intelligence Theory, a correlation matrix was carried out for every learning style and eight intelligence. Table 1 gives insight on the correlation between CE and Multiple Intelligence. As it is reveled from Table 1, there seems to be no relationship between RO and MI.

Table 2 shows, the correlation between CE and MI, as it is revealed by the table, there is a slight positive correlation between CE and Kinesthetic, and CE and Nature.

From Table 3 it is revealed that there is a strong correlation between AC and MI, as it is revealed by the table, there is a positive correlation between AC and the following intelligences: Kinesthetic, Nature, Music,

Table 1. Correlation between RO and MI

		RO	Word	Math	Kinesthetic	Music	Interpersonal	Intrapersonal	Nature	Picture
RO	Pearson Correlation	1	-.012	-.123	-.035	.018	.008	-.088	-.042	.029
	Sig. (2-tailed)		.884	.131	.665	.822	.924	.279	.608	.721
	N Percentage	153 27%	153	153	153	153	153	153	153	153

**. Correlation is significant at the 0.01 level (2tailed).
*. Correlation is significant at the 0.05 level (2-tailed).

Table 2. Correlation between CE and MI

		CE	Word	Math	Kinesthetic	Music	Interpersonal	Intrapersonal	Nature	Picture
CE	Pearson Correlation	1	.097	.034	.332**	.286**	.140	-.073	.386**	.150
	Sig. (2-tailed)		.234	.675	.000	.000	.084	.369	.000	.065
	N Percentage	153 15%	153	153	153	153	153	153	153	153

**. Correlation is significant at the 0.01 level (2tailed).

Table 3. Correlation between AC and MI

		AC	Word	Math	Kinesthetic	Music	Interpersonal	Intrapersonal	Nature	Picture
AC	Pearson Correlation	1	.451**	.304**	.665**	.485**	.444**	.297**	.544**	.395**
	Sig. (2-tailed)		.000	.000	.000	.000	.000	.000	.000	.000
	N Percentage	153 31%	153	153	153	153	153	153	153	153

**. Correlation is significant at the 0.01 level (2tailed).

Word, and Interpersonal. There is also a slight correlation between AC and picture and math.

Table 4. shows, the correlation between AE and MI, as it is revealed by the table, there is a slight positive correlation between AE and Music.

According to this study, there was a significant relationship between Kolb's Learning Style and Multiple Intelligence. The relationship could be seen particularly in AC and Multiple Intelligences which were Nature, kinesthetic, music, word, interpersonal, and picture. There were also a slight relationship between CE and kinesthetic and nature; and also between AE and Music. There was no relationship between RO and Multiple Intelligences. The results show, that the majority of the participants are between AC and AE which means they are convergers and the second in lead is between AE and CE, which means they are accommodators. Since the participants' major is management, that kind of learning style may help them in the future, since it raises their awareness and knowledge on what works best.

CONCLUSION

According to Gardner (1993), all human beings have multiple intelligences. These multiple intelligences can be nurtured and strengthened, or ignored and weakened. Kolb (1984) suggested that each person has a unique way of absorbing and processing experiences and information. He argues that development in learning sophistication results from the integration of the dual dialects of the learning process, these being conceptualizing and acting. Learning theory defines learning as the process whereby knowledge is created through the transformation of experience (Kolb, 1984). According to Kolb (2000, p. 14), certain learning styles tend to gravitate toward certain career types. However, people follow many different patterns. Even within a particular career, there may be sub-patterns of learning styles and interests to consider.

This research has several implications. Firstly, in a diverse work environment, people with different talents and intelligence are essential in order to deal with different problems (Friday, Friday-Stroud, Green, & Hill, 2006). In this case, each individual can know their own strength and weakness, and recognize which position works best from them. The company benefits by knowing how their employees learn and therefore can proceed to plan accordingly. This leads to a workplace that would have significant positive results on organizational structure, planning, development, and operation. The organization will benefit from the increased knowledge and skill of its entire people, resulting in greater productivity, innovation, and economical success (Wilson & Mujtaba, 2007). According to Toms (1997,

Table 4. Correlation between AE and MI

		AE	Word	Math	Kinesthetic	Music	Interpersonal	Intrapersonal	Nature	Picture
AE	Pearson Correlation	1	.149	.069	.231**	.286**	.114	.006	.221**	.084
	Sig. (2-tailed)		.066	.395	.004	.000	.162	.939	.006	.300
	N Percentage	153 26%	153	153	153	153	153	153	153	153

**. Correlation is significant at the 0.01 level (2tailed).

p. 26), 'The market value of companies that succeed in the decades to come will be found principally in their intellectual assets: Their people and the knowledge these people have about the organization's core competencies." This is due to the fact, that for companies to be successful in the future, they must be adaptive, innovative, and creative to be able to respond to changes in the marketplace, technological changes, and social changes. Therefore a more diverse workforce, with continuous learning, is necessary for organizations in order to survive.

Secondly, successful organizations of the future must be prepared to identify and demonstrate its core competencies and the leadership capabilities of its diverse workforce, as this is essential if it wishes to survive and remain as a competitive force in a dynamic, global society. In order to maximize organizational effectiveness, organizations need to focus on implementing practical processes to select, train, and develop leadership. Leadership has become a role for employees of all levels and roles within learning organizations. As people in organizations come from different backgrounds, and often cultures, it is important for leaders to strive to be true cross-cultural leaders who can work effectively in different cultural contexts (Wilson & Mujtaba, 2008). This involves clarifying facts, discussing existing stereotypes and making clear company expectations (Wilson & Mujtaba, 2008). This will in turn create a healthy learning environment for all people present in the organizational structure. In addition, Mujtaba (2010, p.12) suggests that organizations should expect "all professionals to become true diversity champions". This process involves learning to tolerate, respect and understand differences, as well as investigating appropriate options, in order to create an inclusive working environment (Wilson & Mujtaba, 2008). In addition, according to Gardner (1999), leaders like other human beings exhibit several multiple intelligences. Nonetheless the most dominating intelligences are the verbal-linguistic, interpersonal, and intrapersonal intelligences. In other words, leaders are articulate and expressive; and demonstrate a strong sense of their own selves.

Finally, Senge (1990, p.3) defines the learning organization as: 'organizations where people continually expand their capacity to create results they truly desire, where new and expansive patterns of thinking are nurtured, where collective aspiration is set free, and where people continually learn how to learn together'. This makes it necessary for employees to be equipped with skills such as critical thinking or investigative skills. Therefore, learning is not an individual behavioural attribute or capability but a 'double-loop' cognitive learning process that can be shared; and if everyone can participate in shared learning then, in principle, everyone is capable of leading (Senge 2006). By understanding one's potential learning style, it is possible to grow and strive for self-actualization and personal self-mastery. Therefore, by extending the scope of individual autonomy, learning can be enhanced, and there will be a boost in knowledge creation and innovation in organizations (Nonaka & Takeuchi, 1995).

REFERENCES

Armstrong, T. (2009). *Multiple intelligences in the classroom.* Alexandria, VA: Assn for Supervision & Curriculum.

De Leenheer, P. (2004). Revising and managing multiple ontology versions in a possible worlds setting. In *Proc. of On the Move to Meaningful Internet Systems Ph.D. Symposium (OTM 2004), Agia Napa, Cyprus,* (LNCS 3292) (pp. 798-818). Berlin, Germany: Springer.

Freifeld, L. (n. d.). 2012 Training industry report. *Training.* Retrieved from http://www.trainingmag.com/content/2012-training-industry-report

Friday, E., Friday-Stroud, S. S., Green, A. L., & Hill, A. Y. (2006). A multi-semester comparison of student performance between multiple traditional and online sections of two management courses. *Journal of Behavioral and Applied Management*, *8*(1), 66–81.

Gardner, H. (1983). *Frames of mind: The theory of multiple intelligences.* New York: Basic Books.

Gardner, H. (1993). Frames of mind: The theory of multiple intelligences (10th anniversary ed.). New York: Basic Books.

Gardner, H. (1999). *Intelligence reframed.* New York: Basic Books.

Gardner, H., & Hatch, T. (1989). Multiple intelligences go to school: Educational implications of the theory of multiple intelligences. *Educational Researcher*, *18*(8), 4–10.

Hoffman, B. J., & Frost, B. C. (2006). Multiple intelligences of transformational leaders: An empirical examination. *International Journal of Manpower*, *27*(1), 37–51. doi:10.1108/01437720610652826

Kessels, J. W. M. (1996). Knowledge productivity and the corporate curriculum. In J. F. Schreinemakers (Ed.), *Knowledge management, organisation, competence and methodology* (pp. 168–174). Würzburg, Germany: Ergon Verlag.

Kessels, J. W. M. (2001). Verleiden tot kennisproductiviteit [Tempting towards knowledge productivity]. Inaugural Lecture, University of Twente, Enschede, The Netherlands.

Knox, A. (1986). Helping adults learn. *Improving Learning Skills*, *4*(4), 15–17.

Kolb, D. (1984). *Experiential learning: Experiences as the source of learning and development.* Upper Saddle River, NJ: Prentice Hall.

Mujtaba, B. G. (2010). *Workplace diversity management: Challenges, competencies and strategies* (2nd ed.). Davie, FL: ILEAD Academy Publications.

Pink, D. H. (2010). *Drive: The surprising truth about what motivates us.* New York: Penguin.

Riggio, R. E., Murphy, S. E., & Pirozzolo, F. (2002). *Multiple intelligences and leadership.* Mahwah, NJ: Lawrence Erlbaum Associates, Inc.

Senge, P. M. (1990). The leader's new work: Building learning organizations. *Sloan Management Review*, (Fall): 7–23.

Senge, P. M. (1992). *The fifth discipline – The art & practice of the learning organization.* London: Century Business.

Toms, W. (1997). *Corporate instinct: Building a knowing enterprise for the 21st century.* New York: Van Nostrand Reinhold.

van Lakerveld, J. (2005). *Het Corporate Curriculum, Onderzoek naar werk-leeromstandigheden in instellingen voor Zorg en Welzijn* (thesis). Universiteit Twente, Enschede, The Netherlands.

Warmerdam, J., & van den Berg, J. (1992). *Scholing van werknemers in veranderende organisaties*. Den Haag: Ministerie van Sociale Zaken en Werkgelegenheid/ITS Vuga.

Wilson, S. D. (2005). *The relationship between leadership and domains of multiple intelligences*. ProQuest Information and Learning Company. (UMI No: 3151206).

Wilson, S. D., & Mujtaba, B. G. (2007). The relationship between multiple intelligences, culture and diversity. *International Business & Economics Research Journal*, *6*(8), 9–22.

Wilson, S. D., & Mujtaba, B. G. (2008). Intelligence and diversity: A western and eastern view from a global paradigm. *International Business and Economics Research Journal*, *7*(6), 29–39.

Chapter 10
Argument Extraction in Opinion Analysis:
Identifying the Reasons Behind Consumer Evaluations

Maria Paz Garcia-Villalba
IRIT-CNRS Toulouse France

Patrick Saint-Dizier
IRIT-CNRS Toulouse France

ABSTRACT

In this chapter, the authors present foundational elements related to argument extraction in opinion texts to design a model of how consumers develop argumentation in such texts. A second goal of the chapter is to analyze and synthesize user preferences and therefore user value systems from these arguments. The authors show that (1) that the association of an evaluative expression with a discourse structure such as an elaboration, an illustration, or a reformulation must be interpreted as an argument and (2) that the link between a consumer statement and a related argument often requires domain knowledge and dedicated inference schemas. This chapter develops a conceptual semantics of these discourse structures.

AIMS AND CHALLENGES

In the framework of opinion analysis, besides determining whether consumers or citizens are happy or unhappy with a given product or decision, it is of utmost importance to be able to identify *why* they like or dislike a product, or approve or disapprove of a decision. These reasons are mainly provided by arguments associated with the evaluations of product attributes. At the present stage of opinion analysis, there is no 'deep' analysis of the satisfaction or dissatisfaction of consumers or citizens that would provide such an insight on

DOI: 10.4018/978-1-4666-4711-4.ch010

the arguments behind these evaluations. On a large set of texts, over a closely related range of products, this analysis would allow the induction of the main priorities, value systems or preferences of consumers or citizens. This is however a difficult task, as illustrated in Van Eemeren et al. (1984, 1992), among others. Argument extraction in texts in general and in opinion texts in particular is an emerging area. Applied to opinion analysis, to the best of our knowledge, and besides principles given in Fiedler et al. (2001) and the results presented in Delmonte et al. (2012), this constitutes a relatively innovative step that should allow the capture of consumers underlying motivations.

Furthermore, a system of consumer preferences can be induced for each feature from these arguments. Given a recommendation (e.g. *I strongly recommend it, do not stay here, go there if no alternative,* etc.) and a list of attributes which are positively evaluated at various degrees (e.g. *very well located, quite cheap*) as well as another list of attributes which are negatively evaluated (e.g. *not so clean, small rooms, quite noisy*), it is possible to elaborate a system of user preferences or system of values. For a given consumer, it is indeed possible to identify their preferences: if the overall evaluation is positive, this roughly means that the positive attributes are globally more important than the negative ones. For a given product, on a larger scale, considering the pros and cons and the recommendations over a set of consumer evaluations, it is then possible to infer that some features are more essential than others, e.g. that localization and fares are more important than comfort for young consumers. In general, a system of values or preferences must be elaborated by consumer categories, (e.g. by age and aims), since priorities may be different.

From an application point of view, identifying arguments related to opinion expression and making a synthesis is very important for the service provider or decision-maker who can then focus on the criteria which need to be improved first.

In this chapter, from a linguistic and cognitive point of view, we show that the association of an evaluative expression with a discourse structure such as an elaboration, an illustration, or a reformulation must also be interpreted as an argument. These constructions are central to identify the *why* behind the evaluated statement. We then identify the necessary types of inferences and world or domain knowledge which are needed to be able to link an opinion statement and its related arguments so that the relation between the evaluative expression and the arguments is clear and straightforward. For that purpose, we develop a number of cases based on examples that we analyze in depth.

In this chapter we develop a global conceptual semantic representation for opinion expression, since opinions need to be interpreted to infer user preferences and to construct a synthesis. We feel this is also an important step in this type of work, since a conceptual representation should allow the abstraction of natural language utterances, therefore allowing their interpretation, inference and synthesis. Finally, we show how an automatic recognition of these structures can be implemented in the Dislog programming language on the <TextCoop> platform, dedicated to discourse analysis (Saint-Dizier, 2012).

RELATED WORK

Research Overview in Opinion Analysis

Opinion analysis applies to various areas, from the evaluation of a product or a cultural event to the approval or disapproval of a certain social attitude or a political decision. Most opinion analysis systems are based on a global and shallow statistical analysis of positive or negative terms found close to another given term (e.g. a product name). This approach gives interesting general trends when applied to large sets of documents (Breck et al., 2005). In a second stage, language models of opinion expression have been developed to refine this initial schematic view. These models are much more elaborated and may include e.g. taking into account figures of communication such as irony or emphasis, as in the CRYSTAL system (Kim et al., 2007; Popescu et al., 2005). A recent synthesis and analysis of the main trends in this area can be found in Pang et al. (2008) and Liu (2012). These models however do not allow a deep analysis of the author's motivations and reasons for such opinions.

The results produced by the still scarce opinion analysis systems based on a semantic analysis of evaluative expressions (basically the evaluated attribute, the polarity of the associated value and the role played by adverbs to reinforce or weaken the evaluation) are of much interest and can produce relatively accurate opinion analysis in context, most notably Taboada et al. (2009, 2011), but also Bal et al. (2008), Bethard et al. (2004), Breck et al. (2007), and Fiedler et al. (2001). More recently, within the framework of conversation analysis, Pallotta et al. (2011) and Delmonte et al. (2011) show the need for deep linguistic knowledge and processes to be able to correctly and accurately extract arguments in general and from opinions in particular.

The results elaborated in the area of lexical semantics are of much interest to our approach, with the development of strategies to create large general purpose lexicons for sentiment or opinion analysis (SemEval 2007 workshop). Simancik et al. (2009) develop an interesting valence annotation and valence shifting operations for opinion analysis which take into account the variability of opinion statements. However, our experience with users and opinion analysts shows that these resources and processes need quite a complex tuning to be really adapted to a precise area and also to the goals behind surface analysis (e.g. how the analysis is interpreted by analysts taking into account authors' profiles and value systems).

Finally, the importance of discourse analysis for opinion analysis and the need to select relevant text portions has been outlined in the past e.g. in Kim et al. (2007) and Taboada et al. (2009, 2011). However, as noted in Pang et al. (2008), so far these investigations lead to rather informal and general considerations on the need for discourse analysis.

Discourse Structure and Argument Analysis

Discourse structure analysis is a very challenging task because of the large diversity of discourse structures, the various forms they take in language and the importance of knowledge and pragmatics for their identification (Longacre, 1982; Keil, 2000). Recognizing discourse structures cannot in general be based solely on purely lexical or morphosyntactic considerations: subtle kinds of knowledge associated with reasoning schemas are often necessary. The latter capture some facets of the influence of pragmatic factors in our understanding of texts, as described in Kintsch (1988) and Di Eugenio et al. (1996).

Rhetorical structure theory (RST) (Mann et al., 1988, 1992) is a major attempt to organize discourse analysis, with the definition of 22 basic structures. Since then, almost 200 relations have been introduced which are more or less clearly defined. Background information about RST, annotation tools and corpora are accessible at http://www.sfu.ca/rst/. A recent overview is developed in Taboada et al. (2006). Very briefly, RST poses that coherent texts consist of minimal units, which are all linked to each other, recursively, through rhetorical relations. No unit is left pending: all units are connected to others. Some text spans appear to be more central to the text purpose, these are called nuclei (or kernels), whereas others are somewhat more secondary, they are called satellites. Satellites must be associated with nuclei. Relations between nuclei and satellites are one-to-one or one-to-many. For example, an argument conclusion may have several supports, possibly with different orientations. Conversely, a given support can be associated with several distinct conclusions. In our context, kernels, as shall be seen, are evaluative expressions.

Within the domain of computational linguistics, RST has been mainly developed in natural language generation for content planning purposes, (e.g. Kosseim et al., 2000; Reed et al., 1998). Besides language generation, Marcu (1997, 2000) developed a general framework and efficient strategies to recognize a number of major rhetorical structures in various kinds of texts. The main challenges are the recognition of textual units and the identification of relations that hold between them. His work is based on a number of psycholinguistic investigations carried out by Grosz et al. (1986), which show that discourse markers are used by human subjects both as cohesive links between adjacent clauses and as connectors between larger textual units. An important result is that discourse markers are used consistently with the semantics and pragmatics of the textual units they connect and they are relatively frequent and unambiguous.

An argumentation framework is a complex graph structure which exhibits the various conceptual relations that hold between arguments (support and attack are the most well-known, but there are many others, e.g. of a rhetorical nature). We will not develop this aspect here since there is abundant literature on argument typology and argument schemes. Walton et al. (2008), among others, is a good analysis of the functional and logical aspects of argumentation. A synthesis of computational models for processing arguments is reported in Reed et al., (2007).

Arguments are often closely associated with various types of discourse structures, in particular those related to explanation, which contribute to their strength, communicative goals and persuasion effects (e.g. Reed et al., 1997; Masthoff et al., 2008). This view is central in the pragma-dialectical theory (Eemeren et al., 1984, 1992; Eemeren, 2002) which considers the entirety of an argumentation as a discourse activity. More recent developments, from a philosophical and linguistic point of view can be found in Budzynska, (2010) and Budzynska et al. (2012).

Argumentative Inferences and Connectives

Within the field of natural language processing, an argumentation framework needs to be decomposed into its constitutive elements (premises, inferences, conclusions) in order to create conceptual representations which can therefore be integrated to an automated system for their recognition and/or synthesis. The study of inferences dates back to Ancient Greek Philosophy with the development of logic and inductive reasoning, and numerous distinctions and taxonomies have been introduced since Grice's Theory of Implicature (Grice, 1975). We will not enter into such considerations here, focusing on lexical inferences (Anick & Bergler, 1992) made between particular text spans or discourse relations in a text. Mirkin et al. (2009) call this type of inferences 'sub-sentential textual entailment', limiting the scope of an inference to a sub-sentential level, as is the case of the inferences which arise between certain evaluative expressions and their arguments.

The importance of establishing a methodology to access these lexical inferences has been highlighted on numerous occasions, (e.g. Kayser, 1997; Wedekind, 1996), with an emphasis on the utility of connectives in determining inferences coming into play between discourse relations. Within inferential approaches to the study of cue phrases or connectives, Relevance Theory (see Sperber & Wilson, 1986; Luscher, 1989; Moeschler, 2003), LDRT (Spenader & Maier, 2009) and the Theory of Argumentation in Language (Anscombre & Ducrot, 1997) all consider that connectives encode or trigger procedural information which determines the relation holding between text spans. More recently, Winterstein (2012) analyzes the nature of the argumentative inferences made accessible by the connective *but* in the light of these inferential approaches. According to him, all these theories agree on the necessity of determining a 'pivotal inferential element' activated by the first conjunct and then denied by the second in a contrast relation, but they disagree on the status of that element (Wintestein, 2012, pp. 1867-1868). In the present chapter, we will refer to that pivotal element as the glue bonding an evaluative statement to its arguments, similar to the 'dialogue glue' which logically connects dialogical moves in Asher & Lascarides (2003) and Reed (2011).

Winterstein (2012) argues that the nature of such inferences, or the argumentative goals activated by an assertion, are of two types: world-knowledge goals and mechanical goals calculated from the content and from constituents of the utterance alone (see Winterstein, 2012, p. 1877, for a more detailed explanation of the latter as defined by the author). Here we provide with a more detailed taxonomy of inferences in order to better capture the relation between an evaluative statement and its arguments, focusing on the contrast and concession relations, as well as introducing a preliminary analysis of the consequence relation.

SOME MOTIVATIONAL EXAMPLES

Constructing and validating a corpus of texts for a given investigation is a crucial preliminary step. The work reported here has been carried out on a development corpus of French opinion texts in the domains of hotels and restaurants, audio and video products, and the French political campaign. A smaller corpus was developed for English.

Here is a motivational example extracted from our development corpus which has been manually annotated. It includes most of the structures introduced in this chapter:

1. **HOTEL Lone Pine:** I was in a road trip with some friends and we booked a room for one night at the Lone Pine Hotel because there was no other hotel close enough to Death Valley which would take four people in the same room. We were really surprised at the great quality of this hotel, [$_{\text{JUSTIFICATION}}$ especially **since** it is located in the middle of nowhere.] Our room was big, [$_{\text{COMPARISON}}$ **as** is often the case with American hotels.] It was clean and well-furnished, [$_{\text{PRECISION}}$ **with** two King-size beds large enough for six people, enough storage space, flat screen

TV and quite a large fridge, [$_{\text{CONSEQUENCE}}$ **so** we could put all the food we had left so it wouldn't go to waste.]] [$_{\text{CONCESSION}}$ **However**, the bathroom was not very practical.] [$_{\text{CONCESSION}}$ **Although** it was big enough,] we didn't have enough towels. The shower run well [$_{\text{CONTRAST}}$ **but** it had no door,] [$_{\text{CONSEQUENCE}}$ **so** the water kept leaking long after you had a shower.]] The staff was friendly and really helpful [$_{\text{ILLUSTRATION}}$ (**for example**, we didn't know how to get to the entrance of Death Valley so they even printed maps and directions for us)]. Breakfast was excellent and very original [$_{\text{ENUMERATION}}$ **:** coffee, hot chocolate, tea of all sorts, juice, toast, meat and mashed potatoes, pastry, fruit, even croissants…] [$_{\text{REFORMULATION}}$ **in other words**, generous and tasty!] We felt we were getting good value [$_{\text{COMPARISON}}$ **for** the price we were paying.] All in all it was a very good experience and I think I would come back if I ever were to visit Death Valley again. ***Would definitely recommend it***.

In this typical example, we have a number of attribute-value pairs which are underlined. While some expressions are rather neutral such as 'our room was big', others have a higher semantic load such as '*breakfast was very original'* which indicates that breakfast is positively evaluated, with a specific motivation, namely that it includes unusual products. It is clear that the importance of the semantic contents is a fuzzy notion which is highly domain and author dependent. However, some criteria can be introduced such as the strength of the expression, its frequency or the degree of metaphorical use, to evaluate this importance or salience. This is addressed in the methodology section, where we show that salience must be defined jointly by discourse analysts and domain experts. In most cases, evaluative expressions are rather simple, with moderate language diversity, since authors want their text to be easy to understand and a number of them have a moderate literacy level.

In a different register, we find that such texts display a very large number of discourse structures associated with evaluative expressions (justification, comparison, elaboration, etc.) that make the evaluation more precise. We have labeled in the text those discourse structures which can be interpreted as arguments justifying the evaluation. The text ends by an overall recommendation. It is globally positive, but it also has some restrictions on some attributes that reflect a complex argumentation process over several features, with more or less explicit weights and preferences.

Let us have a look at another localized example of a contrast relation extracted from our corpus in French. We have translated this example for the sake of readability, including the original between brackets:

2. Located right in the city center [$_{\text{CONTRAST}}$ **but** quiet] (>Situé en plein centre mais calme)

Here we can see that the link between the first evaluation and the contrast relation is not completely straightforward. If we interpret 'central location' as an evaluative expression orienting the argumentation towards a positive conclusion, and the adjective 'quiet' also as orienting towards a positive conclusion, then the contrast relation may seem unjustified and yet this sentence appears perfectly natural and understandable to the reader. To understand the felicity of this argumentation, we need to take into account all the inferences that are made accessible by the first conjunct. Indeed, 'central location' does not only imply positive values such as 'close to tourist attractions' or 'luxurious', but also potential negative aspects, such as 'expensive' or 'noisy'. The second conjunct therefore selects only one of all the possible inferences, in this case a negative one, 'noisy', which is subsequently denied by 'quiet', thus justifying the contrast relation.

These inferences are the glue between evaluative expressions and arguments and they can be inferred from the lexical elements in the sentence, be made accessible by world-knowledge or be domain-dependent. For instance, in the previous example, the inference in the first conjunct is selected via a general rule or axiom stored in the world-knowledge of the interlocutors, namely the fact that the city center is bound to be noisy. Since these rules can be domain-dependent, their stability will partially depend on the precision of the attributes and values defined in the opinion analysis of the corpus. For example, in this evaluation from our corpus on French politicians:

3. Sarkozy is more about actions than about explanations, he has got the crisis under control [$_{\text{CONTRAST}}$ **but** French people need to hear him]. (>Sarkozy est plus dans l'action que dans l'explication, il gère la crise mais les français ont besoin de l'**en**tendre)

Is there a rule which determines the relation between the values attached to the attribute 'competence' and the attribute 'communication'? *To whi*ch extent are politicians valued solely on the basis of their actions or on the basis of their words? In the section about identifying and characterizing the glue between evaluative expressions and arguments we provide with a first attempt at classifying the different types of knowledge involved, giving some examples of general rules or axioms found in our corpus of hotels and politicians. Finally, we also take an interest on how inferences influence the conclusion reached through complex argumentation, so for instance, if a general rule is identified stating that "in politics, actions or words alone do not suffice," the conclusion in the previous example could be that Sarkozy needs to improve his communication skills.

METHODOLOGY AND EXPERIMENTS

The Corpus

The results presented below are based on a manual analysis of a corpus of texts in French, which is our development corpus. For the sake of readability, English glosses are given in the paper. This corpus has the overall structure shown in Table 1 for the domains considered.

Table 1. The Corpus

Domain	Number of Texts	Average Number of Words per Text	Average Number of Evaluative Expressions per Text
Politics	80	250	7
Hotels	130	220	12
Restaurants	65	140	11
Hifi products	75	170	6

In terms of corpus validation, for the politics domain the corpus is composed of readers' answers to on-line newspaper articles, blog and forum posts from various political orientations and concerning various candidates. Hotels and restaurants texts come from consumer evaluations posted on various evaluation sites, which have more or less precise authoring recommendations. They concern products from various countries for business or tourism, and are written by authors of various ages and profiles. Audio and video product opinions also come from consumer evaluations found on on-line commercial sites. From this corpus, a total of 45 texts for hotels and restaurants have been extracted for evaluation.

The Annotation Process

The analysis and the annotation of our texts is not a standard process as can be found in computational linguistics to annotate e.g. verb structure from examples, as shown in SemEval (2007) workshop and Simancik et al. (2009). The two main reasons are (1) that discourse annotation is a very difficult task, with low inter-annotator agreement in general, and (2) that in our context decisions about relevance and attribute salience are highly dependent on the domain and on the kind of opinion analysis to be carried out. We feel that this analysis process, although somewhat informal, constitutes a method to reproduce our system over various opinion domains.

We first annotate opinion statements, which are under an attribute-value form. This aspect will not be investigated here, since it is developed in (Garcia-Villalba et al., 2012). The main annotation stage is the discourse level. It is well-known that annotating discourse structures is in general a very difficult task. In our case, we considered only a small number of relations, listed below. These relations have already been investigated in a previous work (Bourse et al., 2012) dedicated to explanation analysis in didactic texts. In the present case, we adapt the analysis taking into account a manual inspection of texts. Similarly to didactic texts, opinion texts are in general very explicit at the discourse level in the sense that typical marks for each relation are used in order to make sure that the opinion is clear and easy to understand. Texts which are not sufficiently well-written are simply ignored: there is so much redundancy in opinion expression that ignoring even 20% of the texts is not a major issue.

There are more specialized domains where this approach, while remaining valid, could be more difficult to carry out. Let us note some examples of very specialized domains such as book reviews (poetry, fantasy) or musical interpretation analysis on CDs where the identification of attributes and values is really very complex. Similarly, opinion analysis in specialized areas such as the legal domain is also very challenging, because texts have a complex style and are very rich in technical terms and embedded discourse structures. In terms of robustness, the results given in the last section of this chapter show that the identification of discourse structures, as shown in (Bourse et al., 2012), works well in this context.

EVALUATIVE EXPRESSIONS IN OPINION TEXTS

The expression of opinion about a product or an event in a text is in general a set of sequences of language utterances, each evaluating an attribute or a facet of that product or event. We will not address here the topic of attribute analysis which has been the subject of many debates in AI and language, (e.g. Lakoff, 1988). Let us call each element in such a sequence ***an evaluative expression***: it provides an evaluation about a given attribute. An evaluative expression is often rendered in a rather direct style. However, it can be constructed from metaphors or from forms of irony, dramatization or emphasis. To avoid this, on most specific systems where consumers are invited to express their opinion, style guidelines are provided to avoid unclear or too personal descriptions. In the case of products for the general public, attributes or properties to be evaluated are suggested to consumers because they do not necessarily have a high literacy level.

Although this is not an issue in this chapter, and only for the sake of clarity, let us develop some elements concerning evaluative expressions in opinion analysis, since argumentation is related to this primitive form of opinion expression. An evaluative expression is in general realized in natural language by a short expression which, conceptually speaking, has the form of an **attribute-value** pair. The attribute is the head of the structure, it semantically 'subcategorizes' for a value and, since it conveys the context, it gives the evaluative expression its interpretation. Language realizations of this form may be very diverse. The attribute is in general realized as a noun phrase (NP) (nice <u>design</u>, I like <u>the design</u> of…) or an event, which may be an NP or a proposition (S) (<u>They decorated the room</u>…). Over a set of texts, a given attribute may be expressed by several synonymous or quasi-synonymous words or expressions.

The value has its own head term, often an adjective, which may be modified by several types of constructions, in particular adverb phrases. In: *very good communication system*, *'communication system'* is the attribute while 'very *good*' is the value, composed of a head, the adjective 'good' with a positive orientation (or polarity). This positive character is reinforced by the modifier *'very'*, an adverb phrase. The value can also be a verb of the *like* semantic class (I <u>like</u> this design), although quite similar to an evaluative adjective, this structure will not be investigated here.

In most cases, the syntactic structure of the value is an adjective phrase (AP), and the syntactic structure of an evaluative expression is a noun phrase (NP):

$[_{NP}$ attribute $[_{AP}$ value]] or $[_{NP}$ $[_{AP}$ value] attribute]

We have, for example:

3a. **Adjective:** Breakfast was **generous.**
3b. **Noun:** Breakfast in the terrace was **a real pleasure.**
3c. **Verb:** La propreté **laisse à desirer** (approximate gloss: The room was lacking in cleanness).

An evaluative expression integrates several aspects:

- A positive or a negative orientation,
- The strength of that orientation,
- A detailed semantic characterization of the orientation, which is often very rich and entails very subtle conceptual interpretations. For example *cheap fares*, *competitive fares* and *good quality/fare ratio*, where 'fares' is the attribute, do not convey exactly the same meaning, e.g. fares are good (1) because they are low, (2) because they are lower than those of equivalent products, (3) because you get good value for your money.

Finally, as shown in the above motivational example, an evaluative expression can be associated with several discourse elements, interpreted as arguments, such as illustrations, elaborations, or reformulations. These are viewed syntactically as adjuncts to the evaluative expression where the attribute has wider scope over the adjunct(s):

$[_{NP} [_{NP}$ attribute $[_{AP}$ value $]$ $[_{S}$ sentential adjunct $]]]$

DISCOURSE RELATIONS AS ARGUMENT SUPPORTS

Evaluative Elements and Explanation

As advocated above, evaluative expressions quite frequently come with additional elements such as comments, elaborations, comparisons, illustrations, etc. which are forms of explanation (Keil, 2000; Bourse et al., 2012) that partly realize argument schemas (Walton et al., 2008). In our view, explanation is not a basic rhetorical relation as introduced in RST (Mann et al., 1988), but a very generic construction, a *proto-relation*, which covers a large number of communication situations, realized in language by means of several types of rhetorical relations which can be combined, possibly using a planning strategy.

For example, in:

4. very well located (close to the railway station, restaurants and cinemas)

the expression:

4b. '(close to the railway station, restaurants and cinemas)'

can be analyzed either as an elaboration or as an illustration of the head expression:

4a. 'very well located'.

According to RST theory (Mann et al., 1988), revised in Taboada et al. (2006) and implemented in Marcu (1997), this head expression is a nucleus while the elaboration or illustration is its satellite.

In this chapter, we argue that rhetorical elements related to explanation behave as argument supports. Their conceptual semantics define the semantic and pragmatic function(s) of the support: e.g. they justify, illustrate, develop the evaluative expression. The main hypothesis of our approach is that while rhetorical relations related to explanation do not have any argumentative power or orientation a priori, they acquire such power or orientation when combined with an evaluative expression. Consider the contrast between:

5. Red fruit tart (strawberries, raspberries).
6. Excellent location (3 mns from the Capitole, 5 mns from St Sernin Cathedral...).

In (5), the illustration relation simply provides more detailed information about red fruits, while in (6), the proximity of touristic spots justifies the value *'excellent'*: the location is excellent because tourist spots are very close-by. The pair evaluative expression - discourse relation becomes an argument with a conclusion and one or more support(s), with the general form:

- evaluative expression - reasons for that evaluation.

Each type of rhetorical relation introduces a particular reason or support, with a specific semantics, communicative goal and orientation. This is investigated below through a conceptual analysis.

Investigating these discourse relations allows a better understanding of argument elaboration and how they function in opinion expression. Besides evaluations involving a single relation, we frequently observed sequences (or networks) of rhetorical elements associated with an evaluative expression, as illustrated below.

An Analysis of Discourse Relations Conveying Arguments

Let us now investigate how rhetorical relations related to explanation give an argumentative interpretation to evaluative expressions and exactly what kind of role they play w.r.t. the evaluative expression. For each relation, besides a semantic analysis, we provide recognition rule samples in Dislog (Saint-Dizier, 2012), as they run on our <TextCoop> platform, specifying connectors and structures. The overall processing strategy and the accuracy of the analysis is provided in the next section. Besides linguistic elements such as connector analysis (e.g. Miltasaki et al., 2004), a global and recent view of discourse analysis is provided in Stede (2012).

Justification

Justification clarifies the reasons of an evaluation:

7. The hotel is 2 stars [$_{\text{JUSTIFICATION}}$ due to the lack of bar and restaurant facilities].
8. It was good [$_{\text{JUSTIFICATION}}$ for seeing all the attraction points in town].

The general abstract schema is: *X is Eval because of Fact**

Where Eval denotes the evaluative expression and Fact* a set of facts acting as justifications. The construction is basically causal, but in the context of an evaluative expression it is interpreted as a justification.

The conceptual interpretation of a justification is:

Fact* provide reasons, based on inherent properties of the object being evaluated, for the Eval which is given. Justification supports the evaluative expression; it does not change the orientation and does not add a priori any strength to the evaluation.

Note that while the polarity of example (7) is neutral, the introduction of an adverb such as 'only' introduces a negative polarity to the evaluative expression, without changing the effect of the justification:

7a. The hotel is only 2 stars [$_{\text{JUSTIFICATION}}$ due to the lack of bar and restaurant facilities].

To recognize and tag this relation in opinion texts, a number of corpus samples have been investigated, resulting in six rules, among which:

Justification →
conn(justif), gap(G), ponct(comma). /
conn(justif), gap(G), eos.
conn(justif): *because, because of, due to, for, in order to.*

where eos: end of sentence, gap(G) indicates a finite sequence G of words to skip, which are of no interest for the rule definition.

These rules seem, so far, to cover a large number of prototypical justification structures.

Reformulation

Reformulation (also called restatement) is a relation where the support rephrases the evaluative expression without adding any significant information, the goal being e.g. to make sure that the evaluation is clear and unambiguous:

9. Could be improved [$_{\text{REFORMULATION}}$ in other words, not so good].
10. Localization is perfect for a stay in town, [$_{\text{REFORMULATION}}$ it cannot be better located.]

The general abstract schema is: *X is Eval, in other words, B.*

A total of nine rules have been defined for the reformulation relation, among which:

Reformulation →
    ponct(opening_parenthesis),
        exp(restate), gap(G), ponct(closing_parenthesis). /
    exp(restate), gap(G), eos.

Cue terms introducing reformulations are in particular:

exp(restate): *In other words, to put it another way, that is to say, i.e., put differently*.

The conceptual interpretation of a reformulation is: B provides another way of saying 'X is Eval', without adding any informational contents. Reformulation supports the evaluative expression but does not add any substantial strength to the evaluation. If the repetition of the informational contents with a different formulation is viewed as a form of insistence, then it may add a slight strength to the statement.

Elaboration by Illustration or Enumeration

We consider that the Elaboration relation is a kind of proto- or very generic relation. We decompose it into several relations in our context.

Illustration is a relation where the support instantiates the segment 'X is Eval' via an example:

11. The bathrooms were in a bad condition: [$_{\text{ILLUSTRATION}}$ the shower leaked and the plug mechanism in the bath jammed ...]
12. The staff went out of their way to be helpful: [$_{\text{ILLUSTRATION}}$ (I had thrown away my return ticket by mistake and they emptied their rubbish sack to find it).]

The general abstract schema is: *X is Eval, for example B*.*

Where B* denotes a set of examples illustrating 'X is Eval'. B denotes objects or events. Examples are introduced by a large variety of markers, including typographic markers and punctuation.

Twenty rules have been defined for this relation, among which:

Illustration →
    exp(illus eg), gap(G), eos. /
    [here], auxiliary(be), gap(G1), exp(illus exa), gap(G2), eos. /
    [let,us,take], gap(G), exp(illus bwe), eos.

with:

exp(illus eg): *e.g., including, such as*
exp(illus exa): *example, an example, examples*
exp(illus bwe): *by way of example, by way of illustration*

Punctuation marks such as ':' are also relevant.

The conceptual interpretation of an illustration is: B* are instances of 'X is Eval' which illustrate this statement. They all have the same polarity, which is shared with 'X is Eval' (an illustration cannot be in contradiction with its head, unless it is a form of irony). Depending on the amount of elements in B* and their prototypicality, illustration is a support that adds more or less strength to the argument, without affecting its polarity.

Illustration is called an enumeration when all the elements are explicit:

13. Breakfast selection is very good [$_{\text{ENUMERATION}}$ with a range of cereals, tea and coffee, cold meats and cheese, fresh and canned fruit, bread, rolls and croissants, and a selection of cooked items.]

An enumeration denotes a strong communicative intention: it has a higher strength than an illustration and clearly supports an evaluative expression adding a substantial strength.

Elaboration via Precision

Precision is a relation which adds specific information to the evaluative expression or focuses on a specific point. This specific information confirms the orientation, adding some strength:

14. It is great value being able to accommodate a family of four in one room [$_{\text{PRECISION}}$ (99 Euros including breakfast).]
15. The wine and coffee are included [$_{\text{PRECISION}}$ (our wine glasses were refilled a number of times, all included)]
16. Friendly and helpful staff, [$_{\text{PRECISION}}$ especially the service executives at the counter.]

The general schema is: *X is Eval, in particular B.*

Only prototypical cases have been investigated in the corpus, resulting in five quite generic rules, such as the following:

Precision →
    conn(precis), gap(G), ponct(comma). /
    conn(precis), gap(G), eos.
conn(precis): *with, especially, more precisely, in particular.*

Most of the other structures related to the precision rules are close to the illustration relation. The two notions are indeed quite close.

The conceptual semantics of 'precision' is that B adds specific information and somewhat confirms the statement 'X is Eval'. Precision supports the evaluative expression and adds some strength, depending on the importance and impact of the precision.

Elaboration via Comparison

Comparison is a strong means to reinforce a statement, making a parallel with a better or worse situation or object, more or less explicit:

17. These head phones are excellent, [$_{\text{COMPARISON}}$ as if you were in a concert room.]
18. The room was typically small [$_{\text{COMPARISON}}$ as in all European hotels]
19. [$_{\text{COMPARISON}}$ unlike so many haute cuisine restaurants,] we didn't leave the restaurant hungry.
20. The price is high [$_{\text{COMPARISON}}$ compared with the comfort.]
21. The food in the restaurant was OK [$_{\text{COMPARISON}}$ for the price].

The comparison relation introduces different forms of support, essentially depending on the semantics of the connector:

- In (17), the connector 'as' reinforces the positive orientation of the evaluation,
- In (18), the same connector applied to a negative evaluation tends to justify it: it does not reinforce the negative evaluation,
- In (19), 'unlike' contradicts the rather neutral evaluation, leading to a globally positive evaluation,

- In (20), 'compared' reinforces the negative evaluation,
- In (21) 'for' makes the neutral evaluation slightly positive.

This analysis remains informal: it shows the complexity of the interpretation of the role of the support. A more in-depth study of the semantics of these connectors in various contexts is needed. The same holds for the contrast relation, presented below.

The general schema for the comparison relation is: *X is Eval, like B**.

A single rule has been implemented for this relation, which is quite generic:

comparison →
    conn(comp), gap(G), ponct(comma). /
    conn(comp), gap(G), eos.
conn(comp): *compared with, for, as, unlike, like, such as, as if.*

Elaboration via Consequence

Consequence is here used in a rather limited way. It mainly develops the advantages of a positive or a negative evaluation:

22. A high soundproofing [$_{\text{ELAB-CONSEQUENCE}}$ that allows you to have a rest after a long day of work].
23. A large fridge, [$_{\text{ELAB-CONSEQUENCE}}$ so we could put all the food we had.]

In general, the support stresses the importance of the attribute or value rather than adding any real strength to the evaluation itself.

Rules are similar to the preceding ones. It is interesting to note that elaboration occurs at the end of a sentence, to limit their scope. Cue markers are not very typical. Ambiguities are relatively limited and may be resolved by considering the type of the verb of the embedded clause; however, this is the type of relation that needs knowledge to be accurately identified.

Contrast

Contrast introduces a statement which is somewhat symmetric but in opposition with the evaluation:

24. It was clean and comfortable, [$_{\text{CONTRAST}}$ but the carpet was in need of replacing.]
25. The price is very reasonable [$_{\text{CONTRAST}}$ but comfort is rather poor.]

The support is not in total opposition with the evaluation (it may deal with a different but related property) but weakens it because the elements in the evaluative expression and in the contrast have different polarities.

Due to this partial opposition, contrast can co-occur with relations that reinforce the evaluation without introducing inconsistencies:

26. A nice room [$_{\text{PRECISION}}$ with a flat screen TV] [$_{\text{CONTRAST}}$ but with no real charm.]

It can also modify another relation such as precision:

27. A nice room [$_{\text{PRECISION}}$ with a flat screen TV [$_{\text{CONTRAST}}$ but without any interesting channels.]]

The general schema is: *X is Eval but (with/without) B**.

This relation has a large diversity of realizations. We have developed twelve rules, among which:

Contrast →
    conn(contrast whe), gap(G),
        ponct(comma)./

conn(contrast whe), gap(G), eos. /
conn(contrast how), gap(G), eos.
conn(contrast whe): *whereas, but, while*
conn(contrast how): *however*

The conceptual semantics states that B* is opposed to 'X is Eval' to a certain degree or along a certain meaning component related in some way to 'X is Eval', weakening its argumentative value. A contrast is therefore not a support but an attack of the evaluative expression. Contrast is often used in forms of irony; in that case, the argumentative value is reversed, not weakened.

Concession

Similarly to contrast, concession introduces a form of 'indirect' contradiction between the evaluation and the support. This contradiction weakens or reinforces the evaluative expression depending on the polarity of the connector:

28. The hotel has a nice 'modern' bar and restaurant, [$_{\text{CONCESSION}}$ although not particularly cheap.]

'although' is negatively oriented, the evaluation of the restaurant is affected on a specific property, its fares.

29. Very quiet [$_{\text{CONCESSION}}$ in spite of its downtown location in a nightlife area.]

'in spite of' is positively oriented and supports the evaluation.

The linguistic structure is very close to contrast, but a number of linguistic markers are specific to concession: *however, although, though, even though, even if, notwithstanding, despite, in spite of.* Similarly to contrast, a detailed analysis of connectors in such contexts needs to be realized, as shown in (28) and (29).

Nine rules have been defined to characterize the notion of concession. Here are a few:

Concession →
conn(opposition alth), gap(G1), ponct(comma), gap(G2), eos. /
conn(opposition alth), gap(G), eos. /
conn(opposition how), gap(G), eos.
conn(opposition alth): *although, though, even though, even if, notwithstanding, despite, in spite of*
conn(opposition how): *however*

Overall Recommendation Processing

Finally, consumer opinions end (or sometimes start, e.g. using an introductory sentence or a title) with an overall recommendation. It is composed of a few words that conclude on the product (or event) global opinion, given the different evaluated attributes:

30. …I strongly recommend it. / ...buy it. / ...go there if no alternative.

The recommendation attribute has a 'value' which is not clear-cut positive/negative. It is very difficult, if not impossible, to provide a semantic representation of these recommendations or even organize them along a linear scale. It would make sense to define groups of recommendations which would have approximately the same kind of impact on the reader. This is obviously simpler when marks or a number of stars are provided instead of a natural language expression.

Identifying and Characterizing the Glue between Evaluative Expressions and Arguments

We argue that the rhetorical relations described above can be understood as argument supports. However, as mentioned before, the argumentative link between an evaluative statement and a rhetorical relation is not always straightforward, but rather subject to interpretation. This means that, in order to understand the *why* behind a particular evaluation, the reader unconsciously processes a certain quantity of implicit information, which needs to be made explicit if we want an automated system to access the structure of the argumentative discourse.

Roughly speaking, each evaluative expression activates a number of implicit propositions or inferences in the mind of the reader, only some of which are subsequently selected by the rhetorical relation that complements the evaluation. Understanding the relation between the two is what allows the reader to reach a conclusion. In order to illustrate how complex the process of accessing the implicit information or inferring can be, even for a normal reader with access to all the lexical, world and domain knowledge required, let us have a look at some real examples extracted from our French corpus. For the sake of simplicity, these examples have been translated into English, including French glosses between brackets only in those cases where the original expression can contribute to the analysis.

31. Located in a quiet area **but** next to a vaporetto[1] stop!

If we now add some of the possible inferences (hereinafter introduced by the symbol ⇨) which can be made in this case, we observe that (31) is a potential source of ambiguity:

31a. Located in a quiet area **but** next to a vaporetto stop!
⇨ isolated ⇨ noisy
⇨ off-centered ⇨ accessible by public transport

Indeed, during a preliminary analysis of our corpus, two annotators interpreted this sentence in different ways: either the first pair of inferences are selected, putting the emphasis on the fact that being close to a *vaporetto* stop can be noisy, thus leading to a negative conclusion, or the second pair of inferences is selected, highlighting the convenience of public transportation and therefore implying a positive conclusion. A similar difficulty arises in the case of semantically complex evaluations which make it difficult for the reader to select among all the possible inferences, or even to identify the intention of the reviewer, leading to incongruous or even shallow argumentations. This is more often the case of opinions about politicians, where the boundaries between attributes are extremely fuzzy and there is little or no agreement on the values that can be attached to a certain attribute:

32. Hollande represents the novelty, the unknown,
⇨ good change
⇨ something to be afraid of but he is also the kitchen wallpaper we have grown accustomed to.
⇨ tradition

33. He is a friendly man, always telling jokes, but that is not what is expected of him.
⇨ good relational skills
⇨ sense of humor
⇨ sense of humor is not indispensable/desirable for a presidential candidate?

Notice that in both (32) and (33) it is quite difficult to reach a definite conclusion as regards the opinion of the writer on this particular politician. In (32), up to three conflicting general rules arise: (1) that novelty is usually welcome in the domain of politics, (2) that novelty can also generate a fair amount of fear or confusion, and (3) that old habits die hard and can be reassuring. Moreover, the presence of the additive adverb 'also' suggests that the final conclusion must be reached through a combination of the three inferences, rather than a contrast. In (33) we find ourselves confronted to an undefined general rule: which are the actual indispensable or desirable personality traits of a presidential candidate?

However, in more stable domains such as the hotel domain, where attributes are clearly defined and reviewers are given writing guidelines, we find relatively high inter-agreement. In order to identify and characterize the types of inferences involved in these two domains, we extracted evaluations involving contrast and concession, an argumentative relation which has been largely explored from both a formal and inferential perspective in the past. Our study of inferences in the contrast / concession relation focuses only on a certain number of linguistic markers or connectives in French (*mais*, *par contre*, *en revanche*, *bien que*, *même si*, *pourtant* and *alors que*). We also extracted opinions involving another important argumentative relation, consequence (focusing mainly on the French connectives *donc* and *alors*). Approximately 100 evaluations were annotated for the domain of hotels and restaurants, and almost 200 evaluations of French politicians were extracted, but only about half of them were found suitable for annotation, taking into account methodological constraints such as the need for at least one evaluative expression to be clearly stated in the sentence.

The first step in the analysis is the identification of the recurrent structure in the extracted evaluations and its formalization. These logic-based formalizations prove useful in identifying the types of inferences to be found in each conjunct and inferring the relation between them, but since they bear no significant difference with formalizations proposed by other authors (e.g. Anscombre & Ducrot, 1997; Moeschler, 2003; Winterstein, 2012), they will not be developed here.

Then possible inferences are developed for each of the extracted evaluations by several annotators. A deeper analysis of these inferences is necessary in order to draw conclusions with regard to the possible categories of knowledge required to understand the argumentation in these opinions. Broadly speaking, we identify four categories of knowledge which speakers unconsciously turn to when processing inferential information: lexical knowledge, domain knowledge, world knowledge and other logical inference mechanisms. It is important to note that the boundaries between those categories are not always clear-cut and that some types of knowledge, such as lexical knowledge, are pervasive and, even when other types of knowledge are involved, should not be overlooked during the analysis.

We will now define and illustrate each of the categories which resulted from our analysis:

Lexical Knowledge

This category includes all the linguistic constituents in the sentence other than linguistic markers which, as mentioned before, provide with procedural information about the argumentation, and certain words such as quantifiers which, according to (Winterstein, 2012), play the role of information foci and 'mechanically' affect the content of the proposition.

Instead, our analysis focuses on the identification of the conceptual information encoded in open-class words such as adjectives or nouns, their lexical meaning and the possible connotations which trigger particular inferences.

34. The design is modern, but cozy.
    ⇨ functional ⇨ **warm**
    ⇨ simple
    ⇨ high-tech
    ⇨ **cold**

35. He is distant, but close.
    ⇨ cold ⇨ **friendly**
    ⇨ **not friendly**
    ⇨ not solicitous

In (34) and (35) we can see how even if the inferences activated by these sentences are purely lexical, they are not totally straightforward. In (34), the adjective 'modern' applied to the sub-attribute 'interior design' belonging to the rooms of a hotel, activates a number of properties listed above, many of which seem to orientate the first conjunct to a positive conclusion, such as 'functional' or 'high-tech'. The reviewer knows, though, that 'modern design' might also lead some readers to picture a room with a simple decoration or a cold style. The adjective 'cozy' in the second conjunct therefore selects this last property and cancels it out. At first sight, (35) may seem a paradox, but if we understand 'close' as selecting only one of the properties which can be inferred from 'distant', then the statement does no longer appear as entirely infelicitous.

Domain Knowledge

These inferences concern the knowledge of the particular domain of the product or event reviewed. Since evaluations and the evaluative expressions used in them are generally domain-dependent, this has also an impact on the inferences which can be made. Domain knowledge can be characterized in the form of general rules or axioms that are generally shared among speakers by convention and they can be divided into three types:

- Knowledge of the specific attributes in a domain.

36. I received a warm welcome even though I arrived very late (11 pm!)
37. Eva Joly has no interest in money, but she has got strong convictions. [⇨ so] That's disturbing.

In (36), for instance, the inference being made and cancelled out by the concession is the general rule that hotel staff can be less qualified or less solicitous (i.e. because there are less employees available) during the night shift. In (37), the conclusion, made explicit by the reviewer, seems unexpected. Indeed, there is a contrast being made between the absence of materialistic ambition (from which we can infer ⇨ *honesty)* and strong political convictions (from which we can infer ⇨ *morality*) and this is, in the eyes of the reviewer, unexpected in a politician.

- Knowledge of the specific values which can be applied to an attribute, or the specific connotations that a value can take in a particular domain.

38. The rooms are spacious, because they're *old (> anciennes), but comfortable.
39. I consider myself an apolitical person, anti-Sarkozy and anti-Peggy[2] as well, of course, so I count on the PS.

In (38), the French original 'anciennes' convey a positive sense of 'antique' but includes also the pejorative connotation of 'old'. If furniture in the room is antique, this may also imply that it is uncomfortable, and this is precisely the inference selected and cancelled out by the contrast. (39) is a slightly different example from the preceding ones. Although 'apolitical' literally means that the writer is not interested in politics or does not have any particular political affiliation, the rest of the sentence introduces a nuance to this first statement. Indeed, the reviewer has a preferred political party (the PS), so what the reader infers from the first evaluation is that his/ her political views are not very strong.

- **Specific Realizations:** Or occurrences of certain attributes or values in the domain, which possess special properties which are not necessarily paradigmatic.

40. You should avoid the rooms in the ground floor, especially room N° 4, because it is so close to the reception and the breakfast room.
41. And so it is enough to appear twice on TV to forget three years of disenchantment? Even though we know that the G20 summit was a fiasco…

The inference to be made in (40) is that rooms in the ground floor, as a rule, tend to be noisier, especially if they are close to the reception or to the room where breakfast is served. In (41), the rhetorical question implies a rise in the popularity of the politician concerned, Nicolas Sarkozy, after his appearances on TV, but this idea is cancelled out by the evaluation of the G20 summit. These inferences are not only domain-dependent, but also specific to the particular circumstances at the moment when the review was written.

World Knowledge

Although inferences requiring general world knowledge are probably the easiest to access for the reader, they are the most difficult to characterize, precisely because they summon a lot of abstract shared knowledge. Similarly to domain knowledge inferences, they can be characterized by means of general rules or axioms. However, whereas creating a list of general rules representative enough of a particular domain would be laborious but feasible, exhaustivity in characterizing world knowledge would be impossible.

42. Every day a different breakfast, but every day a table that looks like a Christmas table.
    ⇨ varied ⇨ **good quality**
    ⇨ **not always good?** ⇨ quantity ⇨ decorated
43. Defending your country is not fascist. Making it sink, however…
    ⇨ the right is considered fascist because of their policies on immigration and terrorism
    ⇨ **bad management of economic crisis is seen as morally incorrect**
    ⇨ **self-defense is morally ok**

For instance, in order to understand the inferences being made in (42), the reader would need to know what a Christmas table generally looks like, and in order to understand (43), the reader requires some background information about right-wing and left-wing policies, as well as the concepts of fascism and self-defense. Understanding these inferences makes it clear for the reader that the conclusion implied by the reviewer is that it is the socialists who are doing something immoral.

Other Logical Inference Mechanisms

This category includes a number of recurrent mechanisms used by reviewers in order to logically imply information by association of ideas. They can also be considered as higher order world knowledge, since they are ways of reasoning generally accepted by convention. Here we propose a list of logical inference mechanisms found in our corpus, although this list is, by no means exhaustive:

- **Generalization**

44. Excellent breakfast, but I haven't tried the restaurant though.
    ⇨ By generalization, if breakfast was good, we may infer the restaurant's cuisine will be good as well.

- **Relativization**

45. There are many stairs, a steep and spiral staircase, but in the long run, you get used to it.
    ⇨ By relativization (here, the action of time), the problem is no longer seen as a real obstacle.

- **Elimination**

46. Aubry and Hollande have no charisma whatsoever and their ideas are outdated. Marine is completely out of the game. So, by default, Nicolas Sarkozy.
    ⇨ The reviewer implies that Sarkozy is the only worthy candidate by elimination.

- **Cause and Effect**

47. In the evening, they are short in staff, so if you want to take a beer at the bar, you should be patient.
    ⇨ The lack of staff logically results in a slow service at the bar.

- **Part for the Whole**

48. Nice and clean room. The hotel, however, is really in need of a makeover.
    ⇨ If the rooms are ok, we may infer that the rest of the hotel is ok too, but this implied idea is refused by the contrast here.

All in all, although our classification does not aim at being exhaustive, we believe it is representative enough of the major inferential knowledge encoded between evaluative expressions and rhetorical relations. Also, we suggest that in order to improve the characterization of arguments in opinion analysis, the next step in our approach would be a more thorough study of domain-dependent inferences in relatively stable domains, such as the domain of hotels and restaurants, or the domain of audio and video products, since this type of knowledge enables the access to a lot of relevant information which proves useful in understanding the reasoning behind the evaluation.

IMPLEMENTATION IN <TEXTCOOP>

Overview of the <TextCoop> System

To process these relations, we use <TextCoop>, which is a platform we designed for discourse analysis, with a logic and linguistic perspective (Saint-Dizier, 2012). <TextCoop> is basically a meta-interpreter written in Prolog. The language used to describe rules, lexical resources and constraints is called Dislog (for Discourse in Logic).

Rules in Dislog basically recognize basic discourse units. These are then bound to form larger discourse units via selective binding rules. Structural constraints limit combination possibilities.

Basic Features

A rule in Dislog has the following form:

L(Representation) → R, {P}.

where:

1. L is a non-terminal symbol.
2. Representation is an XML structure with attributes, or a (partial) dependency structure.
3. R is a set of symbols as described below, and
4. P is a set of predicates and functions implemented in Prolog to deal with various forms of reasoning (e.g. to check for types based on ontological knowledge, etc.).

R is a finite sequence of the following main elements:

- **Terminal Symbols:** That represent words, expressions, punctuations, various existing html or XML tags,
- **Preterminal Symbols:** Which are derived directly into terminal elements. These are used to capture various forms of generalizations, facilitating rule authoring and update. Symbols can be associated with a typed feature structure,
- **Non-Terminal Symbols:** Implement 'local grammars', i.e. grammars that encode specific syntactic constructions.
- **Optionality and Iterativity Marks:** Over non-terminal and preterminal symbols, as in regular expressions,
- **Gaps:** Which are symbols that stand for a finite sequence of words of no present interest for the rule which must be skipped. A gap can appear only between terminal, preterminal or non-terminal symbols. Dislog offers the possibility to specify in a gap a list of elements which must not be skipped.

A cluster of Dislog rules is in general needed to recognize a given basic discourse unit (e.g. illustration, elaboration).

Selective Binding Rules

Selective binding rules allow the linking of two or more already identified basic discourse units: e.g. to bind a kernel with its satellite or with another kernel. These are expressed using the Dislog language formalism. Selective binding rules are used to construct hierarchical discourse structures from elementary ones. Different situations occur that make binding rules complex, e.g. adjacent or non-adjacent structures, one-to-many relations. Constraints can be imposed on the 'textual distance' between units: this is implemented via the notion of bounding node (or barriers) restricting the way in which long distance dependencies can be established.

Structural Constraints

Dislog offers the possibility of introducing various types of constraints related to selective binding, for example:

- **Dominance Constraints:** dom(instruction, condition).

states that a conditional expression is always dominated by an instruction.

Similarly, non-dominance constraints can be stated to ensure that two discourse functions appear in different branches of a discourse representation, e.g.:

not_dom(instruction, warning).

Finally, precedence constraints may be stated. We only consider here the case of immediate linear precedence:

prec(elaborated, elaboration).

indicates that an elaboration must follow what is being elaborated.

For the present purpose, we have designed argument extraction rules which precisely correspond to the types of discourse structures that appear in consumer opinion texts. These rules have been adapted from our rule repository dedicated to explanation structures (Bourse & Saint-Dizier, 2012). Adaptation involves developing additional lexical resources (terms expressing polarity, adverbs of intensity, domain verbs and connectors), revising the structure of rules (in particular characterizing their boundaries in more depth) and adding a few more rules (Bethard et al., 2004; Bal & Saint-Dizier, 2008).

We will not go into the details of the processing strategy here. The explanation structures developed here can be recognized in any order, with no specific dominance constraints. The structures are processed one after the other on the whole text, via a cascade of automata. The system processes about 12 Megs of text per hour, it has now run for almost 6 months without any incident, processing every day about 5000 texts coming from the Web and from various domains.

Results and Performances

Our aim in terms of evaluation is to carry out an indicative evaluation that globally shows the overall quality of the results and indicates the points which need significant improvements. Considering the complexity of the present investigation, we cannot provide at this stage more definitive results.

From a test corpus (21.500 words, 50 texts), we have the following coverage and accuracy rates, expressed in terms of recall and precision. Our strategy was to favor precision over recall since some discourse structures may be somewhat ambiguous or close to each other. We propose here an indicative evaluation that gives the main trends of our results. The goal is to identify components which need to be revised and improved before carrying out a more elaborated evaluation. Since we essentially made some limited modifications to the rules developed in (Bourse et al., 2012), the results, in terms of discourse relation recognition, still proved satisfactory. An important point is that most consumers do their best to make their evaluation explicit and easy to understand. This consideration has obviously an impact on the results.

Table 2. Textcoop performances

Structures	Manually Annotated Structures	Precision	Recall
justification	49	92	86
reformulation	28	85	76
illustration	114	91	83
precision	58	90	85
comparison	59	88	84
consequence	16	89	83
contrast	49	86	78
concession	37	88	81
Total	410		

The figures in Table 2 are based on a comparison of the system performances w.r.t. manual annotations on a test corpus of 45 texts from the hotel, restaurant and audio and video domains, with 410 explanation rhetorical relations interpreted as arguments. A structure is correct if it is correctly identified and well-delimited. Context and recommendation are not included here. This evaluation was carried out on a rather limited set of texts; we therefore consider it as an indicative evaluation:

The global results are quite satisfactory. We have also carried out limited tests on the political domain, but these gave much poorer results because of the authoring style with many indirect discourse forms. This probably means that our approach can be applied to texts with a relatively stable and controlled language in the first instance, i.e. for products where consumers express themselves in a relatively standard and accessible way.

Therefore, we feel our system is relatively robust for a certain type of opinion texts, and this validates our initial hypothesis. By robust we mean that its principles, its rules and to some extent some of its lexical resources are re-usable. We feel we have initiated a kind of method which can be reproduced for a number of application domains, possibly generalizing the values for some attributes which turn out to be quite universal (such as price or design). Moving on to less standard text types, where modes of expression are more complex or deteriorated, affects robustness and recognition accuracy, as in any language processing application. For texts such as those from the political domain, which are probably among the most difficult to process, it is necessary to include modules that can handle e.g. irony, various forms of emphasis and metaphors.

CONCLUSION AND PERSPECTIVES

In this paper, we have developed an approach to argument identification and analysis as they appear in opinion texts. We have shown by means of examples that arguments may originate from an evaluation (conclusion) combined with one or more discourse structures such as justification, elaboration or illustration (support) whose goal is to persuade the reader of the relevance of the evaluation.

Identifying those relations in opinion analysis is essential in order to be able to determine why consumers are happy or not with a certain product or decision, and what their preferences and values are. Arguments partly convey this information. We have shown how in order to characterize the arguments supported by rhetorical relations we need to reconstruct the inferring process employed by consumers, identifying the glue between evaluative expressions and discourse structures such as contrast or consequence.

We have outlined four categories of knowledge involved in the inference process: lexical, domain and world knowledge, and other logical inference mechanisms. We believe that further exploration of domain knowledge by extraction of domain-dependent general rules could significantly contribute to the characterization of arguments in sentiment analysis.

Finally, we have briefly shown how the rules and the lexical structures can be implemented in the <TextCoop> platform and have given results of an indicative evaluation.

ACKNOWLEDGMENT

We thank Leila Amgoud and Florence Bannay for their insightful discussions, and Chloé Cimpello for her contribution to inference annotation.

REFERENCES

Anick, P., & Bergler, S. (1992). Lexical structures for linguistic inference. In J. Pustejovsky, & S. Bergler (Eds.), *Lexical semantics and knowledge representation*. Berlin: Springer Verlag. doi:10.1007/3-540-55801-2_31

Anscombre, J. C., & Ducrot, O. (1997). *L'argumentation dans la langue*. Belgium: Mardaga.

Asher, N., & Lascarides, A. (2003). *Logics of conversation (Studies in natural language processing)*. Cambridge, UK: Cambridge University Press.

Bal, B. K., & Saint-Dizier, P. (2008). Towards building annotated resources for analyzing opinions and argumentation. In *News editorials*. Malta: LREC.

Bethard, S., Yu, H., Thornton, A., Hatzivassiloglou, V., & Rafsky, D. (2004). Automatic extraction of opinion propositions and their holders. In *Proceedings of AAAI04*.

Bourse, S., & Saint-Dizier, P. (2012). A repository of rules and lexical resources for discourse structure analysis: the case of explanation structures. In *Proceedings of LREC 2012*, Istanbul.

Breck, E., Choi, Y., & Cardie, C. (2007). Identifying expressions of opinion in context. In *Proceedings of the Twentieth International Joint Conference on Artificial Intelligence (IJCAI-2007)*.

Budzynska, K. (2010). Argument analysis: Components of interpersonal argumentation. In *Proceedings of COMMA 2010*.

Budzynska, K., & Reed, C. (2012). The structure of ad hominem dialogues. In *Proceedings of COMMA 2012*.

Cruse, A. (1986). *Lexical semantics*. Cambridge, UK: Cambridge University Press.

Delmonte, R., & Pallotta, V. (2011). Opinion mining and sentiment analysis need text understanding. In Studies in Computational Intelligence, 361, 81-95.

Di Eugenio, B., & Webber, B. L. (1996). Pragmatic overloading in natural language instructions. *International Journal of Expert Systems*, *9*(3).

Fiedler, A., & Horacek, H. (2001). Argumentation in explanations to logical problems. In *Proceedings of ICCS 2001, LNCS 2073*. Springer.

Garcia-Villalba, M. P., & Saint-Dizier, P. (2012). A framework for extracting arguments in opinion texts. *International Journal of Cognitive Intelligence and Natural Intelligence*, *6*(4).

Grice, H. P. (1975). Logic and conversation. *Syntax and Semantics*, *3*, 41–58.

Grosz, B., & Sidner, C. (1986). Attention, intention and the structure of discourse. *Computational Linguistics*, *12*(3).

Kayser, D. (1997). La sémantique lexicale est d'abord inférentielle. *Langue Française*, *113*, 92–106. doi:10.3406/lfr.1997.5372

Keil, F. C., & Wilson, R. A. (2000). *Explanation and cognition*. Cambridge, MA: Bradford Books.

Kim, S. M., & Hovy, E. H. (2007). CRYSTAL: analyzing predictive opinions on the Web. In *Proceedings of the EMNLP conference*, Prague.

Kintsch, W. (1988). The role of knowledge in discourse comprehension: A construction integration model. *Psychological Review*, *9*(2). PMID:3375398

Kosseim, L., & Lapalme, G. (2000). Choosing rhetorical structures to plan instructional texts. *Computational Intelligence*, *12*(3).

Lakoff, G. (1988). Cognitive semantics. In U. Eco, M. Santambrogio, & P. Violi (Eds.), *Meaning and mental representations*. Bloomington, IN: Indiana University Press.

Liu, B. (2012). *Sentiment analysis and opinion mining*. San Rafael, CA: Morgan and Claypool.

Longacre, R. (1982). Discourse typology in relation to language typology. In S. Allen (Ed.), *Text processing, proceeding of Nobel symposium, 51* (pp. 457–486). Stockholm, Sweden: Almquist and Wiksell.

Luscher, J. M. (1989). Connecteurs et guidage inférentiel, propositions pour une perspective interlingue. In Bulletin CILA (Commission interuniversitaire suisse de linguistique appliquée) 50, 48-58.

Mann, W., & Thompson, S. (1988). Rhetorical structure theory: Towards a functional theory of text organisation. *Text*, *8*(3). doi:10.1515/text.1.1988.8.3.243

Mann, W., & Thompson, S. (Eds.). (1992). *Discourse description: Diverse linguistic analyses of a fund raising text*. Philadelphia, PA: John Benjamins. doi:10.1075/pbns.16

Marcu, D. (1997). The rhetorical parsing of natural language texts. In *Proceedings of ACL 1997*.

Marcu, D. (2000). *The theory and practice of discourse parsing and summarization*. Cambridge, MA: MIT Press.

Masthoff, J., Reed, C., & Grasso, F. (Eds.). (2008). *Symposium on persuasive technology*. Edinburgh.

Miltasaki, E., Prasad, R., Joshi, A., & Webber, B. (2004). Annotating discourse connectives and their arguments. In *Proceedings of New Frontiers in NLP Conference*.

Mirkin, S., Dagan, I., & Shnarch, E. (2009). Evaluating the inferential utility of lexical-semantic resources. In *Proceedings of the 12th Conference of the European Chapter of the ACL*, (pp. 558-566). Athens.

Moeschler, J. (2003). Connecteurs et inférence. In G. Gobber (Ed.), *Syndesmoi: Il connettivo nella realta del testo*. Milano: Vita e Pensiero.

Pallotta, V., & Delmonte, R. (2011). Automatic argumentative analysis for interaction mining. *Argument and Computation, 2*(3).

Pang, B., & Lee, L. (2008). Opinion mining and sentiment analysis. *Foundations and Trends in Information Retrieval, 2*(1).

Popescu, A.-M., & Etzioni, O. (2005). Extracting product features and opinions from reviews. In *Proceedings of HLTEMNLP*.

Reed, C. A. (2011). Implicit speech acts are ubiquitous. Why? They join the dots. In *Proceedings of the Conference on Argumentation: Cognition and Community (OSSA-2011)*, Windsor, ON.

Reed, C. A., & Long, D. P. (1997). Content ordering in the generation of persuasive discourse. In *Proceedings of 15th International Joint Conference on Artificial Intelligence*, Nagoya.

Reed, C. A., & Long, D. P. (1998). Generating the structure of argument. In *Proceedings of COLING-ACL98*, Montreal, Canada.

Saint-Dizier, P. (2012). processing natural language arguments with the <TextCoop> platform. *Argumentation and Computation, 3*(1).

Simancik, F., & Lee, M. (2009). A CCG-based system for valence shifting for sentiment analysis. In A. Gelbukh (Ed.), *Advances in computational linguistics (Research in computing science, 41)*. Germany: Springer.

Spenader, J., & Maier, E. (2009). Contrast as denial in multi-dimensional semantics. *Journal of Pragmatics, 41*(9), 1707–1726. doi:10.1016/j.pragma.2008.10.005

Sperber, D., & Wilson, D. (1986). *Relevance: Communication and cognition*. Oxford, UK: Basil Blackwell.

Stede, M. (2012). Discourse processing, Graeme Hirst (Ed.). Toronto, Canada: Morgan and Claypool Publishers.

Taboada, M., Brooke, J., & Stede, M. (2009). Genre-based paragraph classification for sentiment analysis. In *Proceedings of 10th Annual SIGDIAL Conference on Discourse and Dialogue*. London.

Taboada, M., Brooke, J., Tofiloski, M., Voll, K., & Stede, M. (2011). Lexicon-based methods for sentiment analysis. *Computational Linguistics, 37*(2). doi:10.1162/COLI_a_00049

Taboada, M., & Mann, W. C. (2006). Rhetorical structure theory: Looking back and moving ahead. *Discourse Studies, 8*(3). doi:10.1177/1461445606061881

Van Eemeren, F. H. (Ed.). (2002). *Advances in pragma-dialectics*. Newport News, VA: Vale Press.

Van Eemeren, F. H., & Grootendorst, R. (1984). *Speech acts in argumentative discussions: A theoretical model for the analysis of discussions directed towards solving conflicts of opinion*. Edinburgh, UK: Floris Publications. doi:10.1515/9783110846089

Van Eemeren, F. H., & Grootendorst, R. (1992). *Argumentation, communication, and fallacies: A pragma-dialectical perspective*. Hillsdale, NJ: Lawrence Erlbaum Associates.

Walton, D., Reed, C., & Macagno, F. (2008). *Argumentation schemes*. Cambridge, UK: Cambridge University Press. doi:10.1017/CBO9780511802034

Wedekind, J. (1996). On inference-based procedures for lexical disambiguation. In *Proceedings of COLING 1996*.

Winterstein, G. (2012). What *but*-sentences argue for: An argumentative analysis of *but*. *Lingua, 122*, 1864–1885. doi:10.1016/j.lingua.2012.09.014

ENDNOTES

1 A waterbus in Venice, Italy.

2 ‘Peggy’ is a nickname given to Marine Le Pen, French right-wing politician and president of the Front National (FN). The use of this nickname already provides with significant domain information about the political views of the speaker (probably left-wing), which are confirmed later on in the sentence. In this case, we could consider the information as falling into the following sub-category of domain knowledge: ‘specific realizations’.

Chapter 11
Current Trends and Developments, Future Requirements, and Predictions for Computer Mediated Communications and E-Collaboration

Alfie Keary
Cork Institute of Technology, Ireland

Sam Redfern
National University of Ireland, Galway, Ireland

Paul Walsh
Cork Institute of Technology, Ireland

ABSTRACT

This chapter provides a revision and update to the authors' original 2012 research that discussed fifteen semi-structured interviews carried out with international industry experts and thought leaders within the computer mediated communications and e-collaboration field. The original interviews focused on 5, 10, and 15-year time frames, and sought to elicit predictions on the components and services of future platforms, as well as their likely impact on business processes and value chains. Affinity Diagramming/KJ Analysis techniques on the original interview transcripts exposed a number of key tenets that are now revisited, discussed in a current context, revised and updated in this chapter. Following a similar structure to the 2012 paper, the authors discuss the origins of the field, main providers and platforms, related software development technologies, W3C standards, video conferencing, telepresence, cloud computing and Enterprise 2.0. The authors provide a synopsis of the original interviews and have updated their

DOI: 10.4018/978-1-4666-4711-4.ch011

conclusions and findings in light of most recent research and developments. With reference to future requirements, they have also updated their discussions on a next generation architecture proposal/model with additional insights from the authors' research work and that of others in the computer mediated communication and e-collaboration field.

INTRODUCTION

This chapter provides a revision and update to our original 2012 paper, "Future Directions of the Conferencing and Collaboration Field." The paper presented 2010/2011 research from a series of fifteen intensive one to one interviews with conferencing and collaboration industry experts and influential thought leaders across business, education and scientific sectors. A range of issues related to the future directions of the conferencing and collaboration (C&C) field were raised, including technical, social, organisational and educational. The research aimed to provide a forecast into the short and long term directions for the C&C field as predicted by current practitioners and users.

This 2013 revised chapter will revisit the original work and provide new technical insights, service developments, innovations and current research and development trends for the C&C field. For the purpose of this chapter it was decided to expand the context of our research. With this in mind we have expanded our research remit to include a range of computer mediated communications (CMC) technologies such as video, audio and Web conferencing, collaborative virtual environments (CVE), virtual worlds, computer supported cooperative work (CSCW) and e-research environments. From thence any reference to C&C will be incorporated in the CMC term.

Our work will roughly follow the structure of the original paper. Section one will provide a historical research context and an update on new research directions. Section two and three will present a commercial focus from a market and CMC provider perspective with relevant updates on main players in the sector. Section four will address software development in relation to CMC and will discuss recent advances. Following this, section five discusses recent research and developments in relation to video conferencing, telepresence, CMC related standards, cloud computing and Enterprise 2.0. Section six will review the detailed interview analysis from our original paper with full revision and updated comments in relation to findings and conclusions. The final section (section seven) will re-visit our proposed CMC architecture and will also provide input on our current research work and its relevance to the future directions of the CMC sector.

1. CMC ORIGINS

The theoretical and technical origins of CMC can be traced back to the Computer Supported Cooperative Work (CSCW) developments of some 20 years ago. In research published in 1994, Grudin remarks that "CSCW started as an effort by technologists to learn from economists, social psychologists, anthropologists, organizational theorists, educators, and anyone else who could shed light on group activity." (Grudin, 1994). During the early 90s, groupware emerged and was seen as an able technology for CSCW.

As CSCW evolved, the term Group Decision-Support Systems (GDSS) began to emerge (Palmer, Fields, & Brouse, 1994). The GDSS approach supports both synchronous and asynchronous collaboration of multiple groups. In GDSS, the emphasis is not just on CSCW concepts, but also on the decision-making requirements of dispersed groups.

During 1999 Wheeler was researching geographically dispersed teams (Wheeler, Dennis, & Press, 1999). At the time Wheeler stressed that "the implication for researchers is to move beyond the study of just face-to-face teams or just distributed teams to include research of teams that work both face-to-face and distributed."

Goossenaerts et al. (2007) provide a deep insight into the issues in collaborative engineering at both inter-company and partner levels. They state that "the next step will be systematic, networked engineering approaches that link the expertise and knowledge of past engineering projects with new engineering tasks across interdepartmental and intercompany boundaries" (Goossenaerts, Possel-Dölken, & Popplewell, 2007). Today issues of distributed teams and requirements engineering has moved on to address more managerial aspects. Work by Hashmi et al. (Hashmi, Ishikawa, & Richardson, 2013) presents a communications process methodology in relation to global software development and dispersed teams. Their work addresses the non-verbal aspects of collaboration across global sites and more specifically the situations that arise as software requirement engineering is passed from one site to another. With reference to virtual research environments (VRE), Ponti (2010) states that "collaboration is not necessarily natural and straightforward but is likely to raise personal, political and professional challenges, and to put at stake identities and interests of some of the participants" (Ponti, 2010). As CMC technologies mature and permeate more processes the need is emerging for applied business re-engineering as raised by Hashmi et al. and Ponti above. Duranti and de Almeida (2012) also research virtual teams but from a cultural position. Their paper "Is more technology better for communication in international virtual teams" looks at CMC technologies from a cultural perspective across teams. Their research points out that "mere usage" of the best technology (CMC) may not be in the best interests of the project. Technologies deemed adequate for virtual interactions by one culture may be seen as totally inadequate by another cultural group. The authors remind us of the idea that "more technology does better cannot be taken for granted" when cultural issues form a core aspect of virtual teams.

This section provided a review of the origins of the CMC field and how it has developed. More current research work highlights a move away from just the technology aspects to more focus on process change and business re-orientation/application. The next section presents a discussion on the current CMC market and also reviews current offerings from established global providers.

2. CURRENT AND FUTURE CMC MARKET

In the 2012 version of its annual technology report, the Gartner Magic Quadrant (MQ) for Web conferencing sees no major change from the 2011 MQ. Cisco, Citrix OnLine, Adobe, Microsoft, IBM and Saba all sit close to one another in the leaders quadrant. Dialcom and PGi fit into the visionaries quadrant with AT&A positioned in the challengers quadrant. Intercall, FuseBox and Blackboard are in the niche players quadrant. According to the 2011

MQ, the main mover for the 2012 MQ has been AT&T moving into the challenger quadrant. A certain stabilisation has happened in the market during 2012 following a number of mergers, acquisitions and integrations in 2011.

2011 saw salcsforcc.com (Salesforce.com, 2013) enter the market with acquisition of Dim Dim (integrated as Chatter) for integration with its flagship product. Blackboard purchased Wimba and Elluminate (Blackboard, 2013) with the intent of expanding its niche market in CMC technologies for the education sector. Google closed their Wave project and launched a new free offering of community based video conferencing, Google+ Hangouts (Google, 2013). July 2012 saw Microsoft purchase Perceptive Pixel (Microsoft, 2013), a specialist in multi-touch display technologies. Last year also saw extreme activity by the video conferencing vendors Cisco, AT&T, Polycom and others. December 2012 headlines covered how commercial telepresence robots are entering mainstream with continual use cases during 2013 (AnyBots, 2013). Further evidence of CMC robotic developments is the recent collaboration announcement between Cisco and iRobot (Cisco and iRobot, 2013).

We conducted Google research in relation to some emerging CMC related trends. Trending under "Telepresence Robots" (Figure 1) shows major search activity for the first half of 2013.

Trending analysis on "Internet of Things" (Figure 2) shows the concept has been searched

Figure 1. Google trends "Telepresence Robots"

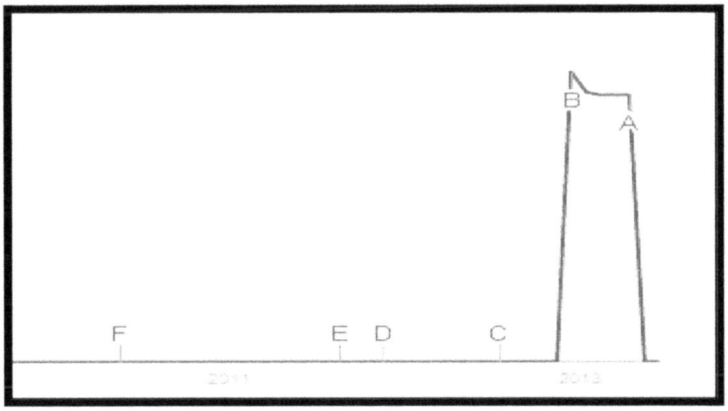

Figure 2. Google trends "Internet of Things"

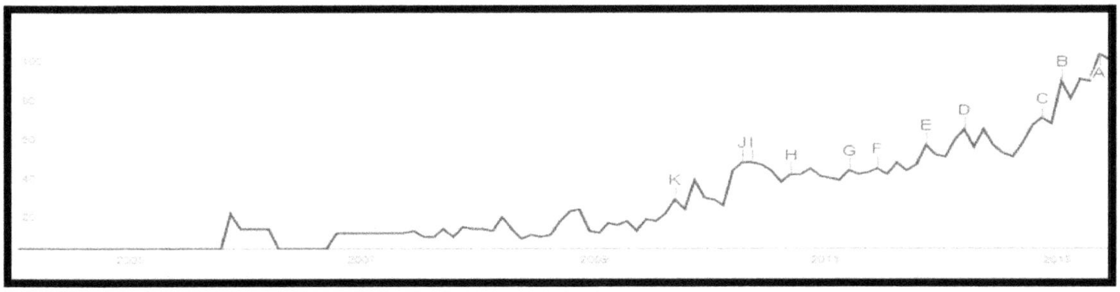

since around 2006 with ever increasing search interest since then. The more recent "Internet of Everything" (Figure 3) is also provided and shows the rise of its search popularity since 2013.

Web Real Time Communications (WebRTC), (Figure 4) a project designed to create standards for real time communication on the Web, has also had major search increases for 2012 and 2013. WebRTC will be discussed later in this paper.

A 2009 report from Gartner (Smith, 2009) suggests that virtual meetings involving human-controlled avatars are likely to be commonplace in the future, driven largely by economic pressures which are leading companies to move some of their larger conferences and events to virtual deployments. Kock wrote a 2008 paper that discussed the growth of virtual worlds and how more large events are also having a virtual aspect. Kock's paper states that "if a virtual community of users is

Figure 3. Google trends "Internet of Everything"

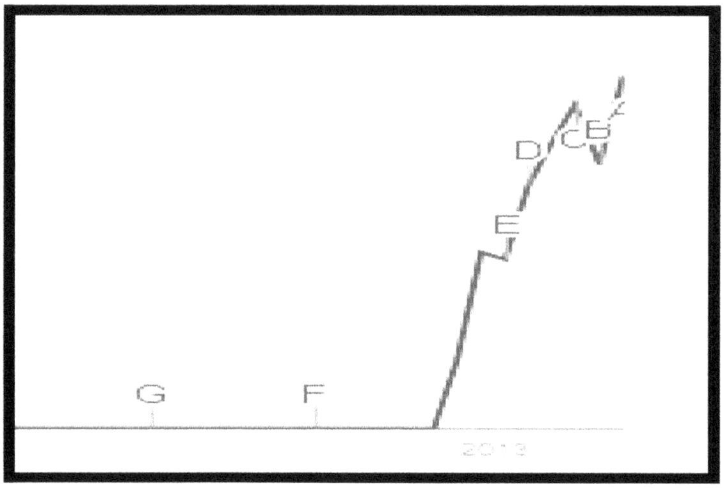

Figure 4. Google trends "WebRTC"

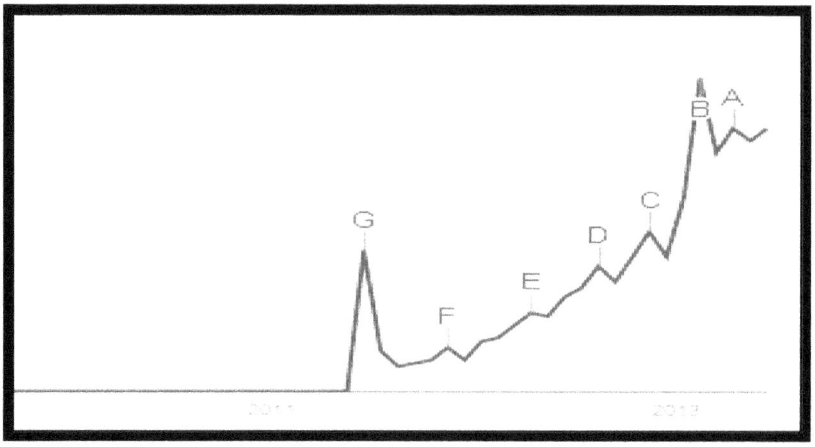

created around a technology and grows beyond a critical mass, then practical e-collaboration applications will follow" (Kock, 2008). He explains that "any virtual world that attracts a large number of users on a global scale will eventually have a business impact, even if for no other reason than its marketing appeal." We return to virtual worlds and more recent developments later in our paper.

In relation to the Internet of Things/Everything, we believe that CMC infrastructure and related services will have a major role in the enablement of such a connected vision. Padmasree Warrior, Cisco's chief technologist and strategist did a recent interview with McKinsey (McKinsey & Company, 2013) under their disruptive technologies series with worldwide experts. Speaking from a Cisco perspective, Warrior believes that "today only 1% of what can be connected in the world is actually connected." She says that it took about 20 years to connect 1% of the world and that in the next ten years the numbers will go up dramatically to address a major part of the remaining 99%. Warrior discusses connecting people, devices, objects and also the data that flows between. In relation to the "Internet of Everything" she refers to "an intelligent way to connect processes with data and things...... not just connecting the devices onto the network, but how can you use the information that's being collected to drive better processes, better decision making for businesses, and better lifestyles for users and consumers."

Warrior sees the upsurge in massive connectivity leading to two main types of connectivity. One kind will deliver very rich media experiences through video, with video being a lot more prevalent than it is today. The other connectivity she refers to involves sensors that will enable connectivity of a continuous stream of low bit-rate data. The merging of people, devices, objects and data are discussed further in her interview where she also discusses future applications for such connectivity.

Our original IJeC paper found evidence of future devices such as digital rooms, HDTVs and interactive table top devices emerging from academic research to commercial application. Today there is increasing evidence of multi-modal devices with Android and Windows 8 providing the required OS functionality. Microsoft has been working on table top technologies for a number of years and the acquisition of Perceptive Pixel has fuelled further innovation. Recent launch of PixelSense (Microsoft, 2013) has brought the Samsung SUR40 to the marketplace. According to the PixelSense site the Samsung SUR40 with Microsoft PixelSense brings people together to connect, learn, and decide. Microsoft state that PixelSense will enable experiences that change the way people collaborate and connect by providing a 360-degree intuitive interface. The SUR40 sees and responds to touch and real world objects and can support more than 50 simultaneous inputs. The PixelSense Samsung SUR40 display can be used as a table top, on the wall I/O device, or embedded in other fixtures or furniture.

This section has provided a general review and update on CMC current and future developments. Core technology leaders are clearly dominating, specifically in relation to audio, Web and video conferencing. As price points adjust, services become more innovative and with increased focus on trust, cloud security and availability we believe that only the players with trusted global infrastructure will continue to provide platforms to the corporate CMC sector. Outside of this, opportunities will also continue to exist for niche and consumer players and for those that are integrating CMC into specialised software platforms. One rapid change has been the increased research and commercial interest in the Internet of Everything (IOE). Evidence suggests that IOE is no longer an academic concept that may impact on CMC, rather it is now a matter of when.

The next section provides a quick review of some of the key technologies from a number of Gartner MQ leaders. This is then followed with an update on how providers are opening up their CMC platforms for software developers.

3. CMC SOFTWARE AND SERVICE PROVIDERS

This section provides a short review of the providers and their CMC offerings. Our original 2012 paper (Keary & Redfern, 2012) provides additional technical detail for the reader if required.

Cisco

In 2007, Cisco Systems, Inc. announced the completion of its acquisition of WebEx Communications. Since then Cisco has been integrating WebEx into its products family, and WebEx is now seen as a core part of Cisco's CMC strategy. Cisco has a family of collaboration applications; Cisco WebEx Web Conferencing, Cisco Jabber and Cisco WebEx Social (Cisco, Collaboration Family, 2013). Cisco have considered Collaboration as a whole and structured it as: Communication, People and Information Management & Business Processes. *Communication* incorporates video, voice, chat, messaging, conferences, meetups and meetings. *People* covers find and connect services (identity, directories, presence, notifications) and social workspaces (social graphs, communities, activity streams). *Information Management & Business Processes* includes create, share, consume services (documents, media content, file share, desktop share) and personal workspace (contacts, calendar, projects, virtual desktop). WebEx still offers Meeting, Event, Training and Support Centre (Cisco WebEx, Collaboration Platforms and Services, 2013). Recent developments include the integration of WebEx with Jabber and Cisco Telepresence. Also Cisco is offering private (on-premises) cloud deployment for in data centre behind firewall conferencing.

Jabber is a unified communication platform aimed at enterprises, enabling collaboration from any workspace on multiple communication channels (Web, IM, Voice, Mobile, Messaging) with seamless WebEx integration. Jabber is specifically focused at connecting knowledge workers across enterprises. The most recent addition, WebEx Social, is an enterprise social networking, content creation and integrated real time communications platform. The WebEx Social platform is a major step into a social media based dashboard that can launch context related collaboration sessions with both internal and external work colleagues. Knowledge tagging, security policies and expertise on demand features are all part of the platform.

Microsoft

The Microsoft family of collaboration products and services has undergone major re-structuring. Lync (Microsoft Lync, 2013) and Skype is the core focus of the Microsoft collaboration strategy. On the 29th May 2013, Microsoft released Lync-Skype connectivity (Microsoft, 2013). This functionality will enable users to add each other as contacts and communicate using IM, see presence data and set up audio calls (video calls expected to follow in the future) across platforms. Such interoperability development is clearly aimed at platform integration and further development of the Skype client for interfacing across Microsoft collaboration platforms. Skype ubiquity has been advanced with its recent integration into Facebook for video calling and messaging.

Adobe

Adobe describes Connect Pro as a "complete Web communications and collaboration application suite that enables live, interactive Web meetings; virtual classes; on-demand presentations and courses; and real-time and asynchronous group collaboration" (Adobe, 2009). This is still Adobe's core focus with Connect Pro 9 the current version of the service. With Connect Pro a meeting room can be provided with a selection of CMC functionality components Adobe call "pods." Pods (extensions) can be tailored for specific use cases, such as project management, emergency response, command and control centers, virtual classrooms, large seminars, and more (Adobe, 2009). Connect has matured as an enterprise platform and offers pods for learning management systems, event management, mobile apps, customised meeting pods, content management and integration with Refined Data and Vidyo (Adobe, 2013). Adobe remains fully focused on the Meeting, Training and Webinar Connect services. The most recent developments have been around mobile and tablet connectivity to Connect services.

Google

As of August 2010, Google announced that it has stopped development on the Wave platform. Since then Google has consolidated its services on collaboration with a focus on Google+ Hangouts (Google, Hangouts, 2013). Hangouts is primarily a 10 user video conferencing service that is part of the Google+ platform. Use of the service for broadcasting and recording live activity is increasing, with Google acting similar to a TV station by advertising programme schedules of '*On Air*' and '*Scheduled Hangout*' activity. Combining the asynchronous social aspects (Circles) of Google+ with the synchronous capabilities of Hangouts is the main strategy for Google and a direct assault on the Facebook + Skype service. From a consumer perspective both Google+ Hangouts and Facebook + Skype may fuel a revolution in more consumer driven real-time interactions (audio and video) across the Web.

IBM

In our 2012 paper we reported that IBM Research and Lotus were joining forces to deliver new innovation on the Web through the "creation of LotusLive Labs -- a proving ground for advances in business-driven collaboration in the cloud" (IBM, 2010). January 2012 saw a further announcement on the integration of LotusLive into the IBM Smart Cloud service (IBM, Connections, 2012). IBM Smart Cloud "Social Business" (IBM, Smart Cloud, 2013) provides "enterprise file sharing, communities, IM, Web meetings, user profiles, mail and calendar." IBM is leveraging its global reputation in connected enterprise while also adding remote working, remote team management, staff, partners and supplier interactions all from the one cloud platform. Social Business compares in some way with the Office 365 offering from Microsoft (Microsoft Office365, 2013) but with considerable additional functionality.

Citrix Online

The Citrix family of collaboration products primarily includes GoToMeeting, GoToTraining, GoToWebinar and GoToAssist (Citrix, 2013). More recent developments have added GoToAssist Service Desk which provides a full suite of services for managing remote support for customers. Podio (Citrix Podio, 2013) for social collaboration is defined by Citrix as a "collaborative work platform where you can build apps and setup workspaces to support your preferred workflows." Podio provides a suite of apps that can be client configured and that have ease of integration with the GoTo CMC family. Citrix is clearly adding application and business process support on top of its collaboration suite.

4. CMC DEVELOPMENT PLATFORMS

In this section, we provide a high-level review of CMC vendors from a software engineering perspective. We briefly discuss the platform Application Programming Interfaces (APIs), SDKs and related technologies for CMC software developers.

Cisco WebEx Connect

WebEx Meetings offer an "Integration Platform" (Cisco WebEx, Development, 2013) that can be used to integrate enterprise applications and make them "WebEx Enabled." Three distinct APIs are provided by the Cisco WebEx Integration Platform:

- The URL API, which provides browser-based, external hooks into the WebEx services.
- The XML API, which is a comprehensive set of services supporting most aspects of WebEx. This provides user management, meeting scheduling and attendee management.
- The Teleconference Service Provider API, which is a full-featured XML-based interface to allow integration with audio conferencing networks. This feature is designed for telecommunications providers to seamlessly integrate their services with Cisco WebEx.

The Cisco Jabber SDKs and APIs (Cisco, Jabber Development, 2013) are available to developers that want to integrate presence, IM, voice, video, voice messaging, desktop sharing and conferencing into their applications. Cisco Jabber SDKs are available for browser based and mobile app developers who wish to embed Jabber functionality. According to Cisco the WebEx Social API (Cisco, WebEx Social, 2013) provides for the creation, updating, deletion, searching, sorting and filtering of WebEx Social resources. Cisco has a dedicated collaboration developer hub available at http://developer.cisco.com/web/collaboration-developer (Cisco, 2013).

Adobe Live Cycle Collaboration Services

The Adobe platform for collaboration development is Live Cycle Collaboration Services (LCCS): this enables developers to add real-time collaboration and social capabilities to their applications. LCCS is a development platform hosted by Adobe: therefore the responsibility of deployment, maintenance and scalability rests with Adobe, leaving developers to concentrate on application development. Recently Adobe and Influxis made an announcement about LCCS in relation to a new joint consulting development service called "Influxis Collaboration Service" (Adobe Influxis, 2013). This may be seen as a move by Adobe to develop the knowledge base and services around embedded applications using the LCCS backend. LCCS provides the following features:

- Real-time push messaging, enabling the creation of collaboration-aware components and applications;
- The use of pre-built components such as a white board, chat window, and Webcam;
- Audio and video sharing, with support for P2P (RTMFP) streaming;
- The detection of changes to presence, status, and roles.

The LCCS protocol stack has four core layers (Adobe LCCS Developer, 2013); *Sessions and authentication; Shared model components*; *Shared managers*; and *Collaboration UI components*. A full discussion on LCCS architecture is outside the scope of this paper. Adobe provides a dedicated site for developers working with LCCS (Adobe LCCS Developer, 2013).

Microsoft Lync 2013 Development

Albert Kooiman (Microsoft Lync, 2013) from Microsoft presents the new unified communication (UC) architecture and strategy for Lync and Exchange 2013. This video describes a number of APIs such as the Unified Communications Web API, Lync Managed API, Persistent Chat API, Unified Communications API, Exchange Web Services API, and Mail Apps for Office 2013. Kooiman presents Microsoft's UC vision that incorporates "communications enabled applications" using an IP powered network. Essentially Microsoft envisions that every application will eventually have some universally accessible communications enabled endpoint. Such universal deployment may be on-premises, online, hybrid or federated. Developers will see requirements for applications that streamline communications such as: enhanced presence, click to communicate, and contextual in-app communication. The second layer of development according to Microsoft will aim to reduce human latency. Applications with focused notification and alert services, interactive outbound targeted communications and finding correct human expertise on-demand all fall into this category. The final layer of development for UC relates to extending the application reach and tends more toward human to machine interactions. Such applications will increasingly use smart "bot" technologies for context based Web chats, interactive voice response and query-response interactions prior to human intervention. These services are explained in further detail by Kooiman. Microsoft expects that their UC platform will be a major component in the re-engineering of future business processes for user empowerment, economical reasons, organisational efficiencies and for the overall in-app user experience.

From a CMC perspective it is clear that Cisco, Adobe and Microsoft are fully committed to providing developers with services and platforms that will acts as a backend set of UC cloud services. In conclusion of this section we will review two further development services from Google and IBM.

Google+ Hangout Development

The Google Developers site provides details on the Hangouts API (Google, Hangouts API, 2013). The API provides the programming reference to Hangout video calls and enables an app to do such things as list Hangout participants, share data between instances of apps in the Hangout, control aspects of the user interface, and control the microphone, camera and speaker settings. Sound effects and image overlays to faces can also be implemented using the API. The Developer Channel provides early access to features under development that may become part of the API. Features that enable background blur or replacement and a hand tracking feature are in development and may be formally integrated into a future version of the Hangout API.

IBM Smart Cloud Development

IBM provide a Social Business Toolkit (SBTK) (IBM, Social Business Toolkit, 2013) which acts as a single source for developers using their SmartCloud for Social Business. IBM discusses "Inside-Out" integrations which refer to the expansion of the SmartCloud for Social Business platform to provide bespoke functionality. Integrations that are "Outside-In" relate to expanding an existing in-house application/SaaS with Social Business functionality. The SBTK provides API calls for files, activities, meetings, contacts, profiles and communities.

The CMC/UC development space has seen considerable activity in the past eighteen months. It is clear that global vendors have identified the criticality of having a platform that is robust, scalable, multi-device and open standards based. The next section presents recent relevant research and developments in a number of inter-related CMC topics. Topics covered include interoperability, standards, video conferencing, telepresence, virtual worlds, cloud computing and Enterprise 2.0.

5. CMC RECENT RESEARCH AND DEVELOPMENTS

Today some of the main concerns with CMC relate to standards, security, transparency and interoperability. The ability to easily move across platforms is still a highly complex process specifically if intellectual property has been developed throughout organisations. In 2003 the Internet Engineering Task Force (IEFT) set up a working group for the specific standardisation of Web conferencing called Centralised Conferencing (XCON). According to the IEFT Website the deliverables for the XCON working group are:

- A mechanism for membership and authorization control
- A mechanism to manipulate and describe media "mixing" or "topology" for multiple media types (audio, video, text)
- A mechanism for notification of conference related events/changes (for example a floor change)
- A basic floor control protocol

Request for comment (RFC) 6503 was last submitted August 03 2011. The RFC presents the proposed standard for Centralized Conferencing (XCON) (IETF XCON, 2013). XCON is a step in the direction of improved interoperability across CMC enabled processes. If approved and implemented as a standard by software manufacturers, XCON has potential to truly exploit interrelationships across platforms thus providing increased opportunities for truly innovative engineering of next generation computer mediated communication services.

As discussed earlier WebRTC has seen increased search activity since 2013. An extract from a draft submission to the IETF describes Web Real-Time Communication (WebRTC) as a framework that provides support for direct interactive rich communication using audio, video, text, collaboration, games, etc. between two peers' Web-browsers. The Real-time Transport Protocol (RTP) is used as the underlying technology of WebRTC. RTP provides a framework for delivery of audio and video conferencing data and other real-time media applications (IEFT WebRTC, 2012). Work by Davis et al. (Davies, Joachim, & Gabner, 2012) compared WebRTC against an alternative solution called APSINT that used a Javascript API and framework. In their research they found that their solution was more developer friendly and productive. Even so, the researchers believe WebRTC will gain momentum as issues such as standardisation, browser support and better documention are addressed. They suggest that "with the use of open standards, its efficient media transmission, and no need of plugins or additional software WebRTC has a lot of potential." Writing for Network World, Hippensteel explain how any end-point (person, sensor, device, object) can be enabled with CMC features once it has a built-in browser. He also stresses the core advantage of only requiring a browser that supports the WebRTC standard, no other software is required. According to Hippensteel, WebRTC support is currently built into Chrome 21, Opera 12, Firefox 17, and Internet Explorer (via Chrome Frame) (Hippensteel, 2013). He believes that Micrsoft is the one to watch and advises that "Microsoft's official position is that they will support it when it becomes a standard." Depending how fast the W3C IETF moves on this may dictate the fortunes of WebRTC. Currently the momentum is there and with a number of telecommunication manufacturers incorporating the standard into new offerings WebRTC cannot be ignored.

Video Conferencing and Telepresence

A report by Lombardi (2008) outlines the primary video-conferencing (VC) systems as conference room, telepresence, desktop, rolling, set-top, portable and videophones. VC as described has primarily remained static with telepresence, Cloud VC, HD Web VC and new innovations such as telepresence robotics as the most recent developments. The effectiveness of telepresence in relation to business meetings has been researched by Standaert et al. (Standaert, Muylle, & Basu, 2013). They surveyed 248 users of CMC technologies and found that "social presence provided by telepresence is significantly more effective than the social presence provided by (traditional) video-conferencing for giving or receiving feedback and for building relationships and trust." The research conducted also found major limitations with telepresence and other forms of VC technologies when it comes to idea generation, communicating confidential/sensitive information, communicating emotions and feelings, making decisions, garnering buy-in and finding solutions. Their 2013 paper identifies the current limitations that exist with VC technologies but it identifies telepresence as the one technology that offers real potential in terms of addressing the social presence aspects that are severely lacking in VC/telepresence but so prevalent in typical face to face meetings. Perceived cost, scarce resources and limited deployment of telepresence systems are seen as current barriers in terms of telepresence uptake across organisations (Standaert, Muylle, & Basu, 2013).

Video is proliferating and interweaving itself into all forms of software services. New standards and technologies are aimed at addressing both video and data explosions across all forms of devices. Costa-Perez et al. (2013) present their current findings in relation to the latest trends in telecommunications standards. Their paper discusses the increasing requirement for interoperability across various standards and development organisations such as 3rd Generation Partnership Project (3GPP), IEEE 802.11, IETF, Open Networking Foundation for Software-Defined Networking (ONF SDN), Industrial Specification Group for Network Functions Virtualization (ETSI ISG NFV), Machine-to-Machine communication (oneM2M) and Intelligent Transportation Systems (ETSI TC ITS). Their paper presents current research on new standards along with their thoughts on '*disruptive technologies*' that are expected to impact in the not too distant future. According to their research, increasing system interdependencies are accelerating the collaboration between standards development organisation which is primarily being driven by fixed-mobile network convergence. A quote from their paper most pertinent to our research is that "wireless technologies are spending most efforts in dramatically increasing future peak data rates" (Costa-Perez, et al., 2013). Increased collaboration between fixed and mobile networks is also projected to deliver major cross platform and device interconnectivity. At a network level Software Defined Networking (SDN) is expected to be critical from an operator's perspective in terms of service productivity and innovation. With direct reference to CMC, disruptive technologies such as machine to machine (M2M) software services and Intelligent Transport Systems (ITS) are expected to increase the overall market size for telecommunication/CMC systems.

As large screen public display systems proliferate across organisations and public areas, Häkkilä et al. (Häkkilä, Koskenranta, Posti, Ventä-Olkkonen, & Colley, 2013) see a role for VC integration with gesture based computing. Their research describes trials they conducted with two VC linked public display systems. Each local and remote display screen was equipped with a Microsoft Kinect depth camera for the capture and processing of interactive user gestures. The researchers used the metaphor of an iced window on each display screen. Users made wiping gestures at the 'Ice Window' (Häkkilä, Koskenranta, Posti, Ventä-Olkkonen, & Colley, 2013) to virtually melt the ice, thus clearing a view to the video stream from the remote location. During non-activity the window to the remote location frosted up again till the next user interacted with the system. The ability to notice when someone else was peeking through the window was one of the unique aspects identified by users during their trials of the system. The research by Häkkilä et al. provides an insight into how gesture based interfaces are driving demand for more embedded intelligent processing of video data. Ice Window and similar interface projects could well be a major driver of future innovation/research in VC/CMC technologies.

The future of personal video communication was the subject of a workshop conducted at the ACM SIGCHI Conference on Human

Factors in Computing Systems in April 2013. The workshop objective was to conduct outside the box brainstorming on how the existing paradigm of video 'talking heads' could evolve into personal video systems that can share everyday experience. Oduor et al. (Oduor, Venolia, Neustaedter, & Judge, 2013) explain their vision of personal video systems encompassing everyday experiences such as dining, watching TV, storytelling, attendance at weddings, parties, graduations or indeed any random aspect of daily living.

The Google Glass project relates to the work of Oduor et al. and is also addressing pervasive personal video. Glass is the subject of a paper by Elise Acherman (2013). In her paper she describes the look and feel of the Google Glass head mounted point of eye device. Glass will run apps such as Google+, Google Search and is designed to feel more natural and immersive than a PC or smartphone (Acherman, 2013). Hayes (2013) describes Glass as a hands-free display of information currently available on a smartphone but with gesture and voice based interactions. One very interesting observation made by Hayes with reference to Glass is his concept of '*you are the camera*'. He argues that if Glass becomes as pervasive as the mobile phone then such a continual stream of visual data will have major implications across many aspects of society. Unwilling to wait for the Google developer edition of Glass, Furlan an artificial intelligence researcher went and built his own prototype device from readily available components bought on the Internet. He refers to the Glass device as a "brain-prosthesis" and believes that the real potential will be in second-generation applications that provide total recall and augmented cognition (i.e. ability to call up and share everything you have ever seen) (Furlan, 2013) services to users.

Video Playdate is a Microsoft Research project that uses video conferencing to provide play between children over distances. The research work of Yarosh et al. (Yarosh, Inkpen, & Brush, 2009) is at a very early stage and several limitations have been identified by the researchers but overall they are 'enthusiastic' on the potential for free play systems (Video Playdate) over distance using next generation video conferencing systems. Nokia Research is also innovating in the device VC space. The 'Family Story Play' system is aimed at grandparents reading books together with their grandchildren. The paper explains that Family Story Play is designed to improve communication across generations and over a distance. The system interface combines a paper book, a sensor-enhanced frame, video conferencing technology, and video content of a Sesame Street Muppet (Elmo). In software trials the researchers found that children preferred Story Play and responded well to the physical aspect of the book as well as the video coach and assistant Elmo. Grandparents preferred the larger images in the alternative Skype system (alternative system also tested) and were more at home with a computer rather than the Story Play device. The research concludes that their Story Play system has "shown that communications, education and entertainment can converge in a shared activity context …" (Raffle, et al., 2010).

Video and related intelligent services are set for major growth. As the video data is processed in real-time the embedded intelligence in the image offers the promise of a new generation of applications never thought possible. Image processing technologies such as Microsoft's Kinect, Intel's 3D Gesture Camera (Intel, Gesture Camera, 2013) and related SDKs, offer increasing intelligent processing capabilities to developers working in the VC space. Such developments around video are expected to drive new innovations in what Intel refers to as perceptual computing (Intel, Perceptive Computing, 2013). Expected future innovations in telepresence and personal/consumer VC, interoperability of standards and the Internet of Everything look set to prove the analysts correct in terms of a '*video everywhere*' future. Since our 2012 paper cloud computing has dominated the headlines. A short summary of our findings in relation to cloud and enterprise 2.0 is provided below.

Cloud Computing, SaaS, and Enterprise 2.0

The work of Youseff et al. (Youseff & Dilma Da Silva, 2009) presents relevant research on cloud computing. Cloud computing is expected to be the dominant infrastructure for the delivery of CMC services in the future. Youseff presents a five layer reference ontology of cloud computing:

Layer 5 - Cloud Application: Software as a Service (SaaS)
Layer 4 - Cloud Software Environment: Platform as a Service (PaaS)
Layer 3 - Cloud Software Infrastructure:
- **Computational Resources:** Infrastructure as a Service (IaaS)
- **Storage:** Data-Storage as a Service (DaaS)
- **Communications:** Communications as a Service (CaaS)

Layer 2 - Software Kernel: Software kernels at this level can be implemented as an OS kernel, hypervisor, virtual machine monitor and/or clustering middleware
Layer 1 - Firmware/Hardware: Hardware as a Service (HaaS)

Cloud computing and SaaS are the enabling technologies of Web 2.0 and the core concept of Enterprise 2.0. The AIIM Market Intelligence (Frappaolo, 2008) report analysed discussions with more than 400 Enterprise 2.0 users, and provides a comprehensive insight into the acceptance of Enterprise 2.0 technologies across organisations.

The AIIM report attempted to establish a formal definition of Enterprise 2.0, and the result from a panel of experts was the following. "Enterprise 2.0 [is] a system of Web-based technologies that provide rapid and agile collaboration, information sharing, emergence, and integration capabilities in the extended enterprise" (Frappaolo, 2008). The authors point out that the first clause in the definition "indicates that Enterprise 2.0 is a collection, not a single entity or tool, the fact that it leverages Web-based technologies and its need for an (eco) system to thrive." They go on to state that the terms rapid and agile implies that there is a low barrier to entry and that Enterprise 2.0 is dynamic by nature. The last part of the definition is clearly positioning the functionality within a robust enterprise setting rather than merely generic Web services. The use of "extended enterprise" also refers to the potential for inter–company collaborations, and collaborations with partners and customers.

Related to Enterprise 2.0 is the idea of Web-Based Knowledge Communities (WKC). A paper by Lin et al. (Lin, Fan, & Zhang, 2009) highlights the fact that "WKCs have become prevalent and useful tools for knowledge acquisition, exchange, and collaborative decision making." In their paper they define a WKC as a "virtual community comprised of individuals who share common interests for a knowledge domain and who work together to expand their understanding of the knowledge domain through on-going knowledge sharing and acquisition." Lin et al. explore the success factors of WKCs, and their conclusions are relevant to the development of Enterprise 2.0.

Increasing evidence of Enterprise 2.0 is emerging as platforms such as Oracle Beehive (2013), Microsoft Office 365 Enterprise (Microsoft Office365, 2013), IBM Smart Cloud for Social Business and Cisco WebEx Social aim to securely bridge the gap between enterprise and social computing. These platforms also incorporate some form of WKC functionality as discussed by Lin et al. but under the security, control and scrutiny of the Enterprise 2.0 platform.

From our research, it is evident that the past number of months has seen exceptional activity across numerous aspects of the CMC field. In the next section we revisit our visionary interviews with industry and thought leaders. We provide an edited version of the original interview outcomes and have also updated our conclusions considering the most recent research we have conducted.

6. INTERVIEWS WITH INDUSTRY EXPERTS AND THOUGHT LEADERS

Fifteen industry experts and thought leaders were interviewed using semi-structured techniques from December 2009 to April 2010. The following is an edited version of the results and findings from our 2012 paper (Keary & Redfern, 2012).

Interview Process

Interviewees were selected across a range of sectors. The interviewees were asked to consider the following five questions from a conferencing and collaboration (CMC) perspective:

Q1. What should you be able to do with CMC environments?
Q2. What services should be included?
Q3. What is missing from CMC services?
Q4. How can CMC change business value chains?
Q5. What are the barriers to CMC uptake?

Following the conclusion of all interviews, the transcripts were analysed and cross-referenced using the Affinity Diagram technique (Kawakita, 1975). This technique is used to put structure on ideas and concepts that may be compiled from meetings, brainstorming sessions, interviews, Web collaborations or any other means of collecting opinions and ideas.

Discussion of Interview Contents

This section provides edited key points from the KJ analysis.

Q1. What should you be able to do with CMC environments?

This question gathered technical and user issues with existing CMC platforms.

Q1.A. CMC platforms must be simple to use:

Platforms must become more intuitive and aim to make the interaction as close to face-to-face as possible.

Q1.B. Skype/VoIP is driving innovation across CMC providers:

Interviewees generally agreed that Skype and VoIP is forcing innovation across CMC providers and that they are using VoIP throughout their networks to drive down costs of service delivery.

Q1.C. Increased access via mobile apps is vital:

Many interviewees stressed that all of the existing platforms must provide CMC access capabilities via mobile devices.

Q1.D. More reliable integration of CMC with backend business systems is required:

The lack of robust back-end integration with business systems was identified as a limitation in existing platforms.

Q1.E. The CMC services model is changing:

One-price bundles and fixed pricing is changing the pricing models for audio and Web services. This trend is compared with payment models in the mobile phone sector.

Q1.F. Issues persist with existing CMC services:

Existing services are generally delivering on user expectations and have had major improvement in terms of reliability over the last five years. Document sharing features are seen as not being intuitive and easy to use in a number of platforms. It was also mentioned that it is not easy to integrate audio services into platforms.

Q1.G. Recording of CMC sessions needs to be more straightforward:

Session recording is not as intuitive as it should be: it should be a lot easier to record, store and track session activity. Hotlinks could be added during a CMC session or edited post-session with further tagging details by the moderator or the participant. Such a feature has the potential to provide a multi-contextual view of a specific CMC session as seen by the moderator and each attending participant.

Q1.H. Professional backup and maintenance by the CMC provider is important:

The secure back-up and support services of established providers are seen as key to the integration of CMC services into organisations.

Q1.I. Critical issues with current platforms persist:

Firewall issues came up as one of the main recurring problems.

Q2. What services should be included?

This question aimed to elicit information on the types of services that should be available in today's platforms but are either non-existent or are too complex to use.

Q2.A. Improvements are required in services across platforms:

The development of a "meeting dashboard" with key functions to get meetings set up quickly was discussed. Better tools to manage, schedule and market Web casts and to manage archiving were called for. Moderator-less breakout rooms that could be monitored and reported on was also mentioned by an industry expert.

Q.2.B. Real-time support and new services are required:

Online intelligent assistance either by machine or human is seen as a core service for the future. Also raised was the expected increase in language translation and transcription services that may create new offerings for global providers.

Q2.C. New platform trends include Audio, Unified Communication, and WiFi:

There is growth in the trend for CMC providers to provide a branded hub that appears to exist privately on the corporate network. This is expected to increase as more companies move to dedicated conferencing hubs.

Q2.D. CMC needs to integrate social media services:

The future employee will be from the YouTube/Facebook generation and services will need to take account of this fact. Mobile CMC clients will need to be engineered for social media interactions between users. Presence was also raised in a social media context.

Q2.E. Presence functionality needs to mature:

Presence functionality is increasing in popularity and has an increasing role to play in the creation of the true "Multi-Media Phone Call." Today visual calling is increasing in availability with providers adding screens to their telephone handsets, while traditional audio conference call providers are integrating more Web based features into their services which can be used as a gateway into launching a full CMC or social media session if required.

Q2.F. Templates and automated procedures are required:

On-board templates should be developed that would guide a user through the type of tasks they wish to carry out. Overall the research points to the need for job-role based instructions on the usage of key features to be made available online to presenters/moderators.

Q2.G. IBM 'Global Jam'-like services are required:

The IBM Global Jam technology uses Web components to connect thousands of experts for a set time period, normally three to four days, to discuss multiple research tracks. IBM pioneered this collaboration technology as a knowledge management and processing environment. This type of global Web based collaboration can be expected to grow as more organisations realise the potential of the technology for innovation, idea generation and problem resolution.

Q3. What is missing from CMC services?

The interviewer shifted focus and encouraged the interviewee to discuss their thoughts on the medium and long-term futures of CMC technologies and platforms.

Q3.A. Virtual reality and 3D is missing:

The integration of commercial business oriented Virtual Worlds (VWs) was discussed by a number of industry and thought leaders. Work by Redfern & Naughton (2002) on virtual learning environments (Redfern & Naughton, 2002), Ponti (2010) on virtual research environments, and Goossenaerts et al. (2007) on virtual engineering environments, are examples of academic research relating to this question.

Q3.B. Better social media integration is required:

A "Magic Button" with reference to social media integration could take 5 people from Facebook into an audio conference and back again seamlessly. In the future it was suggested that special "Social Media Workbenches" should be developed with such a "Magic Button" concept.

Q3.C. Digital rooms and archives are a future feature:

Digital Object Archives would be capable of using presence services to establish instant conferencing and collaboration with the owners of digital artefacts in an archive. Social media could also be used to reach out to those involved with an object from the archive.

Q3.D. Embedded platform intelligence will evolve:

Intelligence was discussed in relation to the CMC sessions that take place. Meta knowledge that captures the details on why a session was set-up was discussed. When knowledge based activities are passed along, the meta-knowledge for those involved relates to "What to work on," "What not to work on," and "Where help is needed." CMC environments in the future must provide access to this type of task intelligence which is developed and added to as the task progresses through a series of CMC activities in its lifecycle. Some interviewees suggested that it should be easy to track the knowledge sources and expert interactions that take place within a CMC session. This could be software tools that enable quick revisions of a meeting to identify where attendees currently are in a meeting/decision process.

Q3.E. CMC analytics and data mining services should improve:

Interviewees suggested that there should be improved meeting analytics and data mining services capable of monitoring meeting behaviours. A suggested drill-down service could also be used to search and deliver digital media relevant to the current CMC session.

Q3.F. Machine translation services should be integrated:

Machine translation services will need to be integrated into platforms in the future, rather than having to reach out to external service providers via Web links.

Q3.G. Trust, security and certification will be vital:

One third of those interviewed raised the areas of trust and security in their interview. They believe that these factors are limiting CMC uptake, especially in sectors such as pharmaceutical. Such trust and security is expected to come at a price and is seen as a counteraction to the 'Freemium' model. External CMC providers to enterprises must ensure at all times that client services will be maintained and never compromised. Such dedicated infrastructure and certification standards may see a number of providers exit the traditional CMC market in the future.

Q3.H. Education related requirements:

Developments in CMC based education services are expected to advance such that true remote monitoring and assessment can be carried out. CMC needs to look at what can be learnt from the Nintendo Wii and similar innovative input devices. Kock (2008) also addresses this topic under a discussion on user interface problems in virtual worlds: "as the huge success of the Nintendo Wii has taught us, one possible direction for progress is improvement in interactivity support through interface devices whose use are more natural than mice and keyboards." (Kock, 2008). Gesture based computing was also discussed in relation to intelligent observation by remote intelligent agents capable of monitoring a user in a live session aided by some form of gesture based analysis.

Q3.I. CMC and ICT corporate integration:

All of the previous headings clearly indicate that in the future there will be an ever-increasing needs for seamless integration of CMC into existing corporate applications.

Q3.J. CMC interoperability standards:

Two interviewees discussed the Sharable Content Object Reference Model (SCORM) (Buendía & Hervás, 2006), which is a standard for sharing content across eLearning platforms. A type of SCORM compliance standard for CMC session content would enable increased integration across platforms.

Q3.K. Visual based services:

While most interviewees did not raise issues on visual interaction it was agreed that the future is likely to be highly focused on HD and telepresence. Developments in HD and perhaps full screen body imagery via telepresence are likely to deliver closer body language functionality that is evidently lacking in CMC systems currently in use.

Q3.L. Trends and future services:

"Find an Expert" services were discussed as a potential value-added service that conferencing providers may develop in the future. Such services would provide instant access to certified expertise made available from within a CMC session. The service could be provisioned to provide access to internal or external experts as specified by client requirements.

Q4. How can CMC change business value chains?

This question switched from a technology focus to consider how CMC is changing work processes, service and support and how industry value chains may be transformed.

Q4.A. CMC changing the value chain:

CMC technologies are expected to enable the creation of virtual companies in the future; equally, CMC may be a disruptive technology for traditional siloed organisations. Future developments should aim to alleviate cultural barriers, thus creating seamless integration across global business value chains.

Q4.B. CMC value chain drivers:

It was generally discussed that CMC deployments should deliver substantial contributions to profitability and productivity. The concept of Key Performance Indicators (KPIs) and their achievement using CMC is an area to consider in terms of value chain impact. A number of participants raised the fact that CMC and social networking can be expected to have a considerable impact on siloed organisations, and that major transformation is underway (in the midst of the current economic difficulties) and corporations are re-engineering their organisational ICT and business architectures.

Q4.C. Inter-organisation value chain trends:

Topics discussed here relate to the development of inter-organisational and inter-government collaboration in the future. This will lead to deeper integration across organisations, across digital cities, borders and continents. Also mentioned was the potential for CMC to play a major role in domestic and social applications.

Q4.D. Workplace value chain transformations:

Continued Professional Development (CPD) services in the future may be enabled by CMC providers thus ushering in authorised and monitored interaction with social networking technologies to the corporate space. The idea of a Knowledge Factory (KF) was discussed. The concept is that knowledge workers (KW) work on the same problem on a 24-hour basis across multiple time zones. Tracking of knowledge sources and the expert communications relating to a knowledge-based activity is a core feature of CMC if it is to be used in a KF type scenario. The use of CMC to enable real-time interaction with internal experts and authorised external pools was also discussed. Management will require tools and services to control and audit the virtual and social enterprise for compliance and legal purposes. CMC is also expected to be increasingly used for idea generation and knowledge worker engagement and exchange.

Q4.E. New CMC delivery models:

In general it is believed that 'Freemium' services will grow in the consumer sector. As organisations incorporate CMC into their value chains and cultures, the interviewees agree that companies will continue to pay for innovative leading edge CMC services and platforms.

Q5. What are the barriers to CMC uptake?

The final question addressed the uptake and limitations of CMC from an organisational perspective.

Q5.A. Managerial and business barriers to CMC uptake:

Management must be educated on how the technologies relate to the business and its value chain. There is still a reluctance to change from the top down and CMC is coming up against political, cultural and social barriers. As the next generation of employees emerge this is likely to change. It was also noted that in large organisations there is no central focus or person responsible for the deployment of CMC services. CMC in its current form has various services that are consumed by different parts of an organisation. Without a central home, proper integration across an organisation will remain a problematic area. It was also discussed that there tends to be a range of incompatible technologies across organisations today and there is a lack of consistent knowledge on how to use such services and infrastructure. Cost was identified as still being a major barrier to uptake but this is starting to change as providers reduce costs across their networks in order to offer more cost-effective services.

Q5.B. User barriers to CMC uptake:

There is customer confusion in having to deal with multiple interfaces and feature sets across platforms. Corporate education programmes should provide a common set of the main features that can be learnt by users in a very short time.

Q5.C. Provider barriers and delivery issues:

Strategic and effective CMC operations management will increase in importance as demand for services grows over the decade.

Research Interviews: Discussion and Conclusion

The key research findings have been summarised above (see original paper for detailed analysis with industry and user references) in relation to each of the research questions presented to the interviewees. This section provides our original conclusions and analyses. We also link in our research presented in previous sections (in italics) as applicable to the discussion.

Existing CMC platforms must be a lot easier to use with more intuitive interfaces, offer increased mobile access and must be easier to configure and deploy across an organisation. Developments of existing services should include meeting dashboards, online assistance, more integrated presence, social media integration and the ability to configure a platform based on the roles and tasks to be carried out. *Research presented in our paper suggests that CMC providers have increased their focus on usability, social media integration and the development of hub/dashboard functionality. Today services such as WebEx Social, Citrix Podio, Google+ Hangouts, Skype, IBM SmartCloud and Facebook + Skype all appear to be addressing a number of the issues raised by the interviewees.*

3D, virtual worlds, and avatars are technologies that are expected to increase in usage as more intuitive interfaces to CMC services are demanded in the future. Digital rooms, HDTVs and interactive tabletops will also appear as future user interfaces for CMC. *Increased integration of the real and virtual world is evident with 3D worlds entering many domains. Developments around the Internet of Everything, and smart devices such as the SUR40 and Glass are recent developments in relation to the points raised above.*

Meta-knowledge, context capture, auto review, meeting analytics and machine translation are research areas that will influence the development of next generation CMC platforms. Identity and trust are critical to the secure uptake of CMC across organisations. *The work of Kooiman on Microsoft's UC strategy* (Microsoft Lync, 2013) *is perhaps most relevant to the above. The vision of more embedded intelligence around communication enabled processes has potential to address some of points raised such as meta-knowledge, context capture, analytics and translation services.*

Interoperability between CMC platforms, and standards for content sharing, are critically important. There are also requirements for integration with corporate applications and improved access via Web services and APIs. *There has been a lot of recent activity in relation to these requirements. It remains to be seen what the W3C and IEFT deliver in terms of XCON and WebRTC. The work of Costa-Perez et al.* (Costa-Perez, et al., 2013) *also highlights the increased activities across standards organisations. In parallel there is the drive by the main players to embed their CMC infrastructure/services into the software development strategies of large organisations thus positioning CMC as a functional (SaaS) component of next generation applications.*

Social networking will be more formalised across the enterprise in the future. There will also be a requirement for services to manage increased inter-organisation collaboration. These developments are expected to transform the traditional siloed organisation. *As already discussed, providers such as IBM, Cisco, Microsoft and Oracle are presenting Enterprise 2.0 type platforms with a complete range of CMC services. Such platforms are being positioned to larger organisations as secure and trusted conferencing and collaboration services for both internal and external activities.*

From a management perspective, selecting the correct applications for CMC and a focused collaboration strategy is vital. The education of management and the integration of CMC into business and knowledge worker processes are an integral part of ensuring continual increases in effectiveness, efficiencies, and productivity across an organisation. *Hashmi et al., Duranti & de Almeida, Goossenaerts et al. and Ponti all identify the increased management focus around CMC related technologies and process change. Their overall research stresses that change should be gradual, strategy based, introduced via management education, and not just technology for the sake of technology.*

7. CMC PROPOSED NEXT GENERATION ARCHITECTURE

The primary scope of our original research concerned the conceptual underpinnings of and industry insights into CMC futures. We also provided a brief summary of a proposed future CMC (C&C) architecture. The architecture was based on our belief that a number of leading providers with established CMC platforms can be expected to dominate the market for the foreseeable future. There is evidence of this from the recent Garner MQ research. This led us to accept the core functionality of current CMC platforms as an underlying infrastructure service to our proposed architecture. As discussed above, existing CMC platforms are being exposed as Web services/APIs and they are expected to form the de facto standard on which the next generation of CMC services will be constructed. The assumption is that a reinvention of existing CMC functionality is not required and that it provides an accepted set of standards that enable basic conferencing and collaborative communication services.

The second pre-requisite we proposed was in relation to the fact that as more and more content is used and accessed during synchronous and asynchronous CMC activities, a purpose built storage and mining facility will be required. In the future we propose that this will be in the form of a knowledge warehouse (KW). KW infrastructure is central for interfacing and service provision to a number of the modules in our proposed CMC architecture.

The following nine modules were presented in our 2012 work: 3D – SVW (Social Virtual Worlds), CMC Session Management, CMC Context Services, NG (Next Generation) – Interface Services, NG – Services, Trust Services, Communication Services, Development & API Services and CMC Enterprise Services (Keary & Redfern, 2012). The original architecture presented was based on forecasts over a five to ten year period. For the purpose of this updated paper we have revisited each module in our architecture proposal. We discuss each module in the architecture and present new thinking and relate it to recent developments in the CMC field.

For clarification purposes, we do not see that our architecture will result in one colossal software platform but rather a suite of SaaS applications with defined interfaces that will enable the next generation of CMC capabilities. As discussed, existing Web conferencing functionality (audio, video, screen share, whiteboard, file share, desktop/application share) and the KW can be taken as SaaS application modules in addition to the nine modules discussed below. This section will also discuss the various CMC research activities of the authors and will relate expected contributions and relevance to the overall architecture proposal.

a. 3D: SVW

This module provides for 3D and virtual reality interfaces for CMC platforms. It is anticipated that integration of CMC with social virtual worlds will reach into enterprise applications in the future. This will also see the integration of smart spaces and objects into virtual worlds.

This is already happening with providers such as ON24 (ON24, 2013) Second Life (Second Life, 2013) and World of Warcraft (Blizzard Games, 2013) as examples of corporate and consumer virtual worlds. Redfern and Naughton discuss developments in 3D virtual interaction spaces involving avatars and support for the key tenets of effective CSCW, such as shared interaction awareness (WYSIWIS), persistence of place, and chance meetings (Redfern & Naughton, 2002). The term 'Collaborative Virtual Environment' (CVE) is used to refer to CSCW platforms involving strong spatial metaphors in which fully integrated work tools, data, and avatars co-exist (see also Churchill et al. 2001). Kock's (2008) paper, "E-Collaboration and E-Commerce In Virtual Worlds" highlights the potential of Second Life and World of Warcraft as an enabler of "actual work" and "trade." Kock also discusses whether virtual worlds "can serve as a platform for credible studies of e-collaboration behaviour and related outcomes." Virtual worlds are gaining popularity in academia and commercial sectors. Current EU led research relating to a CVE (S-Cube) for soft skills' training and development is one of our current research projects. The S-Cube uses virtual world scenario based simulations to help players develop their interpersonal communications skills. This free online serious games platform will be available to the general public in 2013 and will be discussed later in this paper (S-Cube Partners, 2013). Related research by Mavridis et al. (2012) compared two collaborative virtual learning environments (CVLES): Open Sim vs. Second Life for education purposes. Their research concludes that open source CVLEs "are not mature enough yet to accommodate collaborative activities and allow educators to utilise them effectively." While the issues identified during their research are not insurmountable they suggest that future work must focus on total CVLE immersion thus facilitating more engagement and motivation by learners.

Our work (Keary and Walsh) on S-Cube is also researching the current limitations of computer mediated communications in online game based learning (GBL) and relates to the field of perceptive (Intel, Perceptive Computing, 2013) and affective computing (Picard, 1997). Research already discussed from Häkkilä, et al., 2013, Oduor, et al., 2013, Yarosh, et al., 2009 and Raffle, et al., 2010 provides an insight into how smart spaces and objects may be integrated into CMC based SVW. There has been a lot of recent CMC activity in relation to virtual worlds and it is expected to grow as tablets, smartphones, interactive touch displays/TVs become the platform of choice for SVW.

Much of the current development of 3D worlds in a 'serious work' context has been enabled by the maturation of the Games Engines industry. We are now in the 2nd generation of affordable Games Engines, driven by an explosion in the (programmer) user base and fuelled by the increasingly low barriers-to-entry into the mobile and desktop games markets. The long and well-funded history of computer games technology development has brought about a revolution in terms of accessible and affordable underpinning technology.

There is also a mature body of research into CVEs, which has been an academic focus since the late 1990s and which provides a strong theoretical context by which effective 3D virtual environments may be built for work applications (see Churchill et al. 2001, Redfern & Naughton 2002). Much of the research in CVEs has considered and adapted the tenets of CSCW to the context of multi-user interaction spaces, and we are now seeing this theory maturing into commercial products.

b. CMC Session Management

Sessions are defined as the core CMC user activity that compiles all data and knowledge assets used during an interaction. Sessions may be synchronous or asynchronous. This module provides all of the services such that knowledge workers are able to create, control, manage and mine all of the session activities they are involved with. The module will primarily interface with the proposed knowledge warehouse. As knowledge workers collaborate across multi-CMC platforms in their daily activities the capabilities to effectively mine their session (knowledge) assets will be required. Here we see developments in XCON (IETF XCON, 2013) and WebRTC (IEFT WebRTC, 2012) as key enablers of cross platform standardisations. The development of a typical SCORM (Buendía & Hervás, 2006) compliant standard for CMC session content will be a mandatory requirement to enable knowledge management services across platforms.

c. CMC Context Services

This module supports the Session Management module and provides context capture, provenance and machine learning services to knowledge workers. Faced with ever increasing CMC activities, the ability to capture session context information in real time on behalf of a knowledge worker will be an important development. Machine learning techniques that know and understand the knowledge worker offer the potential of intelligent assistance prior, during and post CMC sessions. We also see the ability to easily track the originality of any content used/referenced in CMC sessions as a vital service in terms of supporting real-time decision making. Such a provenance service may also be used to validate archived CMC sessions and content from the knowledge warehouse.

d. NG (Next Generation): Interface Services

This module manages the next generation of interfaces that will interact with CMC platforms. The range of interfaces can be expected to include HDTVs, IPTVs, tabletops, interactive walls, Augmented Reality (AR) devices, tablets and Brain Machine Interfaces (BMIs).

This module will also handle interface integration with external platforms and interfaces with smart objects and smart spaces.

One of our own research projects involves the development of new interfaces using 3D depth camera and body sensor technology for the S-Cube. Affective and perceptive computing software services will not only transform CMC interfaces but will also provide intelligent processing capabilities to additional layers in the architecture. Related work by Smith and Redfern (2012) and Murphy and Redfern (2011) has developed an Emotion Tracking Agent (ETA) for use in distributed e-research environments. The authors explain that the ETA is intended as an innovative solution to the impaired awareness and attention resulting from continuous task switching or multitasking behaviour of collaborating remote team members. The ETA was integrated into a CMC environment and initial studies were undertaken to analyse the benefits and impact of real-time emotion tracking, by informing remote participants of important changes in the emotional states of fellow collaborators. This research found that vocal, textual and visual cue reporting of such changes can increase attention to and awareness of the meaning of important information presented by co-workers. Affective and perceptive computing, Internet of Everything and BMI interfaces, application and trials will be the main focus of our CMC related research over the coming years.

e. NG – Services

This module provides for social media integration services, culture and language services, knowledge worker task supports and global reach-out platform services for enterprises. The module provides a range of business services that should be easily accessible from a CMC platform. Effort by vendors in relation to 'social business' are addressing social media platform integration and are also providing knowledge/expertise tracking services to users. As discussed most of these service developments are primarily deployed in platforms such as WebEx Social (Cisco, WebEx Social, 2013). With vendors currently developing their own unique social services we envision that these services should be abstracted as independent from any specific platform and should have non-proprietary interface capabilities. These services are also relevant to the Composite Persona and 24 Hours Knowledge Factory concepts discussed later.

f. Trust Services

Presence, trust and security services are provided in this module, which is designed to ensure that organisations can monitor their CMC activities and have knowledge and trust in what is happening across their CMC infrastructure. As already discussed, the rise of Enterprise 2.0 platforms is starting to address the control and monitoring of CMC activities. This needs to be extended to federated services where the interactions with trusted parties may also be monitored. Our thesis is that there is an additional requirement for this layer of services that not only provides presence, trust and security analytics but also uses machine learning algorithms to report on '*what the organisation is actually doing*'. We believe that such management insights into CMC activity offers enormous potential for business, process, social and emotional intelligence and may well be seen as a corporate asset of the future. Google Recorded

Future (Google Recorded Future, 2013) is an example of the type of service proposed for this module.

g. Communication Services

This module relates to developments in the underlying platform (PaaS) communication infrastructure. In this paper we have already presented the most recent developments from the W3C IETF that are most likely to influence the CMC sector. As discussed by Costa-Perez, et al. (2013) in their paper on emerging standards, mobile-fixed convergence and increased spectrum availability will be the main game-changers over the next few years. In our opinion new technologies and standardisation at the communication services layer of our proposed architecture will position CMC as one of the key enablers of the Internet of Everything.

h. Development and API Services

Development services will be critical over the next decade and will be used to seamlessly integrate CMC business and value chain activities across enterprises. The discussion on development in this paper confirms how major vendors are already positioning their services for integration with any type of application that needs to use CMC services. This module is perceived as a suite of generic standard based APIs and SDKs that will work cross platform and that will provide interface configuration, inter-organisation integration services, embedded CMC functionality, knowledge warehouse integration and semantic Web functionality. As we have seen all vendors are currently developing their own technologies for integrating CMC. As standards develop across the sector we believe that similar standards need to be developed for CMC application development and integration.

i. CMC Enterprise Services

The final module provides for enterprise supports in terms of knowledge workers and value chain analytics. Specific human resource (HR) supports for the management of Composite Persona is provided. The uptake of CMC across an enterprise is also supported with training services and online support available to knowledge workers on demand. The Composite Persona (CP) is defined as a "highly cohesive micro-team that, like a corporation, has simultaneous properties of both individual and collective natures" (Denny, et al., 2008). Although a CP acts as a singular entity, it is the composition of several individuals: the CP entity spans the globe and "as the world turns and sites turn on and off, each CP remains active, but the driver of each CP changes with each site" (Denny, et al., 2008). Hybrid offshoring is the focus of the paper by Denney et al. and also discusses the concept of the '24 Hour Knowledge Factory (24-KF)'. CP and CMC are central to the 24-KF and perhaps a concept that will take some time to infiltrate global business. There are considerable challenges ahead for organisations as processes, people, communications and work transformation projects get underway. We are reminded of the research of Hashmi et al. in that even at the basic level of platform selection (Hashmi, Ishikawa, & Richardson, 2013) such CMC related transformation projects should be handled with extreme care and attention to fine detail. The Enterprises Services module should produce a process change methodology to be applied across organisations and will be used to integrate and manage the underlying modules (1 – 8) already discussed above.

The objective of this section was to provide a high-level overview of parallel research that has been conducted in conjunction with the primary research documented in this paper. As part of our research and development activities we are currently working on research projects relating to layers four, five and six. The above architecture has been formally documented with use cases and additional specification details and is the subject of ongoing research by all involved with this paper. While we do not see our work addressing every single module discussed above, our research is advancing with reference to our architecture proposal and will address future innovations and applications for CMC platforms.

ACKNOWLEDGMENT

The authors would like to thank all of the industry experts and thought leaders that participated in the original research.

REFERENCES

Acherman, E. (2013). Google gets in your face. *Spectrum IEEE, January*, 26-29.

Adobe. (2009). *Building toward a unified communications strategy*. Retrieved August 25, 2010, from http://www.adobe.com/products/acrobatconnectpro/webconferencing/pdfs/connectpro_unifiedcommwhitepaper_1_09.pdf

Adobe. (2013). *Adobe extensions*. Retrieved June 28, 2013, from http://www.adobe.com/ie/products/adobeconnect/extend.html

Adobe Influxis. (2013). *Influxis collaboration service*. Retrieved July 03, 2013, from http://www.adobe.com/devnet/livecycle/collaboration.html

Adobe LCCS Developer. (2013). *Adobe LCCS Developer.* Retrieved July 03, 2013, from https://learn.adobe.com/wiki/display/lccs/LiveCycle+Collaboration+Service

AnyBots. (2013). *Telepresence robots - AnyBots*. Retrieved June 27, 2013, from https://www.anybots.com/

Blackboard. (2013). *Blackboard services*. Retrieved June 27, 2013, from http://www.blackboard.com/Platforms.aspx

Blizzard Games. (2013). *World of Warcraft*. Retrieved July 05, 2013, from https://us.battle.net/account/creation/wow/signup/

Buendía, F., & Hervás, A. (2006). An evaluation framework for e-learning platforms based on educational standard specifications. In *Proceedings of the Sixth International Conference on Advanced Learning Technologies (ICALT'06)*. IEEE. doi:0-7695-2632-2/06

Churchill, E., Snowdon, D., & Munro, A. (2001). *Collaborative virtual environments: Digital places and spaces for interaction*. London: Springer-Verlag. doi:10.1007/978-1-4471-0685-2

Cisco. (2013). *Cisco collaboration developer hub*. Retrieved June 29, 2013, from http://developer.cisco.com/web/collaboration-developer

Cisco. (2013). *Collaboration family*. Retrieved June 28, 2013, from http://developer.cisco.com/web/collaboration-developer/collaboration-tools-overview

Cisco. (2013). *Jabber development*. Retrieved June 29, 2013, from Jabber http://developer.cisco.com/web/jabber-developer/cisco-jabber-and-the-sdks

Cisco. (2013). *WebEx social*. Retrieved June 29, 2013, from http://developer.cisco.com/web/webexsocial-developer

Cisco and iRobot. (2013). *Cisco and iRobot telepresence*. Retrieved June 27, 2013, from http://www.irobot.com/us/learn/commercial/ava500.aspx

Cisco Jabber. (2013). *Cisco Jabber for Web*. Retrieved June 29, 2013, from http://developer.cisco.com/web/jabber-developer/overview

Cisco WebEx. (2007). *WebEx meeting service API technical overview*. Retrieved March 26, 2010, from http://static.webex.com/fileadmin/webex09/files_en_us/pdf/webex_wp_MeetingServiceAPI.pdf

Cisco WebEx. (2013). *Collaboration platforms and services*. Retrieved June 28, 2013, from http://www.webex.com/products/enterprise.html

Cisco WebEx. (2013). *Development*. Retrieved June 29, 2013, from http://developer.cisco.com/web/webex-developer/developer-platform-overview

Citrix. (2013). *Citrix GoTo family*. Retrieved June 2013, 2013, from http://www.citrix.com/products.html

Citrix Podio. (2013). *Citrix Podio*. Retrieved June 28, 2013, from https://podio.com/?c_name=ctxs

Costa-Perez, X., Festag, A., Kolbe, H.-J., Quittek, J., Schmid, S., Stiemerling, M., & van der Veen, H. (2013). Latest trends in telecommunication standards. *SIGCOMM Computer Communication Review*, *43*(2), 64–71. doi:10.1145/2479957.2479968

Davies, M., Joachim, Z., & Gabner, R. (2012). Evaluating two approaches for browser-based real-time multimedia communication. In *Proceedings of 10th International Conference on Advances in Mobile Computing & Multimedia (MoMM2012)*. Bali, Indonesia: ACM.

Denny, N., Mani, S., Sheshu, R., Swaminathan, M., Samdal, J., & Gupta, A. (2008). Hybrid offshoring: Composite personae and evolving collaboration technologies. *Information Resources Management Journal*, *21*(1), 89–104. doi:10.4018/irmj.2008010106

Duranti, C. M., & de Almeida, F. C. (2012). Is more technology better for communication in international teams. *International Journal of e-Collaboration*, *8*(1), 36–52. doi:10.4018/jec.2012010103

Frappaolo, C. (2008). *Enterprise 2.0: agile, emergent and integrated AIIM, MarketIQ*. AIIM. Retrieved July 25, 2010, from htttp://www.aiim.org/Research/Industry-Watch/Enterprise-20-Agile-Emergent-Integrated

Furlan, R. (2013). Build your own Google Glass. Spectrum, IEEE, 1-2.

Google. (2013). *Google+ Hangouts*. Retrieved June 27, 2013, from http://www.google.com/+/learnmore/hangouts/

Google. (2013). *Hangouts*. Retrieved June 28, 2013, from http://www.google.com/+/learnmore/hangouts/

Google. (2013). *Hangouts API*. Retrieved July 03, 2013, from https://developers.google.com/+/hangouts/api/

Google Recorded Future. (2013). *Google recordedfuture API*. Retrieved July 08, 2013, from https://code.google.com/p/recordedfuture/wiki/RecordedFutureAPI#Introduction

Goossenaerts, J., Possel-Dölken, F., & Popplewell, K. (2007). Vision, trends, gaps, and a broad road map for future engineering. *International Journal of e-Collaboration*, *3*(4), 1–20. doi:10.4018/jec.2007100101

Grudin, J. (1994). Computer-supported cooperative work: History and focus. *Computer*, *27*(5), 19–26. doi:10.1109/2.291294

Häkkilä, J., Koskenranta, O., Posti, M., Ventä-Olkkonen, L., & Colley, A. (2013). Clearing the virtual window - Connecting two locations. In *Proceedings of PerDis '13, International Symposium on Pervasive Displays*. California.

Hashmi, S. I., Ishikawa, F., & Richardson, I. (2013). A communication process for global requirements engineering. *International Conference on Software and System Processes 2013,* (pp. 136 - 140). San Francisco, CA.

Hayes, A. (2013). Cyborg cops, googlers, and connectivism. *IEEE Technology and Society Magazine*, (Spring): 23–24. doi:10.1109/MTS.2013.2247731

Hippensteel, P. (2013, July 01). *What is WebRTC*. Retrieved July 02, 2013, from Network World: http://www.conferencingnews.com/news/48432

IBM. (2010, January 18). *IBM accelerates cloud computing with LotusLive*. Retrieved August 19, 2010, from http://www-03.ibm.com/press/us/en/pressrelease/29210.wss?S_CMP=swnews_210

IBM. (2012). *Connections*. Retrieved June 28, 2013, from https://www-304.ibm.com/connections/blogs/socialbusiness/entry/ibm_lotuslive_is_becoming_ibm_smartcloud_for_social_business3?lang=en_us

IBM. (2013). *Smart cloud*. Retrieved June 28, 2013, from http://www.ibm.com/cloud-computing/social/us/en/benefits/

IBM. (2013). *Social business toolkit*. Retrieved July 03, 2013, from http://www.ibm.com/cloud-computing/social/us/en/

IEFT WebRTC. (2012). *WebRTC draft specification*. Retrieved July 03, 2013, from http://tools.ietf.org/html/draft-ietf-rtcweb-rtp-usage-06#page-4

IETF XCON. (2013). *XCON Centralized Conferencing Manipulation Protocol*. Retrieved May 17, 2013, from http://datatracker.ietf.org/doc/draft-ietf-xcon-ccmp/

Intel. (2013). *Gesture camera*. Retrieved May 17, 2013, from http://click.intel.com/intelsdk/Creative_Interactive_Gesture_Camera_Developer_Kit-P2061.aspx

Intel. (2013). *Perceptive computing*. Retrieved July 25, 2013, from Intel Software: http://software.intel.com/en-us/vcsource/tools/perceptual-computing-sdk

Kawakita, J. (1975). *The KJ method A scientific approach to problem solving*. Tokyo: Kawakita Research Institute.

Keary, A., & Redfern, S. (2012). Future directions of the conferencing and collaboration field. *International Journal of e-Collaboration*, *8*(2), 78–98. doi:10.4018/jec.2012040104

Kock, N. (2008). E-Collaboration and E-Commerce in virtual worlds: The potential of Second Life and World of Warcraft. *International Journal of e-Collaboration*, *4*(3), 1–13. doi:10.4018/jec.2008070101

Lin, H., Fan, W., & Zhang, Z. (2009). A qualitative study of Web-based knowledge communities: Examining success factors. *International Journal of e-Collaboration*, *5*(3), 39–57. doi:10.4018/jec.2009070103

Lombardi, C. (2008). *Videoconferencing equipment selection guide*. Retrieved July 19, 2010, from http://www.iuma.ulpgc.es/~nunez/clases-micros-para-com/varios/faulknertoc_fait.pdf

Mavridis, A., Konstantinidis, A., & Tsiatos, T. (2012). A comparison of 3D collaborative virtual learning environments: OpenSim vs. Second Life. *International Journal of e-Collaboration*, *8*(4), 8–12. doi:10.4018/jec.2012100102

McKinsey & Company. (2013). *McKinsey - Disruptive technologies. Interviews with industry thought leaders*. Retrieved May 17, 2013, from http://www.mckinsey.com/insights/high_tech_telecoms_internet/connecting_everything_a_conversation_with_ciscos_padmasree_warrior

Microsoft. (2013). *Lync-Skype connectivity*. Retrieved June 28, 2013, from Lync-Skype Connectivity: http://blogs.skype.com/2013/05/29/skype-and-lync-connecting-the-living-room-to-the-board-room/

Microsoft. (2013). *Microsoft pixel sense*. Retrieved May 17, 2013, from http://www.microsoft.com/en-us/pixelsense/whatissurface.aspx

Microsoft. Office365. (2013). *Microsoft Office 365 Enterprise*. Retrieved July 05, 2013, from http://office.microsoft.com/en-ie/business/office-365-enterprise-e3-business-software-FX103030346.aspx

Microsoft Lync. (2013). *Microsoft Lync*. Retrieved June 28, 2013, from http://office.microsoft.com/en-us/microsoft-lync-video-conferencing-and-instant-messaging-FX102004552.aspx

Microsoft Lync. (2013). *New capabilities in Lync 2013*. Retrieved July 03, 2013, from http://msdn.microsoft.com/en-US/lync/fp179716

Murphy, A., & Redfern, S. (2011). Non-verbal communication assisted serious gaming applications. In *GAME-ON 2011 International Conference on Intelligent Games and Simulation* (pp. 63-66).

ON24. (2013). *ON24 virtual show*. Retrieved May 17, 2013, from http://www.on24.com/products/virtual-show/

Oduor, E., Venolia, G., Neustaedter, C., & Judge, T. K. (2013). The future of personal video communication: Moving beyond talking heads to shared experiences. In *Proceedings of ACM SIGCHI Conference on Human Factors in Computing Systems*. Paris.

Oracle Beehive. (2013). *Beehive*. Retrieved July 05, 2013, from Beehive: http://www.oracle.com/technetwork/middleware/beehive/overview/index.html

Palmer, J., Fields, N., & Brouse, P. L. (1994). Multigroup decision-support systems in CSCW. *Computer*, *27*(5), 67–72. doi:10.1109/2.291289

Picard, R. (1997). *Affective computing*. Cambridge, MA: MIT Press.

Ponti, M. (2010). Socio-technical influences on virtual research environments. *International Journal of e-Collaboration*, *6*(2), 33–44. doi:10.4018/jec.2010040102

Raffle, H., Ballagas, R., Revelle, G., Horii, H., Follmer, S., Go, J., & Spasojevic, M. (2010). Family story play: Reading with young children (and Elmo) over a distance. In *Proceedings of ACM SIGCHI Conference on Human Factors in Computing Systems*. Atlanta, Georgia.

Redfern, S., & Naughton, N. (2002). Collaborative virtual environments to support communication and community in Internet-based distance education. *Journal of Information Technology Education*, *1*(3), 201–211.

S-Cube Partners. (2013). *S-Cube E-MORPG video*. Retrieved June 20, 2013, from http://www.s-cubeproject.eu/gettingstarted

Salesforce.com. (2013). *Salesforce.com chatter*. Retrieved June 27, 2013, from https://www.salesforce.com/chatter/overview/

Second Life. (2013). *Second Life*. Retrieved July 05, 2013, from http://secondlife.com/?gclid=CNWyu7KfmLgCFcmQ4QodVVwAlw

Skype, M. (2013). *Microsoft Skype*. Retrieved June 28, 2013, from http://www.skype.com/en/

Smith, M. D. (2009, July 26). *Magic quadrant for Web conferencing*. Retrieved 2013, from http://www.corp.att.com/awards/docs/gartner_mq_0709.pdf

Smith, P., & Redfern, S. (2012). Artificial intelligence supported non-verbal communication for enriched collaboration in distributed e-research environments. In A. Juan, T. Daradoumis, M. Roca, S. Grasman, & J. Faulin (Eds.), *Collaborative and distributed e-research: innovations in technologies, strategies and applications* (pp. 135–164). Hershey, PA: IGI-Global. doi:10.4018/978-1-4666-0125-3.ch007

Standaert, W., Muylle, S., & Basu, A. (2013). Assessing the effectiveness of telepresence for business meetings. In *Proceedings of 46th Hawaii International Conference on System Sciences* (pp. 549-558). Hawai.

Wheeler, B., Dennis, A., & Press, L. (1999). Groupware comes to the Internet: Charting a new world. *SIGMIS Database*, *30*(3-4), 8–21. doi:10.1145/344241.344242

Yarosh, S., Inkpen, K. M., & Brush, A. (2009). Video playdate: Toward free play across distance. In *Proceedings of ACM SIGCHI Conference on Human Factors in Computing Systems*. doi:978-1-60558-246-7/09/04.

Youseff, L., & Dilma Da Silva, M. B. (2009). *Toward a unified ontology of cloud computing*. Retrieved April 8, 2010, from http://www.silicon.com/white-papers/it-infrastructure/2008/10/13/toward-a-unied-ontology-of-cloud-computing-60829795/2/

Related References

To continue our tradition of advancing information science and technology research, we have compiled a list of recommended IGI Global readings. These references will provide additional information and guidance to further enrich your knowledge and assist you with your own research and future publications.

Abril, R. M. (2011). The quality attribution in data, information and knowledge. In D. Schwartz, & D. Te'eni (Eds.), *Encyclopedia of knowledge management* (2nd ed., pp. 1343–1354). Hershey, PA: Information Science Reference.

Abufardeh, S. (2013). KM and global software engineering (GSE). In S. Saeed, & I. Alsmadi (Eds.), *Knowledge-based processes in software development* (pp. 12–34). Hershey, PA: Information Science Reference. doi:10.4018/978-1-4666-4229-4.ch002

Aggestam, L., Backlund, P., & Persson, A. (2010). Supporting knowledge evaluation to increase quality in electronic knowledge repositories. *International Journal of Knowledge Management*, *6*(1), 23–43. doi:10.4018/jkm.2010103002

Aggestam, L., Backlund, P., & Persson, A. (2012). Supporting knowledge evaluation to increase quality in electronic knowledge repositories. In M. Jennex (Ed.), *Conceptual models and outcomes of advancing knowledge management: New technologies* (pp. 24–44). Hershey, PA: Information Science Reference. doi:10.4018/978-1-4666-0035-5.ch002

Aiken, P., Gillenson, M., Zhang, X., & Rafner, D. (2011). data management and data administration: Assessing 25 years of practice. *Journal of Database Management*, *22*(3), 24–45. doi:10.4018/jdm.2011070102

Akabawi, S., & Hodeeb, H. (2013). Implementing business intelligence in the dynamic beverages sales and distribution environment. In M. Khosrow-Pour (Ed.), *Cases on performance measurement and productivity improvement: Technology integration and maturity* (pp. 194–221). Hershey, PA: Business Science Reference.

Al-Busaidi, K. A. (2011). A social and technical investigation of knowledge utilization from a repository knowledge management system. In M. Al-Shammari (Ed.), *Knowledge management in emerging economies: social, organizational and cultural implementation* (pp. 122–139). Hershey, PA: Information Science Reference. doi:10.4018/978-1-60960-783-8.ch815

Al-Busaidi, K. A. (2012). The impact of supporting organizational knowledge management through a corporate portal on employees and business processes. In M. Jennex (Ed.), *Conceptual models and outcomes of advancing knowledge management: New technologies* (pp. 208–229). Hershey, PA: Information Science Reference. doi:10.4018/978-1-4666-0035-5.ch011

Alaraifi, A., Molla, A., & Deng, H. (2013). An empirical analysis of antecedents to the assimilation of sensor information systems in data centers. *International Journal of Information Technologies and Systems Approach*, *6*(1), 57–77. doi:10.4018/jitsa.2013010104

Alguezaui, S., & Filieri, R. (2010). Social capital: Knowledge and technological innovation. In P. López Sáez, G. Castro, J. Navas López, & M. Delgado Verde (Eds.), *Intellectual capital and technological innovation: knowledge-based theory and practice* (pp. 271–296). Hershey, PA: Information Science Reference. doi:10.4018/978-1-61520-875-3.ch013

Alhashem, A., & Shaqrah, A. A. (2012). Exploring the relationship between organizational memory and business innovation. *International Journal of Knowledge-Based Organizations*, *2*(3), 32–46. doi:10.4018/ijkbo.2012070102

Allan, M. B., Korolis, A. A., & Griffith, T. L. (2011). Reaching for the moon: Expanding transactive memory's reach with wikis and tagging. In M. Jennex (Ed.), *Global aspects and cultural perspectives on knowledge management: Emerging dimensions* (pp. 144–156). Hershey, PA: Information Science Reference. doi:10.4018/978-1-60960-555-1.ch010

Alsmadi, I., & Alda, S. (2013). Knowledge management and Semantic Web services. In S. Saeed, & I. Alsmadi (Eds.), *Knowledge-based processes in software development* (pp. 35–48). Hershey, PA: Information Science Reference. doi:10.4018/978-1-4666-4229-4.ch003

Alstete, J. W., & Meyer, J. P. (2011). Expanding the model of competitive business strategy for knowledge-based organizations. *International Journal of Knowledge-Based Organizations*, *1*(4), 16–31. doi:10.4018/ijkbo.2011100102

Alstete, J. W., & Meyer, J. P. (2013). Expanding the model of competitive business strategy for knowledge-based organizations. In J. Wang (Ed.), *intelligence methods and systems advancements for knowledge-based business* (pp. 132–148). Hershey, PA: Information Science Reference.

Alves da Silva, N. S., Alvarez, I. M., & Rogerson, S. (2011). Glocality, diversity and ethics of distributed knowledge in higher education. In G. Morais da Costa (Ed.), *Ethical issues and social dilemmas in knowledge management: Organizational innovation* (pp. 131–159). Hershey, PA: Information Science Reference.

Anantatmula, V. S., & Kanungo, S. (2011). Strategies for successful implementation of KM in a university setting. In M. Jennex, & S. Smolnik (Eds.), *Strategies for knowledge management success: Exploring organizational efficacy* (pp. 262–276). Hershey, PA: Information Science Reference.

Andreu, R., & Sieber, S. (2011). External and Internal Knowledge in Organizations. In D. Schwartz, & D. Te'eni (Eds.), *Encyclopedia of Knowledge Management* (2nd ed., pp. 298–307). Hershey, PA: Information Science Reference.

Andriessen, D. (2011). Metaphor use in knowledge management. In D. Schwartz, & D. Te'eni (Eds.), *Encyclopedia of knowledge management* (2nd ed., pp. 1118–1124). Hershey, PA: Information Science Reference.

Angelopoulos, S., Kitsios, F., & Moustakis, V. (2012). Transformation of management in the public sector: Exploring the strategic frameworks of e-government. In T. Papadopoulos, & P. Kanellis (Eds.), *Public sector reform using information technologies: Transforming policy into practice* (pp. 44–58). Hershey, PA: Information Science Reference. doi:10.4018/978-1-4666-1740-7.ch060

Anselma, L., Bottrighi, A., Molino, G., Montani, S., Terenziani, P., & Torchio, M. (2013). Supporting knowledge-based decision making in the medical context: The GLARE approach. In J. Wang (Ed.), *Intelligence methods and systems advancements for knowledge-based business* (pp. 24–42). Hershey, PA: Information Science Reference.

Arh, T., Dimovski, V., & Blažic, B. J. (2011). ICT and Web 2.0 technologies as a determinant of business performance. In M. Al-Mutairi, & L. Mohammed (Eds.), *Cases on ICT utilization, practice and solutions: Tools for managing day-to-day issues* (pp. 59–77). Hershey, PA: Information Science Reference. doi:10.4018/978-1-60960-783-8.ch312

Ariely, G. (2011). Operational knowledge management in the military. In D. Schwartz, & D. Te'eni (Eds.), *Encyclopedia of knowledge management* (2nd ed., pp. 1250–1260). Hershey, PA: Information Science Reference.

Assefa, T., Garfield, M., & Meshesha, M. (2014). Enabling factors for knowledge sharing among employees in the workplace. In Y. Al-Bastaki, & A. Shajera (Eds.), *Building a competitive public sector with knowledge management strategy* (pp. 246–271). Hershey, PA: Business Science Reference.

Assudani, R. H. (2011). Negotiating knowledge gaps in dispersed knowledge work. *International Journal of Knowledge-Based Organizations*, *1*(3), 1–21. doi:10.4018/ijkbo.2011070101

Assudani, R. H. (2013). Negotiating knowledge gaps in dispersed knowledge work. In J. Wang (Ed.), *Intelligence methods and systems advancements for knowledge-based business* (pp. 75–96). Hershey, PA: Information Science Reference.

Atkins, R. (2011). Supply chain knowledge integration in emerging economies. In M. Al-Shammari (Ed.), *Knowledge management in emerging economies: Social, organizational and cultural implementation* (pp. 104–121). Hershey, PA: Information Science Reference.

Aung, Z., & Nyunt, K. K. (2014). Constructive knowledge management model and information retrieval methods for software engineering. In I. Management Association (Ed.), Software design and development: concepts, methodologies, tools, and applications (pp. 253-269). Hershey, PA: Information Science Reference. doi: doi:10.4018/978-1-4666-4301-7.ch014

Aziz, M. W., Mohamad, R., & Jawawi, D. N. (2013). Ontology-based service description, discovery, and matching in distributed embedded real-time systems. In M. Nazir Ahmad, R. Colomb, & M. Abdullah (Eds.), *Ontology-based applications for enterprise systems and knowledge management* (pp. 178–190). Hershey, PA: Information Science Reference.

Badia, A. (2011). Knowledge management and intelligence work: A promising combination. In D. Schwartz, & D. Te'eni (Eds.), *Encyclopedia of knowledge management* (2nd ed., pp. 612–623). Hershey, PA: Information Science Reference. doi:10.4018/978-1-60960-783-8.ch411

Badr, K. B., & Ahmad, M. N. (2013). Managing lessons learned: A comparative study of lessons learned systems. In M. Nazir Ahmad, R. Colomb, & M. Abdullah (Eds.), *Ontology-based applications for enterprise systems and knowledge management* (pp. 224–245). Hershey, PA: Information Science Reference.

Bakshi, K. (2014). Technologies for big data. In W. Hu, & N. Kaabouch (Eds.), *Big data management, technologies, and applications* (pp. 1–22). Hershey, PA: Information Science Reference.

Ballou, D. P., Belardo, S., & Pazer, H. L. (2012). A project staffing model to enhance the effectiveness of knowledge transfer in the requirements planning phase for multi-project environments. In M. Jennex (Ed.), *Conceptual models and outcomes of advancing knowledge management: New technologies* (pp. 77–98). Hershey, PA: Information Science Reference. doi:10.4018/978-1-4666-0035-5.ch005

Baporikar, N. (2011). Knowledge management and entrepreneurship cases in India. In M. Al-Shammari (Ed.), *Knowledge management in emerging economies: Social, organizational and cultural implementation* (pp. 325–346). Hershey, PA: Information Science Reference. doi:10.4018/978-1-60960-783-8.ch420

Baporikar, N. (2014). Knowledge management initiatives in Indian public sector. In Y. Al-Bastaki, & A. Shajera (Eds.), *Building a competitive public sector with knowledge management strategy* (pp. 53–89). Hershey, PA: Business Science Reference.

Baporikar, N. (2014). Organizational barriers and facilitators in embedding knowledge strategy. In M. Chilton, & J. Bloodgood (Eds.), *Knowledge management and competitive advantage: Issues and potential solutions* (pp. 149–173). Hershey, PA: Information Science Reference.

Barioni, M. C., Kaster, D. D., Razente, H. L., Traina, A. J., & Júnior, C. T. (2011). Querying multimedia data by similarity in relational DBMS. In L. Yan, & Z. Ma (Eds.), *Advanced database query systems: Techniques, applications and technologies* (pp. 323–359). Hershey, PA: Information Science Reference. doi:10.4018/978-1-60960-475-2.ch014

Baroni de Carvalho, R., & Tavares Ferreira, M. A. (2011). Knowledge management software. In D. Schwartz, & D. Te'eni (Eds.), *Encyclopedia of knowledge management* (2nd ed., pp. 738–749). Hershey, PA: Information Science Reference.

Barroso, A. C., Ricciardi, R. I., & Junior, J. A. (2012). Web 2.0 and project management: Reviewing the change path and discussing a few cases. In I. Boughzala, & A. Dudezert (Eds.), *Knowledge management 2.0: Organizational models and enterprise strategies* (pp. 164–189). Hershey, PA: Information Science Reference.

Baskaran, V., Naguib, R., Guergachi, A., Bali, R., & Arochen, H. (2011). Does knowledge management really work?: A case study in the breast cancer screening domain. In A. Eardley, & L. Uden (Eds.), *Innovative knowledge management: concepts for organizational creativity and collaborative design* (pp. 177–189). Hershey, PA: Information Science Reference. doi:10.4018/978-1-60960-783-8.ch106

Bebensee, T., Helms, R., & Spruit, M. (2012). Exploring the impact of Web 2.0 on knowledge management. In I. Boughzala, & A. Dudezert (Eds.), *Knowledge management 2.0: Organizational models and enterprise strategies* (pp. 17–43). Hershey, PA: Information Science Reference.

Becerra-Fernandez, I., & Sabherwal, R. (2011). The role of information and communication technologies in knowledge management: A classification of knowledge management systems. In D. Schwartz, & D. Te'eni (Eds.), *Encyclopedia of knowledge management* (2nd ed., pp. 1410–1418). Hershey, PA: Information Science Reference.

Benbya, H. (2013). Valuing knowledge-based initiatives: What we know and what we don't know. In M. Jennex (Ed.), *Dynamic models for knowledge-driven organizations* (pp. 1–15). Hershey, PA: Business Science Reference.

Berends, H., van der Bij, H., & Weggeman, M. (2011). Knowledge integration. In D. Schwartz, & D. Te'eni (Eds.), *Encyclopedia of knowledge management* (2nd ed., pp. 581–590). Hershey, PA: Information Science Reference.

Berger, H., & Beynon-Davies, P. (2011). Knowledge-based diffusion in practice: A case study experience. In A. Eardley, & L. Uden (Eds.), *Innovative knowledge management: Concepts for organizational creativity and collaborative design* (pp. 40–55). Hershey, PA: Information Science Reference.

Berio, G., Di Leva, A., Harzallah, M., & Sacco, G. M. (2012). Competence management over social networks through dynamic taxonomies. In I. Boughzala, & A. Dudezert (Eds.), *Knowledge management 2.0: Organizational models and enterprise strategies* (pp. 103–120). Hershey, PA: Information Science Reference.

Bhatt, S., Chaudhary, S., & Bhise, M. (2013). Migration of data between cloud and non-cloud datastores. In A. Ionita, M. Litoiu, & G. Lewis (Eds.), *Migrating legacy applications: Challenges in service oriented architecture and cloud computing environments* (pp. 206–225). Hershey, PA: Information Science Reference.

Bloodgood, J. M., Chilton, M. A., & Bloodgood, T. C. (2014). The effect of knowledge transfer motivation, receiver capability, and motivation on organizational performance. In M. Chilton, & J. Bloodgood (Eds.), *Knowledge management and competitive advantage: Issues and potential solutions* (pp. 232–242). Hershey, PA: Information Science Reference.

Boersma, K., & Kingma, S. (2011). Organizational learning facilitation with Intranet (2.0), a socio-cultural approach. In D. Schwartz, & D. Te'eni (Eds.), *Encyclopedia of knowledge management* (2nd ed., pp. 1280–1289). Hershey, PA: Information Science Reference. doi:10.4018/978-1-60960-783-8.ch517

Bond, P. L. (2010). Toward a living systems framework for unifying technology and knowledge management, organizational, cultural and economic change. In D. Harorimana (Ed.), *Cultural implications of knowledge sharing, management and transfer: Identifying competitive advantage* (pp. 108–132). Hershey, PA: Information Science Reference.

Bordogna, G., Bucci, F., Carrara, P., Pepe, M., & Rampini, A. (2011). Flexible querying of imperfect temporal metadata in spatial data infrastructures. In L. Yan, & Z. Ma (Eds.), *Advanced database query systems: Techniques, applications and technologies* (pp. 140–159). Hershey, PA: Information Science Reference. doi:10.4018/978-1-60960-475-2.ch006

Boughzala, I. (2012). Collaboration 2.0 through the new organization (2.0) transformation. In I. Boughzala, & A. Dudezert (Eds.), *Knowledge management 2.0: Organizational models and enterprise strategies* (pp. 1–16). Hershey, PA: Information Science Reference.

Bratianu, C. (2011). A new perspective of the intellectual capital dynamics in organizations. In B. Vallejo-Alonso, A. Rodriguez-Castellanos, & G. Arregui-Ayastuy (Eds.), *Identifying, measuring, and valuing knowledge-based intangible assets: New perspectives* (pp. 1–21). Hershey, PA: Business Science Reference.

Bratianu, C. (2011). Universities as knowledge-intensive learning organizations. In A. Eardley, & L. Uden (Eds.), *Innovative knowledge management: Concepts for organizational creativity and collaborative design* (pp. 1–17). Hershey, PA: Information Science Reference.

Breu, K., Ward, J., & Murray, P. (2000). Success factors in leveraging the corporate information and knowledge resource through intranets. In Y. Malhotra (Ed.), *Knowledge management and virtual organizations* (pp. 306–320). Hershey, PA: Idea Group Publishing. doi:10.4018/978-1-930708-65-5.ch016

Briones-Peñalver, A., & Poças-Rascão, J. (2014). Information technologies (ICT), network organizations, and information systems for business cooperation: A Focus on organization and strategic knowledge management. In G. Jamil, A. Malheiro, & F. Ribeiro (Eds.), *Rethinking the conceptual base for new practical applications in information value and quality* (pp. 324–348). Hershey, PA: Information Science Reference.

Brock, J. K., & Zhou, Y. J. (2011). MNE knowledge management across borders and ICT. In D. Schwartz, & D. Te'eni (Eds.), *Encyclopedia of knowledge management* (2nd ed., pp. 1136–1148). Hershey, PA: Information Science Reference.

Brunet-Thornton, R., & Bureš, V. (2011). Meeting Czech knowledge management challenges head-on: KM-Be.At-It. In M. Al-Shammari (Ed.), *Knowledge management in emerging economies: Social, organizational and cultural implementation* (pp. 20–46). Hershey, PA: Information Science Reference. doi:10.4018/978-1-60960-783-8.ch422

Bucher, T., & Dinter, B. (2012). Situational method engineering to support process-oriented information logistics: Identification of development situations. *Journal of Database Management, 23*(1), 31–48. doi:10.4018/jdm.2012010102

Burstein, F., & Linger, H. (2011). Task-based knowledge management approach. In D. Schwartz, & D. Te'eni (Eds.), *Encyclopedia of knowledge management* (2nd ed., pp. 1479–1489). Hershey, PA: Information Science Reference.

Butler, T. (2011). Anti-foundational knowledge management. In D. Schwartz, & D. Te'eni (Eds.), *Encyclopedia of knowledge management* (2nd ed., pp. 1–11). Hershey, PA: Information Science Reference.

Butler, T., & Murphy, C. (2011). Work and knowledge. In D. Schwartz, & D. Te'eni (Eds.), *Encyclopedia of knowledge management* (2nd ed., pp. 1556–1566). Hershey, PA: Information Science Reference.

Cabrilo, S., & Grubic-Nesic, L. (2013). The role of creativity, innovation, and invention in knowledge management. In S. Buckley, & M. Jakovljevic (Eds.), *Knowledge management innovations for interdisciplinary education: organizational applications* (pp. 207–232). Hershey, PA: Information Science Reference.

Cabrita, M. D., Machado, V. C., & Grilo, A. (2010). Intellectual capital: How knowledge creates value. In E. O'Brien, S. Clifford, & M. Southern (Eds.), *Knowledge management for process, organizational and marketing innovation: Tools and methods* (pp. 237–252). Hershey, PA: Information Science Reference. doi:10.4018/978-1-61520-829-6.ch015

Cagliero, L., & Fiori, A. (2013). Knowledge discovery from online communities. In I. Association (Ed.), *Data mining: Concepts, methodologies, tools, and applications* (pp. 1230–1252). Hershey, PA: Information Science Reference.

Camisón-Zornoza, C., & Boronat-Navarro, M. (2010). Linking exploration and exploitation capabilities with the process of knowledge development and with organizational facilitators. In M. Russ (Ed.), *Knowledge management strategies for business development* (pp. 159–179). Hershey, PA: Business Science Reference. doi:10.4018/978-1-61520-965-1.ch304

Carneiro, A. (2010). Change knowledge management: Transforming a ghost community into a real asset. In E. O'Brien, S. Clifford, & M. Southern (Eds.), *Knowledge management for process, organizational and marketing innovation: Tools and methods* (pp. 120–132). Hershey, PA: Information Science Reference. doi:10.4018/978-1-61520-829-6.ch007

Carrillo, F. J. (2010). Knowledge-based value generation. In K. Metaxiotis, F. Carrillo, & T. Yigitcanlar (Eds.), *Knowledge-based development for cities and societies: Integrated multi-level approaches* (pp. 1–16). Hershey, PA: Information Science Reference. doi:10.4018/978-1-61520-721-3.ch001

Cartelli, A. (2012). Frameworks for the benchmarking of digital and knowledge management best practice in SME and organizations. In A. Cartelli (Ed.), *Current trends and future practices for digital literacy and competence* (pp. 166–175). Hershey, PA: Information Science Reference. doi:10.4018/978-1-4666-0903-7.ch015

Castellano, G., Fanelli, A. M., & Torsello, M. A. (2010). Soft computing techniques in content-based multimedia information retrieval. In K. Anbumani, & R. Nedunchezhian (Eds.), *Soft computing applications for database technologies: Techniques and issues* (pp. 170–192). Hershey, PA: Information Science Reference. doi:10.4018/978-1-60566-814-7.ch010

Chalkiti, K., & Carson, D. (2010). Knowledge cultures, competitive advantage and staff turnover in hospitality in Australia's Northern Territory. In D. Harorimana (Ed.), *Cultural implications of knowledge sharing, management and transfer: Identifying competitive advantage* (pp. 203–229). Hershey, PA: Information Science Reference.

Chang, W., & Li, S. (2011). Deploying knowledge management in R&D workspaces. In A. Eardley, & L. Uden (Eds.), *Innovative knowledge management: Concepts for organizational creativity and collaborative design* (pp. 56–76). Hershey, PA: Information Science Reference. doi:10.4018/978-1-60960-783-8.ch407

Chawla, D., & Joshi, H. (2013). Impact of knowledge management dimensions on learning organization: Comparison across business excellence awarded and non-awarded Indian organizations. In M. Jennex (Ed.), *Dynamic models for knowledge-driven organizations* (pp. 145–162). Hershey, PA: Business Science Reference.

Chen, E. (2012). Web 2.0 social networking technologies and strategies for knowledge management. In I. Boughzala, & A. Dudezert (Eds.), *Knowledge management 2.0: Organizational models and enterprise strategies* (pp. 84–102). Hershey, PA: Information Science Reference.

Chihara, K., & Nakamori, Y. (2013). Clarification of abilities and qualities of knowledge coordinators: The case of regional revitalization projects. In G. Yang (Ed.), *Multidisciplinary studies in knowledge and systems science* (pp. 1–17). Hershey, PA: Information Science Reference.

Christidis, K., Papailiou, N., Apostolou, D., & Mentzas, G. (2011). Semantic interfaces for personal and social knowledge work. *International Journal of Knowledge-Based Organizations*, *1*(1), 61–77. doi:10.4018/ijkbo.2011010104

Christidis, K., Papailiou, N., Apostolou, D., & Mentzas, G. (2013). Semantic interfaces for personal and social knowledge work. In J. Wang (Ed.), *Intelligence methods and systems advancements for knowledge-based business* (pp. 213–230). Hershey, PA: Information Science Reference.

Chua, C. E., Storey, V. C., & Chiang, R. H. (2012). Knowledge representation: A conceptual modeling approach. *Journal of Database Management*, *23*(1), 1–30. doi:10.4018/jdm.2012010101

Clinton, M. S., Merritt, K. L., & Murray, S. R. (2011). Facilitating knowledge transfer and the achievement of competitive advantage with corporate universities: An exploratory model based on media richness and type of knowledge to be transferred. In M. Jennex (Ed.), *Global aspects and cultural perspectives on knowledge management: Emerging dimensions* (pp. 329–345). Hershey, PA: Information Science Reference. doi:10.4018/978-1-60960-555-1.ch020

Colomb, R. M. (2013). Representation of action is a primary requirement in ontologies for interoperating information systems. In M. Nazir Ahmad, R. Colomb, & M. Abdullah (Eds.), *Ontology-based applications for enterprise systems and knowledge management* (pp. 68–76). Hershey, PA: Information Science Reference.

Colucci, S., Di Noia, T., Di Sciascio, E., Donini, F. M., & Mongiello, M. (2011). Description logic-based resource retrieval. In D. Schwartz, & D. Te'eni (Eds.), *Encyclopedia of knowledge management* (2nd ed., pp. 185–197). Hershey, PA: Information Science Reference.

Connell, N. A. (2011). Organisational storytelling. In D. Schwartz, & D. Te'eni (Eds.), *Encyclopedia of knowledge management* (2nd ed., pp. 1261–1269). Hershey, PA: Information Science Reference.

Cooper, L. P., & Rober, M. B. (2012). Moving wikis behind the firewall: Intrapedias and work-wikis. In I. Boughzala, & A. Dudezert (Eds.), *Knowledge management 2.0: organizational models and enterprise strategies* (pp. 44–63). Hershey, PA: Information Science Reference.

Corallo, A., De Maggio, M., & Margherita, A. (2011). Knowledge democracy as the new mantra in product innovation: A framework of processes and competencies. In A. Eardley, & L. Uden (Eds.), *Innovative knowledge management: Concepts for organizational creativity and collaborative design* (pp. 141–156). Hershey, PA: Information Science Reference.

Costa, G. (2011). Knowledge worker fair compensation: Ethical issues and social dilemmas. In G. Morais da Costa (Ed.), *Ethical issues and social dilemmas in knowledge management: Organizational innovation* (pp. 215–231). Hershey, PA: Information Science Reference.

Costello, R. (2014). Evaluating e-learning from an end user perspective. In M. Pańkowska (Ed.), *Frameworks of IT prosumption for business development* (pp. 259–283). Hershey, PA: Business Science Reference.

Crasso, M., Zunino, A., & Campo, M. (2013). A survey of approaches to Web service discovery in service-oriented architectures. In K. Siau (Ed.), *Innovations in database design, Web applications, and information systems management* (pp. 107–138). Hershey, PA: Information Science Reference.

Croasdell, D., & Wang, Y. K. (2011). Virtue-nets. In D. Schwartz, & D. Te'eni (Eds.), *Encyclopedia of knowledge management* (2nd ed., pp. 1545–1555). Hershey, PA: Information Science Reference.

Cucchiara, S., Ligorio, M. B., & Fujita, N. (2014). Understanding online discourse strategies for knowledge building through social network analysis. In H. Lim, & F. Sudweeks (Eds.), *Innovative methods and technologies for electronic discourse analysis* (pp. 42–62). Hershey, PA: Information Science Reference.

Cudanov, M., & Kirchner, K. (2011). Knowledge management in high-growth companies: A case study in Serbia. In M. Al-Shammari (Ed.), *Knowledge management in emerging economies: Social, organizational and cultural implementation* (pp. 227–248). Hershey, PA: Information Science Reference.

Cuel, R., Bouquet, P., & Bonifacio, M. (2011). Distributed knowledge management. In D. Schwartz, & D. Te'eni (Eds.), *Encyclopedia of knowledge management* (2nd ed., pp. 198–208). Hershey, PA: Information Science Reference.

Daidj, N. (2012). The evolution of KM practices: The case of the Renault-Nissan international strategic alliance. In I. Boughzala, & A. Dudezert (Eds.), *Knowledge management 2.0: Organizational models and enterprise strategies* (pp. 190–213). Hershey, PA: Information Science Reference.

Daniel, B. K., Zapata-Rivera, J., & McCalla, G. I. (2010). A Bayesian belief network methodology for modeling social systems in virtual communities: Opportunities for database technologies. In K. Anbumani, & R. Nedunchezhian (Eds.), *Soft computing applications for database technologies: Techniques and issues* (pp. 125–152). Hershey, PA: Information Science Reference. doi:10.4018/978-1-60566-814-7.ch008

Darchen, S., & Tremblay, D. (2010). Attracting and retaining knowledge workers: The impact of quality of place in the case of Montreal. In K. Metaxiotis, F. Carrillo, & T. Yigitcanlar (Eds.), *Knowledge-based development for cities and societies: Integrated multi-level approaches* (pp. 42–58). Hershey, PA: Information Science Reference. doi:10.4018/978-1-61520-721-3.ch003

Davenport, D. L., & Hosapple, C. W. (2011). Knowledge organizations. In D. Schwartz, & D. Te'eni (Eds.), *Encyclopedia of knowledge management* (2nd ed., pp. 822–832). Hershey, PA: Information Science Reference.

Davenport, D. L., & Hosapple, C. W. (2011). Social capital knowledge. In D. Schwartz, & D. Te'eni (Eds.), *Encyclopedia of knowledge management* (2nd ed., pp. 1448–1459). Hershey, PA: Information Science Reference.

De Maggio, M., Del Vecchio, P., Elia, G., & Grippa, F. (2011). An ICT-based network of competence centres for developing intellectual capital in the Mediterranean area. In A. Al Ajeeli, & Y. Al-Bastaki (Eds.), *Handbook of research on e-services in the public sector: E-Government strategies and advancements* (pp. 164–181). Hershey, PA: Information Science Reference. doi:10.4018/978-1-60960-587-2.ch810

Dehuri, S., Patra, M. R., Misra, B., & Jagadev, A. (2013). Intelligent techniques in recommendation systems: Contextual advancements and new methods (pp. 1-350). doi:10.4018/978-1-4666-2542-6

Delbaere, M., Di Zhang, D., Bruning, E. R., & Sivaramakrishnan, S. (2014). Knowledge management and the roles it plays in achieving superior performance. In M. Chilton, & J. Bloodgood (Eds.), *Knowledge management and competitive advantage: Issues and potential solutions* (pp. 90–108). Hershey, PA: Information Science Reference.

Delgado-Verde, M., & Cruz-González, J. (2010). An intellectual capital-based view of technological innovation. In P. López Sáez, G. Castro, J. Navas López, & M. Delgado Verde (Eds.), *Intellectual capital and technological innovation: Knowledge-based theory and practice* (pp. 166–193). Hershey, PA: Information Science Reference. doi:10.4018/978-1-61520-875-3.ch008

Deltour, F., Plé, L., & Roussel, C. S. (2012). Knowledge sharing in the age of Web 2.0: A social capital perspective. In I. Boughzala, & A. Dudezert (Eds.), *Knowledge management 2.0: Organizational models and enterprise strategies* (pp. 122–141). Hershey, PA: Information Science Reference.

Derballa, V., & Pousttchi, K. (2011). Mobile technology for knowledge management. In D. Schwartz, & D. Te'eni (Eds.), *Encyclopedia of knowledge management* (2nd ed., pp. 1158–1166). Hershey, PA: Information Science Reference.

Dieng-Kuntz, R. (2011). Corporate Semantic Webs. In D. Schwartz, & D. Te'eni (Eds.), *Encyclopedia of knowledge management* (2nd ed., pp. 131–149). Hershey, PA: Information Science Reference.

Diosteanu, A., Stellato, A., & Turbati, A. (2012). SODA: A service oriented data acquisition framework. In M. Pazienza, & A. Stellato (Eds.), *Semi-automatic ontology development: Processes and resources* (pp. 48–77). Hershey, PA: Information Science Reference. doi:10.4018/978-1-4666-0188-8.ch003

Donate-Manzanares, M. J., Guadamillas-Gómez, F., & Sánchez de Pablo, J. D. (2010). Strategic alliances and knowledge management strategies: A case study. In M. Russ (Ed.), *Knowledge management strategies for business development* (pp. 240–260). Hershey, PA: Business Science Reference.

Donnet, T., Keast, R., & Pickernell, D. (2010). Up the junction? Exploiting knowledge-based development through supply chain and SME cluster interactions. In K. Metaxiotis, F. Carrillo, & T. Yigitcanlar (Eds.), *Knowledge-based development for cities and societies: Integrated multi-level approaches* (pp. 179–195). Hershey, PA: Information Science Reference. doi:10.4018/978-1-61520-721-3.ch011

Douglas, I. (2011). Organizational needs analysis and knowledge management. In D. Schwartz, & D. Te'eni (Eds.), *Encyclopedia of knowledge management* (2nd ed., pp. 1290–1297). Hershey, PA: Information Science Reference.

Edvardsson, I. R., & Oskarsson, G. K. (2013). Outsourcing in knowledge-based service firms. In J. Wang (Ed.), *Intelligence methods and systems advancements for knowledge-based business* (pp. 97–113). Hershey, PA: Information Science Reference.

Elenurm, T. (2013). Knowledge management and innovative learning. In S. Buckley, & M. Jakovljevic (Eds.), *Knowledge management innovations for interdisciplinary education: Organizational applications* (pp. 108–131). Hershey, PA: Information Science Reference.

Eppler, M. J., & Burkhard, R. A. (2011). Knowledge visualization. In D. Schwartz, & D. Te'eni (Eds.), *Encyclopedia of knowledge management* (2nd ed., pp. 987–999). Hershey, PA: Information Science Reference.

Ergazakis, K., Metaxiotis, K., & Ergazakis, E. (2011). Exploring paths towards knowledge cities developments: A research agenda. In D. Schwartz, & D. Te'eni (Eds.), *Encyclopedia of knowledge management* (2nd ed., pp. 288–297). Hershey, PA: Information Science Reference. doi:10.4018/978-1-60960-783-8.ch814

Eri, Z. D., Abdullah, R., Jabar, M. A., Murad, M. A., & Talib, A. M. (2013). Ontology-based virtual communities model for the knowledge management system environment: Ontology design. In M. Nazir Ahmad, R. Colomb, & M. Abdullah (Eds.), *Ontology-based applications for enterprise systems and knowledge management* (pp. 343–360). Hershey, PA: Information Science Reference.

Erickson, G. S. (2014). Government as a partner in knowledge management: Lessons from the US Freedom of Information Act. In Y. Al-Bastaki, & A. Shajera (Eds.), *Building a competitive public sector with knowledge management strategy* (pp. 90–103). Hershey, PA: Business Science Reference.

Erickson, G. S., & Rothberg, H. N. (2011). Assessing knowledge management needs: A strategic approach to developing knowledge. *International Journal of Knowledge Management*, *7*(3), 1–10. doi:10.4018/jkm.2011070101

Erickson, G. S., & Rothberg, H. N. (2011). Assessing knowledge management needs: A strategic approach to developing knowledge. *International Journal of Knowledge Management*, *7*(3), 1–10. doi:10.4018/jkm.2011070101

Erickson, G. S., & Rothberg, H. N. (2011). Protecting knowledge assets. In D. Schwartz, & D. Te'eni (Eds.), *Encyclopedia of knowledge management* (2nd ed., pp. 1336–1342). Hershey, PA: Information Science Reference.

Erickson, G. S., & Rothberg, H. N. (2013). Assessing knowledge management needs: A strategic approach to developing knowledge. In M. Jennex (Ed.), *Dynamic models for knowledge-driven organizations* (pp. 180–189). Hershey, PA: Business Science Reference.

Evermann, J., & Wand, Y. (2011). Ontology based object-oriented domain modeling: Representing behavior. In K. Siau (Ed.), *Theoretical and practical advances in information systems development: Emerging trends and approaches* (pp. 37–60). Hershey, PA: Information Science Reference. doi:10.4018/978-1-60960-521-6.ch003

Fadel, K. J., Durcikova, A., & Cha, H. S. (2011). An experiment of information elaboration in mediated knowledge transfer. In M. Jennex (Ed.), *Global aspects and cultural perspectives on knowledge management: Emerging dimensions* (pp. 311–328). Hershey, PA: Information Science Reference. doi:10.4018/978-1-60960-555-1.ch019

Fazel-Zarandi, M., Fox, M. S., & Yu, E. (2013). Ontologies in expertise finding systems: Modeling, analysis, and design. In M. Nazir Ahmad, R. Colomb, & M. Abdullah (Eds.), *Ontology-based applications for enterprise systems and knowledge management* (pp. 158–177). Hershey, PA: Information Science Reference.

Ferri, F., & Grifoni, P. (2011). Sketching in knowledge creation and management. In D. Schwartz, & D. Te'eni (Eds.), *Encyclopedia of knowledge management* (2nd ed., pp. 1438–1447). Hershey, PA: Information Science Reference.

Filho, C. G., Baroni de Carvalho, R., & Jamil, G. L. (2011). Market knowledge management, innovation and product performance: Survey in medium and large Brazilian industrial firms. In M. Jennex, & S. Smolnik (Eds.), *Strategies for knowledge management success: Exploring organizational efficacy* (pp. 32–50). Hershey, PA: Information Science Reference.

Fink, D., & Disterer, G. (2011). Knowledge management in professional service firms. In D. Schwartz, & D. Te'eni (Eds.), *Encyclopedia of knowledge management* (2nd ed., pp. 650–659). Hershey, PA: Information Science Reference.

Fink, K. (2011). Process model for knowledge potential measurement in SMEs. In M. Jennex, & S. Smolnik (Eds.), *Strategies for knowledge management success: Exploring organizational efficacy* (pp. 91–105). Hershey, PA: Information Science Reference. doi:10.4018/978-1-60960-783-8.ch210

Fink, K., & Ploder, C. (2011). Knowledge management toolkit for SMEs. In M. Jennex (Ed.), *Global aspects and cultural perspectives on knowledge management: Emerging dimensions* (pp. 49–63). Hershey, PA: Information Science Reference. doi:10.4018/978-1-60960-555-1.ch004

Flynn, R., & Marshall, V. (2014). The four levers for change in knowledge management implementation. In Y. Al-Bastaki, & A. Shajera (Eds.), *Building a competitive public sector with knowledge management strategy* (pp. 227–245). Hershey, PA: Business Science Reference.

Fortier, J., & Kassel, G. (2011). Organizational Semantic Webs. In D. Schwartz, & D. Te'eni (Eds.), *Encyclopedia of knowledge management* (2nd ed., pp. 1298–1307). Hershey, PA: Information Science Reference.

Framinan, J. M., & Molina, J. M. (2010). An overview of enterprise resource planning for intelligent enterprises. In I. Management Association (Ed.), Business information systems: Concepts, methodologies, tools and applications (pp. 60-68). Hershey, PA: Business Science Reference. doi: doi:10.4018/978-1-61520-969-9.ch005

Franco, M., Di Virgilio, F., & Di Pietro, L. (2014). Management of group knowledge and the role of E-WOM for business organizations. In M. Chilton, & J. Bloodgood (Eds.), *Knowledge management and competitive advantage: Issues and potential solutions* (pp. 71–89). Hershey, PA: Information Science Reference.

Franke, U. J. (2000). The knowledge-based view (KBV) of the Virtual Web, the virtual corporation and the net-broker. In Y. Malhotra (Ed.), *Knowledge management and virtual organizations* (pp. 20–42). Hershey, PA: Idea Group Publishing. doi:10.4018/978-1-930708-65-5.ch002

Freivalds, D., & Lush, B. (2012). Thinking inside the grid: Selecting a discovery system through the RFP Process. In M. Popp, & D. Dallis (Eds.), *Planning and implementing resource discovery tools in academic libraries* (pp. 104–121). Hershey, PA: Information Science Reference. doi:10.4018/978-1-4666-1821-3.ch007

Frieß, M. R., Groh, G., Reinhardt, M., Forster, F., & Schlichter, J. (2012). Context-aware creativity support for corporate open innovation. *International Journal of Knowledge-Based Organizations*, *2*(1), 38–55. doi:10.4018/ijkbo.2012010103

Fuller, C. M., & Wilson, R. L. (2011). Extracting knowledge from neural networks. In D. Schwartz, & D. Te'eni (Eds.), *Encyclopedia of knowledge management* (2nd ed., pp. 320–330). Hershey, PA: Information Science Reference.

Furquim, T. D., & do Amaral, S. A. (2011). Knowledge management practices in Brazilian software organizations: The case of SERPRO. In M. Al-Shammari (Ed.), *Knowledge management in emerging economies: Social, organizational and cultural implementation* (pp. 213–226). Hershey, PA: Information Science Reference. doi:10.4018/978-1-60960-783-8.ch421

Gaál, Z., Szabó, L., Obermayer-Kovács, N., Kovács, Z., & Csepregi, A. (2011). knowledge management profile: An innovative approach to map knowledge management practice. In A. Eardley & L. Uden (Eds.), Innovative knowledge management: Concepts for organizational creativity and collaborative design (pp. 253-263). Hershey, PA: Information Science Reference. doi: doi:10.4018/978-1-60566-701-0.ch016

Ganguly, A., Mostashari, A., & Mansouri, M. (2013). Measuring knowledge management/knowledge sharing (KM/KS) efficiency and effectiveness in enterprise networks. In M. Jennex (Ed.), *Dynamic models for knowledge-driven organizations* (pp. 318–336). Hershey, PA: Business Science Reference.

Gaumand, C., Chapdaniel, A., & Dudezert, A. (2012). Strategic knowledge management system framework for supply chain at an intra-organizational level. In I. Boughzala, & A. Dudezert (Eds.), *Knowledge management 2.0: Organizational models and enterprise strategies* (pp. 142–163). Hershey, PA: Information Science Reference. doi:10.4018/978-1-4666-2625-6.ch028

Ghazali, R., & Zakaria, N. H. (2013). Knowledge management processes in enterprise systems: A systematic literature review. In M. Nazir Ahmad, R. Colomb, & M. Abdullah (Eds.), *Ontology-based applications for enterprise systems and knowledge management* (pp. 1–24). Hershey, PA: Information Science Reference. doi:10.4018/978-1-4666-4153-2.ch010

Ghosh, B. (2011). Cross-cultural knowledge management practices to support offshore outsourcing. In M. Al-Shammari (Ed.), *Knowledge management in emerging economies: Social, organizational and cultural implementation* (pp. 249–260). Hershey, PA: Information Science Reference. doi:10.4018/978-1-60960-783-8.ch623

Gohil, U., Carrillo, P., Ruikar, K., & Anumba, C. (2013). Development of a business process model for a project-based service organisation. *International Journal of Knowledge-Based Organizations*, *3*(1), 37–56. doi:10.4018/ijkbo.2013010103

Goldsmith, R. E., & Pillai, K. G. (2011). Knowledge calibration and knowledge management. In D. Schwartz, & D. Te'eni (Eds.), *Encyclopedia of knowledge management* (2nd ed., pp. 497–505). Hershey, PA: Information Science Reference.

Gomes de Andrade, F., & Baptista, C. D. (2013). An ontology-based approach to support information discovery in spatial data infrastructures. In C. Rückemann (Ed.), *integrated information and computing systems for natural, spatial, and social sciences* (pp. 369–387). Hershey, PA: Information Science Reference.

Gonçalo, C. R., & Jacques, E. J. (2010). Best practices of knowledge strategy in hospitals: A contextual perspective based on the implementation of medical protocols. In D. Harorimana (Ed.), *Cultural implications of knowledge sharing, management and transfer: Identifying competitive advantage* (pp. 180–202). Hershey, PA: Information Science Reference.

Górniak-Kocikowska, K. (2011). Knowledge management and democracy: A critical review of some moral issues and social dilemmas. In G. Morais da Costa (Ed.), *Ethical issues and social dilemmas in knowledge management: Organizational innovation* (pp. 28–44). Hershey, PA: Information Science Reference. doi:10.4018/978-1-60960-783-8.ch704

Gottschalk, P. (2014). Police knowledge management strategy. In M. Chilton, & J. Bloodgood (Eds.), *Knowledge management and competitive advantage: Issues and potential solutions* (pp. 202–220). Hershey, PA: Information Science Reference.

Goudos, S. K., Peristeras, V., & Tarabanis, K. (2010). Application of Semantic Web technology in e-business: case studies in public domain data knowledge representation. In I. Management Association (Ed.), Business information systems: Concepts, methodologies, tools and applications (pp. 1223-1233). Hershey, PA: Business Science Reference. doi: doi:10.4018/978-1-61520-969-9.ch075

Govindarajan, M., & Chandrasekaran, R. (2012). A hybrid multilayer perceptron neural network for direct marketing. *International Journal of Knowledge-Based Organizations*, *2*(3), 63–73. doi:10.4018/ijkbo.2012070104

Grant, J., & Minker, J. (2011). Logic and knowledge bases. In D. Schwartz, & D. Te'eni (Eds.), *Encyclopedia of knowledge management* (2nd ed., pp. 1022–1033). Hershey, PA: Information Science Reference.

Green, A. (2011). Engineering business reasoning, analytics and intelligence network (E-BRAIN), a new approach to intangible asset valuation based on Einstein's perspective. In B. Vallejo-Alonso, A. Rodriguez-Castellanos, & G. Arregui-Ayastuy (Eds.), *Identifying, measuring, and valuing knowledge-based intangible assets: New perspectives* (pp. 232–253). Hershey, PA: Business Science Reference.

Greenaway, K. E., & Vuong, D. C. (2010). Taking charities seriously: A call for focused knowledge management research. *International Journal of Knowledge Management*, *6*(4), 87–97. doi:10.4018/jkm.2010100105

Greenaway, K. E., & Vuong, D. C. (2012). Taking charities seriously: A call for focused knowledge management research. In M. Jennex (Ed.), *Conceptual models and outcomes of advancing knowledge management: New technologies* (pp. 333–344). Hershey, PA: Information Science Reference. doi:10.4018/978-1-4666-0035-5.ch017

Gunjal, B., Gaitanou, P., & Yasin, S. (2012). Social networks and knowledge management: An explorative study in library systems. In I. Boughzala, & A. Dudezert (Eds.), *Knowledge management 2.0: Organizational models and enterprise strategies* (pp. 64–83). Hershey, PA: Information Science Reference.

Habhab-Rave, S. (2010). Knowledge management in SMEs: A mixture of innovation, marketing and ICT: Analysis of two case studies. In E. O'Brien, S. Clifford, & M. Southern (Eds.), *Knowledge management for process, organizational and marketing innovation: Tools and methods* (pp. 183–194). Hershey, PA: Information Science Reference. doi:10.4018/978-1-61520-829-6.ch011

Habicht, H., Möslein, K. M., & Reichwald, R. (2012). Open innovation maturity. *International Journal of Knowledge-Based Organizations*, *2*(1), 92–111. doi:10.4018/ijkbo.2012010106

Hamburg, I., & Hall, T. (2010). Readiness for knowledge management, methods and environments for innovation. In E. O'Brien, S. Clifford, & M. Southern (Eds.), *Knowledge management for process, organizational and marketing innovation: Tools and methods* (pp. 1–15). Hershey, PA: Information Science Reference. doi:10.4018/978-1-61520-829-6.ch001

Hamza, S. E. (2011). Capturing tacit knowledge from transient workers: Improving the organizational competitiveness. In M. Jennex (Ed.), *Global aspects and cultural perspectives on knowledge management: Emerging dimensions* (pp. 172–188). Hershey, PA: Information Science Reference. doi:10.4018/978-1-60960-555-1.ch012

Harorimana, D. (2010). Knowledge, culture, and cultural impact on knowledge management: Some lessons for researchers and practitioners. In D. Harorimana (Ed.), *Cultural implications of knowledge sharing, management and transfer: Identifying competitive advantage* (pp. 48–59). Hershey, PA: Information Science Reference. doi:10.4018/978-1-61520-965-1.ch419

Hasan, H. (2011). Formal and emergent standards in KM. In D. Schwartz, & D. Te'eni (Eds.), *Encyclopedia of knowledge management* (2nd ed., pp. 331–342). Hershey, PA: Information Science Reference.

He, G., Xue, G., Yu, K., & Yao, S. (2013). Business process modeling: Analysis and evaluation. In Z. Lu (Ed.), *Design, performance, and analysis of innovative information retrieval* (pp. 382–393). Hershey, PA: Information Science Reference.

Heiman, B. A., & Hurmelinna-Laukkanen, P. (2010). Problem finding and solving: A knowledge-based view of managing innovation. In P. López Sáez, G. Castro, J. Navas López, & M. Delgado Verde (Eds.), *Intellectual capital and technological innovation: Knowledge-based theory and practice* (pp. 105–130). Hershey, PA: Information Science Reference. doi:10.4018/978-1-61520-875-3.ch005

Hendriks, P. H. (2011). Organizational structure. In D. Schwartz, & D. Te'eni (Eds.), *Encyclopedia of knowledge management* (2nd ed., pp. 1308–1318). Hershey, PA: Information Science Reference.

Hercheui, M. D. (2012). KMS for fostering behavior change: A case study on Microsoft Hohm. In I. Boughzala, & A. Dudezert (Eds.), *Knowledge management 2.0: Organizational models and enterprise strategies* (pp. 214–232). Hershey, PA: Information Science Reference.

Hipkin, I. (2011). Perceptions of factors influencing knowledge-based technology management in conflict areas. In M. Al-Shammari (Ed.), *Knowledge management in emerging economies: Social, organizational and cultural implementation* (pp. 294–307). Hershey, PA: Information Science Reference.

Hofer, F. (2011). Knowledge transfer between academia and industry. In D. Schwartz, & D. Te'eni (Eds.), *Encyclopedia of knowledge management* (2nd ed., pp. 977–986). Hershey, PA: Information Science Reference.

Holjevac, I. A., Crnjar, K., & Hrgovic, A. V. (2013). Knowledge management and quality in Croatian tourism. In S. Buckley, & M. Jakovljevic (Eds.), *Knowledge management innovations for interdisciplinary education: Organizational applications* (pp. 178–192). Hershey, PA: Information Science Reference.

Holsapple, C. W., & Joshi, K. D. (2011). Knowledge management ontology. In D. Schwartz, & D. Te'eni (Eds.), *Encyclopedia of knowledge management* (2nd ed., pp. 704–711). Hershey, PA: Information Science Reference.

Holsapple, C. W., & Oh, J. (2014). Reactive and proactive dynamic capabilities: Using the knowledge chain theory of competitiveness. In M. Chilton, & J. Bloodgood (Eds.), *knowledge management and competitive advantage: Issues and potential solutions* (pp. 1–19). Hershey, PA: Information Science Reference.

Huang, A., Xiao, J., & Wang, S. (2013). A combined forecast method integrating contextual knowledge. In G. Yang (Ed.), *Multidisciplinary studies in knowledge and systems science* (pp. 274–290). Hershey, PA: Information Science Reference.

Huff, C. (2011). What does knowledge have to do with ethics? In G. Morais da Costa (Ed.), *Ethical issues and social dilemmas in knowledge management: Organizational innovation* (pp. 17–27). Hershey, PA: Information Science Reference. doi:10.4018/978-1-60960-783-8.ch708

Hürster, W., Wilbois, T., & Chaves, F. (2010). An integrated systems approach for early warning and risk management systems. *International Journal of Information Technologies and Systems Approach*, *3*(2), 46–56. doi:10.4018/jitsa.2010070104

Iyer, S. R., Sharda, R., Biros, D., Lucca, J., & Shimp, U. (2011). Organization of lessons learned knowledge: A taxonomy and implementation. In M. Jennex (Ed.), *Global aspects and cultural perspectives on knowledge management: Emerging dimensions* (pp. 190–209). Hershey, PA: Information Science Reference. doi:10.4018/978-1-60960-555-1.ch013

Jacobson, C. M. (2011). Knowledge sharing between individuals. In D. Schwartz, & D. Te'eni (Eds.), *Encyclopedia of knowledge management* (2nd ed., pp. 924–934). Hershey, PA: Information Science Reference.

Jakovljevic, M. (2013). A conceptual model of creativity, invention, and innovation (MCII) for entrepreneurial engineers. In S. Buckley, & M. Jakovljevic (Eds.), *Knowledge management innovations for interdisciplinary education: Organizational applications* (pp. 66–87). Hershey, PA: Information Science Reference.

Jasimuddin, S. M., Connell, N., & Klein, J. H. (2011). Understanding organizational memory. In D. Schwartz, & D. Te'eni (Eds.), *Encyclopedia of knowledge management* (2nd ed., pp. 1536–1544). Hershey, PA: Information Science Reference.

Jennex, M. E. (2010). Do organizational memory and information technology interact to affect organizational information needs and provision? In *Ubiquitous developments in knowledge management: Integrations and trends* (pp. 1–20). Hershey, PA: Information Science Reference. doi:10.4018/978-1-60566-954-0.ch001

Jennex, M. E. (2010). Knowledge sharing model of 24-hour knowledge factory. In *Ubiquitous developments in knowledge management: Integrations and trends* (pp. 141–154). Hershey, PA: Information Science Reference. doi:10.4018/978-1-60566-954-0.ch009

Jennex, M. E. (2010). Operationalizing knowledge sharing for informers. In *Ubiquitous developments in knowledge management: Integrations and trends* (pp. 319–340). Hershey, PA: Information Science Reference. doi:10.4018/978-1-60566-954-0.ch020

Jennex, M. E. (2010). Qualitative pre-processing for semantic search of unstructured knowledge. In *Ubiquitous developments in knowledge management: Integrations and trends* (pp. 252–263). Hershey, PA: Information Science Reference. doi:10.4018/978-1-60566-954-0.ch016

Jennex, M. E. (2010). A specialized evaluation and comparison of sample data mining software. In *Ubiquitous developments in knowledge management: Integrations and trends* (pp. 300–318). Hershey, PA: Information Science Reference. doi:10.4018/978-1-60566-954-0.ch019

Jennex, M. E. (2010). Using soft systems methodology to reveal socio-technical barriers to knowledge sharing and management: A case study from the UK National Health Service. In *Ubiquitous developments in knowledge management: Integrations and trends* (pp. 215–235). Hershey, PA: Information Science Reference. doi:10.4018/978-1-60566-954-0.ch014

Jennex, M. E. (2011). Knowledge management success models. In D. Schwartz, & D. Te'eni (Eds.), *Encyclopedia of knowledge management* (2nd ed., pp. 763–771). Hershey, PA: Information Science Reference.

Jennex, M. E., & Olfman, L. (2011). A model of knowledge management success. In M. Jennex, & S. Smolnik (Eds.), *Strategies for knowledge management success: Exploring organizational efficacy* (pp. 14–31). Hershey, PA: Information Science Reference.

Jennex, M. E., Smolnik, S., & Croasdell, D. (2011). Towards a consensus knowledge management success definition. In M. Jennex, & S. Smolnik (Eds.), *Strategies for knowledge management success: Exploring organizational efficacy* (pp. 1–13). Hershey, PA: Information Science Reference. doi:10.4018/978-1-60960-783-8.ch201

Jewels, T. (2013). Teaching enterprise information systems in the United Arab Emirates. In F. Albadri (Ed.), *Information systems applications in the Arab education sector* (pp. 322–337). Hershey, PA: Information Science Reference.

Jolly, R., & Wakeland, W. (2011). Using agent based simulation and game theory analysis to study knowledge flow in organizations: The KMscape. In M. Jennex (Ed.), *Global aspects and cultural perspectives on knowledge management: Emerging dimensions* (pp. 19–29). Hershey, PA: Information Science Reference. doi:10.4018/978-1-60960-555-1.ch002

Joshi, S. (2014). Web 2.0 and its implications on globally competitive business model. In M. Pańkowska (Ed.), *Frameworks of IT prosumption for business development* (pp. 86–101). Hershey, PA: Business Science Reference.

Judge, R. (2011). A simulation system for evaluating knowledge management system (KMS) implementation strategies in small to mid-size enterprises (SME). In M. Jennex (Ed.), *Global aspects and cultural perspectives on knowledge management: Emerging dimensions* (pp. 92–112). Hershey, PA: Information Science Reference. doi:10.4018/978-1-60960-555-1.ch007

Kalid, K. S. (2011). Transfer knowledge using stories: A Malaysian University case study. In M. Al-Shammari (Ed.), *Knowledge management in emerging economies: Social, organizational and cultural implementation* (pp. 186–198). Hershey, PA: Information Science Reference. doi:10.4018/978-1-60960-783-8.ch812

Kamau, C. (2010). Strategising impression management in corporations: Cultural knowledge as capital. In D. Harorimana (Ed.), *Cultural implications of knowledge sharing, management and transfer: Identifying competitive advantage* (pp. 60–83). Hershey, PA: Information Science Reference.

Kamthan, P., & Fancott, T. (2011). A knowledge management model for patterns. In D. Schwartz, & D. Te'eni (Eds.), *Encyclopedia of knowledge management* (2nd ed., pp. 694–703). Hershey, PA: Information Science Reference.

Kamthan, P., & Pai, H. (2011). Knowledge representation in pattern management. In D. Schwartz, & D. Te'eni (Eds.), *Encyclopedia of knowledge management* (2nd ed., pp. 893–904). Hershey, PA: Information Science Reference.

Kane, G. C., Schwaig, K. S., & Storey, V. C. (2011). Information privacy: Understanding how firms behave online. In K. Siau (Ed.), *Theoretical and practical advances in information systems development: Emerging trends and approaches* (pp. 81–100). Hershey, PA: Information Science Reference. doi:10.4018/978-1-60960-521-6.ch005

Kankanhalli, A., Tan, B. C., & Wei, K. (2011). Knowledge producers and consumers. In D. Schwartz, & D. Te'eni (Eds.), *Encyclopedia of knowledge management* (2nd ed., pp. 867–877). Hershey, PA: Information Science Reference.

Karagiannis, D., Woitsch, R., & Hrgovcic, V. (2010). Industrialisation of the knowledge work: The knowledge conveyer belt approach. In E. O'Brien, S. Clifford, & M. Southern (Eds.), *Knowledge management for process, organizational and marketing innovation: Tools and methods* (pp. 79–94). Hershey, PA: Information Science Reference. doi:10.4018/978-1-61520-829-6.ch005

Karlsson, F., & Ågerfalk, P. J. (2011). Towards structured flexibility in information systems development: Devising a method for method configuration. In K. Siau (Ed.), *Theoretical and practical advances in information systems development: Emerging trends and approaches* (pp. 214–238). Hershey, PA: Information Science Reference. doi:10.4018/978-1-60960-521-6.ch010

Karna, A., Singh, R., & Verma, S. (2010). Knowledge management for an effective sales and marketing function. In M. Russ (Ed.), *Knowledge management strategies for business development* (pp. 324–337). Hershey, PA: Business Science Reference.

Kassim, A. M., & Cheah, Y. (2013). SEMblog: An Ontology-based semantic blogging tool for knowledge identification, organization, and reuse. In M. Nazir Ahmad, R. Colomb, & M. Abdullah (Eds.), *Ontology-based applications for enterprise systems and knowledge management* (pp. 210–223). Hershey, PA: Information Science Reference.

Kayakutlu, G. (2010). Knowledge worker profile: A framework to clarify expectations. In K. Metaxiotis, F. Carrillo, & T. Yigitcanlar (Eds.), *Knowledge-based development for cities and societies: Integrated multi-level approaches* (pp. 162–178). Hershey, PA: Information Science Reference. doi:10.4018/978-1-61520-721-3.ch010

Kettunen, J., & Chaudhuri, M. R. (2011). Knowledge management to promote organizational change in India. In M. Al-Shammari (Ed.), *Knowledge management in emerging economies: Social, organizational and cultural implementation* (pp. 308–324). Hershey, PA: Information Science Reference.

Khalil, O. E., & Seleim, A. (2012). Culture and knowledge transfer capacity: A cross-national study. In M. Jennex (Ed.), *Conceptual models and outcomes of advancing knowledge management: New technologies* (pp. 305–332). Hershey, PA: Information Science Reference. doi:10.4018/978-1-4666-0035-5.ch016

Khasawneh, R., & Alazzam, A. (2014). Towards customer knowledge management (CKM), where knowledge and customer meet. In M. Chilton, & J. Bloodgood (Eds.), *Knowledge management and competitive advantage: Issues and potential solutions* (pp. 109–121). Hershey, PA: Information Science Reference.

Kim, J. (2014). Big data sharing among academics. In W. Hu, & N. Kaabouch (Eds.), *Big data management, technologies, and applications* (pp. 177–194). Hershey, PA: Information Science Reference.

Kim, S., Felan, J., & Kang, M. H. (2011). An ontological approach to enterprise knowledge modeling in a shipping company. *International Journal of Knowledge Management, 7*(4), 70–84. doi:10.4018/jkm.2011100105

Kim, S., Felan, J., & Kang, M. H. (2013). An ontological approach to enterprise knowledge modeling in a shipping company. In M. Jennex (Ed.), *Dynamic models for knowledge-driven organizations* (pp. 351–363). Hershey, PA: Business Science Reference.

King, W. R. (2011). Knowledge transfer. In D. Schwartz, & D. Te'eni (Eds.), *Encyclopedia of knowledge management* (2nd ed., pp. 967–976). Hershey, PA: Information Science Reference.

Kivijärvi, H., Piirainen, K., & Tuominen, M. (2010). Sustaining organizational innovativeness: Advancing knowledge sharing during the scenario process. *International Journal of Knowledge Management, 6*(2), 22–39. doi:10.4018/jkm.2010040102

Kivijärvi, H., Piirainen, K., & Tuominen, M. (2012). Sustaining organizational innovativeness: Advancing knowledge sharing during the scenario process. In M. Jennex (Ed.), *Conceptual models and outcomes of advancing knowledge management: New technologies* (pp. 99–117). Hershey, PA: Information Science Reference. doi:10.4018/978-1-4666-0035-5.ch006

Knyazhansky, M., & Plotkin, T. (2012). Knowledge bases over algebraic models: Some notes about informational equivalence. *International Journal of Knowledge Management, 8*(1), 22–39. doi:10.4018/jkm.2012010102

Kong, E. (2014). The role of social intelligence in acquiring external knowledge for human capital development, organisational learning, and innovation. In M. Chilton, & J. Bloodgood (Eds.), *Knowledge management and competitive advantage: Issues and potential solutions* (pp. 53–70). Hershey, PA: Information Science Reference.

Kor, A., & Orange, G. (2011). A survey of epistemology and its implications on an organisational information and knowledge management model. In A. Eardley, & L. Uden (Eds.), *Innovative knowledge management: Concepts for organizational creativity and collaborative design* (pp. 95–124). Hershey, PA: Information Science Reference. doi:10.4018/978-1-60960-783-8.ch707

Kostrzewa, A., Laaksoharju, M., & Kavathatzopoulos, I. (2011). Management of moral knowledge and ethical processes in organizations. In G. Morais da Costa (Ed.), *Ethical issues and social dilemmas in knowledge management: Organizational innovation* (pp. 199–214). Hershey, PA: Information Science Reference.

Kraaijenbrink, J., & Wijnhoven, F. (2011). External knowledge integration. In D. Schwartz, & D. Te'eni (Eds.), *Encyclopedia of knowledge management* (2nd ed., pp. 308–319). Hershey, PA: Information Science Reference.

Kraft, T. A., & Steenkamp, A. L. (2012). A holistic approach for understanding project management. In F. Stowell (Ed.), *Systems approach applications for developments in information technology* (pp. 25–39). Hershey, PA: Information Science Reference. doi:10.4018/978-1-4666-1562-5.ch003

Kulkarni, U., & Freeze, R. (2011). Measuring knowledge management capabilities. In D. Schwartz, & D. Te'eni (Eds.), *Encyclopedia of knowledge management* (2nd ed., pp. 1090–1100). Hershey, PA: Information Science Reference.

Kumar, A. S., Alrabea, A., & Sekhar, P. C. (2013). Temporal association rule mining in large databases. In I. Association (Ed.), *Data mining: Concepts, methodologies, tools, and applications* (pp. 586–602). Hershey, PA: Information Science Reference.

Laihonen, H., & Koivuaho, M. (2011). Knowledge flow audit: Indentifying, measuring and managing knowledge asset dynamics. In B. Vallejo-Alonso, A. Rodriguez-Castellanos, & G. Arregui-Ayastuy (Eds.), *Identifying, measuring, and valuing knowledge-based intangible assets: New perspectives* (pp. 22–42). Hershey, PA: Business Science Reference.

Land, F., Amjad, U., & Nolas, S. (2011). Knowledge management processes. In D. Schwartz, & D. Te'eni (Eds.), *Encyclopedia of knowledge management* (2nd ed., pp. 719–727). Hershey, PA: Information Science Reference.

Lavanderos, L. P., & Fiol, E. S. (2011). Production cognitive capital as a measurement of intellectual capital. In B. Vallejo-Alonso, A. Rodriguez-Castellanos, & G. Arregui-Ayastuy (Eds.), *Identifying, measuring, and valuing knowledge-based intangible assets: New perspectives* (pp. 112–132). Hershey, PA: Business Science Reference.

Lavoué, É., George, S., & Prévôt, P. (2011). A knowledge management tool for the interconnection of communities of practice. *International Journal of Knowledge Management, 7*(1), 55–76. doi:10.4018/jkm.2011010104

Lee, H., Chan, K., & Tsui, E. (2013). Knowledge mining Wikipedia: An ontological approach. In G. Yang (Ed.), *Multidisciplinary studies in knowledge and systems science* (pp. 52–62). Hershey, PA: Information Science Reference.

Leung, N. K. (2011). A Re-Distributed Knowledge Management Framework in Help Desk. In D. Schwartz, & D. Te'eni (Eds.), *Encyclopedia of Knowledge Management* (2nd ed., pp. 1374–1381). Hershey, PA: Information Science Reference. doi:10.4018/978-1-60960-783-8.ch221

Li, Y., Guo, H., & Wang, S. (2010). A multiple-bits watermark for relational data. In K. Siau, & J. Erickson (Eds.), *Principle advancements in database management technologies: New Applications and frameworks* (pp. 1–22). Hershey, PA: Information Science Reference.

Lin, C. Y. (2013). Intellectual capital explains a country's resilience to financial crisis: A resource-based view. In P. Ordóñez de Pablos, R. Tennyson, & J. Zhao (Eds.), *Intellectual capital strategy management for knowledge-based organizations* (pp. 52–75). Hershey, PA: Business Science Reference. doi:10.4018/978-1-4666-3655-2.ch005

Lin, Y., & Dalkir, K. (2012). Factors affecting KM implementation in the Chinese community. In M. Jennex (Ed.), *Conceptual models and outcomes of advancing knowledge management: New technologies* (pp. 1–23). Hershey, PA: Information Science Reference. doi:10.4018/978-1-4666-0035-5.ch001

Lindsey, K. L. (2011). Barriers to knowledge sharing. In D. Schwartz, & D. Te'eni (Eds.), *Encyclopedia of knowledge management* (2nd ed., pp. 49–61). Hershey, PA: Information Science Reference.

Liu, K., Tan, H. B., & Chen, X. (2013). Aiding maintenance of database applications through extracting attribute dependency graph. *Journal of Database Management*, *24*(1), 20–35. doi:10.4018/jdm.2013010102

Liu, K., Tan, H. B., & Chen, X. (2013). Automated insertion of exception handling for key and referential constraints. *Journal of Database Management*, *24*(1), 1–19. doi:10.4018/jdm.2013010101

Locuratolo, E., & Palomäki, J. (2013). Ontology for database preservation. In M. Nazir Ahmad, R. Colomb, & M. Abdullah (Eds.), *Ontology-based applications for enterprise systems and knowledge management* (pp. 141–157). Hershey, PA: Information Science Reference.

López-Nicolás, C., & Meroño-Cerdán, Á. L. (2010). A model for knowledge management and intellectual capital audits. In M. Russ (Ed.), *Knowledge management strategies for business development* (pp. 115–131). Hershey, PA: Business Science Reference.

Luck, D. (2010). The implications of the development and implementation of CRM for knowledge management. In M. Russ (Ed.), *Knowledge management strategies for business development* (pp. 338–352). Hershey, PA: Business Science Reference.

Lukovic, I., Ivancevic, V., Celikovic, M., & Aleksic, S. (2014). DSLs in action with model based approaches to information system development. In I. Management Association (Ed.), software design and development: Concepts, methodologies, tools, and applications (pp. 596-626). Hershey, PA: Information Science Reference. doi: doi:10.4018/978-1-4666-4301-7.ch029

Luna-Reyes, L. F., & Gil-Garcia, J. R. (2012). Government and inter-organizational collaboration as strategies for administrative reform in Mexico. In T. Papadopoulos, & P. Kanellis (Eds.), *Public sector reform using information technologies: Transforming policy into practice* (pp. 79–101). Hershey, PA: Information Science Reference.

Lungu, C. I., Caraiani, C., & Dascalu, C. (2013). Sustainable intellectual capital: The inference of corporate social responsibility within intellectual capital. In P. Ordóñez de Pablos, R. Tennyson, & J. Zhao (Eds.), *Intellectual capital strategy management for knowledge-based organizations* (pp. 156–173). Hershey, PA: Business Science Reference. doi:10.4018/978-1-4666-3655-2.ch009

Ma, Z. M. (2011). Engineering design knowledge management. In D. Schwartz, & D. Te'eni (Eds.), *Encyclopedia of knowledge management* (2nd ed., pp. 263–269). Hershey, PA: Information Science Reference.

Maier, R., & Hadrich, T. (2011). Knowledge management systems. In D. Schwartz, & D. Te'eni (Eds.), *Encyclopedia of knowledge management* (2nd ed., pp. 779–790). Hershey, PA: Information Science Reference.

Maria, E. D., & Micelli, S. (2010). SMEs and competitive advantage: A mix of innovation, marketing and ICT—The case of Made in Italy. In M. Russ (Ed.), *knowledge management strategies for business development* (pp. 310–323). Hershey, PA: Business Science Reference.

Mariano, S., & Simionato, N. (2010). Where are we looking? A practical approach to managing knowledge captured from eye-tracking experiments: The experience of Gulf Air. In E. O'Brien, S. Clifford, & M. Southern (Eds.), *Knowledge management for process, organizational and marketing innovation: Tools and methods* (pp. 216–227). Hershey, PA: Information Science Reference. doi:10.4018/978-1-61520-829-6.ch013

Marques, M. B. (2014). The value of information and information services in knowledge society. In G. Jamil, A. Malheiro, & F. Ribeiro (Eds.), *Rethinking the conceptual base for new practical applications in information value and quality* (pp. 134–161). Hershey, PA: Information Science Reference.

Masrom, M., Mahmood, N. H., & Al-Araimi, A. A. (2014). Exploring knowledge types and knowledge protection in organizations. In M. Chilton, & J. Bloodgood (Eds.), *knowledge management and competitive advantage: Issues and potential solutions* (pp. 271–280). Hershey, PA: Information Science Reference.

Masterson, F. (2013). Knowledge management in practice: Using wikis to facilitate project-based learning. In S. Buckley, & M. Jakovljevic (Eds.), *Knowledge management innovations for interdisciplinary education: Organizational applications* (pp. 385–401). Hershey, PA: Information Science Reference.

Mattmann, C. A., Hart, A., Cinquini, L., Lazio, J., Khudikyan, S., & Jones, D. ... Robnett, J. (2014). Scalable data mining, archiving, and big data management for the next generation astronomical telescopes. In W. Hu\ & N. Kaabouch (Eds.), Big data management, technologies, and applications (pp. 196-221). Hershey, PA: Information Science Reference. doi: doi:10.4018/978-1-4666-4699-5.ch009

Maule, R. W. (2011). Military knowledge management. In D. Schwartz, & D. Te'eni (Eds.), *Encyclopedia of knowledge management* (2nd ed., pp. 1125–1135). Hershey, PA: Information Science Reference.

Mavridis, I. (2011). Deploying privacy improved RBAC in Web information systems. *International Journal of Information Technologies and Systems Approach, 4*(2), 70–87. doi:10.4018/jitsa.2011070105

Mavridis, I. (2012). Deploying privacy improved RBAC in Web information systems. In F. Stowell (Ed.), *Systems approach applications for developments in information technology* (pp. 298–315). Hershey, PA: Information Science Reference. doi:10.4018/978-1-4666-1562-5.ch020

McLaughlin, S. (2011). Assessing the Impact of knowledge transfer mechanisms on supply chain performance. In M. Jennex (Ed.), *Global aspects and cultural perspectives on knowledge management: Emerging dimensions* (pp. 157–171). Hershey, PA: Information Science Reference. doi:10.4018/978-1-60960-555-1.ch011

Medina, J. M., & Spinola, M. D. (2011). Understanding the behavior of knowledge management pathways: The case of small manufacturers of footwear in Peru and Brazil. In M. Al-Shammari (Ed.), *Knowledge management in emerging economies: Social, organizational and cultural implementation* (pp. 261–271). Hershey, PA: Information Science Reference.

Meloche, J. A., Hasan, H., Willis, D., Pfaff, C. C., & Qi, Y. (2011). Cocreating corporate knowledge with a wiki. In M. Jennex (Ed.), *Global aspects and cultural perspectives on knowledge management: emerging dimensions* (pp. 126–143). Hershey, PA: Information Science Reference. doi:10.4018/978-1-60960-555-1.ch009

Melzer, S. (2013). On the relationship between ontology-based and holistic representations in a knowledge management system. In M. Nazir Ahmad, R. Colomb, & M. Abdullah (Eds.), *Ontology-based applications for enterprise systems and knowledge management* (pp. 292–323). Hershey, PA: Information Science Reference.

Mendes, E., & Baker, S. (2013). Using knowledge management and aggregation techniques to improve Web effort estimation. In S. Saeed, & I. Alsmadi (Eds.), *Knowledge-based processes in software development* (pp. 64–85). Hershey, PA: Information Science Reference. doi:10.4018/978-1-4666-4229-4.ch005

Metaxiotis, K. (2011). Healthcare knowledge management. In D. Schwartz, & D. Te'eni (Eds.), *Encyclopedia of knowledge management* (2nd ed., pp. 366–375). Hershey, PA: Information Science Reference.

Mikolajuk, Z. (2013). Community-based development of knowledge products. In M. Jennex (Ed.), *Dynamic models for knowledge-driven organizations* (pp. 268–281). Hershey, PA: Business Science Reference.

Mischo, W. H., Schlembach, M. C., Bishoff, J., & German, E. M. (2012). User search activities within an academic library gateway: Implications for Web-scale discovery systems. In M. Popp, & D. Dallis (Eds.), *Planning and implementing resource discovery tools in academic libraries* (pp. 153–173). Hershey, PA: Information Science Reference. doi:10.4018/978-1-4666-1821-3.ch010

Mishra, B., & Shukla, K. K. (2014). Data mining techniques for software quality prediction. In I. Management Association (Ed.), Software design and development: Concepts, methodologies, tools, and applications (pp. 401-428). Hershey, PA: Information Science Reference. doi: doi:10.4018/978-1-4666-4301-7.ch021

Moffett, S., Walker, T., & McAdam, R. (2014). Best value and performance management inspired change within UK councils: A knowledge management perspective. In Y. Al-Bastaki, & A. Shajera (Eds.), *Building a competitive public sector with knowledge management strategy* (pp. 199–226). Hershey, PA: Business Science Reference.

Mueller, C. E., & Bradley, K. D. (2011). Utilizing the Rasch model to develop and evaluate items for the tacit knowledge inventory for superintendents (TKIS). In M. Jennex (Ed.), *Global aspects and cultural perspectives on knowledge management: Emerging dimensions* (pp. 264–284). Hershey, PA: Information Science Reference. doi:10.4018/978-1-60960-555-1.ch017

Muhammed, S., Doll, W. J., & Deng, X. (2011). Impact of knowledge management practices on task knowledge: An individual level study. [IJKM]. *International Journal of Knowledge Management*, 7(4), 1–21. doi:10.4018/jkm.2011100101

Muhammed, S., Doll, W. J., & Deng, X. (2011). Measuring knowledge management outcomes at the individual level: Towards a tool for research on organizational culture. In M. Jennex (Ed.), *Global Aspects and cultural perspectives on knowledge management: Emerging dimensions* (pp. 1–18). Hershey, PA: Information Science Reference. doi:10.4018/978-1-60960-555-1.ch001

Muhammed, S., Doll, W. J., & Deng, X. (2013). Impact of knowledge management practices on task knowledge: An individual level study. In M. Jennex (Ed.), *Dynamic models for knowledge-driven organizations* (pp. 282–301). Hershey, PA: Business Science Reference.

Murata, K. (2011). knowledge creation and sharing in Japanese organisations: A socio-cultural perspective on ba. In G. Morais da Costa (Ed.), Ethical issues and social dilemmas in knowledge management: Organizational innovation (pp. 1-16). Hershey, PA: Information Science Reference. doi: doi:10.4018/978-1-61520-873-9.ch001

Murphy, P. (2013). Systems of communication: Information, explanation, and imagination. In G. Yang (Ed.), *Multidisciplinary studies in knowledge and systems science* (pp. 63–78). Hershey, PA: Information Science Reference.

Nach, H. (2013). Structuring knowledge for enterprise resource planning implementation through an ontology. In M. Nazir Ahmad, R. Colomb, & M. Abdullah (Eds.), *Ontology-based applications for enterprise systems and knowledge management* (pp. 25–42). Hershey, PA: Information Science Reference. doi:10.4018/978-1-4666-4153-2.ch024

Nah, F. F., Hong, W., Chen, L., & Lee, H. (2010). Information search patterns in e-commerce product comparison services. *Journal of Database Management, 21*(2), 26–40. doi:10.4018/jdm.2010040102

Nah, F. F., Hong, W., Chen, L., & Lee, H. (2012). Information search patterns in e-commerce product comparison services. In K. Siau (Ed.), *Cross-disciplinary models and applications of database management: Advancing approaches* (pp. 131–145). Hershey, PA: Information Science Reference.

Natarajan, R., & Shekar, B. (2011). Knowledge patterns in databases. In D. Schwartz, & D. Te'eni (Eds.), *Encyclopedia of knowledge management* (2nd ed., pp. 842–852). Hershey, PA: Information Science Reference.

Nelson, R. E., & Hsu, H. S. (2011). A social network perspective on knowledge management. In D. Schwartz, & D. Te'eni (Eds.), *Encyclopedia of knowledge management* (2nd ed., pp. 1470–1478). Hershey, PA: Information Science Reference.

Neto, R. C., & Souza, R. R. (2010). Knowledge management as an organizational process: From a theoretical framework to implementation guidelines. In E. O'Brien, S. Clifford, & M. Southern (Eds.), *Knowledge management for process, organizational and marketing innovation: Tools and methods* (pp. 16–35). Hershey, PA: Information Science Reference. doi:10.4018/978-1-61520-829-6.ch002

Newell, S. (2011). Understanding innovation processes. In D. Schwartz, & D. Te'eni (Eds.), *Encyclopedia of knowledge management* (2nd ed., pp. 1525–1535). Hershey, PA: Information Science Reference.

Nikabadi, M. S., & Zamanloo, S. (2012). A multidimensional structure for describing the influence of supply chain strategies, business strategies, and knowledge management strategies on knowledge sharing in supply chain. *International Journal of Knowledge Management*, *8*(4), 50–70. doi:10.4018/jkm.2012100103

Nissen, M. (2014). Cyberspace and cloud knowledge. In *Harnessing dynamic knowledge principles in the technology-driven world* (pp. 193–204). Hershey, PA: Information Science Reference.

Nissen, M. (2014). Social media knowledge. In *Harnessing dynamic knowledge principles in the technology-driven world* (pp. 219–227). Hershey, PA: Information Science Reference.

Nissen, M. E. (2014). Harnessing knowledge power for competitive advantage. In M. Chilton, & J. Bloodgood (Eds.), *Knowledge management and competitive advantage: Issues and potential solutions* (pp. 20–34). Hershey, PA: Information Science Reference.

Nissen, M. E., & Levitt, R. E. (2011). Knowledge management research through computational experimentation. In D. Schwartz, & D. Te'eni (Eds.), *Encyclopedia of knowledge management* (2nd ed., pp. 728–737). Hershey, PA: Information Science Reference.

Nisula, A. (2014). Developing organizational renewal capability in the municipal (city) organization. In Y. Al-Bastaki, & A. Shajera (Eds.), *Building a competitive public sector with knowledge management strategy* (pp. 151–172). Hershey, PA: Business Science Reference.

Niu, B., Martin, P., & Powley, W. (2011). Towards autonomic workload management in DBMSs. In K. Siau (Ed.), *Theoretical and practical advances in information systems development: Emerging trends and approaches* (pp. 154–173). Hershey, PA: Information Science Reference. doi:10.4018/978-1-60960-521-6.ch008

Nobre, F. S., & Walker, D. S. (2011). A dynamic ability-based view of the organization. *International Journal of Knowledge Management*, *7*(2), 86–101. doi:10.4018/jkm.2011040105

O'Brien, J. (2014). Lessons from the private sector: A framework to be adopted in the public sector. In Y. Al-Bastaki, & A. Shajera (Eds.), *Building a competitive public sector with knowledge management strategy* (pp. 173–198). Hershey, PA: Business Science Reference.

Omari, A. (2013). Supporting companies management and improving their productivity through mining customers transactions. In I. Association (Ed.), *Data mining: Concepts, methodologies, tools, and applications* (pp. 1519–1533). Hershey, PA: Information Science Reference.

Onwubiko, C. (2014). Modelling situation awareness information and system requirements for the mission using goal-oriented task analysis approach. In I. Management Association (Ed.), Software design and development: Concepts, methodologies, tools, and applications (pp. 460-478). Hershey, PA: Information Science Reference. doi: doi:10.4018/978-1-4666-4301-7.ch023

Orth, A., Smolnik, S., & Jennex, M. E. (2011). The relevance of integration for knowledge management success: Towards conceptual and empirical evidence. In M. Jennex, & S. Smolnik (Eds.), *Strategies for knowledge management success: Exploring organizational efficacy* (pp. 238–261). Hershey, PA: Information Science Reference.

Othman, A. K., & Abdullah, H. S. (2011). The influence of emotional intelligence on tacit knowledge sharing in service organizations. In M. Al-Shammari (Ed.), *Knowledge management in emerging economies: Social, organizational and cultural implementation* (pp. 171–185). Hershey, PA: Information Science Reference. doi:10.4018/978-1-60960-783-8.ch719

Pagallo, U. (2011). The trouble with digital copies: A short KM phenomenology. In G. Morais da Costa (Ed.), *Ethical issues and social dilemmas in knowledge management: Organizational innovation* (pp. 97–112). Hershey, PA: Information Science Reference.

Palte, R., Hertlein, M., Smolnik, S., & Riempp, G. (2013). The effects of a KM strategy on KM performance in professional services firms. In M. Jennex (Ed.), *Dynamic models for knowledge-driven organizations* (pp. 16–35). Hershey, PA: Business Science Reference.

Pańkowska, M. (2014). Information technology prosumption acceptance by business information system consultants. In M. Pańkowska (Ed.), *Frameworks of IT prosumption for business development* (pp. 119–141). Hershey, PA: Business Science Reference.

Pankowski, T. (2011). Pattern-based schema mapping and query answering in peer-to-peer XML data integration system. In L. Yan, & Z. Ma (Eds.), *Advanced database query systems: Techniques, applications and technologies* (pp. 221–246). Hershey, PA: Information Science Reference. doi:10.4018/978-1-60960-475-2.ch009

Papoutsakis, H. (2010). New product development based on knowledge creation and technology education. In E. O'Brien, S. Clifford, & M. Southern (Eds.), *Knowledge management for process, organizational and marketing innovation: Tools and methods* (pp. 148–163). Hershey, PA: Information Science Reference. doi:10.4018/978-1-61520-829-6.ch009

Paquette, S. (2011). Applying knowledge management in the environmental and climate change sciences. In D. Schwartz, & D. Te'eni (Eds.), *Encyclopedia of knowledge management* (2nd ed., pp. 20–26). Hershey, PA: Information Science Reference.

Paquette, S. (2011). Customer knowledge management. In D. Schwartz, & D. Te'eni (Eds.), *Encyclopedia of knowledge management* (2nd ed., pp. 175–184). Hershey, PA: Information Science Reference.

Parker, K. R., & Nitse, P. S. (2011). Competitive intelligence gathering. In D. Schwartz, & D. Te'eni (Eds.), *Encyclopedia of knowledge management* (2nd ed., pp. 103–111). Hershey, PA: Information Science Reference.

Páscoa, C., & Tribolet, J. (2014). Maintaining organizational viability and performance: The organizational configuration map. In G. Jamil, A. Malheiro, & F. Ribeiro (Eds.), *Rethinking the conceptual base for new practical applications in information value and quality* (pp. 266–283). Hershey, PA: Information Science Reference.

Paukert, M., Niederée, C., & Hemmje, M. (2011). Knowledge in innovation processes. In D. Schwartz, & D. Te'eni (Eds.), *Encyclopedia of knowledge management* (2nd ed., pp. 570–580). Hershey, PA: Information Science Reference.

Pawlak, P. (2011). Global knowledge management in humanist perspective. In G. Morais da Costa (Ed.), *Ethical issues and social dilemmas in knowledge management: Organizational innovation* (pp. 45–62). Hershey, PA: Information Science Reference.

Perry, M. (2013). Strategic knowledge management: A university application. In S. Buckley, & M. Jakovljevic (Eds.), *Knowledge management innovations for interdisciplinary education: Organizational applications* (pp. 132–144). Hershey, PA: Information Science Reference.

Pessoa, C. R., Silva, U. P., & Cruz, C. H. (2014). Information management in industrial areas: A knowledge management view. In G. Jamil, A. Malheiro, & F. Ribeiro (Eds.), *Rethinking the conceptual base for new practical applications in information value and quality* (pp. 378–395). Hershey, PA: Information Science Reference.

Peter, H., & Greenidge, C. (2011). An ontology-based extraction framework for a Semantic Web application. *International Journal of Knowledge-Based Organizations*, *1*(3), 56–71. doi:10.4018/ijkbo.2011070104

Peter, H., & Greenidge, C. (2013). An ontology-based extraction framework for a Semantic Web application. In J. Wang (Ed.), *Intelligence methods and systems advancements for knowledge-based business* (pp. 231–246). Hershey, PA: Information Science Reference.

Pham, Q. T., & Hara, Y. (2011). KM approach for improving the labor productivity of Vietnamese enterprise. *International Journal of Knowledge Management*, *7*(3), 27–42. doi:10.4018/jkm.2011070103

Pham, Q. T., & Hara, Y. (2013). KM approach for improving the labor productivity of Vietnamese enterprise. In M. Jennex (Ed.), *Dynamic models for knowledge-driven organizations* (pp. 206–219). Hershey, PA: Business Science Reference.

Philpott, E., & Beaumont-Kerridge, J. (2010). Overcoming reticence to aid knowledge creation between universities and business: A case reviewed. In D. Harorimana (Ed.), *Cultural implications of knowledge sharing, management and transfer: Identifying competitive advantage* (pp. 355–368). Hershey, PA: Information Science Reference.

Pike, S., & Roos, G. (2011). Measuring and valuing knowledge-based intangible assets: Real business uses. In B. Vallejo-Alonso, A. Rodriguez-Castellanos, & G. Arregui-Ayastuy (Eds.), *Identifying, measuring, and valuing knowledge-based intangible assets: New perspectives* (pp. 268–293). Hershey, PA: Business Science Reference.

Pineda, J. L., Zapata, L. E., & Ramírez, J. (2010). Strengthening knowledge transfer between the university and enterprise: A conceptual model for collaboration. In D. Harorimana (Ed.), *Cultural implications of knowledge sharing, management and transfer: Identifying competitive advantage* (pp. 134–151). Hershey, PA: Information Science Reference.

Platonov, V., & Bergman, J. (2013). Cross-border cooperative network in the perspective of innovation dynamics. In J. Wang (Ed.), *Intelligence methods and systems advancements for knowledge-based business* (pp. 150–169). Hershey, PA: Information Science Reference.

Poels, G. (2013). Understanding business domain models: The effect of recognizing resource-event-agent conceptual modeling structures. In K. Siau (Ed.), *Innovations in database design, Web applications, and information systems management* (pp. 72–106). Hershey, PA: Information Science Reference.

Poels, G., Decreus, K., Roelens, B., & Snoeck, M. (2013). Investigating goal-oriented requirements engineering for business processes. *Journal of Database Management, 24*(2), 35–71. doi:10.4018/jdm.2013040103

Pomares-Quimbaya, A., & Torres-Moreno, M. E. (2013). Knowledge management processes supported by ontology technologies. In M. Nazir Ahmad, R. Colomb, & M. Abdullah (Eds.), *Ontology-based applications for enterprise systems and knowledge management* (pp. 125–140). Hershey, PA: Information Science Reference.

Ponis, S. T., Vagenas, G., & Koronis, E. (2010). Exploring the knowledge management landscape: A critical review of existing knowledge management frameworks. In D. Harorimana (Ed.), *Cultural implications of knowledge sharing, management and transfer: Identifying competitive advantage* (pp. 1–25). Hershey, PA: Information Science Reference. doi:10.4018/978-1-61520-965-1.ch103

Powers, S. M., & Salmon, C. (2010). Management of learning space. In D. Wu (Ed.), *Temporal structures in individual time management: Practices to enhance calendar tool design* (pp. 210–219). Hershey, PA: Business Science Reference.

Pretorius, A. B., & Coetzee, F. P. (2011). Model of a knowledge management support system for choosing intellectual capital assessment methods. In B. Vallejo-Alonso, A. Rodriguez-Castellanos, & G. Arregui-Ayastuy (Eds.), *Identifying, measuring, and valuing knowledge-based intangible assets: New perspectives* (pp. 336–359). Hershey, PA: Business Science Reference. doi:10.4018/978-1-60960-783-8.ch222

Pullinger, D. (2011). Mobilizing knowledge in the UK public sector: Current issues and discourse. In G. Morais da Costa (Ed.), *Ethical issues and social dilemmas in knowledge management: Organizational innovation* (pp. 232–249). Hershey, PA: Information Science Reference. doi:10.4018/978-1-60960-783-8.ch322

Rabaey, M. (2013). Complex adaptive systems thinking approach for intelligence base in support of intellectual capital management. In P. Ordóñez de Pablos, R. Tennyson, & J. Zhao (Eds.), *Intellectual capital strategy management for knowledge-based organizations* (pp. 122–141). Hershey, PA: Business Science Reference. doi:10.4018/978-1-4666-3655-2.ch007

Rabaey, M., & Mercken, R. (2013). Framework of knowledge and intelligence base: From intelligence to service. In I. Association (Ed.), *Data mining: Concepts, methodologies, tools, and applications* (pp. 474–502). Hershey, PA: Information Science Reference.

Radziwill, N. M., & DuPlain, R. F. (2010). Quality and continuous improvement in knowledge management. In M. Russ (Ed.), *Knowledge management strategies for business development* (pp. 353–363). Hershey, PA: Business Science Reference.

Rahman, B. A., Saad, N. M., & Harun, M. S. (2010). Knowledge management orientation and business performance: The Malaysian manufacturing and service industries perspective. In K. Metaxiotis, F. Carrillo, & T. Yigitcanlar (Eds.), *Knowledge-based development for cities and societies: Integrated multi-level approaches* (pp. 315–328). Hershey, PA: Information Science Reference. doi:10.4018/978-1-61520-721-3.ch019

Randles, T. J., Blades, C. D., & Fadlalla, A. (2012). The knowledge spectrum. *International Journal of Knowledge Management*, *8*(2), 65–78. doi:10.4018/jkm.2012040104

Real, J. C., Leal, A., & Roldan, J. L. (2011). Measuring organizational learning as a multidimensional construct. In D. Schwartz, & D. Te'eni (Eds.), *Encyclopedia of knowledge management* (2nd ed., pp. 1101–1109). Hershey, PA: Information Science Reference.

Rech, J., & Bogner, C. (2010). Qualitative analysis of semantically enabled knowledge management systems in agile software engineering. *International Journal of Knowledge Management*, *6*(2), 66–85. doi:10.4018/jkm.2010040104

Rech, J., & Bogner, C. (2012). Qualitative analysis of semantically enabled knowledge management systems in agile software engineering. In M. Jennex (Ed.), *Conceptual models and outcomes of advancing knowledge management: New technologies* (pp. 144–164). Hershey, PA: Information Science Reference. doi:10.4018/978-1-4666-0035-5.ch008

Reis, R. S., & Curzi, Y. (2011). Knowledge integration in the creative process of globally distributed teams. In M. Al-Shammari (Ed.), *Knowledge management in emerging economies: Social, organizational and cultural implementation* (pp. 47–65). Hershey, PA: Information Science Reference.

Remli, M. A., & Deris, S. (2013). An approach for biological data integration and knowledge retrieval based on ontology, Semantic Web services composition, and AI planning. In M. Nazir Ahmad, R. Colomb, & M. Abdullah (Eds.), *Ontology-based applications for enterprise systems and knowledge management* (pp. 324–342). Hershey, PA: Information Science Reference.

Reychav, I., Stein, E. W., Weisberg, J., & Glezer, C. (2012). the role of knowledge sharing in raising the task innovativeness of systems analysts. *International Journal of Knowledge Management*, *8*(2), 1–22. doi:10.4018/jkm.2012040101

Reychav, I., & Weisberg, J. (2011). Human capital in knowledge creation, management, and utilization. In D. Schwartz, & D. Te'eni (Eds.), *Encyclopedia of knowledge management* (2nd ed., pp. 389–401). Hershey, PA: Information Science Reference.

Rhoads, E., O'Sullivan, K. J., & Stankosky, M. (2011). An evaluation of factors that influence the success of knowledge management practices in US federal agencies. In M. Jennex, & S. Smolnik (Eds.), *Strategies for knowledge management success: Exploring organizational efficacy* (pp. 74–90). Hershey, PA: Information Science Reference. doi:10.4018/978-1-60960-783-8.ch410

Ribière, V. M. (2011). The effect of organizational trust on the success of codification and personalization KM approaches. In M. Jennex, & S. Smolnik (Eds.), *Strategies for knowledge management success: Exploring organizational efficacy* (pp. 192–212). Hershey, PA: Information Science Reference. doi:10.4018/978-1-60960-783-8.ch516

Ribière, V. M., & Román, J. A. (2011). Knowledge flow. In D. Schwartz, & D. Te'eni (Eds.), *Encyclopedia of knowledge management* (2nd ed., pp. 549–559). Hershey, PA: Information Science Reference.

Ricceri, F., Guthrie, J., & Coyte, R. (2010). The management of knowledge resources within private organisations: Some European better practice illustrations. In E. O'Brien, S. Clifford, & M. Southern (Eds.), *Knowledge management for process, organizational and marketing innovation: Tools and methods* (pp. 36–61). Hershey, PA: Information Science Reference. doi:10.4018/978-1-61520-829-6.ch003

Riss, U. V. (2011). Pattern-based task management as means of organizational knowledge maturing. *International Journal of Knowledge-Based Organizations*, *1*(1), 20–41. doi:10.4018/ijkbo.2011010102

Riss, U. V. (2013). Pattern-based task management as means of organizational knowledge maturing. In J. Wang (Ed.), *Intelligence Methods and Systems Advancements for Knowledge-Based Business* (pp. 1–23). Hershey, PA: Information Science Reference.

Roos, G. (2013). The role of intellectual capital in business model innovation: An empirical study. In P. Ordóñez de Pablos, R. Tennyson, & J. Zhao (Eds.), *Intellectual capital strategy management for knowledge-based organizations* (pp. 76–121). Hershey, PA: Business Science Reference. doi:10.4018/978-1-4666-3655-2.ch006

Rothberg, H. N., & Klingenberg, B. (2010). Learning before doing: A theoretical perspective and practical lessons from a failed cross-border knowledge transfer initiative. In D. Harorimana (Ed.), *Cultural implications of knowledge sharing, management and transfer: Identifying competitive advantage* (pp. 277–294). Hershey, PA: Information Science Reference.

Ruano-Mayoral, M., Colomo-Palacios, R., García-Crespo, Á., & Gómez-Berbís, J. M. (2012). Software project managers under the team software process: A study of competences based on literature. In J. Wang (Ed.), *Project management techniques and innovations in information technology* (pp. 115–126). Hershey, PA: Information Science Reference. doi:10.4018/978-1-4666-0930-3.ch007

Russell, S. (2010). Knowledge management and project management in 3D: A virtual world extension. In E. O'Brien, S. Clifford, & M. Southern (Eds.), *Knowledge management for process, organizational and marketing innovation: Tools and methods* (pp. 62–78). Hershey, PA: Information Science Reference. doi:10.4018/978-1-61520-829-6.ch004

Ryan, G., & Shinnick, E. (2011). Knowledge and intellectual property rights: An economics perspective. In D. Schwartz, & D. Te'eni (Eds.), *Encyclopedia of knowledge management* (2nd ed., pp. 489–496). Hershey, PA: Information Science Reference.

Sabetzadeh, F., & Tsui, E. (2013). Delivering knowledge services in the cloud. In G. Yang (Ed.), *Multidisciplinary studies in knowledge and systems science* (pp. 247–254). Hershey, PA: Information Science Reference.

Sáenz, J., & Aramburu, N. (2011). Organizational conditions as catalysts for successful people-focused knowledge sharing initiatives: An empirical study. *International Journal of Knowledge-Based Organizations, 1*(2), 39–56. doi:10.4018/ijkbo.2011040103

Sáenz, J., & Aramburu, N. (2013). Organizational conditions as catalysts for successful people-focused knowledge sharing initiatives: An empirical study. In J. Wang (Ed.), *Intelligence methods and systems advancements for knowledge-based business* (pp. 263–280). Hershey, PA: Information Science Reference.

Sakr, S., & Al-Naymat, G. (2011). Relational techniques for storing and querying RDF data: An overview. In L. Yan, & Z. Ma (Eds.), *Advanced database query systems: Techniques, applications and technologies* (pp. 269–285). Hershey, PA: Information Science Reference. doi:10.4018/978-1-60960-475-2.ch011

Salem, P. J. (2013). The use of mixed methods in organizational communication research. In M. Bocarnea, R. Reynolds, & J. Baker (Eds.), *Online instruments, data collection, and electronic measurements: Organizational advancements* (pp. 24–39). Hershey, PA: Information Science Reference.

Salisbury, M. (2011). A framework for managing the life cycle of knowledge in global organizations. In M. Jennex (Ed.), *Global aspects and cultural perspectives on knowledge management: Emerging dimensions* (pp. 64–80). Hershey, PA: Information Science Reference. doi:10.4018/978-1-60960-555-1.ch005

Salleh, K. (2014). Drivers, benefits, and challenges of knowledge management in electronic government: Preliminary examination. In Y. Al-Bastaki, & A. Shajera (Eds.), *Building a competitive public sector with knowledge management strategy* (pp. 135–150). Hershey, PA: Business Science Reference.

Salleh, K., Ikhsan, S. O., & Ahmad, S. N. (2011). Knowledge management enablers and knowledge sharing process: A case study of public sector accounting organization in Malaysia. In M. Al-Shammari (Ed.), *Knowledge management in emerging economies: Social, organizational and cultural implementation* (pp. 199–211). Hershey, PA: Information Science Reference.

Saunders, C. (2011). Knowledge sharing in legal practice. In D. Schwartz, & D. Te'eni (Eds.), *Encyclopedia of knowledge management* (2nd ed., pp. 935–945). Hershey, PA: Information Science Reference.

Scarso, E., & Bolisani, E. (2011). Knowledge intermediation. In D. Schwartz, & D. Te'eni (Eds.), *Encyclopedia of knowledge management* (2nd ed., pp. 601–611). Hershey, PA: Information Science Reference.

Scarso, E., & Bolisani, E. (2011). Managing professions for knowledge management. *International Journal of Knowledge Management*, *7*(3), 61–75. doi:10.4018/jkm.2011070105

Scarso, E., & Bolisani, E. (2013). Managing professions for knowledge management. In M. Jennex (Ed.), *Dynamic models for knowledge-driven organizations* (pp. 238–253). Hershey, PA: Business Science Reference.

Scarso, E., Bolisani, E., & Padova, A. (2011). The complex issue of measuring KM performance: Lessons from the practice. In B. Vallejo-Alonso, A. Rodriguez-Castellanos, & G. Arregui-Ayastuy (Eds.), *Identifying, measuring, and valuing knowledge-based intangible assets: New perspectives* (pp. 208–230). Hershey, PA: Business Science Reference.

Schumann, C., & Tittmann, C. (2010). Potentials for externalizing and measuring of tacit knowledge within knowledge nodes in the context of knowledge networks. In D. Harorimana (Ed.), *Cultural implications of knowledge sharing, management and transfer: Identifying competitive advantage* (pp. 84–107). Hershey, PA: Information Science Reference.

Schwartz, D. (2011). An Aristotelian view of knowledge for knowledge management. In D. Schwartz, & D. Te'eni (Eds.), *Encyclopedia of knowledge management* (2nd ed., pp. 39–48). Hershey, PA: Information Science Reference.

Senaratne, S., & Victoria, M. F. (2014). Building a supportive culture for sustained organisational learning in public sectors. In Y. Al-Bastaki, & A. Shajera (Eds.), *Building a competitive public sector with knowledge management strategy* (pp. 118–134). Hershey, PA: Business Science Reference.

Shah, A., Singhera, Z., & Ahsan, S. (2011). Web services for bioinformatics. In M. Al-Mutairi, & L. Mohammed (Eds.), *Cases on ICT utilization, practice and solutions: Tools for managing day-to-day issues* (pp. 28–46). Hershey, PA: Information Science Reference.

Shajera, A., & Al-Bastaki, Y. (2014). Organisational readiness for knowledge management: Bahrain public sector case study. In Y. Al-Bastaki, & A. Shajera (Eds.), *Building a competitive public sector with knowledge management strategy* (pp. 104–117). Hershey, PA: Business Science Reference.

Sharma, A. K., Goswami, A., & Gupta, D. (2011). An extended relational model & SQL for fuzzy multidatabases. In L. Yan, & Z. Ma (Eds.), *Advanced database query systems: Techniques, applications and technologies* (pp. 185–219). Hershey, PA: Information Science Reference. doi:10.4018/978-1-60960-475-2.ch008

Sharma, R., Banati, H., & Bedi, P. (2012). Building socially-aware e-learning systems through knowledge management. *International Journal of Knowledge Management*, *8*(3), 1–26. doi:10.4018/jkm.2012070101

Sharma, R. S., Chandrasekar, G., & Vaitheeswaran, B. (2012). A knowledge framework for development: Empirical investigation of 30 societies. In M. Jennex (Ed.), *Conceptual models and outcomes of advancing knowledge management: New technologies* (pp. 244–265). Hershey, PA: Information Science Reference. doi:10.4018/978-1-4666-0035-5.ch013

Shaw, D. (2011). Mapping group knowledge. In D. Schwartz, & D. Te'eni (Eds.), *Encyclopedia of knowledge management* (2nd ed., pp. 1072–1081). Hershey, PA: Information Science Reference.

Sheluhin, O. I., & Atayero, A. A. (2013). Principles of modeling in information communication systems and networks. In A. Atayero, & O. Sheluhin (Eds.), *Integrated models for information communication systems and networks: Design and development* (pp. 1–15). Hershey, PA: Information Science Reference. doi:10.4018/978-1-4666-2208-1.ch001

Sheluhin, O. I., & Garmashev, A. V. (2013). Numerical methods of multifractal analysis in information communication systems and networks. In A. Atayero, & O. Sheluhin (Eds.), *Integrated models for information communication systems and networks: Design and development* (pp. 16–46). Hershey, PA: Information Science Reference. doi:10.4018/978-1-4666-2208-1.ch002

Siau, K., Long, Y., & Ling, M. (2010). Toward a unified model of information systems development success. *Journal of Database Management*, *21*(1), 80–101. doi:10.4018/jdm.2010112304

Siau, K., Long, Y., & Ling, M. (2012). Toward a Unified model of information systems development success. In K. Siau (Ed.), *Cross-disciplinary models and applications of database management: Advancing approaches* (pp. 80–102). Hershey, PA: Information Science Reference.

Simard, A. J., & Jourdeuil, P. (2014). Knowledge manageability: A new paradigm. In Y. Al-Bastaki, & A. Shajera (Eds.), *Building a competitive public sector with knowledge management strategy* (pp. 1–52). Hershey, PA: Business Science Reference.

Simonette, M. J., & Spina, E. (2014). Enabling IT innovation through soft systems engineering. In M. Pańkowska (Ed.), *Frameworks of IT prosumption for business development* (pp. 64–72). Hershey, PA: Business Science Reference.

Sivaramakrishnan, S., Delbaere, M., Zhang, D., & Bruning, E. (2012). Critical success factors and outcomes of market knowledge management: A conceptual model and empirical evidence. In M. Jennex (Ed.), *Conceptual models and outcomes of advancing knowledge management: New technologies* (pp. 165–185). Hershey, PA: Information Science Reference. doi:10.4018/978-1-4666-0035-5.ch009

Small, C. T., & Sage, A. P. (2010). A complex adaptive systems-based enterprise knowledge sharing model. In D. Paradice (Ed.), *Emerging systems approaches in information technologies: Concepts, theories, and applications* (pp. 137–155). Hershey, PA: Information Science Reference. doi:10.4018/978-1-61520-965-1.ch321

Smedlund, A. (2011). Social network structures for explicit, tacit and potential knowledge. In M. Jennex (Ed.), *Global aspects and cultural perspectives on knowledge management: Emerging dimensions* (pp. 81–90). Hershey, PA: Information Science Reference. doi:10.4018/978-1-60960-555-1.ch006

Smith, A. D. (2013). Competitive uses of information and knowledge management tools: Case study of supplier-side management. *International Journal of Knowledge-Based Organizations*, *3*(1), 71–87. doi:10.4018/ijkbo.2013010105

Smith, P., & Coakes, E. (2011). Exploiting KM in support of innovation and change. In A. Eardley, & L. Uden (Eds.), *Innovative knowledge management: Concepts for organizational creativity and collaborative design* (pp. 242–252). Hershey, PA: Information Science Reference. doi:10.4018/978-1-60960-783-8.ch112

Smith, T. A., Mills, A. M., & Dion, P. (2010). Linking business strategy and knowledge management capabilities for organizational effectiveness. *International Journal of Knowledge Management*, *6*(3), 22–43. doi:10.4018/jkm.2010070102

Smith, T. A., Mills, A. M., & Dion, P. (2012). Linking business strategy and knowledge management capabilities for organizational effectiveness. In M. Jennex (Ed.), *Conceptual models and outcomes of advancing knowledge management: new technologies* (pp. 186–207). Hershey, PA: Information Science Reference. doi:10.4018/978-1-4666-0035-5.ch010

Smuts, H., van der Merwe, A., & Loock, M. (2011). Key characteristics relevant for selecting knowledge management software tools. In A. Eardley, & L. Uden (Eds.), *Innovative knowledge management: Concepts for organizational creativity and collaborative design* (pp. 18–39). Hershey, PA: Information Science Reference. doi:10.4018/978-1-60960-783-8.ch214

Soffer, P., & Kaner, M. (2013). Complementing business process verification by validity analysis: A theoretical and empirical evaluation. In K. Siau (Ed.), *Innovations in database design, Web applications, and information systems management* (pp. 265–288). Hershey, PA: Information Science Reference.

Soffer, P., Kaner, M., & Wand, Y. (2012). Assigning ontological meaning to workflow nets. In K. Siau (Ed.), *Cross-disciplinary models and applications of database management: Advancing approaches* (pp. 209–244). Hershey, PA: Information Science Reference.

Sohrabi, B., Raeesi, I., & Khanlari, A. (2010). Intellectual capital components, measurement and management: A literature survey of concepts and measures. In P. López Sáez, G. Castro, J. Navas López, & M. Delgado Verde (Eds.), *Intellectual capital and technological innovation: Knowledge-based theory and practice* (pp. 1–38). Hershey, PA: Information Science Reference. doi:10.4018/978-1-61520-875-3.ch001

Sohrabi, B., Raeesi, I., Khanlari, A., & Forouzandeh, S. (2011). A comprehensive model for assessing the organizational readiness of knowledge management. In M. Jennex (Ed.), *Global aspects and cultural perspectives on knowledge management: Emerging dimensions* (pp. 30–48). Hershey, PA: Information Science Reference. doi:10.4018/978-1-60960-555-1.ch003

Sparrow, J. (2011). Knowledge management in small and medium sized enterprises. In D. Schwartz, & D. Te'eni (Eds.), *Encyclopedia of knowledge management* (2nd ed., pp. 671–681). Hershey, PA: Information Science Reference.

Stam, C. D. (2011). Making sense of knowledge productivity. In B. Vallejo-Alonso, A. Rodriguez-Castellanos, & G. Arregui-Ayastuy (Eds.), *Identifying, measuring, and valuing knowledge-based intangible assets: New perspectives* (pp. 133–155). Hershey, PA: Business Science Reference.

Stamkopoulos, K., Pitoura, E., Vassiliadis, P., & Zarras, A. (2012). Accelerating Web service workflow execution via intelligent allocation of services to servers. In K. Siau (Ed.), *Cross-disciplinary models and applications of database management: Advancing approaches* (pp. 385–416). Hershey, PA: Information Science Reference.

Sterling, L. (2011). Applying agents within knowledge management. In D. Schwartz, & D. Te'eni (Eds.), *Encyclopedia of knowledge management* (2nd ed., pp. 12–19). Hershey, PA: Information Science Reference.

Su, S., & Chiong, R. (2011). Business intelligence. In D. Schwartz, & D. Te'eni (Eds.), *Encyclopedia of knowledge management* (2nd ed., pp. 72–80). Hershey, PA: Information Science Reference.

Su, W. B., Li, X., & Chow, C. W. (2012). Exploring the extent and impediments of knowledge sharing in Chinese business enterprise. In M. Jennex (Ed.), *Conceptual models and outcomes of advancing knowledge management: New technologies* (pp. 266–290). Hershey, PA: Information Science Reference. doi:10.4018/978-1-4666-0035-5.ch014

Subramanian, D. V., & Geetha, A. (2012). Application of multi-dimensional metric model, database, and WAM for KM system evaluation. *International Journal of Knowledge Management, 8*(4), 1–21. doi:10.4018/jkm.2012100101

Surendran, A., & Samuel, P. (2013). Knowledge-based code clone approach in embedded and real-time systems. In S. Saeed, & I. Alsmadi (Eds.), *Knowledge-based processes in software development* (pp. 49–62). Hershey, PA: Information Science Reference. doi:10.4018/978-1-4666-4229-4.ch004

Takahashi, Y. (2011). The importance of balancing knowledge protection and knowledge interchange. In G. Morais da Costa (Ed.), *ethical issues and social dilemmas in knowledge management: Organizational innovation* (pp. 180–198). Hershey, PA: Information Science Reference.

Talet, A. N., Alhawari, S., & Alryalat, H. (2012). The outcome of knowledge process for customers of Jordanian companies on the achievement of customer knowledge retention. In M. Jennex (Ed.), *Conceptual models and outcomes of advancing knowledge management: New technologies* (pp. 45–61). Hershey, PA: Information Science Reference. doi:10.4018/978-1-4666-0035-5.ch003

Talet, A. N., Alhawari, S., Mansour, E., & Alryalat, H. (2011). The practice of Jordanian business to attain customer knowledge acquisition. *International Journal of Knowledge Management, 7*(2), 49–67. doi:10.4018/jkm.2011040103

Tanner, K. (2011). The role of emotional capital in organisational KM. In D. Schwartz, & D. Te'eni (Eds.), *Encyclopedia of knowledge management* (2nd ed., pp. 1396–1409). Hershey, PA: Information Science Reference. doi:10.4018/978-1-60960-783-8.ch720

Tauber, D., & Schwartz, D. G. (2011). Integrating knowledge management with the systems analysis process. In D. Schwartz, & D. Te'eni (Eds.), *Encyclopedia of knowledge management* (2nd ed., pp. 431–441). Hershey, PA: Information Science Reference.

Tavana, M., Busch, T. E., & Davis, E. L. (2011). Modeling operational robustness and resiliency with high-level petri nets. *International Journal of Knowledge-Based Organizations*, *1*(2), 17–38. doi:10.4018/ijkbo.2011040102

Taxén, L. (2010). Aligning business and knowledge strategies: A practical approach for aligning business and knowledge strategies. In M. Russ (Ed.), *Knowledge management strategies for business development* (pp. 277–308). Hershey, PA: Business Science Reference.

Te'eni, D. (2011). Knowledge for communicating knowledge. In D. Schwartz, & D. Te'eni (Eds.), *Encyclopedia of knowledge management* (2nd ed., pp. 560–569). Hershey, PA: Information Science Reference.

Toiviainen, H., & Kerosuo, H. (2013). Development curriculum for knowledge-based organizations: Lessons from a learning network. *International Journal of Knowledge-Based Organizations*, *3*(3), 1–18. doi:10.4018/ijkbo.2013070101

Tran, B. (2014). The human element of the knowledge worker: Identifying, managing, and protecting the intellectual capital within knowledge management. In M. Chilton, & J. Bloodgood (Eds.), *Knowledge management and competitive advantage: Issues and potential solutions* (pp. 281–303). Hershey, PA: Information Science Reference.

Tsamoura, E., Gounaris, A., & Manolopoulos, Y. (2011). Optimal service ordering in decentralized queries over Web services. *International Journal of Knowledge-Based Organizations*, *1*(2), 1–16. doi:10.4018/ijkbo.2011040101

Tsamoura, E., Gounaris, A., & Manolopoulos, Y. (2013). Optimal service ordering in decentralized queries over Web services. In J. Wang (Ed.), *Intelligence methods and systems advancements for knowledge-based business* (pp. 43–58). Hershey, PA: Information Science Reference.

Tull, J. (2013). Slow knowledge: The case for savouring learning and innovation. In S. Buckley, & M. Jakovljevic (Eds.), *Knowledge management innovations for interdisciplinary education: Organizational applications* (pp. 274–297). Hershey, PA: Information Science Reference.

Turner, G., & Minonne, C. (2013). Effective knowledge management through measurement. In S. Buckley, & M. Jakovljevic (Eds.), *Knowledge management innovations for interdisciplinary education: Organizational applications* (pp. 145–176). Hershey, PA: Information Science Reference.

Uden, L., & Eardley, A. (2011). Knowledge sharing in the learning process: Experience with problem-based learning. In A. Eardley, & L. Uden (Eds.), *Innovative knowledge management: Concepts for organizational creativity and collaborative design* (pp. 215–229). Hershey, PA: Information Science Reference.

Upadhyaya, S., Rao, H. R., & Padmanabhan, G. (2011). Secure knowledge management. In D. Schwartz, & D. Te'eni (Eds.), *Encyclopedia of knowledge management* (2nd ed., pp. 1429–1437). Hershey, PA: Information Science Reference.

Urbancová, H., & Königová, M. (2013). The influence of the application of business continuity management, knowledge management, and knowledge continuity management on the innovation in organizations. In S. Buckley, & M. Jakovljevic (Eds.), *knowledge management innovations for interdisciplinary education: Organizational applications* (pp. 254–273). Hershey, PA: Information Science Reference.

Van Canh, T., & Zyngier, S. (2014). Using ERG theory as a lens to understand the sharing of academic tacit knowledge: Problems and issues in developing countries – Perspectives from Vietnam. In M. Chilton, & J. Bloodgood (Eds.), *Knowledge management and competitive advantage: Issues and potential solutions* (pp. 174–201). Hershey, PA: Information Science Reference.

Vat, K. H. (2011). Knowledge synthesis framework. In D. Schwartz, & D. Te'eni (Eds.), *Encyclopedia of knowledge management* (2nd ed., pp. 955–966). Hershey, PA: Information Science Reference.

Vert, S. (2012). Extensions of Web browsers useful to knowledge workers. In C. Jouis, I. Biskri, J. Ganascia, & M. Roux (Eds.), *Next generation search engines: Advanced models for information retrieval* (pp. 239–273). Hershey, PA: Information Science Reference. doi:10.4018/978-1-4666-0330-1.ch011

Wagner, L., & Van Belle, J. (2011). Web mining for strategic competitive intelligence: South African experiences and a practical methodology. In M. Al-Shammari (Ed.), *Knowledge management in emerging economies: Social, organizational and cultural implementation* (pp. 1–19). Hershey, PA: Information Science Reference.

Wautelet, Y., Schinckus, C., & Kolp, M. (2010). Towards knowledge evolution in software engineering: An epistemological approach. *International Journal of Information Technologies and Systems Approach*, *3*(1), 21–40. doi:10.4018/jitsa.2010100202

Weiß, S., Makolm, J., Ipsmiller, D., & Egger, N. (2011). DYONIPOS: Proactive knowledge supply. In M. Jennex, & S. Smolnik (Eds.), *Strategies for knowledge management success: Exploring organizational efficacy* (pp. 277–287). Hershey, PA: Information Science Reference.

Welschen, J., Todorova, N., & Mills, A. M. (2012). An investigation of the impact of intrinsic motivation on organizational knowledge sharing. *International Journal of Knowledge Management*, *8*(2), 23–42. doi:10.4018/jkm.2012040102

Wickramasinghe, N. (2011). Knowledge creation. In D. Schwartz, & D. Te'eni (Eds.), *Encyclopedia of knowledge management* (2nd ed., pp. 527–538). Hershey, PA: Information Science Reference.

Wickramasinghe, N. (2011). Knowledge management: The key to delivering superior healthcare solutions. In A. Eardley, & L. Uden (Eds.), *Innovative knowledge management: Concepts for organizational creativity and collaborative design* (pp. 190–203). Hershey, PA: Information Science Reference.

Wijnhoven, F. (2011). Operational knowledge management. In D. Schwartz, & D. Te'eni (Eds.), *Encyclopedia of knowledge management* (2nd ed., pp. 1237–1249). Hershey, PA: Information Science Reference.

Williams, R. (2011). A knowledge process cycle. In D. Schwartz, & D. Te'eni (Eds.), *Encyclopedia of knowledge management* (2nd ed., pp. 853–866). Hershey, PA: Information Science Reference.

Wilson, R. L., Rosen, P. A., & Al-Ahmadi, M. S. (2011). Knowledge structure and data mining techniques. In D. Schwartz, & D. Te'eni (Eds.), *Encyclopedia of knowledge management* (2nd ed., pp. 946–954). Hershey, PA: Information Science Reference.

Wimmer, H., Yoon, V., & Rada, R. (2013). Integrating knowledge sources: An ontological approach. *International Journal of Knowledge Management*, *9*(1), 60–75. doi:10.4018/jkm.2013010104

Woods, S., Poteet, S. R., Kao, A., & Quach, L. (2011). Knowledge dissemination in portals. In D. Schwartz, & D. Te'eni (Eds.), *Encyclopedia of knowledge management* (2nd ed., pp. 539–548). Hershey, PA: Information Science Reference.

Worden, D. (2010). Agile alignment of enterprise execution capabilities with strategy. In M. Russ (Ed.), *Knowledge management strategies for business development* (pp. 45–62). Hershey, PA: Business Science Reference.

Wu, D. (2010). Who are effective time managers? Bivariate correlation analysis and hypotheses testing. In D. Wu (Ed.), *Temporal structures in individual time management: Practices to enhance calendar tool design* (pp. 116–138). Hershey, PA: Business Science Reference.

Wu, J., Du, H., Li, X., & Li, P. (2010). Creating and delivering a successful knowledge management strategy. In M. Russ (Ed.), *Knowledge management strategies for business development* (pp. 261–276). Hershey, PA: Business Science Reference.

Wu, J., Liu, N., & Xuan, Z. (2013). Simulation on knowledge transfer processes from the perspectives of individual's mentality and behavior. In G. Yang (Ed.), *Multidisciplinary studies in knowledge and systems science* (pp. 233–246). Hershey, PA: Information Science Reference.

Wu, J., Wang, S., & Pan, D. (2013). Evaluation of technological influence power of enterprises through the enterprise citation network. In G. Yang (Ed.), *Multidisciplinary studies in knowledge and systems science* (pp. 34–44). Hershey, PA: Information Science Reference.

Wu, S. T. (2011). Innovation in new technology and knowledge management: Comparative case studies of its evolution during a quarter century of change. In A. Eardley, & L. Uden (Eds.), *Innovative knowledge management: Concepts for organizational creativity and collaborative design* (pp. 77–93). Hershey, PA: Information Science Reference. doi:10.4018/978-1-60960-783-8.ch803

Xiao, L., & Pei, Y. (2013). A task context aware physical distribution knowledge service system. In G. Yang (Ed.), *Multidisciplinary studies in knowledge and systems science* (pp. 18–33). Hershey, PA: Information Science Reference.

Xu, D., & Wang, H. (2011). Integration of knowledge management and e-learning. In D. Schwartz, & D. Te'eni (Eds.), *Encyclopedia of knowledge management* (2nd ed., pp. 442–451). Hershey, PA: Information Science Reference.

Yaniv, E., & Schwartz, D. G. (2011). Organizational attention. In D. Schwartz, & D. Te'eni (Eds.), *Encyclopedia of knowledge management* (2nd ed., pp. 1270–1279). Hershey, PA: Information Science Reference.

Yeung, C. L., Cheung, C. F., Wang, W. M., & Tsui, E. (2013). A study of organizational narrative simulation for decision support. In G. Yang (Ed.), *Multidisciplinary studies in knowledge and systems science* (pp. 179–192). Hershey, PA: Information Science Reference. doi:10.4018/978-1-4666-3998-0.ch013

Yigitcanlar, T. (2013). Moving towards a knowledge city?: Brisbane's experience in knowledge-based urban development. In J. Wang (Ed.), *Intelligence methods and systems advancements for knowledge-based business* (pp. 114–131). Hershey, PA: Information Science Reference.

Yigitcanlar, T., & Martinez-Fernandez, C. (2010). Making space and place for knowledge production: Socio-spatial development of knowledge community precincts. In K. Metaxiotis, F. Carrillo, & T. Yigitcanlar (Eds.), *Knowledge-based development for cities and societies: integrated multi-level approaches* (pp. 99–117). Hershey, PA: Information Science Reference. doi:10.4018/978-1-61520-721-3.ch006

Yıldırım, A. A., Özdoğan, C., & Watson, D. (2014). Parallel data reduction techniques for big datasets. In W. Hu, & N. Kaabouch (Eds.), *Big data management, technologies, and applications* (pp. 72–93). Hershey, PA: Information Science Reference.

Yoon, K. S. (2012). Measuring the influence of expertise and epistemic engagement to the practice of knowledge management. *International Journal of Knowledge Management, 8*(1), 40–70. doi:10.4018/jkm.2012010103

Yusof, Z. M., & Ismail, M. B. (2011). Factors affecting knowledge sharing practice in Malaysia: A preliminary overview. In M. Al-Shammari (Ed.), *Knowledge management in emerging economies: Social, organizational and cultural implementation* (pp. 157–170). Hershey, PA: Information Science Reference. doi:10.4018/978-1-60960-783-8.ch416

Zapata-Cantú, L., Ramírez, J., & Pineda, J. L. (2011). HRM adaptation to knowledge management initiatives: Three Mexican cases. In M. Al-Shammari (Ed.), *Knowledge management in emerging economies: Social, organizational and cultural implementation* (pp. 273–293). Hershey, PA: Information Science Reference.

Zarri, G. P. (2011). Knowledge representation. In D. Schwartz, & D. Te'eni (Eds.), *Encyclopedia of knowledge management* (2nd ed., pp. 878–892). Hershey, PA: Information Science Reference.

Zarri, G. P. (2011). RDF and OWL for knowledge management. In D. Schwartz, & D. Te'eni (Eds.), *Encyclopedia of knowledge management* (2nd ed., pp. 1355–1373). Hershey, PA: Information Science Reference.

Zhang, Y., Wang, Y., Colucci, W., & Wang, Z. (2013). The paradigm shift in organizational research. In J. Wang (Ed.), *Intelligence methods and systems advancements for knowledge-based business* (pp. 60–74). Hershey, PA: Information Science Reference.

Zhang, Z. J. (2011). Managing customer knowledge with social software. In D. Schwartz, & D. Te'eni (Eds.), *Encyclopedia of knowledge management* (2nd ed., pp. 1046–1053). Hershey, PA: Information Science Reference.

Zyngier, S. (2011). Governance of knowledge management. In D. Schwartz, & D. Te'eni (Eds.), *Encyclopedia of knowledge management* (2nd ed., pp. 354–365). Hershey, PA: Information Science Reference.

Zyngier, S. (2011). Knowledge management: Realizing value through governance. *International Journal of Knowledge Management, 7*(1), 35–54. doi:10.4018/jkm.2011010103

Zyngier, S. (2013). Knowledge management: Realizing value through governance. In M. Jennex (Ed.), *Dynamic models for knowledge-driven organizations* (pp. 36–55). Hershey, PA: Business Science Reference.

Compilation of References

791. *Linked Data in Libraries: Course Blog for SOIS UWM course 791: Linked Data in Libraries: Library Mashups, the Semantic Web and Web 2.0: Yahoo Pipes.* (2011). Retrieved from http://791linkeddata.blogspot.com/2011/03/yahoo-pipes.html

Abuja, G., & Carley, K. M. (2003). Individual centrality and performance in virtual R&D groups: An empirical study. *Management Science*, *49*(1), 21–38. doi:10.1287/mnsc.49.1.21.12756

Acherman, E. (2013). Google gets in your face. *Spectrum IEEE, January*, 26-29.

Adobe Influxis. (2013). *Influxis collaboration service.* Retrieved July 03, 2013, from http://www.adobe.com/devnet/livecycle/collaboration.html

Adobe LCCS Developer. (2013). *Adobe LCCS Developer.* Retrieved July 03, 2013, from https://learn.adobe.com/wiki/display/lccs/LiveCycle+Collaboration+Service

Adobe. (2009). *Building toward a unified communications strategy.* Retrieved August 25, 2010, from http://www.adobe.com/products/acrobatconnectpro/webconferencing/pdfs/connectpro_unifiedcommwhitepaper_1_09.pdf

Adobe. (2013). *Adobe extensions.* Retrieved June 28, 2013, from http://www.adobe.com/ie/products/adobeconnect/extend.html

ALA. (2012). Publishers talk ebooks. *American Libraries*, *43*(11-12), 10.

Al-Akiti, A. (2004). The three properties of prophethood in certain works of Avicenna and al-Ghazali. In J. McGinnis & D.C. Reisman, (Eds.), *Interpreting Avicenna: Science and philosophy in medieval Islam—Proceedings of the 2nd Conference of the Avicenna Study Group* (Islamic philosophy, theology and science: Texts and studies).
Aristotle. (350 BCE). *Poetics.* (S. H. Butcher, Trans.). Retrieved March 31, 2011 from http://classics.mit.edu/Aristotle/poetics.html

Alexander, C. (1979). *The timeless way of building.* Oxford, UK: Oxford University Press.

Alvesson, M. (2004). *Knowledge work and knowledge-intensive firms.* Oxford, UK: Oxford University Press.

Amazon. (2013). Reading on Kindle Fire HD 7”. Retrieved from http://www.amazon.com/gp/help/customer/display.html?nodeId=201009460

Ang, K. H., & Wang, Q. (2006, December). A case study of engaging primary school students in learning science by using Active Worlds. In *Proceedings of the First International LAMS Conference* (pp. 5-14).

Anick, P., & Bergler, S. (1992). Lexical structures for linguistic inference. In J. Pustejovsky, & S. Bergler (Eds.), *Lexical semantics and knowledge representation.* Berlin: Springer Verlag. doi:10.1007/3-540-55801-2_31

Anscombre, J. C., & Ducrot, O. (1997). *L’argumentation dans la langue.* Belgium: Mardaga.

Antonic, S., Mitrovic, J., & Sofronijevic, A. (2011). Fostering open access usage by creation of the library aggregator for Europeana: Project Europeana libraries. In *Proceedings of INFORUM 2011: 17th Conference on Professional Information Resources.* Prague. Retrieved from http://www.inforum.cz/pdf/2011/antonic-sanja.pdf.

AnyBots. (2013). *Telepresence robots - AnyBots.* Retrieved June 27, 2013, from https://www.anybots.com/

Armstrong, T. (2009). *Multiple intelligences in the classroom.* Alexandria, VA: Assn for Supervision & Curriculum.

Arnauld, A., & Nicole, P. (1662). The art of thinking. Port-Royal logic. New York: Bobbs-Merrill. (1964).

Asher, N., & Lascarides, A. (2003). *Logics of conversation (Studies in natural language processing).* Cambridge, UK: Cambridge University Press.

Astrobiology, 9(10), 979-987. doi:10.1089/ast.2009.0384.

Augustine. (397). *De doctrina cristiana*, I-III.

Baker, M. (2010). Relations between two qualities of collaborative dialogue: Knowledge co-elaboration and affective regulation. *Analysing the quality of collaboration in task-oriented computer-mediated interactions* (Workshop at the 9th International Conference on the Design of Cooperative Systems), Aix-en-Provence, France.

Bak, P. (1996). *How nature works: The science of self-organised criticality.* New York: Copernicus Press. doi:10.1007/978-1-4757-5426-1

Bal, B. K., & Saint-Dizier, P. (2008). Towards building annotated resources for analyzing opinions and argumentation. In *News editorials.* Malta: LREC.

Barabási, A.-L. (2003). *Linked. How everything is connected to everything else and what it means for business, science, and everyday life.* New York: Penguin Group.

Barab, S. A., & Duffy, T. (1998). From practice fields to communities of practice. *Learning, 1*, 1–33.

Barbieri, M. (Ed.). (2007). *Introduction to biosemiotics: The new biological synthesis.* Heidelberg, Germany: Springer. doi:10.1007/1-4020-4814-9

Baruch, L., & Juergen, D. (2004). The dominance of intangible assets: Consequences for enterprise management and corporate reporting. *Measuring Business Excellence, 8*(1), 6–17. doi:10.1108/13683040410524694

Baumgarten, A. G. (1750). *Aesthetica.* Frankfurt-an-der-Oder[Kley]. *Impens., I*, C.

Beard, L., Wilson, K., Morra, D., & Keelan, J. (2009). A survey of health-related activities on Second Life. *Journal of Medical Internet Research, 11*(2), e17. doi:10.2196/jmir.1192 PMID:19632971

Bedford, C., Birkedal, R., Erhard, J., Graff, J., & Hempel, C. (2006). Second Life as an educational environment: A student perspective. In *Proceedings of the First Second Life Education Workshop*, (pp. 25-27). San Francisco, CA.

Bellotti, V., Dalal, B., Good, N., Flynn, P., Bobrow, D. G., & Ducheneaut, N. (2004). What a to-do: Studies of task management towards the design of a personal task list manager. In *Proceedings of SIGCHI Conference on Human Factors in Computing Systems* (pp. 735-742). New York: ACM.

Berners-Lee, T. (1998). *Semantic Web roadmap.* Retrieved on March 31, 2011 from http://www.w3.org/DesignIssues/Semantic.html

Bethard, S., Yu, H., Thornton, A., Hatzivassiloglou, V., & Rafsky, D. (2004). Automatic extraction of opinion propositions and their holders. In *Proceedings of AAAI04.*

Bharadwaj, A. S. (2000). A resource-based perspective on information technology capability and firm performance: An empirical investigation. *Management Information Systems Quarterly, 24*(1), 169–196. doi:10.2307/3250983

Birkinshaw, J., & Sheehan, T. (2002). Managing the knowledge life cycle. *MIT Sloan Management Review, 44*(1), 75–83.

Blackboard. (2013). *Blackboard services.* Retrieved June 27, 2013, from http://www.blackboard.com/Platforms.aspx

Blizzard Games. (2013). *World of Warcraft.* Retrieved July 05, 2013, from https://us.battle.net/account/creation/wow/signup/

Borman, W. C., & Motowidlo, S. J. (1993). Expanding the criterion domain to include elements of contextual performance. In N. Schmitt, & W. C. Bormaned (Eds.), *Personnel selection in organizations*. San Francisco: Jossey-Bass.

Bouras, C., & Tsiatsos, T. (2006). Educational virtual environments: Design rationale and architecture. *International Journal of Multimedia Tools and Applications*, *29*(2), 153–173. doi:10.1007/s11042-006-0005-7

Bourse, S., & Saint-Dizier, P. (2012). A repository of rules and lexical resources for discourse structure analysis: the case of explanation structures. In *Proceedings of LREC 2012*, Istanbul.

Brandes, U. (2001). A faster algorithm for betweenness centrality. *The Journal of Mathematical Sociology*, *25*, 163–177. doi:10.1080/0022250X.2001.9990249

Breck, E., Choi, Y., & Cardie, C. (2007). Identifying expressions of opinion in context. In *Proceedings of the Twentieth International Joint Conference on Artificial Intelligence (IJCAI-2007)*.

Bruckman, A., & Hudson, J. M. (2001). Disinhibition in a CSCL Environment. In Proceedings of Computer Support for Collaborative Learning (CSCL), Maastricht, Netherlands (pp. 629-630). Boulder, CO.

Brulé, J., & Bount, A. (1989). *Knowledge Acquisition*. New York: McGraw-Hill.

Bruno, G. (2011). Agility and process agility: ho$w do they relate to each other? In M. M. Cruz-Cunha, & J. Varajão (Eds.), *E-business managerial aspects, solutions and case studies* (pp. 71–89). Hershey, PA: Information Science Publishing.

Bruno, G. (2012). Lecture Notes in Computer Science: Vol. 7447. *Combining information and activities in business processes* (pp. 481–488). Heidelberg, Germany: Springer. doi:10.1007/978-3-642-32597-7_43

Buckley, M. J., & Johnson, M. M. (2013). The why's and how's of integrating academic ebooks: Since ebooks are getting used, it makes sense to ensure that the library provides a full range of functionality to give library users as many options as possible. *Computers in Libraries*, *33*(1), 9.

Budzynska, K. (2010). Argument analysis: Components of interpersonal argumentation. In *Proceedings of COMMA 2010*.

Budzynska, K., & Reed, C. (2012). The structure of ad hominem dialogues. In *Proceedings of COMMA 2012*.

Buendía, F., & Hervás, A. (2006). An evaluation framework for e-learning platforms based on educational standard specifications. In *Proceedings of the Sixth International Conference on Advanced Learning Technologies (ICALT'06)*. IEEE. doi:0-7695-2632-2/06

Burbules, N. C. (2004). Rethinking the virtual. *Learning*, *1*(2).

Buschmann, F., Meunier, R., Rohnert, H., Sommerlad, P., & Stal, M. (1996). *Pattern oriented software architecture. A system of patterns*. New York: John Wiley & Sons.

Butigan, V. T. (2007). *Preporuka formata meta-podataka za objekte digitalizovane nacionalne baštine: (Pokretna kulturna dobra)*. Retrieved from http://www.ncd.matf.bg.ac.rs/?page=news&lang=sr&file=predlogStandardaMetadata.htm

Butigan, V. T. (n. d.). *Nacionalni centar za digitalizaciju*. Retrieved from http://www.nb.rs/view_file.php?file_id=625

Campbell, J. P. (1990). Modeling the performance prediction problem in industrial and organizational psychology. In M. D. Dunnette, & L. M. Hough (Eds.), *Handbook of industrial and organizational psychology*. Palo Alto, CA: Consulting Psychologists Press.

Capra, F., Juarrero, A., Sotolongo, P., & Van Uden, J. (Eds.). (2007). *Reframing complexity*. Mansfield, MA: ISCE Publishing.

Carley, K. M., Martin, M. K., & Hirshman, B. (2009). The etiology of social change. *Topics in Cognitive Science*, *1*(4), 621–650. doi:10.1111/j.1756-8765.2009.01037.x

Cassirer, E. (1923). *Zur Einstein'sche Relativitätstheorie* [Substance and Function and Einstein's Theory of Relativity]. (W. C. Swabey, & M. C. Swabey, Trans.). Chicago: Open Court Publishing Co.

Cassirer, E. (1955). *(1923-1929). Philosophy of symbolic forms* (R. Manheim, Trans.). New Haven, CT: Yale University Press.

Castilla, E. J. (2005). Social networks and employee performance in a call center. *American Journal of Sociology*, *110*(5), 1243–1283.

Chao, T. et al. (2009). Lecture Notes in Computer Science: Vol. 5701. *Artifact-based transformation of IBM Global Financing* (pp. 261–277). Heidelberg, Germany: Springer.

Chen, R. (2004). *The formation and influence of social networks within the organization: Social capital perspective* (PhD Dissertation). Sun Yat-sen University, China.

Chen, I. A., Roberts, R. W., & Szostak, J. W. (2004). The emergence of competition between model protocells. *Science*, *3*(305), 1474–1476. doi:10.1126/science.1100757 PMID:15353806

Churchill, E., Snowdon, D., & Munro, A. (2001). *Collaborative virtual environments: Digital places and spaces for interaction*. London: Springer-Verlag, London Limited. doi:10.1007/978-1-4471-0685-2

Ciljevi i zadaci univerzitetskih repozitorija Zapadnog Balkana. (2010). Retrieved from http://www.westbulnet.com/AmplioCMS2/public/EnterPublic.cms2?langId=74&request_locale=sr_CS#menuId=1347

Cisco and iRobot. (2013). *Cisco and iRobot telepresence*. Retrieved June 27, 2013, from http://www.irobot.com/us/learn/commercial/ava500.aspx

Cisco Jabber. (2013). *Cisco Jabber for Web*. Retrieved June 29, 2013, from http://developer.cisco.com/web/jabber-developer/overview

Cisco WebEx. (2007). *WebEx meeting service API technical overview*. Retrieved March 26, 2010, from http://static.webex.com/fileadmin/webex09/files_en_us/pdf/webex_wp_MeetingServiceAPI.pdf

Cisco WebEx. (2013). *Collaboration platforms and services*. Retrieved June 28, 2013, from http://www.webex.com/products/enterprise.html

Cisco WebEx. (2013). *Development*. Retrieved June 29, 2013, from http://developer.cisco.com/web/webex-developer/developer-platform-overview

Cisco. (2013). *Cisco collaboration developer hub*. Retrieved June 29, 2013, from http://developer.cisco.com/web/collaboration-developer

Cisco. (2013). *Collaboration family*. Retrieved June 28, 2013, from http://developer.cisco.com/web/collaboration-developer/collaboration-tools-overview

Cisco. (2013). *Jabber development*. Retrieved June 29, 2013, from Jabber http://developer.cisco.com/web/jabber-developer/cisco-jabber-and-the-sdks

Cisco. (2013). *WebEx social*. Retrieved June 29, 2013, from http://developer.cisco.com/web/webexsocial-developer

Citrix Podio. (2013). *Citrix Podio*. Retrieved June 28, 2013, from https://podio.com/?c_name=ctxs

Citrix. (2013). *Citrix GoTo family*. Retrieved June 2013, 2013, from http://www.citrix.com/products.html

COBISS.net. (2008). *Platforma COBISS - Kooperativni online bibliografski sistem i servisi*. Retrieved from http://www.cobiss.net/platforma_cobiss-SR.htm

Coleman, V. I. (1998). Investigation of the underlying structure of the contextual performance domain. *Dissertation Abstracts International: Section B: Science and Engineering.*, *58*(8-B), 4499.

COMARC/B Format za bibliografske podatke. (2009). Maribor, Institut informacijskih znanosti.

Conway, J. M. (1999). Distinguishing contextual performance from task performance for managerial jobs. *The Journal of Applied Psychology*, *84*, 3–13. doi:10.1037/0021-9010.84.1.3

Costa-Perez, X., Festag, A., Kolbe, H.-J., Quittek, J., Schmid, S., Stiemerling, M., & van der Veen, H. (2013). Latest trends in telecommunication standards. *SIGCOMM Computer Communication Review*, *43*(2), 64–71. doi:10.1145/2479957.2479968

Coyle, K., & Baker, T. (2009). *Guidelines for Dublin Core application profiles*. Retrieved from http://dublincore.org/documents/profile-guidelines/

Coyle, K. (2005). Understanding metadata and its purpose. *Journal of Academic Librarianship*, *31*(2). doi:10.1016/j.acalib.2004.12.010

Cross, R., & Cummings, J. N. (2004). Tie and network correlates of individual performance in knowledge intensive work. *Academy of Management Journal*, *47*(6), 928–937. doi:10.2307/20159632

Cruse, A. (1986). *Lexical semantics*. Cambridge, UK: Cambridge University Press.

Dalgarno, B., & Lee, M. J. (2010). What are the learning affordances of 3-D virtual environments? *British Journal of Educational Technology*, *41*(1), 10–32. doi:10.1111/j.1467-8535.2009.01038.x

Davenport, T. H., & Short, J. E. (1990). The new industrial engineering: information technology and business process redesign. *Sloan Management Review*, (Summer): 11–27.

Davies, M., Joachim, Z., & Gabner, R. (2012). Evaluating two approaches for browser-based real-time multimedia communication. In *Proceedings of 10th International Conference on Advances in Mobile Computing & Multimedia (MoMM2012)*. Bali, Indonesia: ACM.

De Leenheer, P. (2004). Revising and managing multiple ontology versions in a possible worlds setting. In *Proc. of On the Move to Meaningful Internet Systems Ph.D. Symposium (OTM 2004), Agia Napa, Cyprus*, (LNCS 3292) (pp. 798-818). Berlin, Germany: Springer.

Debenham, J. (1989). *Knowledge system design*. Sidney, Australia: Prentice Hall.

Definition of the Europeana Data Model elements: Version 5.2.1. 2011. (2011). Retrieved from http://group.europeana.eu/c/document_library/get_file?uuid=aff89c92-b6ff-4373-a279-fc47b9af3af2&groupId=10605

Delmonte, R., & Pallotta, V. (2011). Opinion mining and sentiment analysis need text understanding. In Studies in Computational Intelligence, 361, 81-95.

Denny, N., Mani, S., Sheshu, R., Swaminathan, M., Samdal, J., & Gupta, A. (2008). Hybrid offshoring: Composite personae and evolving collaboration technologies. *Information Resources Management Journal*, *21*(1), 89–104. doi:10.4018/irmj.2008010106

Di Eugenio, B., & Webber, B. L. (1996). Pragmatic overloading in natural language instructions. *International Journal of Expert Systems*, *9*(3).

Dickey, M. D. (2010). The pragmatics of virtual worlds for K-12 educators: Investigating the affordances and constraints of Active Worlds and Second Life with K-12 in-service teachers. *Educational Technology Research and Development*, *59*(1), 1–20. doi:10.1007/s11423-010-9163-4

Dieterle, E., & Clarke, J. (2006). Multi-user virtual environments for teaching and learning. *Idea*, (c), 1-11.

Digital Media, J. I. S. C. (2010). *An introduction to metadata. Managing your digital resources*. Retrieved from.

Dillenbourg, P., Baker, M., Blaye, A., & O'Malley, C. (1996). The evolution of research on collaborative learning. In E. Spada, & P. Reiman (Eds.), *Learning in humans and machine: Towards an interdisciplinary learning science* (pp. 189–211). Oxford, UK: Elsevier.

Doerr, M., Gradmann, S., Hennicke, S., Isaac, A., Meghini, C., & van de Sompel, H. (2010). The Europeana Data Model. In *Proceedings of World Library and Information Congress: 76th IFLA General Conference and Assembly*. Gothenburg, Sweden. Retrieved from http://www.ifla.org/files/hq/papers/ifla76/149-doerr-en.pdf

Đukić, P. (2005). Razvoj bibliotečko-informacionog sistema u Srbiji: od Biblisa do Bisisa. *Pančevačko čitalište, 4*, 28-29.

Dumas, M., van der Aalst, W. M. P., & ter Hofstede, A. H. M. (2005). *Process-aware information systems: Bridging people and software through process technology*. New York: Wiley. doi:10.1002/0471741442

Du, R., Ai, S., & Ren, Y. (2007). Relationship between knowledge sharing and performance: A survey in Xi'an China. *Expert Systems with Applications*, *32*(1), 38–46. doi:10.1016/j.eswa.2005.11.001

Duranti, C. M., & de Almeida, F. C. (2012). Is more technology better for communication in international teams. *International Journal of e-Collaboration*, *8*(1), 36–52. doi:10.4018/jec.2012010103

Eco, U. (1975). Preface. In S. Chapman, U. Eco, & J.-M. Klinkenberg (Eds.), *A semiotic landscape/Panorama sémiotique* (pp. v–vii). The Hague, The Netherlands: Mouton.

Eco, U. (1976). *A theory of semiotics (Advances in Semiotics)*. Bloomington, IN: Indiana University Press.

Enis, M. (2012a). Harris County PL to test DCL ebook model. *Library Journal*, *137*(16), 16.

Enis, M. (2012b). 3M makes its presence felt: An ebook platform with easy setup, use, and ILS integration. *Library Journal*, *137*(17), 42.

Enis, M. (2013). Overdrive, 3M debut ebook developments. *Library Journal*, *138*(2), 16.

Europeana Data Model primer. (2010). Retrieved from http://group.europeana.eu/c/document_library/get_file?uuid=718a3828-6468-4e94-a9e7-7945c55eec65&groupId=10605

Europeana Semantic Elements Specification: Version 3.4. 2011. (2011). Retrieved from http://version1.europeana.eu/c/document_library/get_file?uuid=77376831-67cf-4cff-a7a2-7718388eec1d&groupId=10128

Fiedler, A., & Horacek, H. (2001). Argumentation in explanations to logical problems. In *Proceedings of ICCS 2001, LNCS 2073*. Springer.

Filipi-Matutinović, S. (2004). Bibliotečki sistemi i problemi njihovog povezivanja u Srbiji. *Glas biblioteke*, *11*, 5-10.

Flynn, E. (2013). Open access metadata, catalogers, and vendors: The future of cataloging records. *Journal of Academic Librarianship*, *39*, 29–31. doi:10.1016/j.acalib.2012.11.010

Frappaolo, C. (2008). *Enterprise 2.0: agile, emergent and integrated AIIM, MarketIQ*. AIIM. Retrieved July 25, 2010, from htttp://www.aiim.org/Research/Industry-Watch/Enterprise-20-Agile-Emergent-Integrated

Freeze, R., & Kulkarni, U. (2007). Knowledge management capability: Defining knowledge assets. *Journal of Knowledge Management*, *11*(6), 94–109. doi:10.1108/13673270710832190

Freifeld, L. (n. d.). 2012 Training industry report. *Training*. Retrieved from http://www.trainingmag.com/content/2012-training-industry-report

French, J. R. P., & Raven, B. (1959). The bases of social power. In D. Cartwright (Ed.), *Studies in social power*. Ann Arbor, MI: University of Michigan.

Friday, E., Friday-Stroud, S. S., Green, A. L., & Hill, A. Y. (2006). A multi-semester comparison of student performance between multiple traditional and online sections of two management courses. *Journal of Behavioral and Applied Management*, *8*(1), 66–81.

Furlan, R. (2013). Build your own Google Glass. Spectrum, IEEE, 1-2.

Gallese, V. (2001). The shared manifold hypothesis. From mirror neurons to empathy. *Journal of Consciousness Studies*, *8*(5-7), 33.

Gamma, E., Helm, R., Johnson, R., & Vlissides, J. (1994). *Design patterns: Elements of reusable object-oriented software*. Boston: Addison Wesley.

Garcia-Villalba, M. P., & Saint-Dizier, P. (2012). A framework for extracting arguments in opinion texts. *International Journal of Cognitive Intelligence and Natural Intelligence*, *6*(4).

Gardner, H. (1993). Frames of mind: The theory of multiple intelligences (10th anniversary ed.). New York: Basic Books.

Gardner, H. (1983). *Frames of mind: The theory of multiple intelligences*. New York: Basic Books.

Gardner, H. (1999). *Intelligence reframed*. New York: Basic Books.

Gardner, H., & Hatch, T. (1989). Multiple intelligences go to school: Educational implications of the theory of multiple intelligences. *Educational Researcher*, *18*(8), 4–10.

Garner, S., & Mann, P. (2003). Interdisciplinarity: Perceptions of the value of computer-supported collaborative work in design for the built environment. *International Journal of Automation in Construction*.

Gelernter. (1991). *Mirror worlds: Or: The day software puts the universe in a shoebox...How it will happen and what it will mean*. New York: Oxford University Press.

Globus, G. (1995). *The postmodern brain*. Amsterdam, The Netherlands: John Benjamins Publishing Company. doi:10.1075/aicr.1

Gödel, K. (1931). Über formal unentscheidbare Sätze der Principia Mathematica und verwandter Systeme I[On Formally Undecidable Propositions of Principia Mathematica and Related Systems I]. *Monatshefte für Mathematik*, *38*, 173–198. doi:10.1007/BF01700692

Goedertier, S., Haesen, R., & Vanthienen, J. (2008). Rule-based business process modelling and enactment. *International Journal of Business Process Integration and Management*, *3*, 194–207. doi:10.1504/IJBPIM.2008.023219

Goguen, J. (1999). An introduction to algebraic semiotics, with application to user interface design. In C. L. Nehaniv (Ed.), *Computation for metaphors, analogy, and agents* (Vol. 1562, pp. 242–291). Lecture Notes in Computer ScienceBerlin, Heidelberg, New York: Springer. doi:10.1007/3-540-48834-0_15

Gokhale, A. A. (1995). Collaborative learning enhances critical thinking. *Journal of Technology Education*, *7*(1).

Good, J. (2002). *A gentle introduction to metadata*. Retrieved from http://www.language-archives.org/documents/gentle-intro.html

Google Recorded Future. (2013). *Google recorded future API*. Retrieved July 08, 2013, from https://code.google.com/p/recordedfuture/wiki/RecordedFutureAPI#Introduction

Google. (2013). *Google+ Hangouts*. Retrieved June 27, 2013, from http://www.google.com/+/learnmore/hangouts/

Google. (2013). *Hangouts API*. Retrieved July 03, 2013, from https://developers.google.com/+/hangouts/api/

Google. (2013). *Hangouts*. Retrieved June 28, 2013, from http://www.google.com/+/learnmore/hangouts/

Goossenaerts, J., Possel-Dölken, F., & Popplewell, K. (2007). Vision, trends, gaps, and a broad road map for future engineering. *International Journal of e-Collaboration*, *3*(4), 1–20. doi:10.4018/jec.2007100101

Grant, R. (1997). The knowledge-based view of the firm: Implications for management practice. *Long Range Planning*, *30*(3), 450–454. doi:10.1016/S0024-6301(97)00025-3

Grbić, B. (2004). Sadržinska obrada u sistemu COBISS. *Infoteka*, *5*, 53-56. Retrieved from http://www.zbus.rs/cir/infoteka/spec2004/INFOTEKA_V_spec_Maj2004_53-56.pdf

Grbić, B. (n. d.). *Predmetna klasifikacija u sistemu COBISS*. Retrieved from http://www.zbus.rs/cir/pdf/prirucnici/predmetizacija_u_cobissu.pdf

Grbić, B., Đurđulov, J., & Lazarević, G. (2011). *Sadržinska obrada dokumenata u repozitorijumu Phaidra - metapodaci*. [Web seminar]. Retrieved from http://www.westbulnet.com/AmplioCMS2/public/EnterPublic.cms2?langId=74&request_locale=sr_CS#menuId=1569

Grebner, O., & Riss, U. (2008). Implicit metadata generation on the semantic desktop using task management as example. In *Conference on Formal Ontologies Meet Industry* (pp.33-44). Amsterdam, The Netherlands: IOS Press.

Greenberg, J. (2005). *Understanding metadata and metadata schemes*. Retrieved from.

Greenwell, M. (1988). *Knowledge engineering for expert systems*. Chichester, UK: Ellis Horwood Limited.

Grice, H. P. (1975). Logic and conversation. *Syntax and Semantics*, *3*, 41–58.

Grosz, B., & Sidner, C. (1986). Attention, intention and the structure of discourse. *Computational Linguistics*, *12*(3).

Grudin, J. (1994). Computer-supported cooperative work: History and focus. *Computer*, *27*(5), 19–26. doi:10.1109/2.291294

Gudwin, R., & Queiroz, J. (2005). Towards an introduction to computational semiotics. In *Proceedings of the 2005 IEEE International Conference on Integration of Knowledge Intensive Multi-Agent Systems* – KIMAS'05, (pp. 393-398).Waltham, MA.

Guglielman, E., & Vettraino, L. (2007). *Complex learning: A new approach for the age of knowledge.* Retrieved from http://www.scribd.com/doc/20062038/Complex-Learning

Hadlock, K. (2011). *The Anatomy of an RSS Feed.* Retrieved from http://www.webreference.com/authoring/languages/xml/rss/feeds/

Häkkilä, J., Koskenranta, O., Posti, M., Ventä-Olkkonen, L., & Colley, A. (2013). Clearing the virtual window - Connecting two locations. In *Proceedings of PerDis '13, International Symposium on Pervasive Displays.* California.

Harris, C. (2013). Ebooks 2013: New leasing models, cheaper devices, more content. *School Library Journal, 59*(1), 16.

Hashmi, S. I., Ishikawa, F., & Richardson, I. (2013). A communication process for global requirements engineering. *International Conference on Software and System Processes 2013,* (pp. 136 - 140). San Francisco, CA.

Hawking, S. (2000, January 20). *San Jose Mercury News.* Retrieved May 5, 2012, from http://www.comdig.com/stephen-hawking.php

Hayes, A. (2013). Cyborg cops, googlers, and connectivism. *IEEE Technology and Society Magazine*, (Spring): 23–24. doi:10.1109/MTS.2013.2247731

Herman, H., Coombe, R. J., & Lewis, K. (2006). Your Second Life? *Cultural Studies, 20*(2-3), 184–210. doi:10.1080/09502380500495684

Hessel, S. (2011). *Doe er iets aan! (transl. from French).* Amsterdam, The Netherlands: Van Gennep.

Hillmann, D. (2005). *Using Dublin core.* Retrieved from http://dublincore.org/documents/usageguide/

Hippensteel, P. (2013, July 01). *What is WebRTC.* Retrieved July 02, 2013, from Network World: http://www.conferencingnews.com/news/48432

Hjelmslev, L. (1943). *Prolegomena to a theory of language.* Baltimore: Indiana University Publications in Anthropology and Linguistics.

Hobbes, T. (1651). *Leviathan.* London: Andrew Cooke.

Hodge, G. (2004). Metapodaci na lak način. *Glasnik Narodne biblioteke Srbije, 1*, 157-180. Retrieved from http://www.nb.rs/view_file.php?file_id=860

Hoffelder, N. (2012, November 17). Did you know the new Nook HD has text-to-speech? Retrieved from http://www.the-digital-reader.com/2012/11/17/did-you-know-the-new-nook-hd-has-text-to-speech

Hoffman, B. J., & Frost, B. C. (2006). Multiple intelligences of transformational leaders: An empirical examination. *International Journal of Manpower, 27*(1), 37–51. doi:10.1108/01437720610652826

Hoffmeyer, J. (Ed.). (2008). *A legacy for living systems. Gregory Bateson as precursor to biosemiotics.* Berlin, Heidelberg, New York: Springer.

Hopkins, J. (1986). *A new, interpretive translation of St. Anselm's Monologion and Proslogion.* Minneapolis, MN: A.J. Banning Press.

Hordijk, W., Hein, J., & Steel, M. (2010). Autocatalytic sets and the origin of life. *Entropy, 12*(7), 1733–1742. doi:10.3390/e12071733

http://www.ils.unc.edu/mrc/pdf/greenberg05understanding.pdf

http://www.jiscdigitalmedia.ac.uk/crossmedia/advice/an-introduction-to-metadata

Hull, R. (2008). Lecture Notes in Computer Science: Vol. 5332. *Artifact-centric business process models: Brief survey of research results and challenges* (pp. 1152–1163). Heidelberg, Germany: Springer. doi:10.1007/978-3-540-88873-4_17

Hull, R. et al. (2011). Lecture Notes in Computer Science: Vol. 6551. *Introducing the guard-stage-milestone approach for specifying business entity lifecycles* (pp. 1–24). Heidelberg, Germany: Springer. doi:10.1007/978-3-642-19589-1_1

Hutter, J. (2012). E-Readers & E-Books in public libraries: Measuring library patron expectations. *International Journal of Digital Library Systems, 3*(2), 48–59. doi:10.4018/jdls.2012040105

IBM. (2010, January 18). *IBM accelerates cloud computing with LotusLive*. Retrieved August 19, 2010, from http://www-03.ibm.com/press/us/en/pressrelease/29210.wss?S_CMP=swnews_210

IBM. (2012). *Connections*. Retrieved June 28, 2013, from https://www-304.ibm.com/connections/blogs/social-business/entry/ibm_lotuslive_is_becoming_ibm_smartcloud_for_social_business3?lang=en_us

IBM. (2013). *Smart cloud*. Retrieved June 28, 2013, from http://www.ibm.com/cloud-computing/social/us/en/benefits/

IBM. (2013). *Social business toolkit*. Retrieved July 03, 2013, from http://www.ibm.com/cloud-computing/social/us/en/

IEFT WebRTC. (2012). *WebRTC draft specification*. Retrieved July 03, 2013, from http://tools.ietf.org/html/draft-ietf-rtcweb-rtp-usage-06#page-4

IETF XCON. (2013). *XCON Centralized Conferencing Manipulation Protocol*. Retrieved May 17, 2013, from http://datatracker.ietf.org/doc/draft-ietf-xcon-ccmp/

Ilić Kiš, I. (2007). Softverski bibliotečki sistem Bisis: Petnaest godina razvoja i usavršavanja. *Pančevačko čitalište, 6*, 34.

Intel. (2013). *Gesture camera*. Retrieved May 17, 2013, from http://click.intel.com/intelsdk/Creative_Interactive_Gesture_Camera_Developer_Kit-P2061.aspx

Intel. (2013). *Perceptive computing*. Retrieved July 25, 2013, from Intel Software: http://software.intel.com/en-us/vcsource/tools/perceptual-computing-sdk

Ismail, M. B., & Yusof, Z. M. (2009). The relationship between knowledge sharing, employee performance and service delivery in public sector organisations: A theoretical framework. *Public Sector ICT Management Review*, *3*(1), 37–45.

Jackson, M. O. (2008). *Social and economic networks*. Princeton, NJ: Princeton University Press.

Jones, P. (2013, March 15). Supplement: Using semiotics to identify patent-eligible software. *Groklaw*. Retrieved April 2, 2013, from http://www.groklaw.net/article.php?story=20130314152416723#topics

Jörg, T. (2010). A theory of learning for the management of knowledge in learning communities and complex organizations. *International Journal of Knowledge and Systems Science*, *1*(1), 27–42. doi:10.4018/jkss.2010010103

Jörg, T. (2011). *New thinking in complexity for the social sciences and humanities – A generative, transdisciplinary approach*. Dordrecht, The Netherlands: Springer. doi:10.1007/978-94-007-1303-1

Karantzas, G. C., Avery, M. R., Macfarlane, S., Mussap, A., Tooley, G., Hazelwood, Z., & Fitness, J. (2013). Enhancing critical analysis and problem-solving skills in undergraduate psychology: An evaluation of a collaborative learning and problem-based learning approach. *Australian Journal of Psychology*, *65*(1), 38–45. doi:10.1111/ajpy.12009

Kauffman, S. (2011). *The end of a physics worldview: Heraclitus and the watershed of life*. Paper presented at NECSI & MIT/ESD Seminar. Retrieved November 20, 2011, from http://vimeo.com/30875984

Kauffman, S., & Longo, G. (2011). *No law entails the evolution of the biosphere*. Paper presented at Computational Systems Biology, Tampere University of Technology, Finland. Retrieved November 11, 2011, from http://csb.cs.tut.fi/no_law_entails_the_evolution_of_the_biosphere.php

Kauffman, S. A. (1993). *The origins of order. Self-organization and selection in evolution*. Oxford, UK: Oxford University Press.

Kauffman, S. A. (1995). *At home in the universe*. New York: Oxford University Press.

Kauffman, S. A. (2009). Foreword. The open universe. In R. Ulanowicz (Ed.), *The third window. Natural life beyond Newton and Darwin* (pp. ix–xvii). West Conshohocken, PA: Templeton Foundation Press.

Kawakita, J. (1975). *The KJ method A scientific approach to problem solving*. Tokyo: Kawakita Research Institute.

Kayser, D. (1997). La sémantique lexicale est d'abord inférentielle. *Langue Française*, *113*, 92–106. doi:10.3406/lfr.1997.5372

Keary, A., & Redfern, S. (2012). Future directions of the conferencing and collaboration field. *International Journal of e-Collaboration*, *8*(2), 78–98. doi:10.4018/jec.2012040104

Keil, F. C., & Wilson, R. A. (2000). *Explanation and cognition*. Cambridge, MA: Bradford Books.

Kessels, J. W. M. (2001). Verleiden tot kennisproductiviteit [Tempting towards knowledge productivity]. Inaugural Lecture, University of Twente, Enschede, The Netherlands.

Kessels, J. W. M. (1996). Knowledge productivity and the corporate curriculum. In J. F. Schreinemakers (Ed.), *Knowledge management, organisation, competence and methodology* (pp. 168–174). Würzburg, Germany: Ergon Verlag.

Keynes, J. M. (1936). *General theory of employment, interest, and money*. London: Macmillan.

Khoo, M., & Hall, C. (2013). Managing metadata: Networks of practice, technological frames, and metadata work in a digital library. *Information and Organization*, *23*, 81–106. doi:10.1016/j.infoandorg.2013.01.003

Kim, S. M., & Hovy, E. H. (2007). CRYSTAL: analyzing predictive opinions on the Web. In *Proceedings of the EMNLP conference*, Prague.

Kintsch, W. (1988). The role of knowledge in discourse comprehension: A construction integration model. *Psychological Review*, *9*(2). PMID:3375398

Knox, A. (1986). Helping adults learn. *Improving Learning Skills*, *4*(4), 15–17.

Kobbe, L., Weinberger, A., Dillenbourg, P., Harrer, A., Hämäläinen, R., Häkkinen, P., & Fischer, F. (2007). Specifying computer-supported collaboration scripts. *International Journal of Computer-Supported Collaborative Learning*, *2*(2-3), 211–224. doi:10.1007/s11412-007-9014-4

Koblin, A. (2008-present). Aaron Koblin website: Information. Retrieved on April 1, 2011 from http://www.aaronkoblin.com/info.html

Kock, N. (2008). E-Collaboration and E-Commerce in virtual worlds: The potential of Second Life and World of Warcraft. *International Journal of e-Collaboration*, *4*(3), 1–13. doi:10.4018/jec.2008070101

Kojevic, S., Dakic, N., & Nogic, B. (2011). Normativne datoteke ličnih imena. In Standardizacija i kvalitet bibliotečkih usluga (pp. 307-322). Belgrade: Bibliotekarsko drustvo Srbije.

Kolb, D. (1984). *Experiential learning: Experiences as the source of learning and development*. Upper Saddle River, NJ: Prentice Hall.

Konstantinidis, A., Tsiatsos, T., Terzidou, T., & Pomportsis, A. (2010). Fostering collaborative learning in Second Life: Metaphors and affordances. *Computers & Education*, *55*(2), 603–615. doi:10.1016/j.compedu.2010.02.021

Kosseim, L., & Lapalme, G. (2000). Choosing rhetorical structures to plan instructional texts. *Computational Intelligence*, *12*(3).

KPMG. (2011, May). *Confronting complexity. Research findings and insights*. Retrieved May 5, 2012, from http://www.kpmg.com/global/en/issuesandinsights/articlespublications/pages/confronting-complexity-report.aspx

Kreijns, K., Kirschner, P. A., & Jochems, W. (2003). Identifying the pitfalls of social interaction in computer-supported collaborative learning environments: A review of the research. *Computers in Human Behavior*, *19*(3), 335–353. doi:10.1016/S0747-5632(02)00057-2

Kucukoguz, E., & Su, J. (2011). Lecture Notes in Computer Science: Vol. 6551. *On lifecycle constraints of artifact-centric workflows* (pp. 71–85). Heidelberg, Germany: Springer.

Kuhn, L. (1999). *Adventures in complexity. For organizations near the edge of chaos*. Devon, UK: Triarchy Press.

Kuhn, O., & Abecker, A. (1997). Corporate memories for knowledge management in industrial practice: Prospects and challenges. *Journal of Universal Computer Science*, *3*(8), 929–954.

Künzle, V., & Reichert, M. (2009). Towards object-aware process management systems: Issues, challenges, benefits. In *Lecture Notes in Business Information Processing, 29* (pp. 197–210). Heidelberg, Germany: Springer. doi:10.1007/978-3-642-01862-6_17

Künzle, V., & Reichert, M. (2011). PHILharmonicFlows: Towards a framework for object-aware process management. *Journal of Software Maintenance and Evolution: Research and Practice*, *23*(4), 205–244. doi:10.1002/smr.524

Küster, J. M., Ryndina, K., & Gall, H. (2007). Lecture Notes in Computer Science: Vol. 4714. *Generation of business process models for object life cycle compliance* (pp. 165–181). Heidelberg, Germany: Springer. doi:10.1007/978-3-540-75183-0_13

Lakoff, G. (1988). Cognitive semantics. In U. Eco, M. Santambrogio, & P. Violi (Eds.), *Meaning and mental representations*. Bloomington, IN: Indiana University Press.

Lambert, J. H. (1764). *Neues Organon oder Gedanken über die Erforschung und Bezeichnung des Wahren und dessen Unterscheidung vom Irrtum und Schein*. Leipzig, Germany: Johann Wendler.

LaRue, J. (2012). All hat, no cattle: A call for libraries to transform before it's too late. *Library Journal*, *137*(13), 32.

Laughlin, R. B. (2005). *A different universe. Reinventing physics from the bottom down*. New York: Basic Books.

Lazarević, G. (n. d.) *UDK u sistemu Cobiss*. Retrieved from http://www.zbus.rs/cir/pdf/prirucnici/UDK_u_sistemu_COBISS.pdf

Leibniz, G. W. (1672-1696). *Mathematical, Scientific, and technical correspondence* (6 vol.). Hannover, Germany: Leibniz-Archiv Hannover.

Lin, H., Fan, W., & Zhang, Z. (2009). A qualitative study of Web-based knowledge communities: Examining success factors. *International Journal of e-Collaboration*, *5*(3), 39–57. doi:10.4018/jec.2009070103

Liu, B. (2012). *Sentiment analysis and opinion mining*. San Rafael, CA: Morgan and Claypool.

Locke, J. (1690). *Of the division of the sciences: An essay concerning human understanding*. Chapt. XXI. Retrieved from http://www3.nd.edu/~afreddos/courses/439/locke0421.htm

Lombardi, C. (2008). *Videoconferencing equipment selection guide*. Retrieved July 19, 2010, from http://www.iuma.ulpgc.es/~nunez/clases-micros-para-com/varios/faulknertoc_fait.pdf

Longacre, R. (1982). Discourse typology in relation to language typology. In S. Allen (Ed.), *Text processing, proceeding of Nobel symposium, 51* (pp. 457–486). Stockholm, Sweden: Almquist and Wiksell.

Longo, G., Montévil, M., & Kauffman, S. (2012). No entailing laws, but enablement in the evolution of the biosphere. In T. Soule & J. H. Moore (Eds.), *Genetic and Evolutionary Computation Conference, GECCO '12, Philadelphia, PA, Companion Material Proceedings*, (pp. 1379-1392). New York: ACM.

Longo, L. M., Jihun, L., & Blaber, M. (2013). Simplified protein design biased for prebiotic amino acids yields a foldable, halophilic protein. In *Proceedings of the National Academy of Sciences*, (pp. 2135-2139).

Lotman, J. M. (1990). *Universe of the mind: A semiotic theory of culture* (A. Shukman, Trans.). Bloomington, IN: Indiana University Press.

Louie, A. H. (2007). A Rosen etymology. *Chemistry & Biodiversity*, *4*, 2296–2314. doi:10.1002/cbdv.200790188 PMID:17955478

Louie, A. H. (2009). *More than life itself: A synthetic continuation in relational biology (Categories)*. Frankfurt, Germany: Ontos Verlag. doi:10.1515/9783110321944

Luhmann, N. (2002). *Theories of distinction. Redescribing the descriptions of modernity*. Stanford, CA: Stanford University Press.

Luhmann, N. (2003). The cognitive program of constructivism and a reality that remains unknown. In L. E. Cahoone (Ed.), *From modernism to postmodernism: An anthology* (2nd ed.). London: Blackwell Publishing Ltd.

Luisi, P. L. (2003). Autopoiesis: A review and a reappraisal. *Naturwissenschaften*, *90*, 49–59. PMID:12590297

Luo, J. (2005). *Social network analysis notes*. Beijing, China: Social Sciences Academic Press.

Luo, J., Zheng, M., & Xie, Z. (2007). Social capital impact on knowledge sharing within the practical community. *Jiangxi Social Sciences*, *3*, 131–141.

Lu, R., Sadiq, S., & Governatori, G. (2009). On managing business processes variants. *Data & Knowledge Engineering*, *68*(7), 642–664. doi:10.1016/j.datak.2009.02.009

Luscher, J. M. (1989). Connecteurs et guidage inférentiel, propositions pour une perspective interlingue. In Bulletin CILA (Commission interuniversitaire suisse de linguistique appliquée) 50, 48-58.

Macmillan announces library lending pilot. (2013). *Library Journal, 138*(4), 12.

Mainzer, K. (2004). *Thinking in complexity* (4th ed.). New York: Springer Publishers. doi:10.1007/978-3-662-05364-5

Mann, W., & Thompson, S. (1988). Rhetorical structure theory: Towards a functional theory of text organisation. *Text*, *8*(3). doi:10.1515/text.1.1988.8.3.243

Mann, W., & Thompson, S. (Eds.). (1992). *Discourse description: Diverse linguistic analyses of a fund raising text.* Philadelphia, PA: John Benjamins. doi:10.1075/pbns.16

Mans, R. S. et al. (2010). Proclets in healthcare. *Journal of Biomedical Informatics*, *43*(4), 632–649. doi:10.1016/j.jbi.2010.03.010 PMID:20359548

Mansy, S. S., Schrum, J. P., Krishnamurthy, M., Tobé, S., Treco, D. A., & Szostak, J. W. (2008). Template-directed synthesis of a genetic polymer in a model protocell. *Nature*, *454*, 122–125. doi:10.1038/nature07018 PMID:18528332

Marcu, D. (1997). The rhetorical parsing of natural language texts. In *Proceedings of ACL 1997.*

Marcu, D. (2000). *The theory and practice of discourse parsing and summarization.* Cambridge, MA: MIT Press.

Marjanovic, O., & Freeze, R. D. (2011). Knowledge intensive business processes: Theoretical foundations and research challenges. In *Proceedings of the IEEE 44th Hawaii International Conference on System Sciences.* New York: IEEE Press.

Marković, B. (2005). Programski paket BISIS: Iskustva Gradske biblioteke u Novom Sadu. *Pančevačko čitalište, 4*, 30-31.

Marty, R. (1990). *L' Algèbre des Signes: Essai de Sémiotique Scientifique d'après Charles Sanders Peirce (Foundations of Semiotics, 24).* Amsterdam, The Netherlands: J. Benjamins Publishing Co. doi:10.1075/fos.24

Mason, D., & Pauleen, D. (2003). Perceptions of knowledge management: A qualitative analysis. *Journal of Knowledge Management*, *74*, 38–48. doi:10.1108/13673270310492930

Masthoff, J., Reed, C., & Grasso, F. (Eds.). (2008). *Symposium on persuasive technology.* Edinburgh.

Mauboussin, M. J. (2011). Embracing complexity. *Harvard Business Review*, (Sept): 89–92.

Maurer, S. E., Deamer, D. W., Boncella, J. M., & Monnard, P.-A. (2009). Chemical evolution of amphiphiles: Glycerol monoacyl derivatives stabilize plausible prebiotic membranes.

Mavridis, A., Konstantinidis, A., & Tsiatos, T. (2012). A comparison of 3D collaborative virtual learning environments: OpenSim vs. Second Life. *International Journal of e-Collaboration*, *8*(4), 8–12. doi:10.4018/jec.2012100102

McCahill, M. (2004). *Design for an extensible croquet-based framework to deliver a persistent, unified, massively multi-user and self organizing virtual environment.* Paper presented at Second Conference on Creating, Connecting and Collaborating through Computing, Kyoto, Japan.

McClarty, C. (2013). Fermat's last theorem and more can be proved more simply. Retrieved April 2, 2013, from http://www.rdmag.com/news/2013/03/fermat%E2%80%99s-last-theorem-and-more-can-be-proved-more-simply.

McCulloch, W., & Pitts, W. (1943). A logical calculus of the ideas immanent in nervous activity. *The Bulletin of Mathematical Biophysics*, *7*, 115–133. doi:10.1007/BF02478259

McKinsey & Company. (2013). *McKinsey - Disruptive technologies. Interviews with industry thought leaders.* Retrieved May 17, 2013, from http://www.mckinsey.com/insights/high_tech_telecoms_internet/connecting_everything_a_conversation_with_ciscos_padmasree_warrior

Medina-Domínguez, F., Sanchez-Segura, M., Mora-Soto, A., & Amescua, A. (2008). *Patterns in the field of software engineering. Encyclopedia of Information Science and Technology* (2nd ed.). Hershey, PA: Idea Group Publishers.

Medina-Domínguez, F., Sanchez-Segura, M., Mora-Soto, A., & Amescua, A. (2009). Reverse engineering and software products reuse to teach collaborative web portals: A case study with final-year computer science students. *IEEE Transactions on Education*, *53*(4), 595–607. doi:10.1109/TE.2009.2037313

Mesle, R. (2008). *Process-relational philosophy. An introduction to Alfred North Whitehead.* West Conshohocken, PA: Templeton Press.

Meyer, M., & Booker, J. (1991). *Eliciting and analyzing expert judgment. A practical guide*. London: Academic Press.

Microsoft Lync. (2013). *Microsoft Lync*. Retrieved June 28, 2013, from http://office.microsoft.com/en-us/microsoft-lync-video-conferencing-and-instant-messaging-FX102004552.aspx

Microsoft Lync. (2013). *New capabilities in Lync 2013*. Retrieved July 03, 2013, from http://msdn.microsoft.com/en-US/lync/fp179716

Microsoft. (2013). *Lync-Skype connectivity*. Retrieved June 28, 2013, from Lync-Skype Connectivity: http://blogs.skype.com/2013/05/29/skype-and-lync-connecting-the-living-room-to-the-board-room/

Microsoft. (2013). *Microsoft pixel sense*. Retrieved May 17, 2013, from http://www.microsoft.com/en-us/pixelsense/whatissurface.aspx

Microsoft. Office365. (2013). *Microsoft Office 365 Enterprise*. Retrieved July 05, 2013, from http://office.microsoft.com/en-ie/business/office-365-enterprise-e3-business-software-FX103030346.aspx

Miltasaki, E., Prasad, R., Joshi, A., & Webber, B. (2004). Annotating discourse connectives and their arguments. In *Proceedings of New Frontiers in NLP Conference*.

Minati, G., Abram, M., & Pessa, E. (2012). Preface. In G. Minati, M. Abram, & E. Pessa (Eds.), *Methods, models, simulations and approaches towards a general theory of change: Proceedings of the Fifth National Conference on Systems Scienc*e (pp. v-vii). Singapore: Worlds Scientific. Retrieved 20th of April 2013 at http://www.complexityinstitute.it/wp-content/uploads/2013/01/indice-libro-Minati.pdf

Mirkin, S., Dagan, I., & Shnarch, E. (2009). Evaluating the inferential utility of lexical-semantic resources. In *Proceedings of the 12th Conference of the European Chapter of the ACL*, (pp. 558-566). Athens.

Mishra, S. (2009). Really simple syndication. *STRIDE Handbook: E-Learning, 8*, 113-116. Retrieved from http://elf.westernsydneyinstitute.wikispaces.net/file/view/eLearning+STRIDE_Hb8_Full.pdf/114728879/eLearning%20STRIDE_Hb8_Full.pdf#page=120

Mitchell, C. M. (2011). *Complexity. A guided tour*. New York: Oxford University Press.

Mitchell, T. M., Shinkareva, S. V., Carlson, A., Chang, K. M., Malave, V. I., Mason, R. A., & Just, M. A. (2008). Predicting human brain activity associated with the meanings of nouns. *Science*, *320*(4), 1191–1195. doi:10.1126/science.1152876 PMID:18511683

Moeschler, J. (2003). Connecteurs et inférence. In G. Gobber (Ed.), *Syndesmoi: Il connettivo nella realta del testo*. Milano: Vita e Pensiero.

Mohammed, S., Mathieu, J. E., & Barlett, A. L. (2002). Technical administrative task performance, leadership task performance, and contextual performance: Considering the influence of team and task related composition variables. *Journal of Organizational Behavior*, *23*(7), 795–814. doi:10.1002/job.169

Mongré, P. (F. Hausdorff). (1897). Sant' Ilario. Thoughts from Zarathustra's landscape. Leipzig, Germany: C.G. Nauman.

Moore, D., Cheng, Y., McGrath, P., & Powell, N. J. (2005). Collaborative virtual environment technology for people with autism. *Focus on Autism and Other Developmental Disabilities*, *20*(4), 231–243. doi:10.1177/10883576050200040501

Morieux, Y. (2011). Smart rules: Six ways to get people to solve problems without you. *Harvard Business Review*, (Sept): 78–84. PMID:21939130

Morin, E. (2008). *On complexity*. Cresskill, NJ: Hampton Press.

Motowidlo, S. J., & Van Scotter, J. R. (1994). Evidence that task performance should be distinguished from contextual performance. *The Journal of Applied Psychology*, *79*, 475–480. doi:10.1037/0021-9010.79.4.475

Mujtaba, B. G. (2010). *Workplace diversity management: Challenges, competencies and strategies* (2nd ed.). Davie, FL: ILEAD Academy Publications.

Muller, K., & Koubek, A. (2002). Collaborative and virtual environments for learning. In ACM SIG Proceedings, New Orleans, Louisiana.

Müller, D., Reichert, M., & Herbst, J. (2007). Lecture Notes in Computer Science: Vol. 4803. *Data-driven modeling and coordination of large process structures* (pp. 131–149). Heidelberg, Germany: Springer. doi:10.1007/978-3-540-76848-7_10

Mumford, L. (1967). *The myth of the machine: Technics and human development*. New York: Harcourt, Brace Iovanovich.

Murphy, A., & Redfern, S. (2011). Non-verbal communication assisted serious gaming applications. In *GAME-ON 2011 International Conference on Intelligent Games and Simulation* (pp. 63-66).

Murugesan, S. (2007). Understanding Web 2.0. *IT Pro*, 34-41. Retrieved from http://hcotuk.etu.edu.tr/bil554/Understanding_web_2.pdf

Nadin, M. (2005). *E-mail exchange with Clarisse Sieckenius de Souza*.

Nadin, M. (2010). Anticipation and the artificial. Aesthetics, ethics and synthetic life. *AI & Society – Computer Science,* (special issue: *Ethics and Aesthetics of Technologies*), 103-118.

Nadin, M. (1977). Sign and fuzzy automata. *Semiosis*, *1*(5), 19–26.

Nadin, M. (1983). The logic of vagueness and the category of synechism. In E. Freeman (Ed.), *The relevance of Charles Peirce* (pp. 154–166). La Salle, IL: The Monist.

Nadin, M. (1991). *Mind—Anticipation and chaos (Milestones in research and discovery)*. Stuttgart/Zurich, Switzerland: Belser.

Nadin, M. (2003). *Anticipation – The end is where we start from*. Basel, Switzerland: Lars Müller Verlag.

Nadin, M. (2011). Information and semiotics processes. The semiotics of computation (review article). *Cybernetics & Human Knowing*, *18*(1-2), 153–175.

Namani, T., & Deamer, D. W. (2008). Stability of model membranes in extreme environments. *Origins of Life and Evolution of the Biosphere*, *38*(4), 329–341. doi:10.1007/s11084-008-9131-8 PMID:18560991

National Information Standards Organization. (2004). *Understanding metadata*. Retrieved from http://www.niso.org/publications/press/UnderstandingMetadata.pdf

Nayak, A., Takeo, O., Tsuruoka, T., Terabe, K., Hasegawa, T., Gimzewski, J. K., & Aono, M. (2012). Controlling the synaptic plasticity of a Cu_2S gap-type atomic switch. *Advanced Functional Materials*, *22*(17), 3606–3613. doi:10.1002/adfm.201200640

Nessi, M., & Nordberg, M. (September, 2011). *Collaborative effort as an engine for developing strategic capabilities and innovation: Insights from the ATLAS Project at CERN* (Keynote address at the SKM Symposium, Linz).

Network Development and MARC Standards Office. (2006). *Marc 21 – Format for bibliographic data*. Retrieved from http://www.loc.gov/marc/bibliographic/bdintro.html

Newman, M. E. J. (2003). The structure and function of complex networks. *SIAM Review*, *45*, 167–256. doi:10.1137/S003614450342480

Newman, M. E. J. (2005). A measure of betweenness centrality based on random walks. *Social Networks*, *27*, 39–54. doi:10.1016/j.socnet.2004.11.009

Nicolelis, M. A. L., & Shuler, M. (2001). Thalamocortical and corticocortical interactions in the somatosensory system. In M. A.L. Nicolelis (Ed.), Advances in neural population coding (Progress in Brain Research, vol. 130), (pp. 89-110). Amsterdam, The Netherlands: Elsevier Science.

Nietzsche, F. (1975). In G. Colli & Montinari (Eds.), Kritische Gesamtausgabe Briefwechsel. Berlin: Walter de Gruyter.

Nietzsche, F. (1881). *Morgenröte. Gedanken uber die moralischen Vorurteilen*. Chemnitz: Verlag von Ernst Schmeltsner.

Nogić, B. (2004). Uzajamni katalog. *Infoteka, 5,* 47-52. Retrieved from http://www.zbus.rs/cir/infoteka/spec2004/INFOTEKA_V_spec_Maj2004_47-52.pdf

Nonaka, I. (2005). A dynamic theory of organizational knowledge creation. In K. Starkey, S. Tempest, & A. McKinlay (Eds.), *How organizations learn* (2nd ed., pp. 165–201). London: Routledge.

Nonaka, I., & Takeuchi, H. (1995). *The knowledge creating company: How Japanese companies create the dynamics of innovation*. New York: Oxford University Press.

Nonaka, I., & Takeuchi, H. (1997). *The knowledge-creating company*. New York: Oxford University Press.

Nurcan, S. (2008). A survey on the flexibility requirements related to business processes and modeling artifacts. In *Proceedings of the IEEE 41st Hawaii International Conference on System Sciences*. New York: IEEE Press.

Oduor, E., Venolia, G., Neustaedter, C., & Judge, T. K. (2013). the future of personal video communication: Moving beyond talking heads to shared experiences. In *Proceedings of ACM SIGCHI Conference on Human Factors in Computing Systems*. Paris.

OMG-BPMN. (2011). *Business process model and notation*, V.2.0. Retrieved March 13, 2013, from http://www.omg.org/spec/BPMN/

OMG-OCL. (2010). *Object constraint language*, V.2.3.1. Retrieved March 13, 2013, from http://www.omg.org/spec/OCL/

OMG-UML. (2011). *Unified modeling language*, V.2.4. Retrieved March 13, 2013, from http://www.omg.org/spec/UML/2.4

ON24. (2013). *ON24 virtual show*. Retrieved May 17, 2013, from http://www.on24.com/products/virtual-show/

Oracle Beehive. (2013). *Beehive*. Retrieved July 05, 2013, from Beehive: http://www.oracle.com/technetwork/middleware/beehive/overview/index.html

Organization for Economic Cooperation and Development. (2010). *Measuring innovation: A new perspective*. OECD Publishing.

Pallotta, V., & Delmonte, R. (2011). Automatic argumentative analysis for interaction mining. *Argument and Computation, 2*(3).

Palmer, J., Fields, N., & Brouse, P. L. (1994). Multigroup decision-support systems in CSCW. *Computer, 27*(5), 67–72. doi:10.1109/2.291289

Pang, B., & Lee, L. (2008). Opinion mining and sentiment analysis. *Foundations and Trends in Information Retrieval, 2*(1).

Paul, H. (1970). *Principles of the History of Language* (H. A. Strong, Trans.). College Park, MD: McGrath Publishing Company. (Original work published 1880)

Peirce, C. S. (1953). *Letters to Lady Welby* (I.C. Lieb, Ed.). New Haven, CT: Whitlock. Plato. (360 BCE). *Cratylus*. (B. Jowett, Trans.). Retrieved on April 10, 2011 from http://classics.mit.edu/Plato/cratylus.html

Peng, J. (2009). Comparative analysis of the key factors on IT application in Chinese and foreign enterprises. *Business Economics and Management, 8*, 30–35.

Perkins, D. N. (1992). *Smart schools: Better thinking and learning for every child*. New York: Free Press.

Pesic, M., & van der Aalst, W. M. P. (2006). Lecture Notes in Computer Science: Vol. 4103. *A declarative approach for flexible business processes management* (pp. 169–180). Heidelberg, Germany: Springer. doi:10.1007/11837862_18

Piaget, J. (1955). *The child's construction of reality*. London: Routledge and Kegan Paul.

Picard, R. (1997). *Affective computing*. Cambridge, MA: MIT Press.

Pink, D. H. (2010). *Drive: The surprising truth about what motivates us*. New York: Penguin.

Plassard, M. (2001). Authority control in an international environment. Retrieved from http://www.nii.ac.jp/publications/CJK-WS/2-1Plassard.pdf

Plato. (360 BCE). *Sophist*. (B. Jowett, Trans.). Retrieved on April 10, 2011 from http://classics.mit.edu/Plato/sophist.html

Pohorille, A., Schweighofer, K., & Wilson, M. A. (2005). The origin and early evolution of membrane channels. *Astrobiology, 5*(1), 1–17. doi:10.1089/ast.2005.5.1 PMID:15711166

Polanka, S. (2012a). Bibliotheca spices up the library ebook market. *Online, 36*(5), 54.

Polanka, S. (2012b). Lending e-Readers: Legal? Ethical? Practical? *Online, 36*(6), 54.

Pollack, J. (2013). *In defense of the liberal arts: Judah Pollack at TEDxWhitehorse*. Retrieved March 28, 2013from http://www.youtube.com/watch?v=OfTCW-IV8tg

Ponti, M. (2010). Socio-technical influences on virtual research environments. *International Journal of e-Collaboration*, *6*(2), 33–44. doi:10.4018/jec.2010040102

Popescu, A.-M., & Etzioni, O. (2005). Extracting product features and opinions from reviews. In *Proceedings of HLTEMNLP*.

Popović Bošković, G., & Filipi-Matutinović, S. (2001). Virtuelna biblioteka Srbije (VBS) - računarsko povezivanje biblioteka u Srbiji. *Infoteka, 2*, (1- 2), 57-79.

Popper, K. R. (1934/1959). *The Logic of Scientific Discovery*. London: Routledge.

Prasolova-Førland, E. (2008). Analyzing place metaphors in 3D educational collaborative virtual environments. *Computers in Human Behavior*, *24*(2), 185–204. doi:10.1016/j.chb.2007.01.009

Raffle, H., Ballagas, R., Revelle, G., Horii, H., Follmer, S., Go, J., & Spasojevic, M. (2010). Family story play: Reading with young children (and Elmo) over a distance. In *Proceedings of ACM SIGCHI Conference on Human Factors in Computing Systems*. Atlanta, Georgia.

Redfern, S., & Naughton, N. (2002). Collaborative virtual environments to support communication and community in Internet-based distance education. *Journal of Information Technology Education*, *1*(3), 201–211.

Reed, C. A. (2011). Implicit speech acts are ubiquitous. Why? They join the dots. In *Proceedings of the Conference on Argumentation: Cognition and Community (OSSA-2011)*, Windsor, ON.

Reed, C. A., & Long, D. P. (1997). Content ordering in the generation of persuasive discourse. In *Proceedings of 15th International Joint Conference on Artificial Intelligence*, Nagoya.

Reed, C. A., & Long, D. P. (1998). Generating the structure of argument. In *Proceedings of COLING-ACL98*, Montreal, Canada.

Reitmayr, G., & Schmalstieg, D. (2001). Mobile collaborative augmented reality. In *IEEE and ACM International Symposium on Augmented Reality, 2001. Proceedings* (pp. 114-123). IEEE.

Rescher, N. (1998). *Complexity. A philosophical overview*. New Brunswick, NJ: Transaction Publishers.

Rieger, B. B. (1997). Computational semiotics and fuzzy linguistics. On meaning constitution and soft categories. In A. Meystel (Ed.), *A learning perspective: International Conference on Intelligent Systems and Semiotics (ISAS-97)* (pp. 541-551). Washington, DC: NIST.

Rieger, B. B. (2003). Semiotic cognitive information processing: Learning to understand discourse. A systemic model of meaning constitution. In R. Kühn et al. (Eds.), *Adaptivity and learning. An interdisciplinary debate* (pp. 347–403). Berlin, Heidelberg, New York: Springer. doi:10.1007/978-3-662-05594-6_24

Riggio, R. E., Murphy, S. E., & Pirozzolo, F. (2002). *Multiple intelligences and leadership*. Mahwah, NJ: Lawrence Erlbaum Associates, Inc.

Riss, U. V., Rickayzen, A., Maus, H., & van der Aalst, W. M. P. (2005). Challenges for business process and task management. *Journal of Universal Knowledge Management*, *0*(2), 77–100.

Rosen, R. (1985). Organisms as causality systems which are not machines: An essay on the nature of complexity. In R. Rosen (Ed.), *Rosen: Theoretical biology and complexity* (pp. 165–203). Orlando, New York, London: Academic Press. doi:10.1016/B978-0-12-597280-2.50008-8

Rummler, G. A., & Brache, A. P. (1995). *Improving performance: How to manage the white space on the organizational chart*. San Francisco: Jossey-Bass.

Rus, I., Lindvall, M., & Sinha, S. (2001). Knowledge management in software engineering, the Data & Analysis Center for Software (DACS) state-of-the-art-report.

Sabovljev, D. (2008). Četvrta verzija sistema BISIS: Uključivanje u svetsku bibliotečku mrežu. *Pančevačko čitalište, 7*, 28-29.

Sadowski, P. (2010). *Towards systems semiotics: Some remarks and (hopefully useful) definitions*. Retrieved March 16, 2011 from http://www.semioticon.com/semiotix/2010/03/towards-systems-semiotics-some-remarks-and-hopefully-useful-definitions/

Sadun, E. (2009). *Yahoo Pipes: getting started with custom RSS feeds*. Retrieved from http://arstechnica.com/web/guides/2009/03/yahoo-pipes-getting-started-with-custom-rss-feeds.ars

Saint-Dizier, P. (2012). processing natural language arguments with the <TextCoop> platform. *Argumentation and Computation, 3*(1).

Salesforce.com. (2013). *Salesforce.com chatter.* Retrieved June 27, 2013, from https://www.salesforce.com/chatter/overview/

Salomon, L. M. (2000). The impact of personality variables on different facets of contextual performance. *Dissertation Abstracts International. B, The Sciences and Engineering*, *61*(6-B), 3313.

Sánchez-Segura, M., Medina-Domínguez, F., Amescua, A., & Mora-Soto, A. (2010). Improving the efficiency of use of software engineering practices using product patterns. *Information Sciences*, *180*(14), 2721–2742. doi:10.1016/j.ins.2010.03.028

Sandywell, B. (1996). *Reflexivity and the crisis of Western reason. Logological investigations* (Vol. 1). London: Routledge. doi:10.4324/9780203420171

Santarelli, E., & Tran, H. T. (2013). The interplay of human and social capital in shaping entrepreneurial performance: The case of Vietnam. *Small Business Economics*, *40*(2), 435–458. doi:10.1007/s11187-012-9427-y

Sargut, G., & Gunther McGrath, R. (2011). Learning to live with complexity. *Harvard Business Review*, (Sept): 69–76. PMID:21939129

S-Cube Partners. (2013). *S-Cube E-MORPG video*. Retrieved June 20, 2013, from http://www.s-cubeproject.eu/gettingstarted

Second Life. (2013). *Second Life*. Retrieved July 05, 2013, from http://secondlife.com/?gclid=CNWyu7KfmLgCFcmQ4QodVVwAlw

Senge, P. (1997). Sharing knowledge. *Leadership Excellence*, *14*(11), 17–18.

Senge, P. M. (1990). The leader's new work: Building learning organizations. *Sloan Management Review*, (Fall): 7–23.

Senge, P. M. (1992). *The fifth discipline – The art & practice of the learning organization*. London: Century Business.

Shannon, C. E., & Weaver, W. (1949). *The mathematical theory of communication*. Urbana, Chicago, London: University of Illinois Press.

Sheldrake, R. (2011). *Dogs that know when their owners are coming home: And other unexplained powers of animals* (2nd ed.). New York: Crown.

Shukair, G., Loutas, N., Peristeras, V., & Sklarss, S. (2013). Towards semantically interoperable metadata repositories: The asset description metadata schema. *Computers in Industry*, *64*, 10–18. doi:10.1016/j.compind.2012.09.003

Sieckenius de Souza, C. (2005). *The semiotic engineering of human-computer interaction*. Cambridge, MA: MIT Press.

Simancik, F., & Lee, M. (2009). A CCG-based system for valence shifting for sentiment analysis. In A. Gelbukh (Ed.), *Advances in computational linguistics (Research in computing science, 41)*. Germany: Springer.

Skeels, M. M., & Grudin, J. (2009). When social networks cross boundaries: A case study of workplace use of Facebook and LinkedIn. *GROUP '09 Proceedings of the ACM 2009 International Conference on Supporting Group Work*. Sanibel Island, Florida.

Skype, M. (2013). *Microsoft Skype*. Retrieved June 28, 2013, from http://www.skype.com/en/

Slavin, R. E., & Tanner, A. M. (1979). Effects of cooperative reward structures and individual accountability on productivity and learning. *The Journal of Educational Research*, 294–298.

Smalley, R. E. (2001, September). Of chemistry, love and nanobots (Nanofallacies). *Scientific American*, *2001*, 76–77. doi:10.1038/scientificamerican0901-76

Smith, M. D. (2009, July 26). *Magic quadrant for Web conferencing*. Retrieved 2013, from http://www.corp.att.com/awards/docs/gartner_mq_0709.pdf

Smith, P., & Redfern, S. (2012). Artificial intelligence supported non-verbal communication for enriched collaboration in distributed e-research environments. In A. Juan, T. Daradoumis, M. Roca, S. Grasman, & J. Faulin (Eds.), *Collaborative and distributed e-research: innovations in technologies, strategies and applications* (pp. 135–164). Hershey, PA: IGI-Global. doi:10.4018/978-1-4666-0125-3.ch007

Soda, G., & Zaheer, A. (2012). A network perspective on organizational architecture: Performance effects of the interplay of formal and informal organization. *Strategic Management Journal*, *33*(6), 751–771. doi:10.1002/smj.1966

Sofronijevic, A. (2011). Biblioteke Europeane: 24 evropske biblioteke i Univerzitetska biblioteka Svetozar Marković stvaraju bibliotečkiagregator za Europeanu. *Visokoškolske biblioteke, 1*. Retrieved from http://www.zbus.rs/cir/index.php?a=visokoskolske&b=cirilica&c=osam&d=jedan#2.

Solomon, J. (1988). *The signs of our time. Semiotics: The hidden messages of environments, objects, and cultural images*. Los Angeles: Jeremy C. Tarcher.

Sparrowe, R. T., Liden, R. C., Wayne, S. J., & Kraimer, M. L. (2001). Social networks and the performance of individuals and groups. *Academy of Management Journal*, *44*(2), 316–325. doi:10.2307/3069458

Spenader, J., & Maier, E. (2009). Contrast as denial in multi-dimensional semantics. *Journal of Pragmatics*, *41*(9), 1707–1726. doi:10.1016/j.pragma.2008.10.005

Sperber, D., & Wilson, D. (1986). *Relevance: Communication and cognition*. Oxford, UK: Basil Blackwell.

Spretnak, C. (2011). *Relational reality. New discoveries of interrelatedness that are transforming the modern world*. Topsham, ME: Green Horizon Books.

Stam, W., Arzlanian, S., & Elfring, T. (2013). Social capital of entrepreneurs and small firm performance: A meta-analysis of contextual and methodological moderators. *Journal of Business Venturing*.

Standaert, W., Muylle, S., & Basu, A. (2013). Assessing the effectiveness of telepresence for business meetings. In *Proceedings of 46th Hawaii International Conference on System Sciences* (pp. 549-558). Hawai.

Stede, M. (2012). Discourse processing, Graeme Hirst (Ed.). Toronto, Canada: Morgan and Claypool Publishers.

Stephan, P. (1996). Auf dem Weg zu Computational Semiotics. In D. Dotzler (Ed.), *Computer als Faszination* (p. 209). Frankfurt, Germany: CAF Verlag.

Stephens, G. J., Osborne, L. C., & Bialek, W. (2011). Searching for simplicity in the analysis of neurons and behavior. *Proceedings of the National Academy of Sciences of the United States of America*, *107*(32), 14425–14430. doi:10.1073/pnas.1008662107 PMID:21383186

Stevanović, V. (2003). Virtuelna biblioteka Srbije. *Infoteka*, *4*(1), 95–102.

Stevenson, M. A. (1997). *The antecedents and consequences of interpersonal trust in mixed-motive dyadic negotiation* (Doctoral Dissertation). The Ohio State University, OH.

Stoitsev, T., Scheidl, S., & Spahn, M. (2007). A framework for light-weight composition and management of ad-hoc business processes. In *Lecture Notes in Business Information Processing, 4849* (pp. 213–226). Heidelberg, Germany: Springer. doi:10.1007/978-3-540-77222-4_17

Strijbos, J. W., Kirschner, P. A., & Martens, R. L. (2004). *What we know about CSCL: And Implementing it in higher education*. Norwell, MA: Kluwer Academic Publishers. doi:10.1007/1-4020-7921-4

Subramanian, A. M., & Soh, P. H. (2009). Contributing knowledge to knowledge repositories: Dual role of inducement and opportunity factors. *Information Resources Management Journal*, *22*(1), 45–62. doi:10.4018/irmj.2009010103

Sureau, D. (2011). *RSS - Really simple syndication: Building and using an RSS feed*. Retrieved from http://www.xul.fr/en-xml-rss.html#overview

Sveiby, K. E. (2001). A knowledge-based theory of the firm to guide in strategy formulation. *Journal of Intellectual Capital*, *2*(4), 344–358. doi:10.1108/14691930110409651

Taboada, M., Brooke, J., & Stede, M. (2009). Genre-based paragraph classification for sentiment analysis. In *Proceedings of 10th Annual SIGDIAL Conference on Discourse and Dialogue*. London.

Taboada, M., Brooke, J., Tofiloski, M., Voll, K., & Stede, M. (2011). Lexicon-based methods for sentiment analysis. *Computational Linguistics*, *37*(2). doi:10.1162/COLI_a_00049

Taboada, M., & Mann, W. C. (2006). Rhetorical structure theory: Looking back and moving ahead. *Discourse Studies*, *8*(3). doi:10.1177/1461445606061881

Tanoue, R., Higuchi, R., Enoki, N., Miyasato, Y., Uemura, S., & Kimizuka, N. … Kunitake, M. (2011). Thermodynamically controlled self-assembly of covalent nanoarchitectures in acqueous solution. *ACS Nano*. doi: doi:10.1021/nn200393q PMID:21480643

Tejedor, B., & Aguirre, A. (1998). Proyecto Logos: Investigación relativa a la Capacidad de Aprender de las Empresas Españolas. *Boletín de Estudios Económicos*, *53*(164), 231–249.

Thomas, J. A., & Rana, F. R. (2007). The Influence of environmental conditions, lipid composition, and phase behavior on the origin of cell membranes. *Origins of Life and Evolution of the Biosphere*, *37*(4), 267–285. doi:10.1007/s11084-007-9065-6 PMID:17361322

Togo, M. B., & Cantelmi, T. (2012). *Technoliquidity*. Retrieved April 4, 2013, from http://www.upi.com/Science_News/Technology/2012/12/15/Technology-has-spawned-new-brain/UPI-71421355602808/

Toms, W. (1997). *Corporate instinct: Building a knowing enterprise for the 21st century*. New York: Van Nostrand Reinhold.

Trubetzkoy, N. S. (1939/1969). *Principles of Phonology* (C. Baltaxe, Trans.). Berkeley, CA: University of California Press.

Tse, P. U. (2013). *The neural basis of free will. Criterial causation*. Cambridge, MA: The MIT Press. doi:10.7551/mitpress/9780262019101.001.0001

Tsiatsos, T., Konstantinidis, A., & Pomportsis, A. (2009). Collaborative educational virtual environments evaluation: The case of Croquet. Paper presented at *Workshop on Intelligent and Innovative Support for Collaborative Learning Activities (WIISCOLA), Computer Supported Collaborative Learning (CSCL09)*, Rhodes, Greece.

Udicki, V. (2006). BISIS godinu dana posle: Povratak u budućnost. *Pančevačko čitalište, 5*, 25.

UNIMARC/Authorities: Universal Format for Authorities. (1991). München: K. G. Saur.

Uzzi, B. (1997). Social structure and competition in interfirm networks: The paradox of embeddedness. *Administrative Science Quarterly*, *42*(1), 35–67. doi:10.2307/2393808

van der Aalst, W. M. P., Pesic, M., & Schonenberg, H. (2009). Declarative workflows: Balancing between flexibility and support. *Computer Science -. Research for Development*, *23*(2), 99–113.

van der Aalst, W. M. P., Weske, M., & Grünbauer, D. (2005). Case handling: A new paradigm for business process support. *Data & Knowledge Engineering*, *53*(2), 129–162. doi:10.1016/j.datak.2004.07.003

Van Eemeren, F. H. (Ed.). (2002). *Advances in pragma-dialectics*. Newport News, VA: Vale Press.

Van Eemeren, F. H., & Grootendorst, R. (1984). *Speech acts in argumentative discussions: A theoretical model for the analysis of discussions directed towards solving conflicts of opinion*. Edinburgh, UK: Floris Publications. doi:10.1515/9783110846089

Van Eemeren, F. H., & Grootendorst, R. (1992). *Argumentation, communication, and fallacies: A pragma-dialectical perspective*. Hillsdale, NJ: Lawrence Erlbaum Associates.

van Lakerveld, J. (2005). *Het Corporate Curriculum, Onderzoek naar werk-leeromstandigheden in instellingen voor Zorg en Welzijn* (thesis). Universiteit Twente, Enschede, The Netherlands.

Van Scotter, J. R. (1999). *Impact of autonomy on task performance, interpersonal facilitation, job dedication, and their relationships with overall performance.* Paper presented at the 1999 SIOP Conference, Atlanta, GA.

Van Scotter, J. R., & Motowidlo, S. J. (1996). Interpersonal facilitation and job dedication as separate facets of contextual performance. *The Journal of Applied Psychology*, *81*, 525–531. doi:10.1037/0021-9010.81.5.525

Veerman, A., & Veldhuis-Diermanse, E. (2001). Collaborative learning through computer-mediated communication in academic education. In P. Dillenbourg, A. Eurelings, & K. Hakkarainen (Eds.), *European perspectives on computer-supported collaborative learning: Proceedings of the 1st European Conference on Computer-Supported Collaborative Learning* (pp. 625-632). Maastricht: Maastricht University.

Vitek, B., & Jackson, W. (Eds.). (2008). *The virtues of ignorance. Complexity, sustainability, and the limits of knowledge.* Lexington, KY: The University Press of Kentucky.

von Foerster, H. (1981). *Observing systems.* Seaside, CA: Intersystems Publications.

von Kiedrowski, G., & Patzke, V. (2008). Self-replication and autocatalysis. In S. Rasmussen, M. A. Bedau, L. Chen, D. Deamer, D. C. Krakauer, & P. F. Stadler (Eds.), *Protocells: Bridging nonliving and living matter* (pp. 200–316). Boston: MIT Press.

von Uexküll, J. (2010). *A foray into the worlds of animals and humans* (J. D. O'Niell, Trans.). Minneapolis, London: University of Minneapolis Press. (Original work published 1934)

Vosinakis, S., Koutsabasis, P., & Zaharias, P. (2011). An exploratory study of problem-based learning in virtual worlds. *VS-GAMES, 11.*

Vygotsky, L. (1987). *Thought and language* (A. Kozulin (Trans. Ed.)). Cambridge, MA: The MIT Press.

Waber, B. N., Olguin, O. D., Kim, T., & Pentland, A. (2010). Productivity through coffee breaks: Changing social networks by changing break structure. Retrieved from http://ssrn.com/abstract=1586375

Walton, D., Reed, C., & Macagno, F. (2008). *Argumentation schemes.* Cambridge, UK: Cambridge University Press. doi:10.1017/CBO9780511802034

Wang, H., Li, X., & Luo, S. (2003). The validation of two-factor model about task performance and contextual performance. *China Management Science*, *8*, 79–84.

Warmerdam, J., & van den Berg, J. (1992). *Scholing van werknemers in veranderende organisaties.* Den Haag: Ministerie van Sociale Zaken en Werkgelegenheid/ITS Vuga.

Wasko, M. M., & Faraj, S. (2005). Why should I share? Examining social capital and knowledge contribution in electronic networks of practice. *Management Information Systems Quarterly*, *29*(1), 35–57.

Wasserman, S., & Faust, K. (1994). *Social network analysis: Methods and applications.* Cambridge, UK: Cambridge University Press. doi:10.1017/CBO9780511815478

Watzlawick, P. (Ed.). (1984). *The invented reality. How do we know what we believe we know? Contributions to constructivism.* New York: W.W. Norton and Company.

Webster, E., & Jensen, P. (2006). Investment in intangible capital: An enterprise perspective. *The Economic Record*, *82*, 82–96. doi:10.1111/j.1475-4932.2006.00296.x

Wedekind, J. (1996). On inference-based procedures for lexical disambiguation. In *Proceedings of COLING 1996.*

Wellman, B., & Berkowitz, S. D. (Eds.). (1988). *Social structures: A network approach.* Cambridge, UK: Cambridge University Press.

Weske, M. (2007). *Business process management - Concepts, languages, architectures.* Berlin: Springer.

Wheeler, B., Dennis, A., & Press, L. (1999). Groupware comes to the Internet: Charting a new world. *SIGMIS Database*, *30*(3-4), 8–21. doi:10.1145/344241.344242

Wiig, K. (1988). *Management of knowledge: Perspectives of a new opportunity.* Arlington, VA: The Wiig Group.

Wilden, A. (1987). *The rules are no game*. London: Routledge & Kegan Paul.

Wilson, S. D. (2005). *The relationship between leadership and domains of multiple intelligences*. ProQuest Information and Learning Company. (UMI No: 3151206).

Wilson, E. O. (1984). *Biophilia: The human bond with other species*. Cambridge, MA: Harvard University Press.

Wilson, S. D., & Mujtaba, B. G. (2007). The relationship between multiple intelligences, culture and diversity. *International Business & Economics Research Journal*, *6*(8), 9–22.

Wilson, S. D., & Mujtaba, B. G. (2008). Intelligence and diversity: A western and eastern view from a global paradigm. *International Business and Economics Research Journal*, *7*(6), 29–39.

Windelband, W. (1894). *Geschicthte und Naturwissenschaft, Präludien. Aufsätze und Reden zur Philosophie und ihrer Geschichte (History and Natural Science. Speech of the Rector of the University of Straßburg)* (pp. 136–160). Tubingen, Germany: J.C.B. Mohr.

Winn, W. (2002). Current trends in educational technology research: The study of learning environments. *Educational Psychology Review*, *14*(3), 331–351. doi:10.1023/A:1016068530070

Winterstein, G. (2012). What *but*-sentences argue for: An argumentative analysis of *but. Lingua*, *122*, 1864–1885. doi:10.1016/j.lingua.2012.09.014

Yao, J. (2009). Relationship-structure effect of dual social network on the mechanism of job performance-the empirical analysis on real estate sales industry in N City. *Soft*, *23*(3), 134–139.

Yarosh, S., Inkpen, K. M., & Brush, A. (2009). Video playdate: Toward free play across distance. In *Proceedings of ACM SIGCHI Conference on Human Factors in Computing Systems*. doi:978-1-60558-246-7/09/04.

Yelton, A. (2012). The ethics of ebooks: A founding member of Unglue.it ponders the soul of librarianship. *Library Journal*, *137*(15), 30.

Youseff, L., & Dilma Da Silva, M. B. (2009). *Toward a unified ontology of cloud computing*. Retrieved April 8, 2010, from http://www.silicon.com/white-papers/it-infrastructure/2008/10/13/toward-a-unied-ontology-of-cloud-computing-60829795/2/

Zaharias, P., Andreou, I., & Vosinakis, S. (2010). Educational virtual worlds, learning styles and learning effectiveness: An empirical investigation. In A. Jimoyiannis (ed.), *Proceedings of the 7th Pan-Hellenic Conference with International Participation ICT in Education*, (pp.1-6). University of Peloponnese, Korinthos, Greece.

Zhao, C. M., & Kuh, G. D. (2004). Adding value: Learning communities and student engagement. *Research in Higher Education*, *45*(2), 115–138. doi:10.1023/B:RIHE.0000015692.88534.de

zur Muehlen, M., & Indulska, M. (2010). Modeling languages for business processes and business rules: A representational analysis. *Information Systems*, *35*, 379–390. doi:10.1016/j.is.2009.02.006

About the Contributors

Murray E. Jennex is a Professor of Management Information Systems at San Diego State University, editor in chief of the International Journal of Knowledge Management, co-editor in chief of the International Journal of Information Systems for Crisis Response and Management, and president of the Foundation for Knowledge Management (LLC). Dr. Jennex specializes in knowledge management, crisis response, system analysis and design, IS security, e-commerce, and organizational effectiveness. Dr. Jennex serves as the Knowledge Systems Track co-chair at the Hawaii International Conference on System Sciences. He is the author of more than 150 journal articles, book chapters, and conference proceedings on knowledge management, crisis response, end user computing, international information systems, organizational memory systems, ecommerce, cyber security, and software outsourcing. Dr. Jennex is a former US Navy Nuclear Power Propulsion officer and holds a B.A. in chemistry and physics from William Jewell College, an M.B.A. and an M.S. in software engineering from National University, an M.S. in telecommunications management, and a Ph.D. in information systems from the Claremont Graduate University. Dr. Jennex is also a registered professional mechanical engineer in the state of California and a Certified Information Systems Security Professional (CISSP), a Certified Secure Software Lifecycle Professional (CSSLP), and a Project Management Professional (PMP).

* * *

Jelena Andonovski, librarian, (born in Leskovac, 1987) graduated from Library and Information Science at the Faculty of Philology in Belgrade. Since December 2010, she has been working in the University Library "Svetozar Markovic" in Belgrade at the Department for Development of Library System, Funds Digitization and Cultural Activities. She finished her MA studies at the Faculty of Philology, Department of Library and Information Sciences. Since 2012, she has been a student of PhD studies at the Faculty for Philology in Belgrade (Department for Library and Information Science). She is the author of articles in professional periodicals and a participant in national and international conferences.

Giorgio Bruno is an Associate Professor at Politecnico di Torino, Italy, where he teaches courses on software engineering and object-oriented programming. His current interests concern the operational modeling of business processes and collaborative services and the design of information systems and workflow systems. He has authored two books and more than 140 technical papers on the above-mentioned subjects.

Nataša Dakic, library advisor, (born in Belgrade, 1972) graduated from Library and Information Science at the Faculty of Philology in Belgrade. She works as a librarian for expert processing of monographs and analytical processing of monographs and serials in the Book Acquisition and Cataloguing Department at the University Library of Belgrade. She is a member of the State Commission for issuing the permission for shared cataloguing and also the author of articles in professional periodicals and a participant in national and international conferences.

Antonio de Amescua is a full professor in the Computer Science Department at Carlos III University of Madrid. He has been working as software engineer in a public company (Iberia Airlines) and in a private company (Novotec Consultores) as a software engineering consultant. He founded Progresion, a spin-off company, in order to offer advanced Software Process Improvement services. He received his PhD in computer science from the Universidad Politécnica of Madrid. His research interests include Software Process Improvement, Software Reuse, and Software Project Management.

María Paz García-Villalba earned an M.A. in English Studies from the University of Toulouse. She worked as a research assistant at the Toulouse Institute of Computer Science Research (IRIT) in France from 2010 to 2013. Her main research topics range from translation, lexical and cognitive semantics, and discourse analysis to more complex argumentation analysis, dwelling on opinion mining and sentiment analysis and specifically focusing on consumer goods such as hotels, restaurants, or electronic products, but also exploring political opinion. She has also worked on argument fusion techniques for consumer reviews, her research being carried out under the supervision of Patrick Saint-Dizier, CNRS Research Director.

James Hutter is the Head of Technology for the Westbury Memorial Public Library (Long Island, NY). He has an undergraduate degree in Information Technology Management from SUNY Empire State College and received his Master's Degree from the Library and Information Studies program at CUNY Queens College. He is constantly working to utilize new technologies to promote literacy and learning. His current focus is on the use of e-Readers to promote reading amongst both Adults and Young Adults. James's hobbies include biking, hiking, camping, writing, and reading Science Fiction.

Ton Jörg studied Physics and Mathematics with Chemistry (BSc, 1970) at Utrecht University. In 1970, he started to study Psychology at the University of Amsterdam (MA, 1977). He has been working as an evaluation researcher in different national and international projects (SISS-International Science Report). He was affiliated as educational scientist and evaluation researcher at the University of Utrecht, for different departments. In 2008, he retired and became an author. In 2011, his book on "New Thinking in Complexity for the Social Sciences and Humanities – A Generative, Transdisciplinary Approach" was published by Springer Publishers. Recently, he published several articles with 'applications' of thinking in complexity: on topics like innovation, management of knowledge, and education. He is now writing a new book, titled "Towards a New Science of Complexity", which is based on the new paradigm of generative complexity, which is of use for all disciplines, operating in the Age of Complexity.

Alfie Keary has more than 30 years ICT (Information & Communications Technologies) experience and is a director of Informa Europe Limited. His activities with Informa Europe have included the business development of cloud based software services; ICT consulting and education services, as well as interactive web based learning services. This work involved research on Computer Mediated Communications (CMC) technologies, Knowledge Management, x3D, XML and Intelligent Agents. Alfie has taken numerous industry specific training programmes in ICT, has studied management at the Irish Management Institute (IMI), and completed an Enterprise Development Programme managed by the Dublin Institute of Technology. Alfie is a graduate of University College Cork (Mathematics/Computing and Economics), the National College of Ireland (Knowledge Economy Skills Passport), National University of Ireland Galway (NUI-Galway), and Regis University, Denver, Colorado. In 2010, Alfie graduated with an MSc degree in Software Engineering and Database Technologies (MScSED), a joint degree from NUI-Galway and Regis University, Denver. Since then he has been advancing his research in CMC. In 2012, Alfie was awarded a full time PhD Risam scholarship by the Cork Institute of Technology, Ireland. In returning to full-time education, his work now involves research into perceptual and affective computing, Internet of Things/Sensor Web, Artificial Intelligence and Brain Computer Interfaces (BCIs) and how these technologies will drive future CMC innovations and services.

Andreas Konstantinidis holds a BSc in Computer Science, an MSc in ICTE (Information and Communication Technology in Education), and a PhD on the subject of "3D Virtual Environments for Collaborative Learning" from the Aristotle University of Thessaloniki. His research interests are in the areas of Collaborative Virtual Environments, Collaborative Learning, Computer Supported Collaborative Work, and e-Learning Systems. He has published his research in a number of international conferences and journals and has also written chapters in books and encyclopaedias. In the past, he has participated in various European R&D projects through SEERC (South East European Research Centre) and CTI (Computer Technology Institute). He currently holds the position of Technology Enhanced Learning Officer in the Arts and Humanities Department at King's College.

Apostolos Mavridis is a PhD candidate on the subject of "Game Based Learning" in the Department of Informatics, Aristotle University of Thessaloniki, Greece. He holds a BSc in Computer Science and an MSc in ICTE (Information and Communication Technology in Education). Both degrees were obtained from the Aristotle University of Thessaloniki. His research interests are in the areas of eLearning, Instructional Design, Game Based Learning, and Collaborative Virtual Environments. He has published his research in several national and international conferences. He currently participates in a project of the Greek Ministry of Education in the area of eLearning.

Fuensanta Medina-Dominguez is an assistant professor at Carlos III University of Madrid. Her research interests include Software Engineering and software process improvement. Her research interests focus on the software engineering area, specifically in the lines of project management, modeling and process improvement, knowledge reuse, knowledge transfer through the use of new collaborative technology trends, and information technologies for the governance of intelligent organizations. She is the author of articles in books, book chapters, encyclopedias, and relevant journals as *Journal of Systems and Software* and *Journal of Information Science and IEEE Transaction on Education*. Also, she is the author of papers presented at relevant international conferences related to process improvement, reuse, collaborative environments, and patterns and knowledge management. In addition, she is a reviewer in international journals and conferences and participates as a member of the Program Committee of several international conferences. Fuensanta has been a Certified Knowledge Manager for the International Knowledge Management Institute since 2013.

Mihai Nadin's professional life combines engineering, mathematics, digital technology, philosophy, semiotics, mind theory, and anticipatory systems. He has a doctoral degree in Electrical Engineering and Computer Science and a post-doctoral degree in Philosophy, Logic, and the Theory of Science. Nadin introduced semiotics as the underlying foundation for HCI. He also established Computational Design as a distinct knowledge domain. With his book, *Mind—Anticipation and Chaos*, Nadin (in parallel to Robert Rosen) initiated the field of Anticipatory Systems. Nadin established the Institute for Research in Anticipatory Systems (2002) and at the invitation of the University of Texas at Dallas joined the ambitious "MIT of the South" as Ashbel Smith University Professor. He is carrying out research in quantifying anticipatory characteristics, with applications for aging, high-performance and high-attention activities, robotics, computational neuroscience, human-machine hybrid systems, new forms of computation. As a distinguished Fellow of the Hanse Institute for Advanced Study (Germany, since 2011), he researched anticipatory systems within the neuroscience group, and established an international Study Group on anticipation across disciplines. For more information and full access to his publications, see www.nadin.ws and www.anteinstitute.org.

Tse-Kian Neo is the Dean of the Faculty of Creative Multimedia in Multimedia University, Cyberjaya Malaysia. He is also an Associate Professor and has numerous peer-reviewed journals and international conferences. His areas of research include Multimedia in Education, Constructivist learning environment, cooperative learning, learning design, web-based education and others. He is currently a member of the SMILE research group in the university and has been a reviewer for several high-impact journals for a number of years. He has authored several books on multimedia and multimedia tools as well as research books on multimedia learning. He has graduated several post-graduate students and has several grant-related projects involving learning with Web 2.0 tools that have won research awards.

Jianping Peng is an Associate Professor in the Department of Management Science in the School of Business, Sun Yat-sen University. He holds a Ph.D from Sun Yat-sen University. His research interests include enterprise management information systems, electronic commerce and process management, and organizational behavior impact of employee social network. He has published in *Productivity Research (China), Acta Scientiarum Naturalium University Sunyatseni, Management Information Systems (China), China Journal of Information System and Computer Engineering, Decision Support Systems.*

Jing Quan is an Associate Professor in the Department of Information and Decision Sciences in Perdue School of Business at Salisbury University. He holds a Ph.D. from the University of Florida. His research interests include organizational impact of information technology (IT), IS security, and IT professional and personnel issues. His work has appeared in such journals as *Journal of Management Information Systems*, *Communications of the ACM*, *Communications of the AIS*, *Information Resources Management Journal*, *International Journal of Information Management*, *Journal of Global Information Management*, and *Journal of Computer Information Systems.*

Sam Redfern graduated with an MSc and PhD in Information Technology. Sam has subsequently worked as a lecturer in the National University of Ireland, Galway. His research since the mid-1990s has included artificial intelligence and pattern recognition, digital image processing, CSCW, and collaborative virtual environments. In recent years his teaching, research, and consultancy has focused primarily on computer games technologies. Sam's games have won numerous awards and achieved more than 3.5 million downloads.

Sahar Sabbaghan is currently a PhD candidate for University of Auckland. She has a Master's Degree in Knowledge Management from Multimedia University. She has several peer-reviewed publications. Her area of research ranges from Information System, Communication, Knowledge Management, Organizational Behaviour, Innovation Management, Motivation Strategies and Theories, to KM for Environmental Sustainability.

Patrick Saint-Dizier is a CNRS senior researcher in computational linguistics and logic programming. He heads a research group at IRIT-Toulouse on language processing. He is the author of several books and articles on diverse topics in language processing. He also organized a number of conferences and workshops.

María-Isabel Sanchez-Segura is faculty member at Carlos III University of Madrid. She holds a Ph.D. in Computer Science (2001) from the Universidad Politecnica of Madrid, an MSc in Software Engineering (1999), and a BSc in Computer Science (1997). She is author of several books about software analysis and design, interactive systems, and software configuration management, and several courses published under the OCW project lead by the MIT. She is the author of numerous articles published in journals of relevance related to modeling and software process improvement; she is also the author of more than forty papers presented at conferences related to process improvement, reuse, and knowledge management improvement and human aspects of software engineering. She reviews papers for international journals such as *IEEE software*, *Journal of Systems and Software*, *Multimedia tools and applications*, etc.

Adam Sofronijevic was born in Belgrade in 1973. He holds a MSc in management, a MSc in LIS, and a BSc in IT. As of November 2013, Adam is a PhDc in LIS, Faculty of Philology, University of Belgrade. Adam is certified with CISCO CCNA industrial certificate and numerous Coursera, Udacity, and MITx online certificates in fields of ICT, management, and humanities. His first Master thesis was on library business model, and the second one was on Enterprise 2.0, both at University of Belgrade. He has six years of experience in research of Serbian libraries. He has five years of experience in management of a department at University library Belgrade. He is publishing regularly in national and international journals, including the ones with IF, and presents at international conferences. Adam is a member of LIBER annual conference program committee since 2012 and recipient of Belgrade city library ''Best librarian'' award for 2012.

Thrasyvoulos Tsiatsos is currently Assistant Professor in the Department of Informatics, Aristotle University of Thessaloniki, Greece. He obtained his Diploma, his Master's Degree, and his PhD from the Computer Engineering and Informatics Department of Patras University (Greece). His research interests include Networked Virtual Learning Environments, Computer Uses in Education, Evaluation methods of Internet Learning Environments, and Open and Distance Education using Multimedia and Internet Technologies. He has published more than 90 papers in Journals and in well-known refereed conferences, and he is co-author in 3 books. He has been a PC member and referee in various international journals and conferences. He has participated in various national and European R&D projects in the area of e-learning.

Diana-Marcela Vásquez-Bravo has been a member of the Computer Science Department at Carlos III Technical University of Madrid since 2009. She has worked as a teacher at Cauca University in Popayán Colombia. She has the grade of Systems Engineer from Universidad del Cauca (2007). She holds a Master in Computer Science (2010) and PhD in Computer Science (2014) of Carlos III University of Madrid. Diana Marcela works with the Research Group SEL-UC3M (Software Engineering Lab) at Carlos III University of Madrid. Currently, she researches in the fields of Software Engineering and Knowledge Management. Her research interests includes software engineering, software process improvement, strategic management, measurement tools, techniques and methodologies, software metrics, software engineering experimentation, earned value management, process management, knowledge transfer through the use of new collaborative technology trends, and information technologies for the governance of intelligent organizations.

Paul Walsh is an accomplished academic and a leading technical architect with extensive experience in designing and implementing a range of IT Systems. He has published numerous peer reviewed international computer science articles and led and organised academic conferences and committees. He has successfully designed enterprise systems that are secure, auditable, and compliant to FDA standards and is a Microsoft Certified Professional and a certified Project Management Professional. He has architected and implemented Web and CD-ROM E-Learning Software for Literacy Education, www.literacytools.ie (Golden Spider Shortlist), www.readwritenow.ie, Literacy Tools, Technology@Work, Read Write Now I and Read Write Now II E-Learning Applications. He is also honoured to be an International .NET Association (INETA, http://www.ineta.org/) speaker on the latest Microsoft technologies.

Index

K

L

M

N

O

P

R

S

T

V

W

www.ingramcontent.com/pod-product-compliance
Ingram Content Group UK Ltd.
Pitfield, Milton Keynes, MK11 3LW, UK
UKHW050951290926
15470UKWH00005B/1759